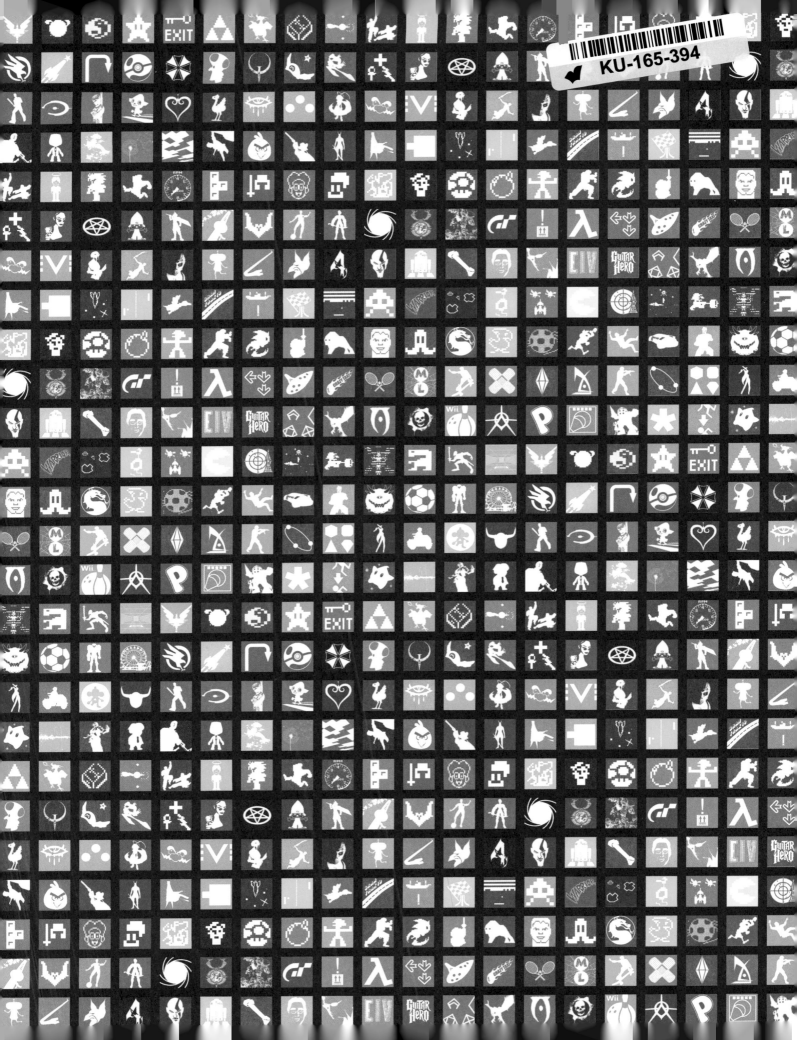

AN ILLUSTRATED HISTORY OF
151 VIDEO GAMES

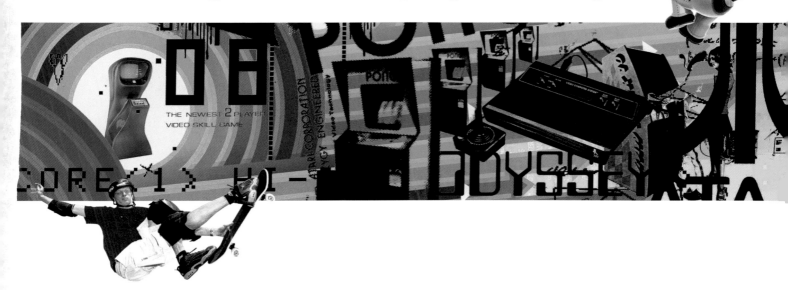

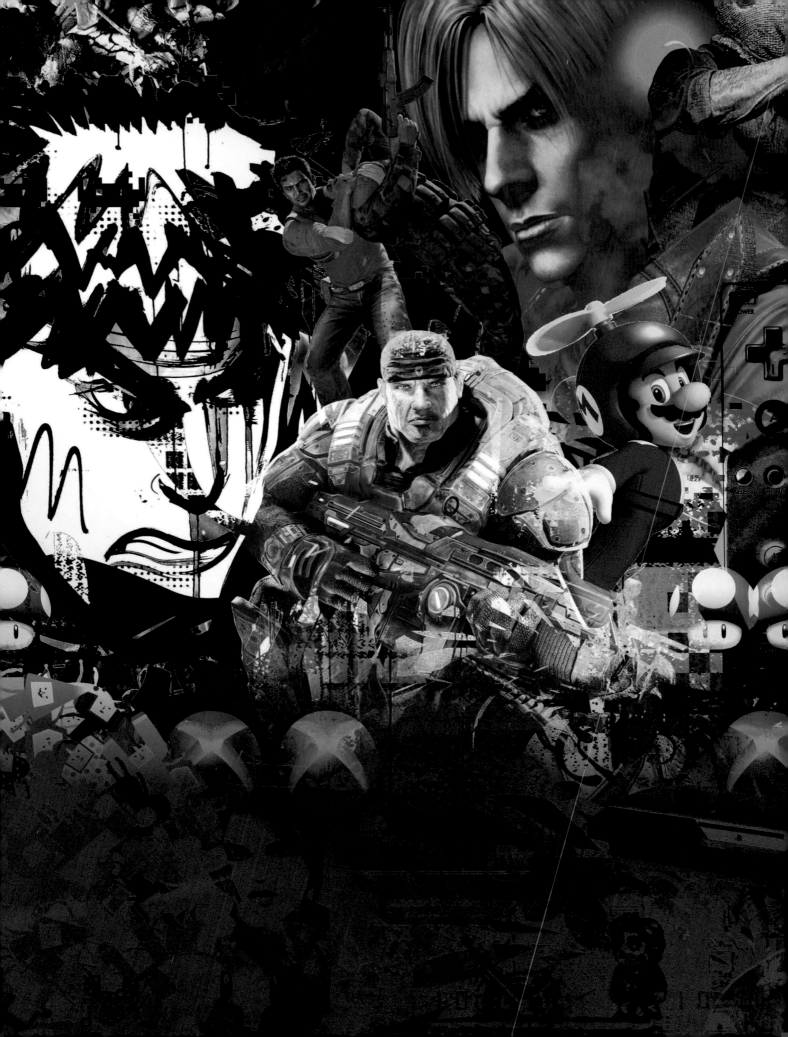

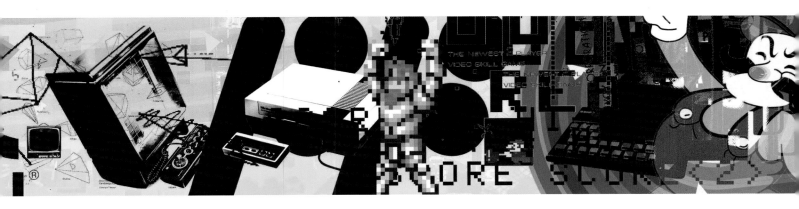

AN ILLUSTRATED HISTORY OF
151 VIDEO GAMES

A DETAILED GUIDE TO THE MOST IMPORTANT GAMES

SIMON PARKIN

LORENZ BOOKS

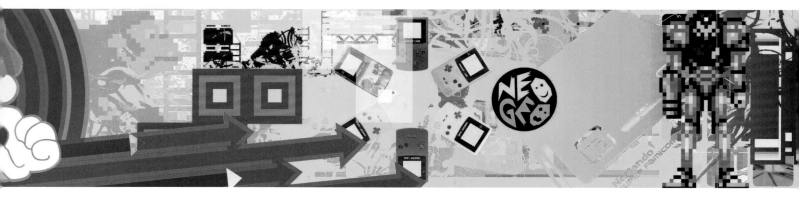

CONTENTS

INTRODUCTION

I t is, as with any attempt to nail down a history, a question of how far back one goes. Is the origin of the video game, a term that has only been in existence for around 30 years, found at 5:29am on 17 July 1945, when the first atomic bomb detonated a technological arms race? Certainly the mainframe computers university students modified in the 1950s to create rudimentary shooting games owe their existence to the missile defence systems of the late 1940s.

Neither could video games exist without the television screen, that indispensable window into their fabricated worlds. Perhaps the origin of games lies here, on 25 March 1925 when Scottish inventor John Logie Baird gave the first public demonstration of televised silhouette images in motion, at Selfridge's Department Store in London. Or maybe in Konosuke Matsushita's 1918 business venture, the Matsushita Electric Housewares Manufacturing Works, a company that led to the formation of Panasonic, and the screen technology that no video game could exist without.

Or perhaps we should rewind a further 40 years, to the moment that Fusajiro Yamauchi established the Marufuku Company in 1889? It was this business that would later blossom into the Nintendo Playing Card Company, sowing the seeds for the most successful video game manufacturer in the world.

No, too short-sighted. Should we not reach back through the centuries in search of the origins of play itself? Dizzy, we dash past playground games of Cops and Robbers, the invention of football, tennis, chess, Go, back into the imaginations of the earliest children, who would mock-hunt their parents in caves as a playful means to learn about their world and the irresistible impulses that drive them to survive within it.

In truth, the story of video games begins at all of these points and 10,000 more besides. This artistic medium exists thanks to a perfect storm of technological advancement, the drive of businessmen

and women to devise new ways to create wealth, and human beings' hard-wired, inescapable desire to play. In this way the story of the video game is the story of humankind: their existence marks the pinnacle of achievement in fulfilling our collective drive to play, one that has propelled humanity forward since life began.

As such, this volume about video games is not an attempt to construct the comprehensive history of the medium. We're not about to return to the primordial soup in search of a proto-Electroplankton. Rather, in selecting a small clutch of titles, this book seeks to pick out the keypoints in the medium's trajectory, examining the broad canvas of gaming through a small selection of lenses. These are the 151 video games that gave birth to trends, or popularized them; that invented genres, or busted them open; that laid down the blueprint for the future, or began its construction.

Each entry treats the game not as a historical artefact, whose origins of existence should be discussed in dry tones while being turned in the hands as a museum piece. Rather, we revisit these experiences with the understanding that video games – despite what their publishers might want us to believe as they promote the next big thing, and the next, and the next again – offer timeless experiences. Popular aesthetics may shift with the plod of technological advance, but the underpinning systems often remain as fresh as the day they were coded; the appeal of their quiddity remains undiminished by time.

This book is a chronological history describing important games, but it's also a celebration of 151 games, holding up each example as a wonderful marriage of art, design and coding waiting to be played, enjoyed and experienced again.

To answer the question, then, this is how far back we go: to the first video game that can be played, enjoyed and experienced today; to the first play space found inside a computer, to Computer Space.

Simon Parkin

THE 1970s

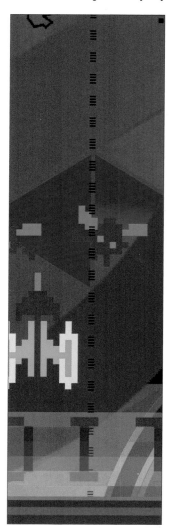

> **"Our Ping-Pong game, courtesy of a little plagiarism by certain parties, spawned the successful start of the arcade video game industry. Not too shabby for such a simple game."**
>
> Ralf Baer, creator of the Magnavox Odyssey

The idea of a game in which you push beams of light around a screen was, in truth, born some time prior to 1970. There was Ralf Baer, a military engineer who captured the concept for an interactive television channel dubbed 'Let's Play' in a four-page document in 1966. And five years earlier than Baer's epiphany a rudimentary video game, *Space War!* debuted on a $120,000 PDP-1 mainframe computer at the Massachusetts Institute of Technology (MIT), created by members of the Tech Model Railroad Club in 1961. These two moments were instrumental in the creation of the first video game console, the Magnavox Odyssey, and the first coin-operated arcade game, *Galaxy Game*.

But it was the 1970s that turned these tentative ideas and prototypes into reality. It was in this decade that the video game was born, growing up from the mewling confusion of infancy to the boisterous adolescent determination of a multi-million dollar industry. In a few short years the video game barged its way into the midst of music, film and literature, declaring itself the fourth pillar in the temple of modern entertainment. In so many of the contemporary digital world's formative moments, video games feature in the background, proving time and again that play is usually the inspiration for progress. In the birth of Atari, video games helped shape the world today in profound, manifest ways, launching the career of Steve Jobs, a young hippy game engineer who, following his experience working on *Breakout* with his friend Steve Wozniak, would go on to form Apple Computer Inc.

Without Will Crowther's *Adventure* – a game designed as a way for this father to stay connected to his daughters following a chaotic divorce – who knows whether he would have remained working at defense contractor Bolt Bernek and Newman, laying the foundations for the Internet by creating data transfer routines for ARPAnet, the US military computer network. It was in the constant drive of the world's earliest arcade game manufacturers to reduce the size of circuit boards and thereby reduce costs, that technology shrank even as its capacity grew.

The industry's adoption of the microprocessor in the late 1970s hauled the development of home computing along with it, helping to accelerate the adoption of the technology that facilitates so much of modern life.

The 1970s saw games evolve faster than at any other time in history, adopting simple animation, imbuing their screens with colour and particles and multiplying their soundtracks from life monitor-esque bleeps and blips to striking melodic arpeggios. Slowly, the familiar activities of 20th-century life were approximated in video game form, from *Pong*'s rudimentary take on table tennis and *Gran Trak 10*'s racing simulation through to *Adventure*, a game based on spelunking, the exploration of a network of underground caves.

In these ten short years video games were propelled from basement university laboratories, where they were available only to the lab-coated high priests of technology, on to the world's stage, the release of *Space Invaders* attracting so much of Japan's attention that the country's national bank launched an investigation into developer Taito following a national shortage of 100 Yen coins.

The 1970s saw game designers move from production line workers to creative artisans tasked with defining the language, vocabulary and boundaries of this new medium. In this decade the floor plans of genres were laid down, echoes of which are still found in the foundations of today's multi-million dollar blockbusters. It's here that we find the first pages of the video game rulebook written down, and begin to investigate why we play games. Is it to go through the experience of learning a skill and perfecting it? Or is it to pit ourselves against technology in a primal contest to prove ourselves master of our machines? Or, perhaps, the appeal is to compete with other humans via the monolithic permanence and irrefutable ranking of a high-score table? Then there's the physical and social appeal: enjoying the camaraderie of standing around an arcade machine, cheering others as they grasp for triumph against the overwhelming odds. Whatever the reason that humans began to play video games en masse, the 1970s were critical for defining *how* we play video games.

[001]
COMPUTER SPACE

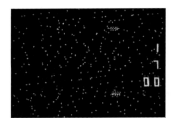

Year: 1971
Developer: Nolan Bushnell & Ted Dabny
Publisher: Nutting Associates
Original format: Arcade
Play today: computerspacefan.com

"People talk about innovation. I say you can't give good ideas away. It's only when they're proven you worry about them."

Nolan Bushnell, creator of
Computer Space

Below: The dramatic space-age design of *Computer Space's* cabinet heightened the game's sci-fi premise.

COMPUTER SPACE

Computer Space wasn't the first commercially available video game but its release lit the torch paper that led to the industry's explosion to life.

It is fitting that the video game should take outer space as its first frontier. This blackness of infinity that envelops humankind, hidden in plain sight, has always fascinated the adventurous storyteller. The obsession has to do with the thrill of the seen but unknown. But in the birth of the video game, these lab-coated pioneers (storytellers boasting perhaps the greatest yearning for adventure of all of us) finally found a way to make the unknown knowable – touchable, even – to explore space's furthest reaches on the near screen. In the video game the galaxy became graspable in the hands, and its wonders and terrors have preoccupied game makers ever since.

It is entirely appropriate then, that the first commercially successful game was named *Computer Space*, a dull, mundane title that nevertheless encapsulates the practicality and mystique of the medium all at once. The game's origins lie in *Spacewar!*, a rudimentary shooting game created for the hulking PDP-1 mainframe computers found on many university campuses across America in the 1960s. Nolan Bushnell fell in love with the game on one such campus while studying at the University of Utah. His ferociously entrepreneurial mind and small-change-sapping interest in the amusements business led him to consider the possibility

of putting a version of *Spacewar!* inside a coin-operated cabinet, to take the game outside the glass-room laboratories, out of the hands of the software priesthood and onto America's streets and piers.

But it was only after graduating in 1968 and taking up a job as an engineer for Ampex Corporation that Bushnell's mind zipped back to his idea for a coin-operated *Spacewar!* when he read about the Data General Nova, a newly released computer on the market for an affordable $3,995. With the help of Ampex colleague Ted Dabney, Bushnell drew up the designs for a cabinet. But it soon became clear that the Nova was insufficiently powered to run *Spacewar!*, proving unable to update the screen at a playable frame rate. Even creating separate, bespoke pieces of hardware to support the Nova, handling jobs such as rendering the stars that formed the game's dark backdrop didn't improve results, and by late 1970 Bushnell was ready to abandon the project and move on.

As work neared completion in the summer of 1971, Bushnell looked for a distributor to produce and market the machines. A conversation with his dentist led to an introduction to the sales manager at Nutting Associates, an amusement machine manufacturer who had a successful coin-operated quiz machine on the market. In August, Bushnell left his job at Ampex

Right: Nolan Bushnell recruited Nutting Associates to produce and market his machines, their experience with quiz machines proving an invaluable asset to the project.

COMPUTER SPACE

NA-2010

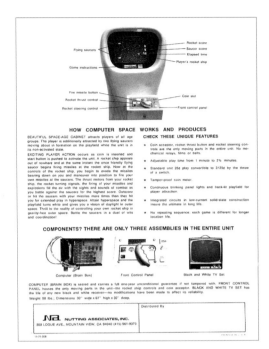

HOW COMPUTER SPACE WORKS AND PRODUCES

CHECK THESE UNIQUE FEATURES

COMPONENTS? THERE ARE ONLY THREE ASSEMBLIES IN THE ENTIRE UNIT

Computer (Brain Box)   Front Control Panel   Black and White TV Set

Above: *Computer Space* heralded the arrival of a new entertainment medium and, while the basic controls of arcade and video games quickly became hard-wired into modern consciousness, in the early 1970s electronic gaming was still a new and unfamiliar concept.

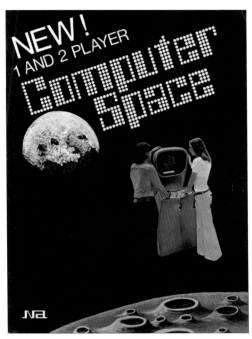

Above: *Computer Space*'s competitive elements made the game ideally suited to bars and restaurants, where patrons could express their tipsy rivalries in the safety of a pixel dimension. It was not until the late 1970s that dedicated amusement arcades first became popular.

"I loved it, and all my friends loved it, but it was a little too complicated for the guy with the beer in the bar."

Nolan Bushnell, creator of *Computer Space*

Above: *Computer Space*'s two-player cabinet featured new joysticks and a wider control panel, but retained the distinctive futuristic curves of the single-player unit.

and joined Nutting to complete work on the game, which he named *Computer Space* as a tribute to Nutting's *Computer Quiz* machine and, of course, the PDP-1's *Spacewar!*, to which the game owed its existence.

It was while working at Nutting, putting the final touches to the game, that Bushnell heard of another, similar project under way to turn *Spacewar!* into a coin-operated game. This rival endeavour came from Bill Pitts and Hugh Tuck, two Stanford University students. Bushnell made contact with the pair and invited them to visit Nutting in order to see his project, with the ulterior motive of discovering how close the competition was to his own work.

Pitts and Tuck agreed to the meeting, but while each party had mutual respect, neither left convinced that the other had the better product. A few weeks later, in September 1971, Pitts and Tuck completed their project and installed their version of *Spacewar!*, a handmade cabinet titled *Galaxy Game*, in the Tressider Union at Stanford University. It was the first coin-operated video game to be positioned

in the semi-public domain. A single game cost 10 cents or players could purchase three games for 25 cents. The game remained popular on campus, players queuing for up to an hour to spend time with this unprecedented novelty.

Computer Space followed in November, Nutting Associates installing their cabinet in the Dutch Goose bar near Stanford University where on sticky carpets, before glinting taps and amid woozy patrons, the video game made its fully public debut.

But while history cites *Galaxy Game* as the first commercial video game, it is the runner-up, Bushnell's title *Computer Space*, which is better remembered and to which the industry owes its existence. The winner, as is so often the case, was decided not by promptness but by business savvy. Though Pitts and Tuck invested $65,000 of their own money into *Galaxy Game*, they had neither the commercial sense nor the drive to turn their project into a serious business. Bushnell, meanwhile, an entrepreneur at heart, was blessed with a surplus of both.

THE KNOWLEDGE
Computer Space features in the classic 1973 science fiction film *Soylent Green* as well as in Steven Spielberg's breakthrough 1975 film, *Jaws*.

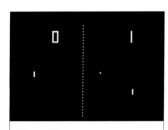

PONG

Pong's visual economy combined with its instantly recognizable rules made this the first iconic video game seated at the heart of the cultural mainstream.

Year: **1972**
Developer: **Atari Inc. (Allan Alcom)**
Publisher: **Atari Inc.**
Original format: **Arcade**
Play today: **http://bit.ly/9UMZ3G**

Avoid missing ball for high score. Few games since have expressed their instructions so concisely. But then few games since have enjoyed such an efficiency of design either. *Pong* reduces tennis to its bare components – two racquets and one ball – a limitation forced by hardware constraints but that, in its bald simplicity, helped introduce the very concept of the video game to a mainstream audience.

Pong's inception came on 24 May 1972, when Magnavox demonstrated its new console, the Odyssey, at the Airport Marina in Burlingame, near San Francisco. One attendee was Nolan Bushnell, co-creator of *Computer Space* who had recently left Nutting Associates to co-found his own arcade game company, Syzygy. Bushnell

was impressed with the machine, but, with a contract to make video games for pinball giant Bally Midway, was too preoccupied to pay much attention to the potential impact such a product might have.

Bushnell intended to create a driving game for Bally Midway and he and his partner, Ted Dabney, agreed to put $250 each into the business in order to incorporate it. However, the pair found out that their chosen name, Syzygy, was taken by another company. Bushnell drew inspiration from his favourite board game, Go, and suggested the name 'Atari', a term from the game similar to 'Check' in chess.

Below: Many copycat developers sought to emulate *Pong*'s success. Taito's *Elepong* is notable for being the first Japanese arcade machine.

THE NEWEST 2 PLAYER VIDEO SKILL GAME

Right After failing to impress Bally Midway with *Pong*, Atari took a risk and decided to manufacture the machines themselves.

On 27 June 1972, Atari Incorporated was born, and that same day hired Al Alcorn, a young engineer who had worked with Bushnell and Dabney at Ampex as a trainee. In search of a simple initial project for Alcorn to get his teeth into, Bushnell cast his mind back to the Magnavox showing, where he had played a rudimentary tennis game that came bundled with the console, *Ping-Pong*.

Bushnell told Alcorn that he had brokered a deal with General Electric to produce a coin-op version of the game. He reasoned that the task of replicating such a simple game on the relatively complicated circuits Bushnell had created would make for excellent training for Alcorn, who would be inspired to work hard if he thought it was a legitimate commercial product. There was, however, no deal. Nevertheless, the trick worked, and Alcorn applied himself to the work, improving the design by having the ball bounce at different angles depending on where it hit the bat and adding sound effects and a scoring mechanism.

The additions, while simple, were enough to make the game compelling enough to keep the three men playing it for an hour or two every evening after work. As a result, Atari changed its plans, deciding to present the game to Bally Midway as the company's first release in place of the driving game. The pinball company was unimpressed, however, owing to the fact it was only a two-player game.

Meanwhile, Atari received word that a *Pong* location test machine it had stationed in a Tavern in Sunnyvale, California had stopped working. Alcorn drove to the bar to investigate the problem. On arrival, he opened the coin box to examine the problem, only to be showered with coins. The game had proved so popular that the coin mechanism had seized. Where the average coin-op machine was earning $50 a

Above and below: From Atari's humble investment in only eight machines, they had soon manufactured and sold 8,000 in the US alone.

"We put the *Pong* prototype on a barrel in Andy Capp's bar. He had old wine barrels to use as tables and we just put it on top of the table. It wasn't even full size."
Nolan Bushnell, co-founder of Atari

week, *Pong* was averaging $200. Despite these figures, Bally Midway remained uninterested, so Atari took a risk, investing the company's money in manufacturing 11 machines and selling 8,000 themselves. The units sold fast, recouping the company's investments with $6,820 profit, enabling Atari to order another 50 units. Word spread quickly and Atari soon had orders from around the country. In total, 8,000 *Pong* units were sold in the US, spawning countless imitators, including *Elepong*, the first Japanese arcade machine.

Thanks to a white lie and a tall gamble, Bushnell had kick-started his company, whose work would come to define the first years of the medium, popularizing video games across the globe.

THE KNOWLEDGE
Nolan Bushnell's first employee was receptionist Cynthia Villanueva, hired to take his calls in order to make it appear as though Atari was a larger company than it really was.

ODYSSEY

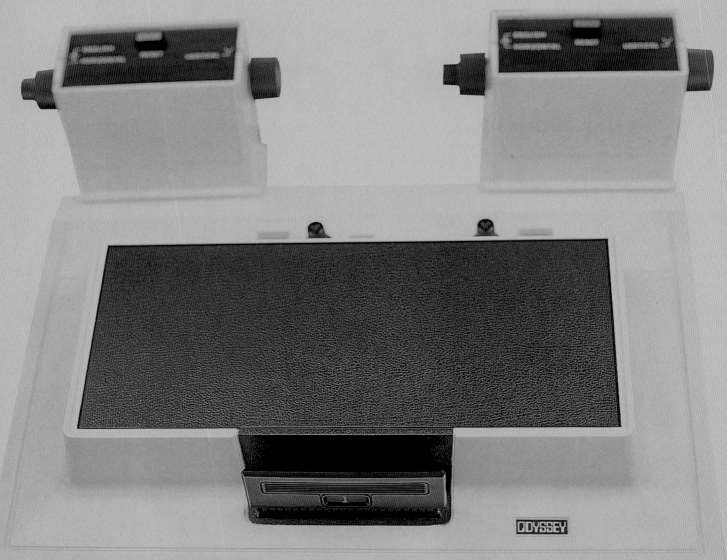

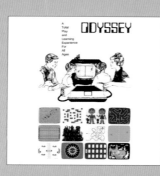

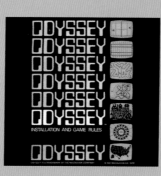

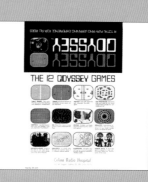

MAGNAVOX ODYSSEY

The first home video game console, named after an epic poem, signalled the start of a revolutionary journey that has ably lived up to its title.

THIS IS **ODYSSEY**

The Magnavox Odyssey was the world's first home video game console. Its Kubrick-esque logo and smooth curved white and black casing, like the dashboard of a newly born space shuttle, was pure science fiction, a far cry from the mythological poem from which it borrowed its name.

And yet, what better word with which to launch both an entirely new entertainment medium and a reimagining of what was possible with the television set? An odyssey: a journey into the long unknown, a voyage fraught with danger and peril, wonder and triumph, the very same words that articulate the base appeal of the video game itself. Indeed, the Odyssey's own journey to life started around such words, although, in this instance, the danger and peril were far from virtual.

August 1938. Ralf Baer, a 16-year-old Jew, and his family fled Germany, three weeks before Kristallnacht saw the Nazis turn cold oppression to hot violence and genocide. Upon his safe arrival in New York, Baer studied television and radio technology, before securing a job at the military contractor Loral Electronics. It was here, in 1951, that Baer and some colleagues were asked to build a television set from the ground up. A piece of test equipment used in the building of the technology drew horizontal and vertical lines across the screen, filling them with colours. Baer could move these lines up and down and wondered whether the test should be built into the set, not necessarily as a game, but as something to do when the owner grew tired of the network television shows. The idea was dismissed by the team but Baer never forgot the concept.

Fifteen years later and Baer's career trajectory had taken him to head of instrument design at New Hampshire-based military contractors Sanders Associates. In August 1966, on a New York business trip, the seed of the idea he had in 1951 broke through the topsoil of his consciousness. While waiting at the East Side Bus Terminal

after the day's work, Baer started to formulate the idea for a game-playing device that plugged into a television set.

The problem was that Sanders Associates only developed military technology, so Baer used his senior position to start work on the project, which he dubbed 'Channel LP', or, 'Let's Play', in secret. Procuring a room on the sixth floor of his office block, Baer set Bill Harrison, a technician at Sanders, to work on the project. A few weeks later, Baer invited Bill Rusch to join as chief engineer, and the three men worked together in secret.

Baer took the prototype to Herbert Chapman, corporate director of research and development, who gave the team a $2,000 grant and five months to turn the idea into something marketable. But despite Baer's small victories, Sanders was unable to find a company with TV expertise with whom to partner, and the project was placed on hold. In late 1969, Baer presented the Brown Box to a host of television manufacturers – General Electric, Magnavox, Motorola, Philco, RCA and Sylvania – in the hope that the similarities in components between the console and television sets would inspire one to jump on board. None did.

Soon after, Bill Enders, one of the RCA execs who had been present at the meeting, moved across to Magnavox, and convinced his new employers to take another look at the system. Baer, Harrison and Rusch presented their machine again and this time Magnavox said yes. The TV manufacturer signed a preliminary deal in January 1971, before redesigning the casing and renaming the project Skill-O-Vision before settling upon Odyssey.

The Magnavox Odyssey launched in May 1972, bundled with 12 games including *Ping-Pong*, the tennis game, which would inspire Atari's *Pong*. To Baer's dismay, his original price tag of $19.95 had ballooned to $99.95 but despite the tall cost, 200,000 consoles had been sold through Magnavox dealerships by 1974.

> **❝**'Are you still screwing around with that stuff, Baer?' That was the question that was asked by my boss, the executive VP, for quite a few years. I was asked that question many times. I'd smile and say nothing.**❞**
>
> Ralf Baer, inventor of the Magnavox Odyssey

Above: Ralf Baer, posed with his invention.

Below: The Odyssey's marketing echoes Nintendo's much later ad campaigns, showing off the players as much as the game itself.

[003]
LASER CLAY SHOOTING SYSTEM

LASER CLAY SHOOTING SYSTEM

The game that started Nintendo on its journey from a small Japanese playing card manufacturer to a behemothic force at the heart of the video game industry.

Year: 1973
Developer: Gunpei Yokoi
Publisher: Nintendo
Original format: Arcade
Play today: Wii Virtual Console

Below: Gunpei Yokoi, the inspirational force behind Nintendo's first video game.

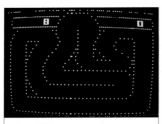

Nintendo's first step toward video game development came from Gunpei Yokoi, a young graduate of Doshinsha University, hired in 1965 by company president, Hiroshi Yamauchi.

It was Yokoi's interest in building gadgets that inspired the creation of the Nintendo Games department in 1969. Following the release of a number of products in the new toy line, Yokoi had the idea for a light beam gun that would register a hit if 'shot' at solar cells placed on targets. Working with Masayuki Uemura from Sharp, Yokoi created a working prototype, which he subsequently developed into the Nintendo Beam Gun. The toy was a gigantic success, selling more than a million units, and Yamauchi suggested using

Above: The game was later released as a launch title, complete with gun peripheral, for Nintendo's Famicom (NES).

the technology to replicate clay pigeon shooting, installing digital representations of the sport in bowling alleys across Japan. The result was *Laser Clay Shooting System*, the first commercial light-gun game in which players had to shoot targets to increase their score.While the launch event was problematic – a fault in the technology meant that a young Nintendo employee, Genyo Takeda, had to manually control the clay pigeons behind the screen, deleting them when shot and raising the score by hand – the game went on to be a launch title for the Famciom (NES).

[004]
GRAN TRAK 10

GRAN TRAK 10

Gran Trak 10 built upon Atari's considerable success with *Pong*. But it was a success that almost led to the company's downfall.

Year: 1974
Developer: Atari Inc.
Publisher: Atari Inc.
Original format: Arcade

It was three years after Atari founder Nolan Bushnell abandoned his idea for a racing video game in favour of releasing Pong that the company would revisit the idea. *Gran Trak 10*, the first racing video game, was the result of months of experimentation looking at ways in which to render the sensation of driving a car on to a screen.

Viewed from a top-down perspective, the game's cabinet featured a steering wheel, a four-position gear shift lever and brake and accelerator pedals. All of these innovations were firsts, but displayed a tendency for game makers

Above: *Gran Trak 10*'s cabinet, featuring a steering wheel and gear shift lever, was the most advanced of its day.

to want the way that players interact with their games to reflect the on-screen action realistically, one that still exists today.

A single-player game, it gives the player a limited amount of time to race around a track, whose curves are rendered with white dots marking out the edge of the road. Collision with the dots causes your car to spin out, as do the oil slicks that punctuate the course as dark splashes.

The game fast became Atari's biggest selling since *Pong*, but the company made an error and underpriced the cabinet, making the game a victim of its success.

Right: Although a success, the money lost on every *Gran Trak 10* cabinet almost brought Atari under.

SEA WOLF

If *Gran Trak 10* laid down the gauntlet for innovative arcade cabinet design, *Sea Wolf* answered the call with a suspended, monolithic periscope.

Atari's *Gran Trak 10* inspired a slew of arcade game manufacturers to look at more elaborate ways to draw players in via their cabinet designs. With *Sea Wolf*, Midway attempted to bring the experience of piloting a military submarine to life, swapping buttons and joysticks for a giant suspended periscope.

While the cabinet was of high quality, it was the control scheme that was completely novel. Peering through the periscope's viewing glass, the player lines up shots against enemy ships, before pressing a button to launch a torpedo at the target. Floating mines obstruct your shots, exploding

Left: The periscope control system added a thrilling element of realism to the game.

torpedoes before they hit their target. The cabinet embellished its graphics with creative hardware effects. A blue transparency placed over the screen created a water effect, while a red reload indicator lights up when five torpedoes have been fired. The game is played under a time limit, with the limit extended when the player passes an operator's preset threshold. The most important innovation, however, was *Sea Wolf's* high score table, the first of its kind and a legacy that stretches through history to the online leaderboards that fuel so many rivalries on contemporary consoles.

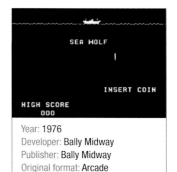

Year: 1976
Developer: Bally Midway
Publisher: Bally Midway
Original format: Arcade
Play today: iOS

Right: *Seawolf's* distinctive cabinet was beautifully constructed and adorned with colourful illustrations.

NIGHT DRIVER

Every contemporary driving simulator, from *Gran Turismo* to *Forza*, has its roots in Atari's *Night Driver*, the first racing game to be viewed from the driver's perspective.

While the principles of how to recreate the visual effect of a vehicle moving down a road into the screen may appear obvious today, in 1976 it was like trying to work out how to draw with perspective for the first time.

Dave Sheppard, a young engineer working at IBM, had been experimenting making games on the Altair 8800, one of the first microprocessor-based home computers (and, incidentally, the hardware that launched the

lucrative careers of Paul Allen and Bill Gates, who formed Microsoft to create software for the machine).

In 1976 Sheppard saw an advert from Atari for programmers, and was hired on the strength of his game experiments. Following his first project, *Flyball*, Sheppard moved on to a driving game project which he chose to develop from the driver's seat perspective.

To simulate the effect of moving along a road, Sheppard created white boxes that emerged from a horizontal plane, growing further apart as the player moved toward them. The prototype dazzled other Atari staff and, once acceleration and steering were introduced, the popularity of the game internally showed that the game would father a genre.

Year: 1976
Developer: Atari Inc.
Publisher: Atari Inc.
Original format: Arcade
Play today: Xbox 360 (Game Room)

Left: The game's night-time setting allows for a lack of scenery along the courses.

Right: The cockpit version of the *Night Driver* cabinet further heightened the driving simulation as it allowed players to brake and accelerate with their feet.

BREAKOUT

Breakout took *Pong's* paddle and ball and repurposed them into something else, while its creation first brought together the duo that would later found Apple Inc.

Year: 1976
Developer: **Atari Inc.**
Publisher: **Atari Inc.**
Original format: **Arcade**
Play today: **Web (atari.com)**

Breakout, a throwaway idea to turn *Pong* into a single-player game, changed the course of gaming history both in the short and long term. As the final game that Atari would release before the industry turned to microprocessors, it was in some ways the last game in the proto-generation of video game hardware. Not only that, but its gigantic sales propelled the software company into its most successful period yet.

But more than this, the game brought together a young hippy technician Steve Jobs and his friend Steve Wozniak, who would later apply lessons learned in creating this game when designing the Apple II computer. In a very real sense, *Breakout* begat Apple, without whom the course of computing history would be drastically different and an entire modern video game publishing platform – the App Store – may not have existed. The idea for *Breakout* was conceived during a weekend break organized by Nolan Bushnell for his engineering team to

spend brainstorming ideas for games by the ocean. One team member suggested taking the bat-and-ball concept of *Pong*, and turning it into a single-player game, in which the aim was to smash bricks.

The design of the game was both elegant and simple. You control a single paddle moving along a horizontal plane at the base of the screen, bouncing a ball upward to knock out bricks in the walled ceiling. Every time the ball strikes a brick, it disappears before knocking the ball back toward the paddle, an upturned version of hitting a tennis ball against a backyard wall. While the idea didn't make the first round of games to be developed from the session, Bushnell liked the idea enough to push it through to development.

Steve Jobs, a young, free-spirited engineer who had taken a job at Atari in order to save enough money to go

Below: Marketing for the game centred around the idea of a prison break.

Below: Because Atari were unable to satisy foreign demand for the *Breakout* cabinets, the Japanese company, Namco, bought the rights to the game and manufactured their own.

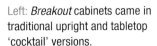

Left: *Breakout* cabinets came in traditional upright and tabletop 'cocktail' versions.

"Woz was here for a Sunday picnic at our house. We were talking and I asked: 'What did you do with that $5000?'. He says: 'What?'. He was visibly upset. I mean, he's a really good guy.**"**
Nolan Bushnell, co-founder of Atari

backpacking in India, was handed the project. Jobs was offered a $100 bonus for every integrated circuit he managed to cull from the game on top of his $750 flat fee for building the game, an incentive designed to help keep production costs down for Atari. Jobs promised he would have the design completed in just four days and, in order to hit the deadline, pulled in the help of his friend Steve Wozniak, a technical whizz-kid who worked for Hewlett Packard. Jobs offered Wozniak half of any bonus Atari paid out.

Wozniak spent every night working on the project without sleep, creating the game from a description Jobs had given him, with neither drawings nor plans. He managed to reduce the number of chips required by the

Below: *Breakout*'s two-player mode required players to alternate turns.

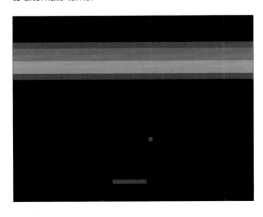

game from between 150 and 200 to just 46. The work netted Jobs a bonus of several thousand dollars, but he told Wozniak that he'd received just $700, passing on $350 to his friend for the help, something he only admitted to after the pair formed Apple Computer later that year.

Breakout generated sales of more than 11,000 units priced at $1,095 a piece, netting Atari huge profits in the short term. The company also sold Japanese arcade manufacturer Namco the rights to the game, but as they couldn't produce units fast enough to supply Japan, Namco ended up creating their own version of the game. Knock-offs of the *Breakout* design soon became as rife as they had for *Pong* in previous years.

Breakout's influence was considerable. In its subtle recasting of the *Pong* concept as a single-player experience, the cornerstone of all abstract sports games was laid. Fresh emphasis was placed on the need to judge angles in order to seek out those last remaining blocks, and the need to clear lines can be seen in *Space Invaders* and beyond. Clones and derivations of the *Breakout* idea can still be found in many contemporary releases, from PopCap's pachinko-hybrid *Peggle* to Q-Games' *Reflect Missile*. But even the vintage game remains playable and exciting today.

THE KNOWLEDGE
The Japanese Yakuza began manufacturing illegal *Breakout* cabinets when Namco, the game's official licensee, couldn't import enough machines from Atari to satisfy demand.

Year: 1977
Manufacturer: Atari
Original Cost: US $249

OCTOBER 1977

[VCS]
ATARI 2600

21

ATARI 2600

Intended by creator Atari to be a short-term Christmas product, the Atari 2600 turned the video game console into a piece of living room furniture around the world.

With its wood panel effect frontage, and black, plastic-rimmed hood leading up to a retro-futuristic panel of orange-rimmed knobs and levers, the Atari 2600 is one of the most iconic machines of the late 1970s and early 1980s. Not only that, but the system provided a crucial step in the evolution of home gaming, taking the focus away from machines dedicated to a single game to a console that could play whatever compatible game was clicked into its cartridge slot.

The machine was conceived by members of an engineering think-tank, Cyan Engineering, which Atari purchased in 1973 to specifically research and develop video game systems. Under the codename 'Stella', the team worked to create a complete CPU capable of reading whatever code was fed into it, a drastic move away from the custom logic-based hardware that was on the market at the time. However, work was slow and, in August 1976, Fairchild Semiconductor released its own CPU-based system, the Video Entertainment System. Atari was still some way off having a machine ready for mass production.

Not only that, but the company did not have sufficient cash-flow to be able to complete the system quickly. Realizing they had to act fast, founder Nolan Bushnell turned to Warner Communications for investment, selling the company to them for $28 million on the understanding that work to finish Stella would be expedited. The next year Stella, initially named the Atari Video Computer System, later changed again to the Atari 2600 after its manufacturing part number CX2600, was released in America for $249. It had cost around $100 million to develop.

Initially the reaction to the machine was lacklustre, the pressure of what looked like a grand failure resulting in the departure of Nolan Bushnell from the company in 1978. The following year, however, through a combination of word of mouth and the release of a home version of *Space Invaders*, the machine gained widespread popularity,

selling a million units in that year alone. With its 8-bit, 1.19 MHz speed processor and palette of 16 colours, the Atari 2600 was far from the most powerful console on the market at the time, technically surpassed by both the Bally Astrocade and Mattel's Intellivision. However, Atari's talent was in software development, and through a steady trickle of compelling, influential titles, the company began converting those who had previously eyed home gaming with scepticism into gamers. Originally intended by Atari to be a short-term product, marketed for one or two holiday seasons, game sales soon made it clear that home video gaming's future lay in a software-led business model. Formative hits such as *Pitfall!*, *Defender*, *Asteroids* and *Missile Command* created a snowball effect in sales, with each success selling more hardware which in turn sold more software, an upward spiral of success that every video game hardware manufacturer since has sought to replicate.

Ports of arcade titles sat alongside games based on licensed names such as *Star Wars*, *G.I. Joe* and *James Bond*, with each success story attracting the attention of yet another Hollywood studio or television company wanting to expand their empire into this brave, new frontier. However, by 1982 the system's software library had reached saturation point, with developers having squeezed the potential from the machine by falling back on uninspired ports, such as *Pac-Man*, or substandard games, such as *E.T. The Extra Terrestrial*. With no Nintendo quality control system in place the ratio of good games to broken ones eroded consumer confidence in the machine and its library of games.

In a few years, success had shifted Atari from a diminutive, agile, fun-obsessed outfit, to a dry corporation apathetic toward developing a follow-up to their once innovative hardware. In 1984 Warner sold Atari to Commodore Business Machines who immediately closed the game publishing wing. With it, the Atari 2600 died.

Above: In 1978 only 550,000 of the 800,000 systems manufactured were sold, so Nolan Bushnell left the company. He then founded the Pizza Time Theatre restaurant chain.

Below: British comedy duo Morecambe and Wise produced a series of TV advertisements in 1982 to promote the system.

"Atari was able to attract the best and the brightest... It was such an exciting thing."

Nolan Bushnell, co-founder of Atari

SPACE INVADERS

Space Invaders' shuffling, monochromatic aliens are hardly the most threatening monsters to contemporary eyes, but their arrival heralded a phenomenon.

Year: **July 1978**
Developer: **Taito (Tomohiro Nishikado)**
Publisher: **Taito**
Original format: **Arcade**
Play today: **iPhone/iPod Touch**

 **= ?**

 **= 30**

 **= 20**

 **= 10**

If *Pong* heralded the emergence of a new form of entertainment from America's primordial digital soup, *Space Invaders* was the alien life form that climbed out from the other side of the pond. No other Japanese video game visually defines the first decade of commercial gaming with such economy and effectiveness, the image of the pixilated alien invader forever burned onto pop culture's collective consciousness.

In its shape it provides a shorthand stamp for gaming's formative days and its ongoing appeal: a simplistic rendering of our worst fears, one that can be overcome with determination and a steady focus, a power fantasy to allow us to, for a moment, take control of our world's fate.

In the game, alien blobs – eleven wide and five deep – sidestep in threatening, hunched, efficient rows down the screen, the only tool in your arsenal to fend off the apocalyptic invasion a pixel peashooter and quick reactions. White bases that protect your ship from the aliens' attacks offer rudimentary cover, at least, until they are chipped away to nothing.

Tomohiro Nishikado was, by 1978, a relatively experienced video game designer for Taito, an arcade game manufacturer that had fast become the Japanese equivalent of Atari. Nishikado, who started work at Taito making electro-mechanical games, had designed numerous Japanese take-offs of Atari games: *Soccer*, a sport-themed rendering of *Pong*, *Speed Race*, a scrolling racing game in the vein of *Gran Trak 10*, and the hugely popular *Western Gun*, a Wild West-themed shooter in which two players attempted to outdraw each other.

Western Gun had been exported to the US and redesigned by Dave Nutting Associates to use microprocessors (later released with the name *Gun Fight*). When Nishikado saw how the Americans had rebuilt his game, he decided to work on a project using the same technology, paying particular attention to the advantages microprocessors offered to game animation.

Nishikado began work on a game in which the gamer had to shoot down aeroplanes but ran into trouble making the movement of the vehicles look smooth. After trying various types of foe, he settled on humans as the most realistic and smooth-moving target. However, as soon as Taito's president got wind of the idea, he baulked, banning the use of human targets in any of Taito's games, setting Nishikado back to square one. The designer decided to try to animate an alien, reasoning that the movement

Left and below: *Space Invaders* was the first non-Atari game licensed by Atari for conversion.

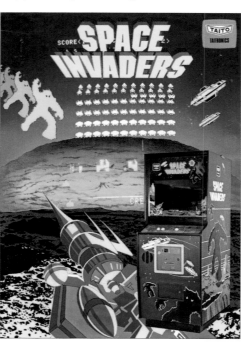

Below: The original Japanese version of the game was released as a 'cocktail table' cabinet, with pure black and white monochrome graphics.

would be similar enough to be able to re-use some of the work he had done on the humans. Drawing inspiration from the bug-like aliens that feature in H. G. Wells' novel *The War of the Worlds*, a book he had loved as a child, Nishikado began to draw Martian enemies using simple pixel patterns.

Nishikado decided that the player's missile launcher should be fixed on the horizontal plane at the base of the screen, like the paddle in Atari's *Breakout*. As with many of the most popular arcade games of the era, failure was an inevitability: the waves of alien invaders in their relentless march are certain to reach Earth in time, so the challenge derived from delaying the inevitable.

The intensity of the experience, and personification of on-screen enemies with a clarity so far unseen in video games, secured its success, and within weeks of the game's Japanese launch it had entered

the national awareness. Pachinko parlours and bowling alleys rebranded themselves as *Space Invaders* arcades, while the novelty pop-group Funny Stuff released a hit single, *Disco Space Invaders*. Within three months *Space Invaders* cabinets had proved so popular that there was a national shortage of 100 Yen coins, prompting an investigation into Taito by the Bank of Japan.

The publisher went on to sell an unprecedented 100,000 *Space Invaders* machines in Japan, while Bally Midway, the game's US distributor, sold around 60,000, tripling US sales figures for coin-op games in 1979 to $1,333 million, up from the previous year's $472 million.

However, more enduring than the profits was *Space Invaders*' legacy, one that runs through every shooting game since, whether the aliens are from outer space in *Halo* or, in the case of *Modern Warfare*, from across the world.

"I anticipated *Space Invaders* would be a hit, but never thought it would be so huge. I wasn't overwhelmed by its popularity though, because I was too busy working on the next project."
Tomohiro Nishikado, creator of *Space Invaders*

Left and right: The British novelist Martin Amis wrote his first non-fiction book, *Invasion of the Space Invaders*, about the game in 1982. "Space isn't for space cadets," he advised.

THE KNOWLEDGE
Nishikado originally titled the game *Space Monsters*, inspired by a popular song in Japan at the time, *Monster*, but the name was changed to *Space Invaders* by his superiors.

[009]

WARRIOR

Presenting conflict as a medieval duel, *Warrior* made one-on-one combat explicit in video games and pioneereed on-screen fighting.

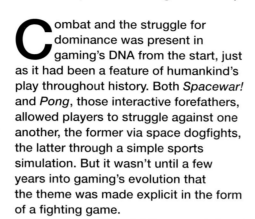

Right: The knights are rendered in monochrome vectors. Due to hardware limitations, the backgrounds are printed.

Combat and the struggle for dominance was present in gaming's DNA from the start, just as it had been a feature of humankind's play throughout history. Both *Spacewar!* and *Pong*, those interactive forefathers, allowed players to struggle against one another, the former via space dogfights, the latter through a simple sports simulation. But it wasn't until a few years into gaming's evolution that the theme was made explicit in the form of a fighting game.

The genesis of the fighting game is found in several unconnected sources, the earliest example being Sega's boxing game, *Heavyweight Champ*, released into arcade in 1976, complete with a boxing glove peripheral. But more significant to the emergence of the genre was Tim Skelly's *Warrior*, an arcade game that presented two armoured knights, viewed from above, duelling in a perilous dungeon.

Where the majority of fantasy games at the time encouraged players to explore, *Warrior*, by contrast, simply asked us to vanquish. Painted in pin-sharp vector lines, like those used in Atari's *Asteroids* (p.25), *Warrior* was let down by Vectorbeam's rudimentary arcade hardware. The unstable electronics were unable to withstand the physical wear and tear that players exerted on the machine, and there are few working examples today.

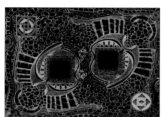

Year: **1979**
Developer: **Vectorbeam (Tim Skelly)**
Publisher: **Vectorbeam**
Original format: **Arcade**
Play today: **MAME**

[010]

GALAXIAN

Gunning to replicate *Space Invaders*' success, *Galaxian* overwhelmed players with swarms of multi-coloured alien invaders and an irresistible soundtrack.

In terms of its raw play mechanics, Namco's *Galaxian* was one step on from *Space Invaders* in the evolution of the shoot 'em up genre. Heavily influenced by Taito's world-conquering arcade game, *Galaxian* adopted the same perspective, removing the shields from which the player could duck and shoot and giving the enemy alien ships the ability to dive bomb the player, swooping down the screen in wild yet elegant lunges.

But in terms of the technology used to power the game, specifically lighting up its world with colour, *Galaxian* represented a giant leap forward for the medium. Prior to 1979, almost every arcade game had been displayed in black and white, with the occasional coloured plastic acetate overlay stuck on a machine's screen to give the illusion of colour, such as that used on *Breakout* to make the bricks appear as different colours.

The restriction was primarily to help keep costs down, as the technology required for colour games had been in existence for years. Technicians, however, didn't think colour would add anything to their games. *Galaxian* proved this accepted wisdom to be untrue, as the introduction of on-screen colour helped the game stand out from its competition, propelling it to global success. Not only that but the faster pace of play kick-started the shoot 'em up genre, resulting in a rapid evolution with innovations added to each successive game, from sequel *Galaga*'s tractor beams, to *Defender's* frantic twitch-scrolling perspective.

Year: **1979**
Developer: **Namco**
Publisher: **Namco**
Original format: **Arcade**
Play today: **Xbox Live Arcade**

Above left: In 1980 Namco partnered with Midway – freshly dumped by Taito - to release *Galaxian* in US.

ASTEROIDS

Piercing white vector lines bisect the screen's black void in Atari's most popular, profitable and visually arresting game.

Before *Asteroids*, video games demanded constant input from their player: remove your hands from the controls and your car would crash, the ball would be missed. Asteroids made inaction a viable strategy, asking players to negotiate an incoming asteroid cluster with tentative bursts of a spaceship's boosters. In this delicate balancing act, players could develop personal strategies, and even express their personalities.

The idea for the game came in an almost complete form from Lyle Rains, who was vice president of Atari's coin-op division at the time. Rains called Ed Logg, one of Atari's programmers, into his office and explained his idea for a game in which a spaceship must destroy incoming asteroids, giant space boulders that divide into smaller

and smaller chunks when hit, until they disappear completely.

While it's possible to simply dodge and weave through the asteroid belt, Logg introduced enemy spaceships that force the player to fire. Offensive players, by contrast, must rein in their attacks, lest the sea of tiny fragments create a maze too difficult to negotiate. Soundtracked by a solitary pulse, designed to mimic the player's rising heartbeat, *Asteroids* become the most popular game ever made by Atari, the second highest grossing in 1979 after *Space Invaders*.

Year: **1979**
Developer: **Atari**
Publisher: **Atari**
Original format: **Arcade**
Play today: **Web (atari.com)**

Left: Logg decided to make the game using a vector monitor, as he had done for his previous project, *Lunar Lander*.

ADVENTURE

Conceived as a way for an absent father to connect with his children, *Adventure* connected a generation of players with the dim-lit joy of spelunking.

Written by Will Crowther, a programmer at defence contractor Bolt Beranek and Newman, *Adventure* began life as a text mission, a way to stay in contact with his two daughters following a messy divorce. Crowther wrote the cave explorations game on his work computer, basing it on the Bed Quilt Cave, part of the Mammoth-Flint Ridge caves of Kentucky that he and his ex-wife used to explore.

He divided the cave system into rooms, giving each a text description before adding treasure to find, monsters to defeat and simple puzzles to solve. The game gained popularity among his colleagues who made copies, which soon began turning up on university networks across the US. In early 1978 Warren Robbinet, a young

Atari engineer, played the game at the Stanford Artificial Intelligence Lab and decided to pitch a graphical remake to his bosses as his next project for the Atari 2600. Robbinet created 29 rooms for the cave system, turning the text adventure into an action game in which players dodge and fight monsters and collect items as they search for an enchanted chalice.

Like many Atari engineers at the time, Robbinet was disillusioned with the company's policy to not credit designers and so added a 30th secret room that, if discovered, revealed the text: 'Created by Warren Robbinet', widely considered the first Easter Egg (hidden feature) in a video game.

Year: **1979**
Developer: **Atari**
Publisher: **Atari**
Original format: **Atari 2600**
Play today: **Web (atari.com)**

Below: The Easter Egg game was not found until after shipping.

THE 1980s

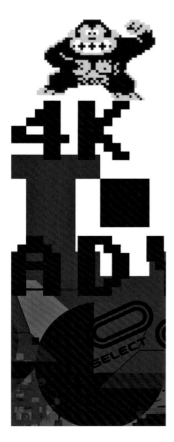

If the 1970s saw the video game industry learn to walk and stand tall, the 1980s brought it back to its knees. A backlash was perhaps inevitable. Ten years earlier, nobody outside a handful of computer science university students had heard of a video game. By 1980, video games had impacted the world in profound ways, invading the town and city centres via amusement arcades and the living room via consoles connected to the family television. What were the long-term effects of all this time and attention people were spending in virtual worlds, precision twitching in front of screens, grasping at high scores meaningless outside their digital context?

On 9 November 1982, Dr Everett Koop, the US Surgeon General, vocalized America's fears that, until that point, had been brewing in the cultural subconsciousness. Speaking at the Western Psychiatric Institute and Clinic in Pittsburgh, Dr Koop challenged America to confront the causes of domestic violence and child abuse. After the speech, he took a question from an audience member asking whether he thought video games had a negative effect on young people. Yes, he replied. Teenagers were becoming addicted 'body and soul' to video games, a form of entertainment in which "everything is 'zap the enemy', there's nothing constructive".

Koop added that there was no scientific evidence to support his view, but by then the newspapers already had their headline. "Surgeon General sees danger in video games" proclaimed the Associated Press news agency the next day, prompting Dr Koop to release a statement emphasizing that his views were not official government policy and that "nothing in my remarks should be interpreted as implying video games are, per se, violent in nature or harmful to children."

These reassurances came too late. Dr Koop had legitimized the fears of a nation of parents, who already viewed the meteoric rise of this new entertainment medium with suspicion. Ten thousand voices of concerned parents and politicking politicians echoed Dr Koop's sentiments. They branded arcades as centres of delinquency and, thanks to abhorrent sex-themed games

such as *Custer's Revenge*, in which players were tasked with raping a Native American woman tied to a post, many called for the wholesale ban of video games. Alongside this gathering storm of moral outrage, the industry was rotting from the inside. The proliferation of substandard games on the Atari 2600 had eroded consumer confidence in the machine. Likewise, the unwillingness of publishers to properly credit or reward the game designers who had made them millions of dollars of profit had created disillusionment at the creative heart of the industry.

Just 28 days after Dr Koop's proclamation, the video game boom turned to bust when Atari announced to investors that its expected growth figures for the fourth quarter of the year had dropped from 50% to between 10–15%. The announcement caused a collapse in confidence among investors, who withdrew their money.

While Atari had pulled the trigger, the causes of the crash were multitudinous. In part the popularity of *Pac-Man* and its ilk had produced too many arcade operators, who bought machines on credit and installed them in locations that weren't profitable. The audience of arcade goers was also fracturing. Enthusiasts were growing in skill and, to keep up, game developers were making their games increasingly difficult. But the mainstream audience, who were responsible for the industry's fast growth, was left behind, finding the new games too difficult.

From the US arcade industry's peak of $4,862 million, sales almost halved by 1984 to just $2,500 million. Shops, saturated with stock for the home consoles, stopped ordering new games and the knock-on effect was that prices were slashed from $30 a game to under $10, and the thousands of start-up developers suffocated.

But from these ashes, new life would rise in the second half of the 1980s. While the US market deflated, the Japanese industry went from strength to strength, in principle thanks to Nintendo's Famicom, the quality assurance controls that the company used to defend against substandard games, and a cultural shift that saw game designers treasured, rather than treated as a commodity.

PAC-MAN

Video gaming's first icon, *Pac-Man* was designed to reach beyond the typical demographic and convince girls to visit the arcade.

Year: **1980**
Developer: **Namco**
Publisher: **Namco**
Original format: **Arcade**
Play today: **Xbox Live Arcade**

Below: Toru Iwatani, *Pac-Man*'s creator, knew that the game's cute, brightly coloured character had massive merchandizing potential.

Right: Having secured exclusive rights to release the game in the US and reaping massive profits as a result, Bally Midway were keen to protect the integrity of their investment.

Modelled on the image of a pizza with a single slice removed, *Pac-Man* was the first iconic lead character that was born of the video game industry. His constantly masticating head is easily as recognizable as *Space Invaders'* solitary alien, yet rather than communicating cold threat, his warm yellow colouring and chirruping theme music make him likeable, not merely recognizable.

That appeal, perhaps, comes from *Pac-Man*'s primary behaviour in the game. If reduced to a single verb, one might describe the interaction of *Pong* as 'bat' or *Space Invaders* as 'shoot'. *Pac-Man*, by contrast, has an innately human defining action: 'eat'. This was no accident.

While Eugene Jarvis was working hard to appeal to highly competitive male gamers in America with his shoot 'em up *Defender*, Japanese designer Toru Iwatani wanted to create a game that would appeal to female players, broadening the demographic of people who played video games in arcades. The thinking was that, if Namco could design a game that appealed to women,

then men and women would want to play arcade games together, meaning that machines could be sold to locations where couples went on dates.

Iwatani's simplistic yet effective line of reasoning was that women particularly enjoy cakes and desserts, so decided to design a game in which eating was the key action. Pac-Man, himself designed to look like a foodstuff, must travel around a maze, eating every dot in the corridors to clear a stage. To introduce the necessary peril to the game, Iwatani designed four ghosts who chase Pac-Man, requiring the player to carefully manoeuvre around the maze in order to eat all the dots without being cut off by the ghosts.

Pac-Man's only defence against the ghosts are four 'power pills', each located in a different corner of the maze. When he eats one of these pills, the ghosts turn blue and sheepishly flee the player, who is temporarily able to gobble them up. The mechanic, whereby the player's role was switched on the fly from prey to pursuer, was new to video games, and introduced a level of unusually deep strategy, elegantly presented so that anyone could grasp the fundamentals within moments.

The game debuted at the same show as Williams' *Defender*, the October 1980 Amusement and Music Operators Association Trade Show in Chicago. As with Jarvis' game, the response of attendees to *Pac-Man* was lukewarm. Namco's US distributor Bally Midway, also a pinball manufacturer, was unsure that players would be interested in a maze game and delegates at the event agreed with them, expressing a preference for Namco's other title on show, *Rally-X*.

As with *Defender*, the response from show delegates proved to be the

Don't Trifle With A Heavyweight

Above: The game has spawned many sequels, including *Super Pac-Man*, which altered the game's mechanics by introducing locked chambers containing fruit and power pellets. Players were required to eat keys to unlock the chambers and complete the levels.

Above: *Pac-Man* is one of the longest running video game series. Perhaps due to this longevity and ubiquity, *Pac-Man* is part of the collection of the Smithsonian Institution in Washington, D.C. and features in New York's Museum of Modern Art. The original English name was 'Puck Man'.

"Pac-Man was planned around the idea of getting girls into arcades. That's also why the enemies are so colorful – they would be harder to hate."
Toru Iwatani, creator of *Pac-Man*

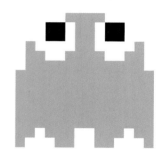

exact opposite to that of the game-playing public. *Pac-Man* immediately attracted huge numbers of female players to the arcade, and the introduction of an entirely new demographic to the industry saw vast numbers of amusement arcades spring up across the whole of the United States.

Not only that, but the iconic design of Pac-Man himself saw video game merchandise take-off in earnest. An ABC-TV spin-off cartoon series featuring the character attracted 20 million viewers on its first broadcast, while lunchboxes, stickers, Frisbees, yo-yos and duvet covers baring Pac-Man's likeness spread across the world. Atari benefited hugely from *Pac-Man*'s success, thanks to a $1 million

exclusivity deal signed with Namco in 1978, before the Japanese publisher had any hits to its name.

As a result, Atari found itself in possession of the rights to release the *Pac-Man* game on all home consoles and computers without limitation. In April 1982 Atari released *Pac-Man* on the Atari 2600, selling more than 12 million cartridges worldwide. The terms of the deal meant that Namco earned just 50 cents from each $25 game sold, netting the US company giant arguably undeserved profits, and ensuring their console dominated the competition in no uncertain terms.

THE KNOWLEDGE
While planning the game *Pac-Man* designer Toru Iwatani sewed stuffed toys and made t-shirts with iron-ons to illustrate to his bosses the merchandizing opportunities the game presented.

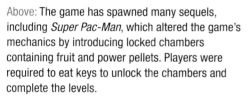

[014]

MISSILE COMMAND

Released while Cold War tensions were taut and high, *Missile Command* was the first mainstream arcade game to take current affairs as its theme.

Year: July 1980
Developer: Atari (Dave Theurer)
Publisher: Atari
Original format: Arcade
Play today: iOS

Below: *Missile Command* was controlled using a unique tracking ball system.

Right: In 1981, an enhancement kit launched to convert *Missile Command* into *Super Missile Attack*, increasing the game's difficulty by adding a UFO enemy, perhaps at the cost of the social commentary.

Without the Cold War driving the advance of military technology, the first mainframe computers that gave birth to the video game as we know it today would not have existed. But it wasn't until the release of *Missile Command* that a video game would explicitly reflect the global anxieties fuelled by nuclear weapons.

Originally known as *Armageddon*, *Missile Command* charged players with staving off the nuclear apocalypse by shooting down incoming missiles as they followed a trajectory toward six cities at the base of the screen; a reflection on the nuclear tensions that still existed between the US and Russia at the start of the 1980s.

Dave Theurer, a young engineer at Atari, was given a simple synopsis for the game by Lyle Rains, vice president of the company's coin-op division. In his idea, the player was charged with protecting the coast of California from incoming missile attacks using carefully positioned counterstrikes to knock them from the air.

The original plan was to have the player detect the position of missiles using a radar read-out, but this idea was dropped in favour of the more immediate, arcade-appropriate task of spatial reasoning in which players must time smart bomb explosions to take down the incoming missiles. Positioning counterstrikes was handled via a trackball used to position a cursor on the screen, a precursor to the mouse technology that would come to define human interaction with computers in subsequent years.

The team stripped the game back to its bare bones, removing geographical features that identified the location as California, and simplifying the mechanics by eliminating submarines, missile transporters and other details they thought made the design too fussy. The result is one of the most pure arcade experiences of 1980.

Theurer worked on the game for six months, during which time he would often wake in the middle of the night in a cold sweat, brought on by the game's terrifying subject matter. However, the game offers no useful commentary on the nuclear weapons issue, other than perhaps making their intransigence explicit. Nevertheless, after *Missile Command*, no subject was too grave for video games.

DEFENDER

Hectic, complex, overwhelming and mad-as-hell, Eugene Jarvis' debut video game defied mastery and yet, in its deviousness, plotted a course to the future.

In contrast to *Space Invaders'* neat mechanical rows of shuffling aliens, *Defender*'s attackers arrive in a squall of chaos. The most uncomfortably difficult game of its time, through a combination of overfussy controls and twitch play that required reactions no game had yet demanded of its player, it was arguably the first video game designed primarily for experts, hostile to beginners.

But there was a great deal riding on *Defender*. For the game's publisher, Williams, it represented the company's comeback attempt to re-enter the video game business from which it had departed years earlier. For the game's designer, Eugene Jarvis, an aspiring pinball designer forced to make video games by virtue of being born too late, it was a chance to prove he had the skill to make the switch.

Jarvis' vision for the project was clear. He wanted to make what he dubbed a 'sperm game', an experience that would appeal to thrill-seeking males, offering the

Below: In 1982 Steve Juraszek from Illinois played *Defender* for over 16½ hours on a single credit.

Out of this world entertainment!

Record-breaking earnings!

player a rush of excitement. Jarvis also believed that defence was a more emotionally engaging play mechanic than offence, and so wanted to introduce something for the player to defend and rescue, rather than merely lash out at.

One of the first games to introduce the concept of saving others, *Defender* tapped into part of the human psyche that video games had yet to discover.

He finished coding the game hours before its debut at the October 1980 Amusement and Music Operators Association Trade Show in Chicago. Williams, nervous about their big comeback game, was disappointed with the game's showing, which saw delegates dismiss the game as too complex.

In the following weeks, their hunch was proved wrong as players flocked to conquer the tough game. Soon after release the game was taking around 150 million quarters per week across the US, securing Williams' place as a publisher, and Jarvis' reputation as a game designer.

Year: 1980
Developer: Williams
Publisher: Williams
Original format: Arcade
Play today: Xbox Live Arcade

"All the best video games are about survival – it's our strongest instinct, stronger than food, sex, lust for money..."
Eugene Jarvis, creator of *Defender*

THE BRAVE NEW WORLD OF *Williams*®

Below: Jarvis designed the controls to emulate *Space Invaders* and *Asteroids* with the left hand manipulating the joystick to reflect Taito's game and the right hand stabbing buttons in a way similar to Atari's.

DONKEY KONG

The furious monkey that kidnapped the Hollywood cliché of blonde girl in *Donkey Kong* also helped her lover become video gaming's most iconic character.

Year: 1981
Developer: Nintendo (Shigeru Miyamoto)
Publisher: Nintendo
Original format: Arcade
Play today: Nintendo Wii (Virtual Console)

Donkey Kong, Nintendo's first global hit, was the game that defined and popularized the platforming genre. Moreover, it launched the career of Shigeru Miyamoto, Nintendo's best-known designer and, in the mustachioed visage of its lead character, video gaming's most recognizable character, Mario, was born.

As Shigeru Miyamoto approached his graduation in the mid-1970s, having been awarded a degree in Industrial Design, his father approached an old family friend, Hiroshi Yamauchi, to see whether he had a job at Nintendo he could offer his son. Miyamoto, a keen artist, was given the task of designing the art for the outside panels of two arcade cabinets the toymaker was building, *Radarscope* and *Sheriff*.

Radarscope, a *Space Invaders'*-style shoot 'em up, went on to be a hit in Japan, but sold only half of the 2,000 machines Nintendo built for the US market. As a result, Nintendo decided to create a new game to run on the unsold *Radarscope* machines and turned to the cabinet's artist, Miyamoto, to conceptualize an idea for the game that would appeal to a Western audience.

Initially the young designer was told to devise a game featuring Popeye. However, unable to obtain the rights to the comic strip, Nintendo left Miyamoto to originate his own character for the game. Drawing inspiration from the classic 1933 film *King Kong* and the fable Beauty and the Beast, he constructed an elaborate story involving a gorilla that had escaped and kidnapped his master's girlfriend, Pauline. In the story, the gorilla climbed to the top of a seven-storey construction site and began hurling barrels at his pursuing master below.

Miyamoto designed the game's characters on square paper, each block representing a single pixel on the screen. The lead character's iconic moustache was a forced design decision. As the character sprite in *Donkey Kong* needed to be so small, it was difficult to display lips in a way that looked believable. The black blocky moustache was an elegant solution to a tricky problem.

When Yamauchi saw the game he asked Miyamoto to find an English name for it. Since Miyamoto spoke only a little English he used a dictionary to look up the words he wanted: 'Donkey', as a synonym for 'Stubborn', and 'Kong' for gorilla. The gorilla's master was just known as 'Jumpman'.

The game was an overnight success in America, selling the entire allocation of *Radarscope* cabinets. Over the course of its production run, *Donkey Kong* sold 67,000 cabinets, making Nintendo's handful of American staff,

Below: *Donkey Kong*'s 22nd level is unofficially known as the 'kill screen'. An error in the game's programming kills Mario after a few seconds, cruelly ending the talented player's game.

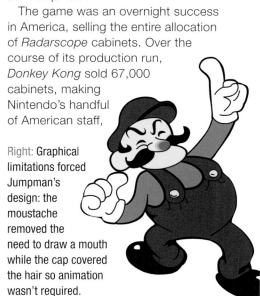

Right: Graphical limitations forced Jumpman's design: the moustache removed the need to draw a mouth while the cap covered the hair so animation wasn't required.

Above: Pauline, Jumpman's girlfriend, was originally known as 'The Lady'.

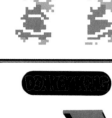

Left and above: Pauline, Jumpman's girlfriend in *Donkey Kong*, provided one of gaming's first damsels-in-distress.

all of whom worked on commission, wealthy. Following the game's success, Nintendo changed Jumpman's name to Mario in honour of its US landlord, Mario Segale, who had generously agreed to give the company's American office more time to pay its rent prior to *Donkey Kong*'s release.

Following the game's success in US arcades, Nintendo granted toy company Coleco exclusive rights to create a home version of the game for its forthcoming Colecovision console. Atari had been offered the rights to the game, but turned Nintendo down on the grounds that the Japanese company wanted too much money. Atari's decision would prove disastrous for the company, as *Donkey Kong*'s success allowed the Colecovision to overtake Atari's new 5200 console, and as such, directly helped bring about the industry crash of 1982.

That same year, the game's triumph almost turned to disaster for Nintendo when Universal Studios threatened to sue the Japanese company claiming that the

"I don't think the Colecovision would have been launched as successfully as it had if we didn't have the exclusive console rights to *Donkey Kong*."
Michael Katz, Coleco's Vice President of Marketing

game infringed copyright on the *King Kong* film. The accusation seemed reasonable; Miyamoto had overtly based the game's antagonist on the great ape. However, rather than simply pay a licensing fee to Universal, Nintendo's lawyer, Howard Lincoln, advised that they stand up to Universal's bullying tactics.

When the case eventually came to court, the judge ruled against Universal Studios after Nintendo demonstrated that, as *King Kong* was more than 40 years old, the character was in the public domain. On 29 July 1985, Universal was ordered to pay Nintendo $1.8 million for "legal fees, photocopying expenses, costs incurred creating graphs and chart, and lost revenues". Howard Lincoln, Nintendo's attorney, was offered a full time job at the company and became senior vice president of Nintendo in the US.

Donkey Kong has remained one of the most popular games of the early 1980s over succeeding decades and players still doggedly compete for the world record score.

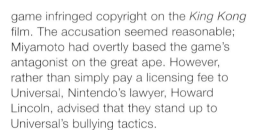

"No matter how good you are there are always ways to improve your game."
Hank Chien, *Donkey Kong* world record-holder

THE KNOWLEDGE
The 2007 film *The King of Kong* documents the real-life rivalry between Billy Mitchell and Steve Wiebe as they vie to set the world record of highest score in *Donkey Kong*.

MUST PLAY:
Manic Miner
Jet Set Willy
Attack of the Mutant
Camels
Knight Lore
Head Over Heels

Year: April 1982
Manufacturer: Sinclair
Original Cost: £125-175 (dependent on size of memory included)

ZX SPECTRUM

The ZX Spectrum was among the first home computers in the UK, bringing computer games to the masses before earning inventor Clive Sinclair a knighthood.

Clive Sinclair, known affectionately as Uncle Clive by his fans and followers, was the embodiment of the British boffin inventor with his bald pate, thin-rimmed spectacles, tidy ginger beard and his determination to retain freedom of action and choice. He built his company and reputation in the 1960s, by reverse engineering the latest, most expensive consumer electronics and releasing his own versions at a fraction of the cost of the originals.

By the early 1980s he'd enjoyed a rich mixture of successes and failures: while his pocket calculators had turned an exclusive technology into a ubiquitous one, his digital Black Watch had almost brought about bankruptcy through defective returns. Sinclair's approach to business was that of the purebred inventor, with his ambition for each invention straining no further than hoping to fund the next.

It was from the ashes of another of Sinclair's failures that his greatest success was born, one that kick-started the British video game industry and inspired the first generation of so-called bedroom coders. By the early 1980s Sinclair was no stranger to home computing. His ZX80 machine, with its extraordinarily low price point of £99.95 (£79.99 if the consumer opted

for the kit version, which they could solder together themselves), had brought computing to the masses, fast becoming the UK's biggest-selling home computer. While the Commodore PET and Apple II were still prohibitively expensive, the ZX80 and its more powerful successor the ZX81 were affordable to most households, and the first British-developed games began to appear.

In 1981 the state-owned British Broadcasting Corporation put out a tender to computer manufacturers inviting pitches to build a standardized computer platform for the country. Sinclair pitched for the contract to build the BBC's machine but lost out to rival Acorn Computers, a computer firm founded by former Sinclair employee Chris Curry. This failure only steeled Uncle Clive's resolve and he launched a savage attack on the corporation, saying: "[The BBC] should not be making computers, any more than they should be making BBC cars or BBC toothpaste."

But Sinclair had more than mere words for a response. Fuelled by disappointment, he started work on the ZX Spectrum, a computer he wanted to release at a fraction of the size and cost of the rival BBC Micro. Released in April 1982 at a starting cost of £125, the Spectrum fast outsold both the Commodore 64 and BBC Micro. It was even singled out by Prime Minister Margaret Thatcher as an example of the UK's technological pre-eminence during a visit from the Japanese premier.

Sinclair's intention was for the spectrum to be an affordable multipurpose computer in the home. However, thanks to its architecture and the ease with which games could be programmed, it was soon defined by interactive entertainment. 226 British-made Spectrum games launched in the console's first 8 months, with no fewer than 1,188 released in 1983.

Almost overnight, the Spectrum spawned the British video game industry, with 95 new game studios opening in 1982, a figure that expanded to 458 in 1983.

Above: Many notable games developers began their careers on the ZX Spectrum, including David Perry, inventor of the cloud-gaming service Gaikai, and Tim and Chris Stamper, founders of Rare.

> "[The BBC] should not be making computers, any more than they should be making BBC cars or BBC toothpaste."
>
> Clive Sinclair on the BBC Micro computer

Below: *Jet Set Willy* was one of the first cassette-based games to come with copy protection – a set of colour codes, one of which had to be entered before the game would load.

Below: Users who purchased the cheaper version of the ZX Spectrum, the 16k memory model, could send their machine for a memory upgrade to bring the spec up to the more expensive 48k model. To save money on these RAM expansions, Sinclair used defective 64K chips with only 32K RAM actually working or available.

[017]

Year: 1982
Developer: Williams (Eugene Jarvis)
Publisher: Williams
Original format: Arcade
Play today: XBox 360 (Arcade)

"Games like *Defender*, *Robotron*, and *Asteroids* give an extra ship every 10,000, 25,000, or what have you. You never feel like you're out of the game. Even if you have the most miserable start, you can always redeem yourself."

Eugene Jarvis, creator of
Robotron 2084

ROBOTRON 2084

Introducing a novel control scheme derived from a temporary handicap, *Robotron'*s punitive rhythms of play still offer perhaps the finest twitch arcade experience.

In every arcade game you are doomed from the first coin: you play to delay the inevitable. These are the in-built economics of the arcade business, an inescapable fact derived from their heritage as an offshoot of the amusement arcade family tree. The game must always win in the end. The trick then, for the game designer, is to convince the player that there's the possibility that they might just, with enough care, practice and stubbornness, beat the machine.

Robotron 2084 is the exception that proves the rule. It gobbles your money without remorse, humiliating its player for

Above and below: The game was developed in six months by Eugene Jarvis and Larry DeMar, founders of *Vid Kidz.*

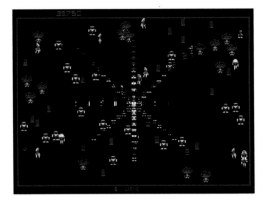

Above: Players must defeat all enemy robots in a 'wave' before the next level starts – a design that has resurfaced as 'Horde' mode in many contemporary titles.

the 15 seconds of play most will, at best, be able to manage before the Game Over screen appears. And yet, somehow *Robotron 2084* manages to keep its player returning for more punishment. Perhaps it's the challenge of insurmountable odds, or in the plight of the human family members that you must rescue from the endless waves of attackers who turn the screen into a pixel bloodbath. Despite being the most difficult game of the 1980s, *Robotron 2084* is also one of the most fondly remembered.

For Eugene Jarvis, the pinball machine designer who had his first video games success with *Defender*, it continued to explore themes of challenge, survival and protecting others. But the game's most enduring legacy to video games, its twin stick control scheme, was one forced by circumstance, not choice. Jarvis worked on *Robotron 2084* following a car crash in which he ended up with a broken hand. Unable to press buttons, Jarvis set the game up to use two arcade sticks, one to move the character, the other to aim and fire its gun.

While the game's notorious difficulty and overwhelming experience limited its appeal – it sold fewer copies than *Defender* – the manoeuverability and precision the control scheme afforded has seen it mimicked throughout gaming's history.

Year: **August 1982**
Manufacturer: **Commodore**
Original Cost: **$595**

AUGUST 1982
[C64]
COMMODORE 64

37

COMMODORE 64

Designed by an Auschwitz survivor, America's first mainstream home computer offered, like the British ZX Spectrum, fertile soil for game developers.

Jack Tramiel, a Polish Jew who survived six years in the Auschwitz concentration camp, was the man responsible for bringing the PC to America. His company, founded in 1955 to design counting machines and calculators, launched the first computer to retail for under $1,000, the Commodore PET and, in his subsequent invention, the Commodore 64, the first computer to function primarily as a video game machine.

Tramiel's venture into the video game industry began in 1976, when he bought the chip manufacturer MOS Technologies for $800,000 (£490,000). MOS built the 6053 processor at the heart of the Apple II, 400 and 800 series computers.

A ruthless businessman, Tramiel was well known for allowing his suppliers to continue to ship product without paying them, stepping in at the last minute to buy the companies out for a fraction of their worth, while simultaneously clearing Commodore's debts. He was obsessed with lowering the cost of his company's products, often employing the slogan: "We're building computers for the masses, not the classes."

In 1981, Commodore released the VIC-20, the company's first foray into video game scene. Just one year later, the company unveiled the VIC-20's follow-up, a vastly more powerful machine marketed as a direct competitor to the $1,000 Apple II, at a fraction of the cost.

As Commodore owned the system's chip maker, the company was able to keep manufacturing costs extremely low, each machine costing an estimated $135 to build, netting the company $460 profit on each unit sold. In this way, the Commodore 64 was able to weather the storm that swallowed the rest of the games industry during the early 1980s and by January 1983, Forbes reported the company was selling 25,000 machines a month.

By the end of 1983 Commodore became the first computer company to report a $1 billion sales year, surpassing Apple for market penetration. Immediately after the announcement, the company reduced the price of the C64 to $200. The new price point made the computer – and its vast library of games – more affordable to families across the Western world, and the system remained in production until 1993.

Jack Tramiel resigned as CEO on 13 January 1984 but remained a name that was synonymous with the industry when he later purchased Atari Corporation.

Above right: The Commodore 64 sold in excess of 12.5 million units over its lifetime, making it the highest-selling personal computer model.

> **"In 1982 no one was buying computers for software, other than for games."**
> Bob Yannes, designer of the Commodore 64

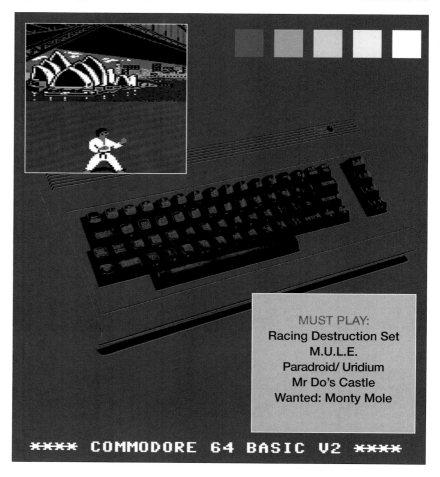

MUST PLAY:
**Racing Destruction Set
M.U.L.E.
Paradroid/ Uridium
Mr Do's Castle
Wanted: Monty Mole**

✳✳✳✳ COMMODORE 64 BASIC V2 ✳✳✳✳

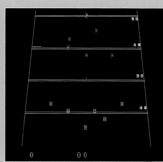

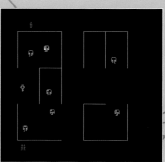

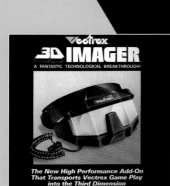

MUST PLAY:
Minestorm
Fortress of Narzod
Scramble
Berzerk
Polar Rescue

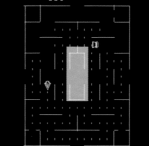

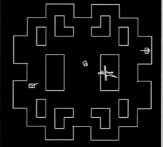

Year: **November 1982**
Manufacturer: **GCE**
Original Cost: **$199**

NOVEMBER 1982
[VEC]
VECTREX

39

VECTREX

The Vectrex's built-in screen, responsive joysticks and high-quality speakers made the system the closest many would come to owning an arcade machine.

The only vector-based home console with an integrated screen, GCE's Vectrex remains desirable and iconic today, decades after its debut and subsequent decline. Where most systems of the era offered embryonic games with rudimentary visuals that have aged poorly, Vectrex's brilliant white vector lines that light up its black screen like laser comets remain irresistibly chic.

The system, on the market for just two years, was home to just 30-odd commercially available games. The Vectrex's rise and fall exactly mirrored that of the wider video game industry, enjoying the boom success of the early 1980s before suffering the obliterating crash of 1984.

The original idea for the machine derived from Western Technologies. One of the company's employees, John Ross, bought a one-inch CRT screen, the type used in aircraft heads-up displays, in a surplus store. He brought it in to work with the idea of using the technology to develop a prototype handheld game. Kenner, best known for its range of *Star Wars* figurines, saw the potential and partnered with Western to build a prototype using a 5-inch screen, before promptly pulling out of the deal. Weeks later, GCE stepped in, changed the hardware design to accommodate a 9-inch monitor and gave the project the name 'Mini-Arcade'. By January 1982 the console was nearing completion but GCE had no games. Ed Smith, Western Technologies'

head of engineering, began to recruit students from Georgia Tech College, setting them the challenge to create 12 games by June that year. One staff member recalls visiting the warehouse at the time: "One programmer used to snort whipped cream gas all night while programming. [People would] trip on the cans when coming in for work the next morning. There were cases of them all over the floor. GCE management apparently put up with this..." The technique appeared to work. By April the games *Mine Storm*, *Berzerk, Rip Off* and *Star Trek* were all complete and, following a brainstorming session, the console's name was changed to Vectrex.

Despite the relatively high price point, the system sold well. In March 1983, the board game developer Milton Bradley bought GCE, just before the market crashed in 1984. MB reportedly lost around $31 million on the Vectrex as the bottom fell out of the market while Atari allegedly threatened to withhold their games and systems from any distributor that also carried Vectrex products.

In recent years, the machine has enjoyed a resurgence of interest thanks to its unique graphical aesthetics. When it comes to vector-based game consoles, the Vectrex has no rival. If you long for a minimalist vector glow to light your living room, there is nowhere else to go.

Below: Smith Engineering's open source policy has spawned a raft of new games for the system.

Above: In 1983 efforts were made to develop a colour Vectrex. One prototype used a TV tube that was prohibitively expensive. Another used a projection TV with three vector scan tubes. This worked well but was also commercially unviable.

"I presented before every major toy studio. I presented to all the major toy companies, venture capitalists, you name it. We probably did fifty presentations in the span of a month."

Hope Nieman, marketing director at GCE

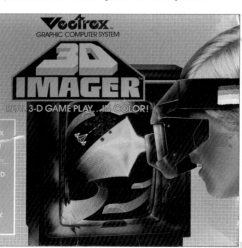

E.T. THE EXTRA TERRESTRIAL

The most expensive video game yet made seeded the young games business' downfall, a commercial catastrophe that saw the game and its industry literally buried.

Year: 1982
Developer: Atari (Howard Scott-Warshaw)
Publisher: Atari, Inc.
Original format: Atari 2600
Play today: MAME

> **"Ross called me and asked me what I thought. I said: 'I think it's a very dumb idea. We've never really made an action game out of a movie'. And he said: 'Well, I've guaranteed Spielberg $25 million royalty regardless of what we did."**
>
> Ray Kassar, CEO of Atari

Below: While the game eventually became one of the best-selling Atari 2600 titles, with sales of 1.5 million copies, between 2.5 and 3.5 million cartridges went unsold.

Multi-million dollar advances, Hollywood directors and the promise of wild riches followed by greedy overproduction, miserable returns, abject commercial failure and, finally, sandy entombment. No video game plots the boom and bust of the early 1980s US video game market better than Atari's *E.T. The Extra Terrestrial*, the game of the movie of the same name. Released as the Atari 2600's 1982 Christmas blockbuster, *E.T.* shouldered financial and creative expectations that would have been a brutal burden for any title, let alone one with a five-week development period.

Steve Ross, chairman of Atari's parent company Warner Communications – the most senior person working in the industry at the time-brokered the deal that led to the game's production. In an unprecedented act of hubris Ross struck a $25 million deal with Hollywood's director-du-jour, Steven Spielberg, gaining the rights to make a game of his new film.

But the offer was made without the consultancy of anyone at Atari who would ultimately be charged with creating the product. Ray Kassar, CEO of Atari, was mortified when he learned of Ross' deal, which afforded the company just five weeks to design and develop the entire game. Kassar pointed out to Ross that, even aside from the unrealistic production window, the film's non-action orientated storyline didn't lend itself well to a video game tie-in and called the entire enterprise "a dumb idea". Ross was adamant: the build must go ahead.

Kassar persuaded 25-year-old Howard Scott-Warshaw to design the game, promising a sizeable bonus in return for his necessarily strenuous efforts. Because he had to throw it together at such short notice and in such a tight timeframe, Scott-Warshaw struggled to create a cohesive experience that meshed with the film's premise and spirit. Players were tasked with exploring various static screens in search of

Above: Atari reportedly earned $25 million in sales of the game, but netted a far greater loss of $100 million.

three randomly placed fragments of an interplanetary telephone which, when combined, would allow the titular character to phone home.

Atari, rather than holding the game back for improvement, went ahead with the deal that had been struck with Spielberg and shipped five million copes to retailers across America in time for Christmas. Within weeks, the majority had been returned, unsold. Ross, as the most senior person at Warner, pushed the blame onto Kassar who was promptly fired from his position as CEO of Atari.

Twelve months after work had begun on the game, the returned cartridges, along with thousands of defective Atari 2600 cartridges, consoles and accessories, were crushed and loaded onto trucks at Atari's El Paso, Texas plant, then dumped into a landfill in New Mexico. On 29 September 1983, they were covered in concrete along with the glory days of the video game industry.

DRAGON'S LAIR

Dragon's Lair's rich and detailed animations proved that visual fidelity could be a short cut to financial success for game makers – even if the game within was ugly.

Everybody remembers the first time they saw *Dragon's Lair*. In the near-instantaneous shift from *Space Invaders'* jaggedy blobs to the curvaceous, cel-animated style of *Dragon's Lair* it was as if video games had skipped five stages of visual evolution and, in this one game, arrived at their final, mesmerizing form.

Rick Dyer's company, Advanced Microcomputer Systems, had been working on an interactive fantasy world game based on *Adventure* for two years when he saw veteran Disney animator Don Bluth's film *The Secret of Nimh*. In that moment Dyer decided to contact Bluth with a view to making an entirely new animated game using the recently unveiled laserdisc technology.

Bluth agreed and, with his team of 300 animators, began work on a game featuring

a hapless knight, Dirk, who storms a booby-trapped castle in order to save a maiden, Daphne, from a fearsome dragon. The team, desperate to be the first to

Left: Bluth's studio couldn't afford to hire any models so the game's animators used *Playboy* magazine photos for inspiration for the character Princess Daphne.

release a laserdisc game, bickered over the story and how best to introduce interactivity. Eventually they settled on the idea of triggering an on-screen flash of light which the player must respond to with directional inputs on the joystick in order to progress the animated story.

With over 50 ways in which Dirk can meet his death through incorrect player inputs, much of the game's attraction comes from players hoping to view every conclusion on offer, whether it's being unceremoniously squashed or eaten by bats. Dyer's company field-tested the game at the Malibu Grand Prix in El Monte, California. Hundreds gathered, standing stationary and agog at the miracle of technology they were witnessing. As the machine itself was so expensive (the laserdisc player alone cost $1,000), *Dragon's Lair* was the first game to increase its cost from a quarter per go to 50 cents, a price point that players were only too happy to pay. Many operators paid off the machines within a fortnight.

Despite the game's gigantic success, the laserdisc phenomenon started and ended with *Dragon's Lair*. The team's two follow-ups, *Space Ace* and *Dragon's Lair II*, failed to inspire passions in the same way. A case of style over substance? Almost certainly. But what substantial style.

Year: **1983**
Developer: **Rick Dyer/Don Bluth Productions**
Publisher: **Cinematronics**
Original format: **Arcade**
Play today: **Nintendo DS, iPhone, iPod touch**

> **"What intrigued me more than anything was all the ways of showing Dirk dying. Because I thought that would be the humor of the thing, you know, how to do it so that it wasn't just gruesome or cruel or anything like that."**
>
> Don Bluth, animator on *Dragon's Lair*

[MSX]

MSX

Year: June 1983
Manufacturer: Various
Original Cost: Various

MSX

Japan's MSX computer sought to standardize the home computing platform, offering full compatibility between different manufacturers' products.

Above: Many major Japanese studios produced software titles specifically for the MSX hardware. However, MSX did not fulfill its potential because it never became popular in the US.

"For a guy from Japan, Kay's more like me than probably anybody I've ever met."

Bill Gates, founder of Microsoft

If the Commodore 64 was America's defining home computer of the early 1980s, and the ZX Spectrum was Europe's machine of choice, it was the MSX that best represented Japan's tentative steps into home computers and games. Unlike its foreign rivals, the MSX was manufactured by various Japanese companies, all of whom had their own version of the machine.

26-year-old Kazuhiko 'Kay' Nishi, vice president of Microsoft Japan and director of ASCII Corporation, originated the idea to introduce a standardized computing format. Nishi wanted to replicate the standard of videocassette recorders established by VHS, hoping that the platform would become as ubiquitous as television or telephones. The idea was that any piece of hardware or software with

Above: In 2001 the MSX Association released an official emulator "MSXPLAYer" allowing a new generation of players access to the system's library of games.

the MSX logo on it would be compatible with any MSX branded product, with the MSX standing for 'Machines with Software eXchangeability'. In other words: the MSX was the first attempt to create a universal video game platform.

Despite finding considerable success with 5 million sales worldwide and launching series as long-running as *Metal Gear* and *Bomberman*, the MSX failed in its intended mission. By the time the system came to America the Commodore 64 was too firmly established in the public's imagination and households to allow room for a computing hardware standard to take root.

It didn't help that the system's internal architecture was difficult to work with for game programmers, particularly because the method by which MSX computers accessed video RAM was far slower than systems that gave direct access to the video memory. As such, early ports of Spectrum and Commodore 64 games were inferior to the originals, leading developers and consumers alike to presume the machine was less capable.

Nishi sought to address these concerns with an updated iteration of the MSX specifications, optimizing graphics and sound for the MSX2, but by then it was too late. Commodore 64 had sold 12 million more machines than the MSX; the war was lost and Japan's dream for a standardized computer game format finished.

MUST PLAY:
Bomberman
Metal Gear
Parodius
Puyo Puyo
Eggerland

Year: July 1983
Manufacturer: Sega
Original Cost: $129

JULY 1983

[SG1]

SG1
SG1000

43

SG1000

Despite a number of bombastic successes in the arcades, Sega's first attempt at a home video game console was a disappointment, anonymous against the competition.

Sega's entry to the video game console market was close to catastrophic. Released on the same day as Nintendo's Famicom, the SG1000's story is one of decline and fall, in contrast to its rival's soaring trajectory. Sega supported the machine for two short years, during which time Nintendo grasped a 90 per cent market share of the home video gaming industry in Japan. And yet, the lessons learned in the system's failure would go into making Sega's subsequent inventions, the Master System and Mega Drive, greater successes, ensuring the system's crucial place in the medium's evolution.

Sega was formed in 1940 in Honolulu, Hawaii, with the name Standard Games, later changed to Service Games, from which the modern-day company derives its name. Founded by three Americans, Marty Bromely, Irving Bromberg and James Humpert, Sega's business was to provide coin-operated amusements for American servicemen on military bases. In 1965 the company merged with a Japanese company, Rosen Enterprises, Inc, which imported mechanical photo-booths, and Sega Enterprises was formed.

With these roots, Sega's entry to the video game business was inevitable, and the company soon became known in the arcades for its spirited, exuberant titles like *Zaxxon* and *Hang-On* – a motorbike racing game designed by Yu Suzuki and the first arcade machine to require the player's full body for control. The success of these

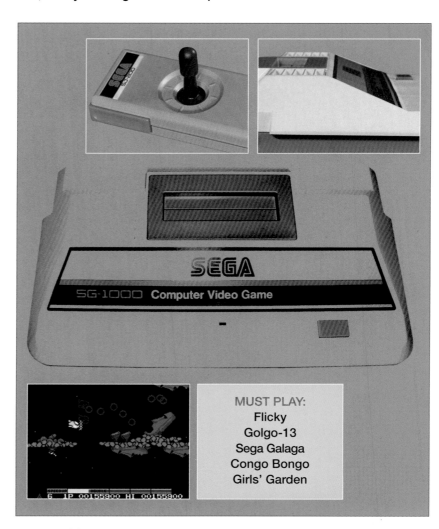

MUST PLAY:
Flicky
Golgo-13
Sega Galaga
Congo Bongo
Girls' Garden

Above: The SG1000 shared a number of internal components (the CPU as well as a video and sound processor) with the American-made Colecovision.

Below: While the SG1000 floundered in Japan, the system found widespread success in the Taiwanese market.

machines drove Sega's profits to $214 million by 1982, funding the SG1000, the company's entry to the home console market.

The cumbersome controller design (a thin waffle of plastic interrupted by a miniature control stick, held vertically in the hand) made games irksome to play. With so much competition from rival systems from companies such as Takara, Bandai, Atari and, of course, Nintendo, the machine quietly disappeared from shelves.

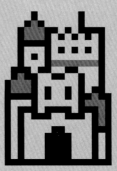

NINTENDO FAMICOM

As the video game business burned in an Arizonan desert, Nintendo's Famicom debuted in Japan with a bold and masterly plan for the industry's resurrection.

Dinky, with red and white plastic casing and rounded edges, you'd be forgiven for thinking Nintendo's defining video game system of the 1980s was a child's toy. It's no accident. Having achieved success with the Color TV Game 6 and 15 systems, Nintendo's CEO Hiroshi Yamauchi wanted to design a more serious home computer disguised as a toy, one to appeal to the entire family: a family computer; or 'Famicom'.

The heart of the machine, based on a Motorola 6502 chip derivative, was nothing unusual. But the system's controllers derived their shape and input dynamics from Gunpei Yokoi's *Game and Watch* LCD games, while the inclusion of a microphone on the second pad showed Nintendo's broadminded industrial creativity. But Yamauchi's inventiveness went further than mere product innovation. In May 1983 he addressed a wholesalers' group, the Shoshin-kai, stating that sellers of the Famicom should not expect to see large profits from system sales. "Forgo profits on the hardware," he said. "It is just a tool to sell software. This is where we shall make our money."

The Famicom launched on July 15 1983 for just ¥14,800, around half the cost of rival systems. Within two months the system had sold over half a million units. Within six, disaster had struck. A bad chipset was causing a crash in certain games. Yamauchi, with typical flourish, recalled every system sold, skirting a crucial sales window in the Japanese New Year holiday, but protecting Nintendo's name.

Nintendo soon learned that software sold hardware, not vice-versa, and Yamauchi appointed a young Shigeru Miyamoto, designer of Nintendo's first global arcade hit, *Donkey Kong*, to head a new game design research group, R&D4. Yamauchi recognized that artists not technicians made the best games and filled R&D4 with similar creative minds. The internal software division established itself as the most successful in Nintendo, launching *Mario Bros.* and *The Legend of Zelda*, triumphs buoyed by Gunpei Yokoi's R&D1 group, which counted

Metroid, *Kid Icarus* and *Excitebike* among its accomplishments.

However, by 1984 Nintendo faced a crisis. The company could not meet the demand with new games. Yamauchi was loath to open the system up to third-party developers, fearing that doing so would dilute the brand with poor games – the Atari effect. In late 1984 he yielded, granting the first three licences to Japanese game makers. The licences were restrictive. Nintendo took an unprecedented ¥2,000 per cartridge, and imposed a minimum order of 10,000 units per game. While many companies were dismayed by the terms, any misgivings were silenced by the size of the potential market. Hudson, one of the first developers to obtain a licence, sold a million copies of its first Famicom title, *Roadrunner*.

While the Famicom's rise to dominance in Japan had been smooth, the journey to the West was tortuous. Following a redesign to make the system look like a more serious computer, Nintendo renamed the machine the Advanced Video System and demonstrated it at the January 1985 CES show in Las Vegas. The reaction was disastrous: not a single order was placed.

Yamauchi ordered another redesign and renamed the machine the Nintendo Entertainment System, while Nintendo of America's Minoru Arakawa offered retailers a bold promise: the company would deliver machines and set up window displays for free. After 90 days, the retailer would pay for what was sold and return anything else they didn't want. The offer broke down barriers and rebuilt trust with the games industry.

Within three months the NES had sold 50,000 systems. Within a year, a million and within three years, three million. By 1990, Nintendo owned a 90 per cent market share of all video games in the West and, by 1991, the company was earning an average $1.5 million per employee, nudging past Toyota to become the most successful company in Japan. Almost single-handedly, Nintendo's machine had resuscitated an industry.

Above: Post-Nintendo licence, Konami, publisher of the Metal Gear series, saw its earnings rise 2,500 per cent from 1989 to 1990.

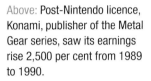

"If you could do a good job in New York, you could pretty much do anything anywhere"
Hiroshi Yamauchi, on deciding to launch the NES in America's toughest market

Below: The 'Azuki' red used as the main colour in the Famicom's iconic two-tone design was selected to keep manufacturing costs down as it was cheaper than other colours at that time in Japan.

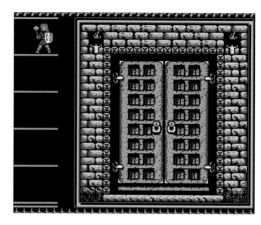

THE BLACK ONYX

The first Japanese role-playing game was designed by an American expatriate, who introduced the nation to the worlds of Tolkein and *Dungeons and Dragons*.

Year: 1983
Developer: Bullet-Proof Software
(Henk Rogers)
Publisher: Bullet-Proof Software
Original format: MSX, NES
Play today: MAME

"When I mention I used to run Bullet-Proof Software Japanese people ask if I had anything to do with Black Onyx. I tell them I designed and developed the game and they'll exclaim: 'You're the reason I'm in this industry!'"

Henk Rogers, creator of
The Black Onyx

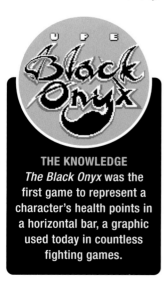

THE KNOWLEDGE
The Black Onyx was the first game to represent a character's health points in a horizontal bar, a graphic used today in countless fighting games.

Final Fantasy and *Dragon Quest* may be synonymous with the Japanese RPG, but both series owe their existence to *The Black Onyx* and its American creator. Henk Rogers moved to Japan in 1976 having graduated from the University of Hawaii where, as a student, he'd while away the hours playing the pen-and-paper RPG *Dungeons and Dragons* with his friends.

By 1982 the home computing storm had travelled to Japan and when Rogers noticed US computer games turning up on cassette tapes in shops, he decided to try his hand at developing a title of his own. He headed to Akihabara, Tokyo's neon-fizz electronics district, and paid $10,000 for a state of the art NEC-8801 PC. With the hardware in place, Rogers needed an idea for a game. He wanted to develop a type of game popular in the US but unknown in Japan at the time, and decided that the RPGs he'd played in his student days would be a perfect fit.

The Black Onyx was designed, drawn and coded over a nine-month period in 1983. Due to the 64k memory constraints only a small per centage of the features he'd hoped to include made it into the game. But scope was just the first of Roger's problems. When the game's publisher pulled out of the deal, leaving Rogers in the lurch, the designer decided to self-publish, borrowing $50,000 from a friend to set up Bullet-Proof Software.

Then there was the difficulty of explaining to Japanese consumers what the game was about. In the first two months following the game's release Bullet-Proof took just four orders for the game. Taking matters into his own hands, Rogers arranged meetings with every game magazine editor in Japan, inputting their name for the lead character and playing for an hour while they watched over his shoulder. It worked. In April 1984 every games

magazine in Japan carried a rave review of the game. Over the next two years, *The Black Onyx* sold 150,000 copies, popularizing RPGs in the Japanese consciousness and inspiring their own creators to try their hand at the genre. In a fitting post-script to the story, Hisashi Suzuki, the Keio University student and part-time employee at Bullet-Proof Software who wrote the manual, went on to become president of Square-Enix, the Japanese corporation that has since dominated the JRPG style of game design for close to 30 years.

Above: Roger's three-year-old son would often sneak into his office and mash at random keys when the designer's back was turned, causing numerous setbacks to development.

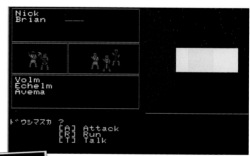

Above left: The first thousand players to complete the game received a certificate signed by Rogers while the first hundred players on each hardware platform received a genuine black onyx gem.

ELITE

Space, always a common locale for the video game, found its boundaries widened to realistic proportions in *Elite*, a game that made the galaxy's edge reachable.

In the 1984 world of *Pac-Man* and *Space Invaders* clones, in which every video game came with a two-minute goal and a high score to chase, *Elite* was a true alien invader, descended from some alternative reality. The space games of the era had traditionally been twitch affairs, testing one's reactions and gall, but rarely one's hunger for exploration. In *Elite* spaceship dogfighting met galaxy-wide capitalism, players ducking laser fire before docking in space stations in order to trade valuable materials – a cerebral test as much as one of muscle memory. Here, finally, was the science fiction epic inpixellate, a true galaxy of peril, wonder and potential to mine and explore.

But even as *Elite* inspired its players to explore its furthermost boundaries, the game almost effortlessly broke its own medium's known boundaries. Employing vector maths that were nothing short of revolutionary to create vast swathes of 3D

space, two university undergraduates, one aged 19, the other 20, worked out of a tiny dormitory in Jesus College, Cambridge on a spaceship game that would change everything, both for the two men and for the industry around them.

At first, few understood what David Braben and Ian Bell had achieved with their game. Thorn EMI turned the game down on the grounds that it was too long, required save slots, used vector graphics and wasn't colourful enough.

Acornsoft was the first publisher to catch the vision, although they did request that the designers reduce the number of galaxies down to eight, from the billions of randomly generated locations in the original. The game's capacity to allow players to engage in gun-running and the drugs trade also was an issue for the publisher, who eventually allowed both to stay in on the grounds that they offered a moral choice.

The game's enduring legacies are numerous. Not only did the opportunity to trade materials in search of a profit add unprecedented depth, the likes of which is still copied today, but also many British game designers and programmers owe the game their profession.

Year: 1984
Developer: David Braben and Ian Bell
Publisher: Acornsoft
Original format: BBC Micro
Play today: bit.ly/71fsgb

"The games industry has been developing on very predictable commercially orientated lines for years now."

Ian Bell, co-creator of *Elite*

Left and below: The *Elite* universe contains eight procedurally generated galaxies, each containing 256 planets to explore.

Below: The commercial success of the BBC Micro version of *Elite* prompted a bidding war for the rights to publish the game in other formats. Eventually around 600,000 copies were sold across all formats.

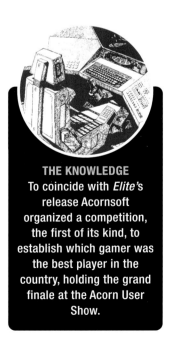

THE KNOWLEDGE
To coincide with *Elite*'s release Acornsoft organized a competition, the first of its kind, to establish which gamer was the best player in the country, holding the grand finale at the Acorn User Show.

MARBLE MADNESS

Controlled with a trackball used to navigate a ball bearing through a series of Escher-esque mazes, *Marble Madness*' placid aesthetic betrays its infuriating challenge.

Year: **1984**
Developer: **Atari (Mark Cerny)**
Publisher: **Atari**
Original format: **Arcade**
Play today: **MAME**

"There was a huge M.C. Escher influence in Marble Madness. I'd seen his lithographs since I was a child, as my parents bought four of them in 1972."

Mark Cerny, creator of *Marble Madness*

In contrast to the contemporary video game industry, in which both consumers and publishers prize the reassurance of familiarity and routine, the arcade development scene of the mid-1980s demanded originality. Atari company policy at the time was that no new game could copy an existing idea, a rule that thwarted as many young designers as it inspired.

Not only that, but the publishing model for games was systematically brutal. A new game would be location-tested in a popular bar and, if it failed to make enough money within a fortnight, would be withdrawn from production. Against this background 17-year-old programmer Mark Cerny conceived *Marble Madness*, a game in which you navigate a ball bearing around an esoteric maze.

It's a dry premise that belies the game's tactile joys. The first game to employ an isometric viewpoint, *Marble Madness* was also significant in its lack of buttons. Players are instead encouraged to be the ball, alternately caressing and swiping at the machine's trackball controller (pioneered in *Missile Command* four years earlier) in order to move the bearing between two points,

while avoiding numerous deadly traps. Just six courses comprise the experience, but each presents enough thrilling ideas, unpredictable layouts and devious conceits to upset progression, that the game feels far more fulsome than its on-paper design might suggest. Likewise, brutal time limits steepen the difficulty yet further, artificial impositions that force mistakes as they panic you into taking unnecessary risks.

Cerny worked on the game sporadically, abandoning the idea after his first sketches to help his colleague Owen Rubin create *Major Havoc*, then returned to the game a year later. While Cerny had wanted the game to be based on custom hardware, Atari insisted he make it for their new System 1 architecture, a move that helped establish the stout background visuals.

Inspired by M.C. Escher's artwork, the game plays with geometry to create an abstract, ethereal ambience, one heightened by the sparse, electronic soundtrack that remains entirely mesmerizing today.

Below: Atari's management wanted the marble to have a smiley face to create an identified character, similar to *Pac-Man*. Cerny refused, but as a compromise, the artwork depicts the ghost of faces on the marbles.

THE KNOWLEDGE
In 1994 Cerny joined Naughty Dog, creator of the *Uncharted* series, to work on a platform game, *Crash Bandicoot*, for Sony's then-forthcoming PlayStation.

THE WAY OF THE EXPLODING FIST

Inspired by Bruce Lee and battling nuns (but not the developer's neighbouring brothels) *The Way of the Exploding Fist* changed game fighting profoundly.

Year: 1985
Developer: Beam Software
Publisher: Melbourne House
Original format: Commodore 64
Play today: MAME

Left: Karate champion Jeoffrey Thompson was signed to promote the game but was not considered sufficiently well known to put his name to the title.

"I went to make a coffee, and when I came back there was a queue of people playing the game. That's when we all knew we had a potential hit."
Gregg Barnett, creator of *The Way of the Exploding Fist*

odged in between two brothels and in full view of a topless beach, Australia's Beam Software developed *The Way of the Exploding Fist* in the heart of Melbourne's red light district. But traces of these salacious surroundings are nowhere to be found in the game, whose serene expression of martial art is in stark contrast to the preceding fighting titles.

No, this is an experience that treasures the understated, concentrating on simulation and the art of blocking and counter-attacking, arts that would, in later years, become so critical to the one-on-one fighting game.

Before any code was written, creator Gregg Barnett would sit with an old joy pad unplugged on his lap, simulating martial arts moves in his mind that mapped to simple movements he made. Barnett wanted the game to be as intuitive as possible, and spent a great deal of time perfecting its 18 moves, ensuring that the on-screen action mapped ideally to the game's inputs. Barnett drew inspiration from Bruce Lee, reading and buying secondhand books and learning everything he could about the fighter. He based the game on the martial artists' interpretation of the Wing Chun style, originally developed so that nuns could protect themselves with small hand movements to shield their breasts, actions epitomized by Lee's iconic one-inch punch.

These slight, powerful moves were well-suited to sprite interpretation, allowing for pixel-faultless collision detection. In this way the game inspired its own rhythms of play, patterns of waiting and blocking that later established the more tactical style of play that would come to characterize fighting games.

Barnett finished the two-player mode first then watched how players acted and reacted for a fortnight before starting development on the AI (artificial intelligence) for the single-player mode. From the information gathered by watching players, Barnett created a set of variables to tweak behaviour: aggression, defensiveness, speed, ability to block, and counterattacks. The result was one of the most realistic and effective fighting games of the 1980s, a forefather to *Street Fighter*'s speed and *Virtua Fighter*'s precision.

THE KNOWLEDGE
The game's exuberant voice samples were recorded by Beam Software staff, who received complaints from neighbours for the high-pitched screaming that went into the game's sound effects.

SUPER MARIO BROS.

Nintendo's venerable, enduring classic established its creator as the world's foremost game designer, and made its hero more recognizable than Mickey Mouse.

Year: 1985
Developer: Nintendo R&D4
Publisher: Nintendo
Original format: Arcade
Play today: Nintendo Wii (Virtual Console)

"Video games are bad for you? That's what they said about rock-n-roll."

Shigeru Miyamoto, creator of *Super Mario Bros.*

It is if not the most important video game yet made then certainly the best known. For over 20 years *Super Mario Bros.* remained the best-selling video game, selling more than 40 million copies worldwide and popularizing a character that by the 1990s had become more recognizable among American schoolchildren than Disney's Mickey Mouse.

Super Mario Bros.' iconography has come to define the medium in popular culture. The red splash of Mario's playful plumbers' costumes, the unfashionable cap and moustache, Koji Kondo's irrepressibly joyful theme tune, the squat, shifty-eyed Goombas and the spike-backed kidnapper, Bowser, all symbolize video games to much of the world.

What can be forgotten then, is that the game these visuals clothe has also come to define video games, both to players and those designers who have drawn never-ending influence from its fine-tuned brilliance. Unusually, this is a classic that remains exciting, playable and mesmerizing today, a fact that bears testament to its exquisite level design, which fills the game's brightly coloured landscapes with treasures and secrets, mushrooms that double Mario's size, flowers that let him to shoot fireballs and stars that make him invulnerable. All still delight in their discovery today.

The game's tall ambition was driven by a number of factors. While Nintendo always intended to debut it in arcades, development was handled with a Famicom version in mind. For designer Shigeru Miyamoto and his team, the project presented a chance to apply all of the technical expertise learned in creating home console titles *Excitebike* and *Kung Fu* in creating something that would bridge the divide between the home and the arcade. Moreover, Miyamoto wanted to create a game that would place a "final exclamation point", as he put it, on the era of cartridge games, which he believed was drawing to a close with the impending release of the Famicom Disk System add-on.

The designer turned to his beloved Mario, star of his first game for Nintendo, *Donkey Kong*, for inspiration. Platform games, or 'Athletic Games' as they were known internally at Nintendo at the time, had been pioneered by Miyamoto, so it seemed appropriate that the designer return to the genre he fathered for what might be his final game for the Famicom.

Additionally, Miyamoto had a slew of ideas for how to improve upon his 1983 game, *Mario Bros.*, which had found only modest success and popularity in arcades. Principle among these was the idea of making the game world larger than the width of the screen, and having the game track the player's movement as they walked Mario to the extreme left and right of the screen. While games had employed this technique before in the guise of *Defender*

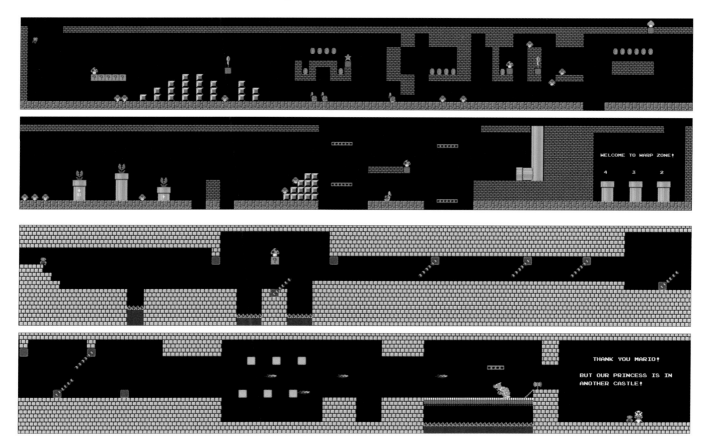

WELCOME TO WARP ZONE!

4 3 2

THANK YOU MARIO!

BUT OUR PRINCESS IS IN
ANOTHER CASTLE!

and *Super Cobra* among others, *Super Mario Bros.* was the first to tie the concept to a platform game. Arnie Katz, editor of US games magazine *Electronic Games* coined the term 'side-scrolling game' to describe the innovation.

Super Mario Bros.' two-button controls, while instinctive and ingrained today, were only changed to the familiar configuration late in development. For much of the game's gestation, one button was used to shoot bullets (which would later become fireballs), another to dash, and 'up' on the direction pad was pressed to jump. Likewise, the idea in which Mario grows to double his size when eating a mushroom came later in the game's development. In the early versions of the game, testers complained that they couldn't see enough of the game world ahead of them as they ran from left to right, but Miyamoto didn't want to shrink the Mario sprite any

more. As a compromise, the team designed the world to scale to a smaller Mario, with the idea of increasing his size in the final version. In that decision the idea to have a power-up item that increased Mario's size in game was born.

With bright, engaging visuals and a host of Easter Egg secrets built into the core gameplay in the guise of entire hidden worlds, *Super Mario Bros.* became a hit in the Japanese arcades. The Famicom version, while not quite identical to the home version, was a close approximation and pushed the system far further than any title before it. Two months after the game's release, Nintendo began packaging *Super Mario Bros.* with the Famicom system itself, capitalizing on the Christmas holiday period. The decision was a masterstroke, extending the life of the Famicom system by years in Japan and resuscitating the American video game industry almost single-handedly.

Above: At the end of each level the player is awarded between 100 and 5,000 points depending on how far up a giant flagpole Mario manages to jump – a piece of design that has subsequently punctuated every Mario platform game.

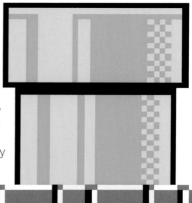

[SMS]

MASTER SYSTEM

Year: October 1985
Manufacturer: Sega
Original Cost: ¥15,500

SEGA MASTER SYSTEM

After a faltering start in the home console business, Sega's Away Team began work on the Master System, hoping to replicate some of Nintendo's dominating success.

"The most important thing is the attractiveness of the contents we will supply. Game hardware is just a box to deliver those contents."

Hideki Sato, creator of the Master System

With the Famicom achieving huge profits in the home video game market, Sega was just one of a number of companies eager to try its hand at launching an alternative, and wrestling some of Nintendo's 90 per cent market share back. The company established an internal division, which was known as Sega Away Team, headed by Hideki Sato, tasked with developing Sega's home consoles. Sato's first hardware release was the Sega-1000, released in 1983 to disastrous response. However, lessons learned were used to design the Mark III, the system that would later be renamed the Sega Master System.

The hardware featured a Zilog Z-80 processing chip and boasted 128 kilobits (a kilobit is one eighth of the size of a kilobyte) of memory, nearly twice that of the Famicom. Despite being more powerful than its rival, Sega lacked the software to make any impact on Nintendo's market share in its homeland, and so began looking to the West in the hope of success, where the Famicom, redubbed Nintendo Entertainment System, had only just been released.

Sega rebranded the Mark III as the Sega Master System, redesigning its futuristic white plastic casing for a black and red rectangular design, more in keeping with Western fashions of the time.

While Nintendo had been steadily pulling away from its arcade business in favour of the home market, Sega emphasized its strong arcade presence. To attract consumers, the company bundled a home version of Yu Suzuki's *Hang On*, its most popular arcade game of the time, with the Master System. However, without the handlebars used to control the arcade version, the home version seemed a little plain by comparison.

With a tiny marketing department run by just two men, Bruce Lowry and Bob Harris, out of a small room in the back of the company's coin-op games offices, Sega lacked the advertising clout that was necessary to rival Nintendo's spread across America. Without a recognizable mascot to set against Mario, the Master System floundered in America and Europe, in the same way that it had in Japan, leaving Sato and his team to return to the console drawing board once more.

"Yes, the Master System was a better piece of hardware than the NES. Remember, they had two extra years to develop it."

Peter Main,
Vice President of Marketing,
Nintendo of America

MUST PLAY:
Dracula X
1941
Soldier Blade
Ninja Gaiden
Splatterhouse

GAUNTLET

Gauntlet, the next game from Atari's wunderkind designer Ed Logg, established the rhythms and ingredients that have come to define multiplayer video games.

I t was in the belly of *Gauntlet*'s ghoul-infested dungeons that multiplayer gaming as we recognize it today was forged. In its rudimentary but pioneering balance of shooting, magic attacks, treasure hunting and griefing, Atari's wunderkind Ed Logg, creator of *Asteroids* (p. 25) and *Centipede*, established the ingredients that go into every four-player video game experience today, from *Halo* to *Left 4 Dead*.

By 1985 Atari was a very different company to the world-conquering arcade developer of just a few years earlier. The business had split in two: Atari Games Corp handling the coin-op division, and Atari Corp handling console games. The pressure was on the arcade game designers who were tasked with developing experiences that players could not find on consoles in order to give people a reason to leave their homes for destination play.

Gauntlet was born in the fire of this challenge. Before its launch, two-player games were either purely competitive, or turn-based. Logg's game, inspired by *Dungeons and Dragons* (it was originally titled simply *Dungeons*) asked four players to work cooperatively in taking on the computer, descending through seemingly endless levels of a perilous dungeon.

Logg's masterstroke was in adding a subtle competitive edge to the game. Players have to compete to collect food, keys and treasure in the synchronous quest to progress, survive

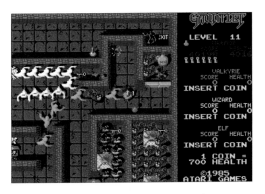

Above: Soon after the game's US release the game designer John Palevich threatened a lawsuit, claiming Gauntlet copied his 1983 title, *Dandy*. The conflict was settled out of court.

and succeed. With four character types to choose between – Wizard, Elf, Valkyrie or Warrior, each with their own strengths and weaknesses – *Gauntlet* became the first class-based team game, one whose immediacy and subtlety rival that of contemporary games.

Within a week of the game's field test at a small arcade in San Jose, California, word had spread about the secret test location, and Logg found Sega's David Rosen and other arcade manufacturers taking pictures of the game to use in developing their own versions. Atari immediately removed the machine, but Logg and his team already knew that something profound about the way in which we play video games together was about to change.

Year: 1985
Developer: In-house
Publisher: Atari
Original format: Arcade
Play today: XBox 360 (Arcade)

"It's obvious from board games that having more people is often more fun than just playing against bots who you cannot taunt or verbally harass."

Ed Logg, creator of *Gauntlet*

Below: Upon *Gauntlet*'s Japanese release some players found a way to play the game indefinitely on a single credit. The team added code to remove food from the level if the game detected players playing too well.

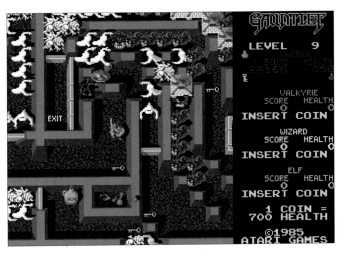

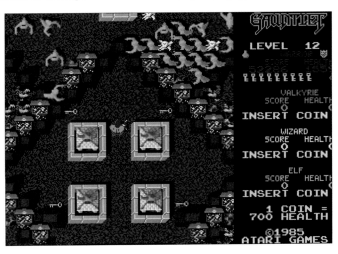

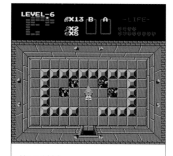

Year: 1986
Developer: Nintendo R&D4
Publisher: Nintendo
Original format: Famicom
Play today: Nintendo Wii (Virtual Console)

Below: Princess Zelda, the object of Link's quest, was named after F. Scott Fitzgerald's wife. Miyamoto believed the name sounded "pleasant and significant".

THE LEGEND OF ZELDA

Link's debut marked a design departure for creator Shigeru Miyamoto, who reconstructed the narrative-heavy Japanese RPG's elements into a bold fairy tale.

Despite the Japanese RPG's burgeoning popularity across Japan, Nintendo remained unconvinced of whether this new style of game had any place in its portfolio of in-house titles.

For one, the genre's favoured dark aesthetic, drawn from the fantasy fiction of British novelist J.R.R. Tolkien, sat somewhat awkwardly with the typical primary cultured exuberance of the Nintendo multiverse. President Hiroshi Yamauchi described role-playing games as being for 'depressed gamers', the type of people who sit in darkened rooms, an audience Nintendo had little interest in serving and growing. But for designer Shigeru Miyamoto, the issue was more fundamental and design-focused. He found the prescribed storylines and level-based character progress ran contrary to the loose, narrative-lite games he had pioneered. Indeed, Mario's creator professed a "fundamental dislike" for the Japanese RPG.

In part it was a response to the dark aesthetic. Nevertheless, with the genre now rivalling the success of Miyamoto's platform games, the designer set about developing a concept for a fantasy game that adhered to the design sensibilities of his previous work. The result was *The Legend of Zelda*, a coming-of-age tale in which a young elf boy, Link, sets out into a sprawling pastoral world, one punctuated by puzzle-filled dungeons that must be overcome as he searches for the titular princess Zelda.

Apocryphal or otherwise, two stories behind *The Legend of Zelda*'s conception bear repeating. The first suggests that the designer came up with the idea for Link's epic adventure while opening and closing the drawers of his desk, daydreaming that each one contained a separate secret garden ripe for exploration.

Still more romantic is Miyamoto's own, evermore embellished claim that the idea for the game was born in his childhood, when he would explore the countryside around his house in the village of Sonobe, 39 miles outside Japan's capital Kyoto. With this action RPG, Miyamoto hoped to recreate the sense of discovery he experienced when discovering waterfalls, caves and rivers as a boy. Regardless of the source of inspiration, Miyamoto succeeded in providing players

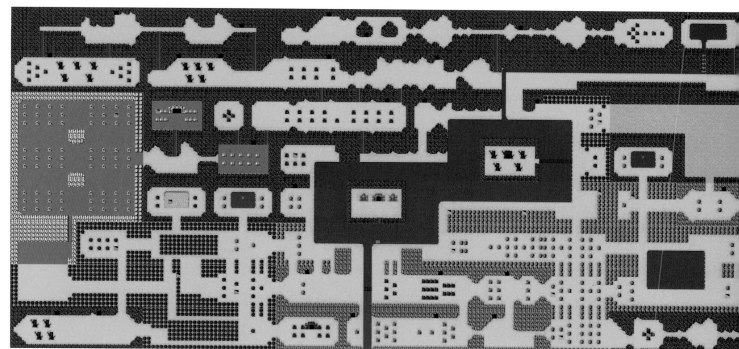

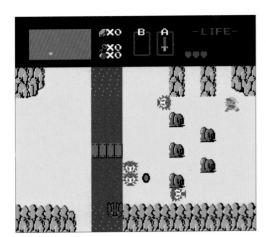

Above: For the first time, the cartridge version of the game let players save onto the battery-powered RAM.

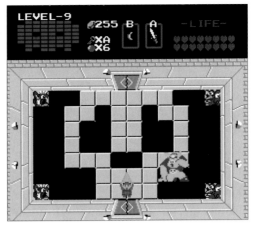

Above: *The Legend of Zelda* was the first NES title to sell over 6.5 million copies in total.

> "It had great mechanics. Typical of Miyamoto, it had puzzles. You would come across things that would be on an island or behind a door or whatever, and you could see them, but you couldn't have them."
>
> Howard Phillips, 'Game Master' at Nintendo of America

with an unrivalled sense of joyful discovery. In contrast to the side-scrolling *Super Mario Bros.*, *The Legend of Zelda* is played from a top-down perspective, Miyamoto's first free-roaming game in which the player could move the character in any compass direction. The game was so expansive that it required an internal battery, the first of its kind, to record the player's progress. The scope of the adventure even filtered down to the packaging, which came with a thick instruction booklet identifying the monsters and weapons in the game, as well as a fold-out map of its knotted world, Hyrule. But Nintendo executives didn't view this sense of

Right: American players could send in the warranty card that came with the game in order to become a member of the Fun Club mailing list. Eventually, the newsletter bloomed into the magazine *Nintendo Power*.

dramatic scale as a positive. When the company tested the game in America, Nintendo president Minoru Arakawa noticed a worrying trend. Players would rate the game highly, but needed ten hours playtime before they understood its complex systems.

As a result of testing Arakawa feared players wouldn't be able to navigate the game and would give up. He ordered the packaging designers to place an 800 telephone number in the game's manual, a free helpline that players could call to receive help and tips on how to play the game.

Immediately after the game's US release on 27 June 1987 the phone began ringing. Within days the number of calls coming in were swamping the four staff members Nintendo had hired to man the phones. Eventually, Arakawa agreed with Nintendo to provide 200 people to answer the phones, by 1990. The support system worked. As a result of its success the game became a series, each subsequent title adding a spattering of fresh new elements. *The Legend of Zelda* gave Nintendo the opportunity to articulate the JRPG's dark aesthetic and rigid storylines in its own lighter way. As with so many of Miyamoto's earliest games, many of the brightest ideas remain relevant today, a testament to the designer's skill in eliciting a human emotion – in this case, the joy of discovery – via a video game.

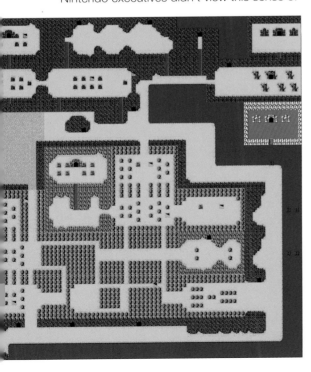

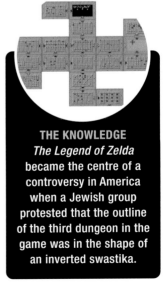

THE KNOWLEDGE
The Legend of Zelda became the centre of a controversy in America when a Jewish group protested that the outline of the third dungeon in the game was in the shape of an inverted swastika.

DRAGON QUEST

Designed by the ex-editor of one of Japan's best-selling manga magazines, *Dragon Quest* is a homely role-playing game that aims to realize a live-in fairy tale.

Year: 1986
Developer: ChunSoft
Publisher: ENIX Corporation
Original format: Famicom

"I came to video games from the Manga tradition so I've always just wanted to tell stories through them. This core aim runs throughout the Dragon Quest series."

Yuji Horii, creator of
Dragon Quest

Right: Yasuhiro Fukushima founded the Eidansha Boshu Service Center in 1975 as a publisher of tabloid magazines to advertise real estate. In 1982, after failing to establish a chain of stores, Fukushima changed the business to focus on games.

While Henk Rogers' *Black Onyx* was the first computerized role-playing game released in Japan, *Dragon Quest* was the first to typify what we now recognize as the Japanese RPG. Released at a time when the question of Japanese uniqueness was a critical topic of political and social discourse, the game exemplifies the nation's skill in borrowing an idea from across seas, and tweaking and absorbing it to become a cornerstone of Japanese culture.

Yuji Horii, designer of the *Portopia Serial Murder Case* adventure game, was hired by Enix after winning a game design talent contest boasting a 1 million Yen prize. Horii, who was editor of the popular manga magazine *Shÿnen Jump*, proposed the idea for *Love Match Tennis*, a game that later became Enix's first commercial release.

Following this unusual success Horii hoped to take the Western RPG typified by *Wizardry* and *Black Onyx*, and infuse it with more mainstream Japanese traits. Eschewing the dark fantasy style of his US influences, Horii hired Akira Toriyama, a manga artist best known for his striking and colourful work on the *Dragon Ball* anime series, to draw the characters and world for his game. He then approached TV composer Koichi Sugiyama to compose the game's soundtrack, asking for a grander,

Above: Koichi Sugiyama was a well-known TV composer when he sent a PC game's feedback questionnaire in to Enix. Company founder Fukushima wrote to him asking if he would consider scoring the company's new title, *Dragon Quest*.

more cinematic approach that ebbed and flowed with the on-screen action.

To reinforce this move toward Japanese mainstream culture, Horii turned his back on the drab, *Dungeons and Dragons*-esque dialogue that typified RPGs, instead using colloquial language and local dialects to give the game a warm, easygoing charm. Finally, in order to best suit the game to the Famicom platform, Horii simplified the RPG's mechanics, reducing the number of buttons and statistical read-outs to create a game that only bore a passing resemblance to those foreign titles that had provided so much influence.

Released in May 1986, *Dragon Quest* was an immediate hit, creating a cultural impact akin to a major Hollywood film release and triggering the first fork in the evolutionary road between Eastern and Western RPGs. Its influence is still felt today, both in the release of the game's contemporary sequels, whose launch day scrambles still bring the country to a standstill, and the emphasis on predefined narrative that continues to define the JRPG.

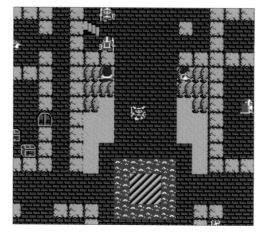

METAL GEAR

The first entry to Hideo Kojima's *Metal Gear* series showed that, when it comes to warfare, stealth can be as exhilarating as combat for the video game player.

When he was ten years old Hideo Kojima's parents would give him the money for a cinema ticket. He was allowed to see whatever he wanted on the sole condition that he would sit with his family and discuss the movie on his return. In this way Kojima's love for film was nurtured from a young age, blossoming into a longing to create his own works when a friend of his was given an 8mm camera and the pair would make ambitious home movies. Kojima's passion grew through his teenage years, the young man even writing a handful of novels in the hope that this might provide him with a route into the Hollywood.

It was while studying economics at a Japanese university that Kojima saw Nintendo's Famicom and, in its rudimentary scenes of action, sensed the emergence of a new digital storytelling medium where he might more easily fulfil his ambition. Despite enduring the scorn of his friends and family for his career move, Kojima joined Konami where he found a community of like-minded individuals, many of whom had arrived at games either through failure or a lack of opportunity in other creative industries.

The young designer's first game, *Lost World*, was cancelled after just six months and Kojima was asked to come up with an idea for a military-themed game.

Below: Following the first game's success Konami commissioned a sequel, paying for its development team to visit a forest in the mountains nearby, wear military uniform and play games for inspiration.

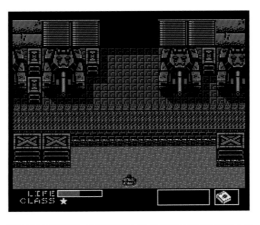

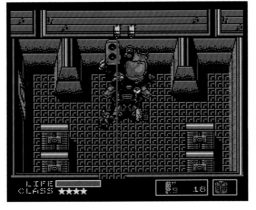

Above: In the game the player must evade enemy capture by hiding from patrolling soldiers' sight lines. If spotted, the player must retreat to a safe distance until the danger has passed.

Year: 1987
Developer: Konami
Publisher: Konami
Original format: MSX2
Play today: PS3, PS Vita

"Konami wanted a war game, because they were incredibly popular at that time. But I didn't want to make the same as everyone else so I started thinking of ways in which I could subvert the genre."

Hideo Kojima, creator of *Metal Gear*

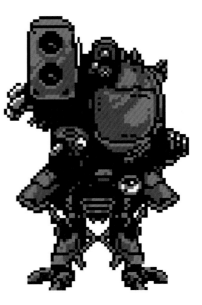

Uninterested in the popular war games of the time, Kojima suggested a sneaking game, drawing influence from *The Great Escape*, a non-combat experience in which you simply had to escape a prison. Despite being the youngest and most junior member of the team, one of Kojima's managers caught the inventiveness of the idea and allowed him to steer the project, dubbed *Metal Gear*, in that direction.

The game introduced one of video games' best-known characters, Solid Snake (named after Snake Plissken from John Carpenter's *Escape from New York*), as well as introducing the concept of a stealth game to a medium hitherto characterized by direct conflict.

[029]
R-TYPE

Year: 1987
Developer: **Irem**
Publisher: **Irem**
Original format: **Arcade**
Play today: **Xbox 360 (XBLA)**

"It started out as a joke, but our idea for the Force came from the dung beetle. We thought of a system where you wouldn't power up your own ship, but would instead power up a ball of dung."

Akibo, designer of *R-Type*

R-TYPE

Brooding, monstrous and relentlessly challenging, Irem's *R-Type*, along with Konami's *Gradius*, typifies the Japanese arcade space game of the late 1980s.

On the edge of a dark empire, you embark on a mission no one has survived. 'Will you?'

The answer to the question posed by the promotional flyer for 1987's *R-Type* is: 'probably not'. If *Defender* originated a trend towards insurmountable odds in video games, Irem's seminal horizontal shooting game presented the pinnacle of the impossible. In these suffocating skies, a players' ambition rarely stretches beyond mere survival, rather than a high score table. For those few who did manage to pilot the R-9 Arrowhead through the last of *R-Type's* 8 brilliant stages, the psychological release of completion was palpable.

But while a 'life' in the game is usually short-lived, *R-Type* remains one of the most enduring shoot 'em ups yet made. Released two years after Konami's *Gradius* made its debut, *R-Type's* maturity of design defied its genre's infancy. Slow-moving by comparison to its rivals of the time,

its primary innovation was in the 'Force', a chunk of alien flesh encased inside a sphere that loyally follows your spaceship around the screen. Indestructible, it matches the player's movements in kind, attaching to either the front or rear of your ship and increasing your firepower while also offering some much-needed defence.

In this way you control two on-screen entities simultaneously, each with its own properties, resulting in an ingenious system whose sophistication still stands out. This core ingenuity is backed with some of the most startling visuals of its time, exquisite parallax-scrolling alien vistas that backdrop choreographed waves of enemy sprites.

With an electrifying chip tune soundtrack, all anthemic rises and flickering percussive beats, *R-Type* set a new benchmark in aesthetics, matching its strange beauty with rare mechanical wonder.

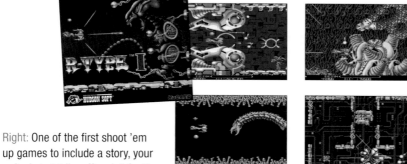

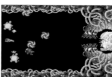

Right: One of the first shoot 'em up games to include a story, your order is to 'strike off and defeat' the Bydo, a biological weapon abandoned in space that has evolved into an empire bent on human destruction.

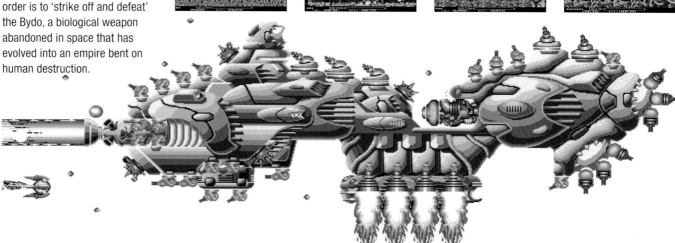

STREET FIGHTER

The first entry to Capcom's definitive fighting game series alienated players and dismayed arcade operators through a fatal design flaw in the hardware.

Konami hired Yoshiki Okamoto, a high school senior, as a graphic artist in 1982. Despite his dislike of video games, Okamoto was a diligent employee and over the next two years was responsible for two of the company's most successful arcade shoot 'em ups, *Time Pilot* and *Gryuss*. In 1984, following his games' widespread success, Okamoto asked for a raise. He was promptly fired.

Capcom, recognizing Okamoto's skill, immediately hired him to work in their R&D department, and his first Capcom title, a top-down World War II shooting game dubbed *1942*, put the five-year-old company on the video game map. Next Capcom tasked Okamoto with challenging his former employer by developing a one-on-one fighting game that could compete with Konami's *Yi-Ar Kung Fu*.

Below: *Street Fighter*'s designer, Keija Inafune, was responsible for Capcom's mascot character, Mega Man, and producer of *Ominusha* and *Dead Rising*. He left Capcom in a storm of controversy in late 2010.

Okamoto gathered a team together that was comprised of director Takashi Nishiyama, planner Hiroshi (two men who were responsible for Capcom's overhead beat-'em-up *Avengers*) and a 22-year-old graphic designer, Keija Inafune, to design the fighters.

The team stuck closely to Konami's games template, borrowing the gauges used to display each fighter's health, while Inafune drew heavily on *Yi-Ar Kung Fu*'s character designs for his fighters. These included Ryu, a solemn, muscle-bound Shotokan karate master, Geki, a shuriken-throwing ninja boy and the tonfa-wielding Eagle. But the execution of the game was anything but derivative, employing devastating special moves such as Hadouken ('wave motion fist') fireball, Shouryuken ('rising dragon fist') uppercut, or Tatsumaki Senpukyaku ('tornado whirlwind kick') spin-kick that, while challenging to pull off, could end a game in moments.

Likewise, Capcom chose to house the game in a unique cabinet, whose buttons would detect the amount of pressure with which they'd been struck and execute a light, medium or heavy attack accordingly.

The team named their new project *Street Fighter* after the Americanized title of Sonny Chiba's 1974 beat-'em-up classic *Clash! Killer Fist* and released it into arcades with some fanfare. However, the game's hardware was plagued with technical faults, failing to detect players' input accurately and being subject to hard button-mashing. The cabinets broke regularly, souring *Street Fighter*'s reputation.

However, in the game's special moves and iconic character designs, the seeds of a revolution had been sown, one that would blossom in the game's first proper sequel, which would be four years later.

Year: **1987**
Developer: **In-house**
Publisher: **Capcom**
Original format: **Arcade**
Play today: **MAME**

"I wanted there to be a story so it would feel like a movie. *Street Fighter* **was different from prior games in terms of the amount of depth we gave the characters."**

Takashi Nishiyama, creator of *Street Fighter*

Below: Capcom initially worked with Atari on a prototype punching bag that could measure the player's punch strength and translate this input on-screen.

1987

[PCE]
PC ENGINE

PC ENGINE

In the US, the PC Engine, or TurboGrafx-16, was marketed as a competitor to the NES with advertisements touting the system's superior graphics and sound.

B y 1986 Japan's home console market was burgeoning thanks to Nintendo's Famicom and its evergreen success. PC manufacturing giant NEC Home Electronics, well aware of the continual drop in chip manufacturing costs, commissioned one of its R&D teams to design a console that could incorporate PC technologies into a video game system.

Tomio Gotoh, one of NEC's top semiconductor engineers, was placed in charge of the project. Gotoh, having been responsible for some of the very first DOS machines, was a highly experienced electronic engineer, but he had no understanding of the console market.

> **"We attempted to position [the PC Engine] as a high-end gaming machine for customers that'd grown up with the NES and were graduating to a more advanced system."**
>
> Ken Wirt, VP of NEC

Above: The PC Engine appeared in the 1998 movie *Enemy Of The State* when the TurboExpress was used as a playback device for video captured onto a PCMCIA card.

As a result, Gotoh approached Hudson, a prolific third-party software developer that had been considering the hardware market, having seen at first hand the profits Nintendo was able to skim from third-party developers. The pair struck a deal to develop the hardware in partnership, and the PC Engine was finally conceived.

Unlike the companies' rivals, NEC and Hudson spent a huge amount of time and money developing the casing for the system, hoping to design a console that looked more like a stylish Walkman than a toy. The casing's dimensions were finally settled on at a slender 135 x 130 x 35 mm, the smallest home console yet released. But it was the system's internal power that really impressed. A 7.16MHz processor was paired with 64Kb of VRAM and four coprocessors to allow 64 sprites to be displayed on screen at a time. With potential for 256 on-screen colours pulled from a palette of 512, the system's raw specs dwarfed those of the Famicom and Mark III. In Japan, at least, the machine's excellent ports of Sega's arcade titles, *OutRun*, *Afterburner 2* and *Thunder Blade*, scuppered the Mega Drive's chances in the region even before it was released.

In 1988 the PC Engine was the best-selling piece of hardware in Japan, and the machine continued to be the second best-selling machine until the release of the Super Famciom. In the US the PC Engine, renamed TurboGrafx-16, fared worse, undermined by smart rival advertising by Sega that dubbed NEC's machine an 8-bit machine and by the poor quality of its pack-in game, *Keith Courage in Alpha Zones*.

MUST PLAY:
Dracula X
1941
Soldier Blade
Ninja Gaiden
Splatterhouse

MANIAC MANSION

LucasArts' debut adventure game brought rationality, accessibility and ripe humour to a style of game previously known for its arcane language and resolute dryness.

Maniac Mansion's achievements are as many and varied as the absurd, lateral-thinking puzzles it houses. One of the few video games to inspire a TV sitcom, its offbeat comedy narrative saw the interactive adventure break away from the worthy, solemn tone of those that had gone before.

Three teenagers (chosen by the player from a pool of seven potential charges) led by class presidential candidate Dave Miller work together to rescue Miller's girlfriend Sandy Pants, who has been kidnapped by Dr. Fred Edison and his family of mutants. It offers wit, humour, pop-culture references and a silliness that few American games had dared attempt before, and set the tone for a decade's worth of LucasArts adventure games that would follow.

Not only that, but the game established an engine, SCUMM (Script Creation Utility for *Maniac Mansion*), that would usher in a new era for adventure games, creating the technology that would drive many of the finest titles of the 1990s, from *Monkey Island* to the game's own sequel, *Day of the Tentacle*.

Maniac Mansion was designer and scriptwriter Ron Gilbert's first commercial title. His previous work at Lucasfilm Games (the company that would later become LucasArts) primarily consisted of porting Atari 800 games to the Commodore 64. But through a conversation with the artist Gary Winnick, the idea for a camp horror

Below: Gilbert made a board game version, creating a paper layout of the *Maniac Mansion*'s floor, with acetate overlays to represent characters and events.

adventure game was born. The pair pulled every horror movie cliché into the game, painting stereotypes in bold colours to comedic effect.

Gilbert began programming the game in 6502 assembly language, but soon realized that the project was becoming unwieldy and over-complex and needed its own scripting language. He spent nearly a year working on the bespoke language, which would come to be known as SCUMM, a tool that allowed the game's designers to control the characters on screen and manipulate the game logic, all using simple near-English commands.

At the time Gilbert was unpopular with LucasArts management. The game was to be the first title film director George Lucas' company self-published (previously all of their titles had been released through Atari, Activision and Epyx) and, because of the time Gilbert had spent on the SCUMM engine, the project was running over 12 months late.

Part of the reason for the delays was Gilbert's decision to remove the text parsing that had previously defined the genre, where players had to enter rudimentary words in order to solve the game's puzzles. Instead, *Maniac Mansion* offered the player an essential but limited dictionary of on-screen verbs, which could be clicked in order to guide the character's actions. While some onlookers in the company worried that limiting the player's options for interaction would oversimplify the game, Gilbert stood firm, arguing that true complexity came not from second-guessing the parser, but from the ways in which different objects could be combined with one another in order to solve puzzles.

The game released to critical and consumer acclaim, the shockwaves of its impact forever changing the landscape of adventure games. The game's success allowed Gilbert and his team to begin work on advancing the SCUMM engine and its application, in doing so birthing an entire genre that would, to many, become known as the 'LucasArts Adventure'.

Year: 1987
Developer: In-house
Publisher: LucasArts
Original format: Commodore 64
Play today: Xbox 360 (XBLA)

Below: An Easter Egg, in which the player can place a hamster in a microwave oven and watch it explode into a charred mess, made it through Nintendo's strict certification process. 250,000 copies were sold before anyone noticed the feature, which was removed for the second production run.

"The first inspirational picture I drew for the game – an exterior of a scary house with the sign 'WARNING: TRESPASSERS WILL BE HORRIBLY MUTILATED' out front as a joke – actually made it into the final game."

Gary Winnick,
Maniac Mansion's artist

FINAL FANTASY

A desperate gamble on a new type of game propelled Square, a struggling Tokyo developer, to become one of Japan's largest and most powerful publishers.

Year: 1987
Developer: **Square**
Publisher: **Nintendo**
Original format: **Famicom**
Play today: **iPhone, iPod Touch**

With over 90 million video games sold worldwide, countless associated spin-offs, movies, television series, figurines, and even soft drinks, *Final Fantasy* is perhaps the most recognizable Japanese RPG franchise around the world. If the series didn't give birth to the JRPG's conventions, then it was certainly responsible for popularizing them.

The random battles, line-dancing combat, angst-ridden teenager protagonists and dizzyingly convoluted stories that have come to embody this, Japan's most popular style of video game, were all present in this game's 1987 debut.

That the template has endured is somewhat surprising: developer Square didn't start off making RPGs and the game was something of a last-ditch attempt at finding success in the industry. *Final Fantasy* creator Hironobu Sakaguchi made three computer games after joining Square in 1983 as a part-time designer. Soon afterwards he switched platforms to the Famicom and developed the racing game

Highway Star (released as *Rad Racer* in the US), *King's Knight* and *World Runner*. The games sold reasonably well (*Highway Star* and *World Runner* securing around half a million sales between them) but Sakaguchi wasn't particularly excited by the designs. His bosses had assigned him to make 3D games for the system because the programmer working with him, Nasir Gebelli, excelled at 3D code.

Bored with these restrictions, Sakaguchi resolved to attempt one last project in a genre that interested him, and wrote the design for a role-playing game, labelling the project with a title that reflected the fact he expected this to be his final game project.

Placed in the position of Director of Planning and Development, Sakaguchi had only to convince the president of the company of his plan in order for the project to go ahead. With just a rudimentary

Above: Composer Nobuo Uematsu joined Square in 1986, when an employee from the game developer walked into the Tokyo music rental shop where he was working and asked if he'd like to write some music for a video game.

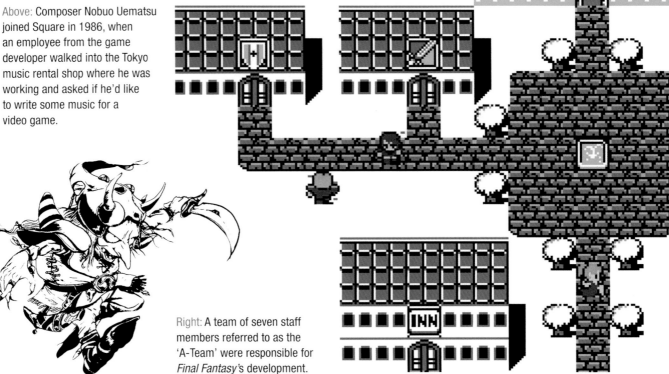

Right: A team of seven staff members referred to as the 'A-Team' were responsible for *Final Fantasy*'s development.

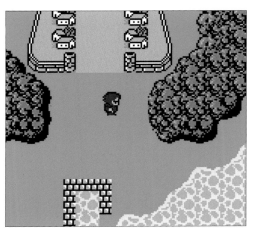

Above: Final Fantasy's divisive random battles – which capriciously interrupt a player's exploration of the world for an impromptu fight – lingered in the series for years.

understanding of games, the president chose to trust Sakaguchi's instinct and assigned him 15 staff to work on the game. Sakaguchi started with the game's story, employing the Klimt-esque Japanese fine artist, Yoshitaka Amano, to conceptualize the game world. Where nowadays Square writes the entire story before development begins, at the time the game world was limited by the technical capacity of the Famicom. So Sakaguchi got his artists to work out how large the world could be and, from that, derived the number of separate towns and dungeons that could fill it, finally writing the story with which to fill the world.

The game, of course, defied its pessimistic title. Not only did Sakaguchi and his team manage to create a rip-roaring video game story of knights, crystals and world-saving but also a team-based battle system that was engaging enough to last the course of the adventure. Far from being the swan song Sakaguchi expected it to be, the game resonated so well with Japanese audiences that, three years later, Nintendo published the game in the US under its own label, establishing a solid relationship between the two companies that would endure till the advent of Sony's PlayStation.

However, despite selling 3 million copies in Japan, six times as many as the most popular Square release had achieved before, the game didn't find the same broad audience in America. While *Final Fantasy* introduced the JRPG to Westerners, catching a generation of American fans who would closely follow the company's releases in subsequent years, the genre struggled to find the mainstream acceptance that *Dragon Quest* had achieved in its homeland.

While the game is at times tortuous to play today (especially in its original NES guise, hamstrung by a lack of world map, the constant flurry of random battles and its rudimentary sprites) the vision and ambition are still clear. Best viewed today as a museum piece, the original *Final Fantasy* should nevertheless be celebrated for laying the foundations upon which all subsequent games bearing its name and style were built.

Above and below: Each subsequent *Final Fantasy* title presented a new universe and set of characters but wrapped these in thematic constants. The details changed, but the tone and systemic DNA remained continuous.

"During those days the development studio was in a rented apartment. Because I was so poor I'd often stay at their premises because they had a bath and air conditioning. I never really went home...."

Hironobu Sakaguchi, creator of *Final Fantasy*

THE KNOWLEDGE
Due to *Final Fantasy's* relatively poor performance in America the second and third entries to the series weren't released in the region, leading to a confusing discrepancy in game numbers when the fourth game was released as *Final Fantasy II* in the US.

The Super SHINOBI

9/ MUSIC ©1989 YUZO KOSHIR

5550 STAGE

3:56

16-BIT

MEGA DRIVE SEGA

TRIES
x03 ITEMS x02 SCORE 00000600

MUST PLAY:
Sonic the Hedgehog
Gunstar Heroes
Alien Soldier
Street of Rage 2
Castle of Illusion

0438

SEGA MEGA DRIVE

After a faltering start in the console business, Sega launched the Mega Drive, a powerful machine that stole crucial ground from its rival, Nintendo.

Sega is nothing. Nintendo President Hiroshi Yamauchi would regret those words – an off-hand remark given to a Japanese journalist – when, four years after its debut, the Sega Mega Drive recorded sales of 7.5 million systems in the US, outselling Nintendo's Super Nintendo by a factor of 2:1. For Sega's staff, Yamauchi's pronouncement acted as a thrown gauntlet. The company's American CEO, Tom Kalinske, went so far as to pin a copy of the phrase on every door in the Sega offices, a challenge to his staff to prove the venerable businessman wrong.

But in 1988, Yamauchi's bullish diagnosis made reasonable sense. Nintendo's Famicom swaggered into its fifth year with a rudely dominant 90 per cent of the video game hardware market share and one machine in every three US homes. Sega's Master System machine, meanwhile, limped behind, having secured fewer than a quarter of a million sales in Europe, showing an equally poor record in America and Japan. Despite its technical superiority over the Famicom, the lack of third-party support, and arrival of the vastly superior PC Engine, ensured Sega's hardware ventures throughout the 1980s were ill-timed and ill-fated.

Believing that Sega's success might lie in porting its arcade hits to the home, CEO Hayou Nakayama took the decision to try the company's hand at a new console launch, developing a domestic version of Sega's successful coin-operated technology, the System 16. Codenamed MK-1601, Sega announced a launch slot of autumn 1988, hoping the system could establish dominance in the next generation of video game hardware as the first '16-bit' system.

On 29 October 1988, Sega launched the MK-1601, now renamed the Mega Drive, in Japan for ¥21,000 (£114) alongside four titles, *Altered Beast*, *Super Thunderblade*, *Space Harrier II* (an exclusive sequel to Yu Suzuki's popular arcade title) and *Osomatsu-kun*. While the ease with which the system handled the arcade ports caused a small stir in Japan, Nintendo's dominance prevented Sega from making the financial impact the company had hoped for.

In a shift of focus, Nakayama decided that the system's fortunes lay in the West and charged the US wing of the company with a Japanese mandate: 'Haku Mandai,' or 'sell one million consoles.' Copyright issues with the 'Mega Drive' name in the US forced a name change, an inconvenience that nevertheless enabled the American team to spell out their aspiration for the machine, nothing short of a rebirth of Sega: Genesis. The team assumed that gamers who had joined the Nintendo camp with the launch of the NES five years earlier would now be looking for more mature content. The marketing team designed a campaign to paint Nintendo as a family and children's company, and Sega as a more grown-up offering.

On 14 August 1989, Sega shipped a limited quantity of console to stores in New York and Los Angeles, priced at $199 (£125). Celebrity-endorsed sports titles *Arnold Palmer Tournament Golf* and *Tommy Lasorda Baseball* were twinned with arcade behemoths *Golden Axe* and *Altered Beast* to reinforce Sega's positioning of the console as a more mature machine. The approach worked and within one week industry figures put Sega as owning 65 per cent of the market share, growing to 90 per cent by the Christmas period.

However, the Nintendo user base remained greater in the West, and Sega began a campaign, using slogans such as 'Sega does what Nintendon't'. In Japan, Sega had all but given up hope of besting Nintendo and now focused all of its energy at beating its rival on foreign soil, now supported by a Mario-beating mascot, Sonic The Hedgehog. While the Mega Drive slid from popularity with the release of a number of ill-advised add-ons, its impact was still significant, moving public perception toward games to send the medium into its cultural adolescence.

> **"The Japanese would never do competitive commercials. They thought they were in bad taste in terms of business ethics, but we convinced them that was what we needed since we were up against Nintendo."**
>
> Michael Katz,
> head of Sega of America

Below: The Mega Drive was the first backward-compatible video game machine, which included a Master System Mark III emulator known as VDP Mode 4 that would allow owners to boot the machine with the Power Base converter.

GHOULS'N GHOSTS

The sequel to Capcom's most demanding arcade title made some concessions to the player, but its difficulty – just like its legions of foes – remains the stuff of night terrors.

Year: 1988
Developer: In-house
Publisher: Capcom
Original format: Arcade
Play today: MAME

Devilishly tough, the first title in Capcom's *Makaimura* series lived up to its Japanese title, which translates as 'Demon World Village'. In the 1985 action game, players assume the role of the chivalrous knight Sir Arthur as he storms a flaming village overrun by occultish monsters – zombies, ogres, demons, Cyclops and dragons – on a quest to rescue Princess Prin Prin from Lucifer himself. Despite the dark premise, the game's cartoonish style and comical art – which has Arthur continue the fight in his underwear after having been struck by an enemy – afforded the game a lighthearted tone at odds with its subject matter.

While the debut found modest success both in the arcades and on the various consoles to which it was ported, it was this 1988 sequel that matured designer Tokuro Fujiwara's blueprint for the game. In between working on the two games, Fujiwara directed the arcade hit *Bionic Commando*, and lessons learned there carried across to the development of this sequel, which saw Sir Arthur gain the ability to throw his spears upward and downward while in the air, a move that levelled the playing field between the player and machine.

Nevertheless, this is a game that delights in killing its player in creative ways, and every mistimed jump is punished. Treasure chests

Above: The original soundtrack was composed by Tamayo Kawamoto, one of the first musicians hired at Capcom, where she went by the aliases Tamayan and Tamatama.

are as likely to contain a spectral magician who'll turn Arthur into a duck or frail elderly gentleman, as they are treasure for hoarding, making every scavenge a gamble. But the game's true masterstroke of cruelty is that, if you make it to the final confrontation with Lucifer, you are sent back to the beginning to search for the weapon necessary to defeat him. Many arcade games offer the chance of looping play-throughs for the skilled, but *Ghouls'N Ghosts* is perhaps the only one to demand it, a design intended to make players part with their money, and do so infuriated, but gladly.

"I think that game trends are like fashion trends. But I believe the desire for playing 2D platformer games will always remain. Perhaps there aren't as many game creators who can really pull off a good 2D game anymore."

Tokuro Fujiwara, creator of *Ghouls'N Ghosts*

Right: A version of the game released for Sega's Master System in 1990 allowed players to upgrade Sir Arthur's armour in shops, offering the player a small advantage in the face of the dispiriting odds.

HARD DRIVIN'

The first polygonal racing game, *Hard Drivin'*'s commitment to realistic car physics set the genre down a track pursued by many successful video games today.

Atari's *Hard Drivin'* presented a pivotal moment not only in the evolution of racing games but also that of the medium. The first title to feature 3D polygonal environments, Atari's game displayed further invention in allowing a player to race against a translucent, ghost-like recording of their previous best time, securing a patent that every racing game to use the 'ghost' data technique since has credited.

But more than these headline innovations, Atari's attempts to create the first realistic driving simulator marked a fork in the road for the genre, one whose effects still delineate racing games today. Previously, car games had presented exaggerations of reality, embellishing speed and understating gravity in the name of fun. Atari's *Hard Drivin'* sought to mimic real-world physics and, in doing so, replicate the feel of a real car on tarmac – albeit one that could do unlikely loop-de-loops on a stunt course.

Featuring a sit-in cabinet designed to look like the front section of a Ferrari Testarossa, limb-rattling force feedback imitates the g-forces applied to a steering wheel when turning into a corner at speed. *Hard Drivin'* was programmed by Max Behensky who worked on modelling the engine, transmission control, suspension, and tyre physics with Doug Milliken. Milliken was a leading expert on car modelling, having written the pioneering book on the subject, *Race Car Vehicle Dynamics*, with his father William F. Milliken. The two men were obsessed with creating an accurate car model to mathematically describe the physics of how

the parts of the car (engine, transmission, springs, shock absorbers, tyres and other parts) react to each other, to the road, and to the driver's inputs. Shrewdly, Atari listed Milliken as a Test Driver in the game's credits because they didn't want rivals to know they were conducting real car modelling.

But the feel of the virtual car in the hands was so obviously based on reality, that Atari's rivals soon realized the race was on to create the flawless racing simulator, an obsession that continues today in Sony's work with *Gran Turismo* and Turn10's with the *Forza* series.

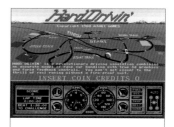

Year: 1988
Developer: Atari Games Applied Research Group, Tengen, Sterling Silver Software, Domark
Publisher: Atari Games
Original format: Arcade
Play today: MAME

"Hard Drivin' was easily one of the most innovative coin-ops of the late eighties: its filled-vector graphics and tactile feedback, as well as its original stunt tracks, caused a sensation in the arcades."

Matt Regan, *Mean Machines*

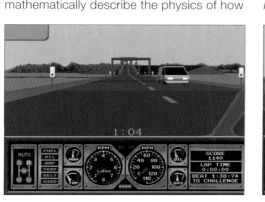

[035]

Year: 1984
(Game Boy: June 1989)
Developer: Alexey Pajitnov
Publisher: N.A.
Original format: Electronica 60
Play today: Various

TETRIS

One of the few games from Soviet-era Russia, Alexey Pajitnov's tetronimo-stacking conundrum remains one of the most enduring and widely played video games yet.

The rules can be almost written down as a mathematical formula. Four squares arranged into seven different shapes drop consecutively at random into a bucket ten squares wide, 20 squares deep. Arrange the shapes in order to stretch across the width of the screen and the line will disappear, making room in the bucket for yet more shapes to fall. Repeat forever.

And repeat forever we have. *Tetris*, a game that was in no small part responsible for selling 120 million Nintendo Game Boys, has been ported and re-ported onto almost every computer, video game system and mobile phone since its invention. Its popularity and appeal is unprecedented, the closest that any game has come to realizing the fundamental goal of being timelessly captivating to a human, no matter how many times you have played it. In terms of ubiquity and range of appeal,

Below: Nintendo's Game Boy version of *Tetris*, released in 1989, became the most widely-known version of the game, selling over 33 million copies.

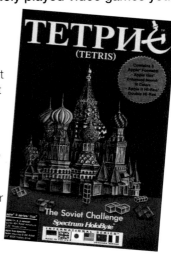

who could argue that *Tetris* is anything but the greatest video game design yet conceived? Frightening, then, that it so very nearly never found its way out of its Mother Russia.

Alexey Pajitnov was a Russian researcher working on artificial intelligence systems at Moscow Academy of Science when he stumbled across the *Tetris* formula. Pajitnov had a special interest in exploring the relationship between computers and the human mind, and he spent a lot of time talking with psychologists and trying to create small games and puzzles that explored their findings out of these conversations.

It was while browsing a local toyshop that Pajitnov discovered a game called *Pentominoes*, a box containing 12 different shapes constructed from five squares. In the game the challenge is to put all of the pieces back into the box, a sort of geometrical tidying riddle. At once Pajitnov decided to make a computer game version of *Pentominoes*.

Pajitnov couldn't create graphics for the alphanumeric screen on his Electronica 60 from open and closed bracket symbols. A prototype was completed in just 14 days but he discovered that the 12

"I never thoughts that Tetris would become so big, but later on in the computer centre I didn't see anybody who wasn't addicted."

Alexey Pajitnov

pentominoes were too many, overwhelming the player. He swapped the pentominoes for tetrominoes and everything slotted into place. Pajitnov's productivity reduced dramatically. He still has to add in scoring, adjust the speed of the game and tweak the difficulty, but all of those adjustments had to wait – not because he had other work but because Pajitnov could not stop playing his incomplete game.

Interested to see if the obsession was unique to him, Pajitnov loaded his prototype onto his colleagues' computers and left the room. When he returned, everyone was hunched over their screens; eyes locked ahead, compulsively tidying the blocks.

Pajitnov knew that he had struck psychological gold.

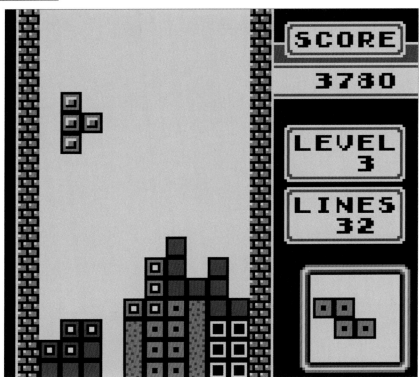

Over the following six months Pajitnov and a 16-year-old local schoolboy, Vadim Gerasimov, ported the game to the company's only IBM PC. The work was arduous and as he concentrated on tweaking and balancing the game, Pajitnov had little time to worry about copyright as his creation spread across Moscow businesses.

In the spirit of Russian law Pajitnov's game belonged to the state, but software licensing was a grey area for the Soviets, a fact that would lead to the rights to *Tetris* becoming the most contested in gaming's history. By 1986 *Tetris* had made it to Hungary, where a London-based software agent, Robert Stein, recognized its potential and sought to acquire the rights to produce a Western version. Stein sent telex messages to Pajitnov over the next two years, receiving a verbal agreement to distribute the game, but no written contract. Believing he owned the rights, Stein searched for a buyer.

Above: Pajitnov's original version for the Elektronica 60 computer used green brackets to represent blocks, but these were completely redrawn for the Game Boy release.

At an arcade show in June 1988, Arakawa, president of Nintendo America, saw *Tetris* for the first time. The graphics and design were in stark contrast to anything Arakawa had seen, and within minutes he was hooked. This, he reasoned, was the puzzle game he needed to fuel demand for Nintendo's new handheld system. Arakawa approached Henk Rogers, creator of the first JRPG, *The Black Onyx* (p. 46), to hammer out a deal with the Russians. At the same time Stein was carrying out his own negotiations. After the show, Rogers had secured the console and handheld rights to *Tetris*, Stein the coin-op rights. Nintendo had acquired the secret Russian formula that would make the Game Boy a global success.

THE KNOWLEDGE
In 1985 *Tetris* became so popular among employees of local Moscow businesses than an anti-*Tetris* program was created in an attempt to restore productivity.

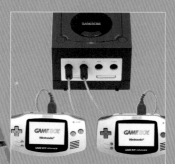

MARIO×02 WORLD TI
0 0×00 1-1 (

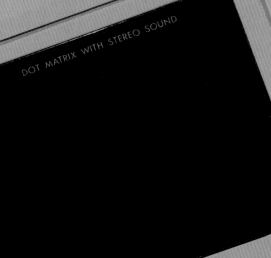

OFF ON

DOT MATRIX WITH STEREO SOUND

BATTERY

Nintendo GAME BOY™

B

A

SELECT START

B [L-1] A [000

MUST PLAY:
Super Mario Land
Tetris
The Legend of Zelda:
Link's Awakening
Pokémon
Metroid II: Return of
Samus

SCORE
6629

LEVEL
3

LINES
33

NINTENDO GAME BOY

Built with outmoded components to drive down manufacturing costs, Nintendo's Game Boy demonstrated that affordability could trump technological prowess.

Nintendo's Game Boy became synonymous with handheld gaming overnight. A system with interchangeable games, it could be played anywhere, combining portability, miniaturization and entertainment – three of the most important attributes of today's emerging technology – into a single, affordable, power-light device.

Not only that, but the Game Boy is arguably the most iconic piece of video game hardware design. Its light grey casing is punctuated by two maroon buttons and a jet black d-pad, while a single bright red power light winks to life on the left of a square, luminous green screen, a miniature window into a world of two-tone possibility.

The system's marriage to Alexey Pajitnov's *Tetris* is a pairing of hardware and software that is yet to be bettered, establishing the handheld's place as a near-universally recognizable cultural artefact. Not only that, but this was the system to establish Nintendo's most successful line of gaming hardware, one that stretches across the years in numerous iterations, leading up to the Nintendo 3DS, a handheld system in whose three-dimensional face the bold likeness of the original Game Boy can still be recognized.

And yet, even at launch, the Game Boy's components were technically obsolete. Its creator, Gunpei Yokoi, the man almost single-handedly responsible for Nintendo's entry to the video game market (page 16), had been responsible for Nintendo's range of Game & Watch handhelds, LCD-based machines dedicated to a single game. The Game & Watch games were created to make use of cheap LCD screens, a re-purposing of elderly technology that Yokoi imaginatively described as: 'Lateral Thinking of Withered Technology.'

It was this same philosophy that directed Yokoi and his 45-man team of designers, programmers and engineers to create the Game Boy, a system assembled from inexpensive, near-obsolete components that kept manufacturing costs to a minimum. While Sega and Atari busied themselves working with high-powered handhelds with colour graphics and impressive sound capabilities (the Game Gear and Atari Lynx respectively), Yokoi and his team opted for a monochrome screen and a tinny speaker. As a result, the Game Boy outlasted its rivals by several times over.

The biggest benefit to Yokoi's decision to use outdated technology was lowered manufacturing costs. As a result of the team's insistence on using cheap components inside the Game Boy shell, the launch price was set at just $89.99 in the US, $100 cheaper than Atari's rival Lynx, and $60 cheaper than Sega's Game Gear. Nintendo's competitors were quick to jump upon the Game Boy's weaker specifications. Sega aired a number of negative advertising campaigns in the US that mocked the Game Boy's monochrome display in comparison to Game Gear's full colour display. But despite the jibes, the Game Boy's popularity rose. The system's affordability also elevated Nintendo's own expectations, with company president Hiroshi Yamauchi predicting sales of 25 million within the first three years of its release. In reality, three years after its launch, the Game Boy had sold 32 million units, far exceeding Yamauchi's seemingly wild speculation.

In contrast to the console side of its business, Nintendo subjected the Game Boy technology to a series of iterations, releasing the Game Boy Pocket, then the Game Boy Color, small upgrades on the original hardware, that allowed the hardware to develop without rendering its back catalogue of over 650 games obsolete. While risky, the approach proved savvy. Across its various versions the Game Boy remains the best-selling handheld yet made.

> "**Nobody, including me, thought that Game Boy would take off like it did. Anytime that someone shows me something that I have doubts about, I remind myself that I had doubts about Game Boy too.**"
>
> Don Thomas, former director of customer service and marketing, Atari Corporation

Above: **More than 200 million Game Boys have been sold across the handheld's various hardware iterations since 1989.**

[036]

POPULOUS

A serendipitous misreading of the phonebook led to *Populous'* creation, and the birth of a divine new style of game with it, the God Sim.

Year: 1989
Developer: Bullfrog
Publisher: Electronic Arts
Original format: Amiga
Play today: Emulation

"I feel like *Populous* created me, I didn't create *Populous*. The reason that it was so good, I think, is because we played it a massive amount. We played *Populous* again and again."

Peter Molyneux, creator of *Populous*

Right: The game found unexpected success in Japan. As a result Molyneux and Les Edgar, co-founder of Bullfrog, were flown to Tokyo to take part in competition against the Japanese national champion. Molyneux, who hadn't played the game in two months, was soundly thrashed.

There's some irony in the fact that the game that would establish so-called 'God Sim' should come about by way of an act of human fallibility. Commodore, hoping to foster industry support for its fledgling Amiga in the mid-1980s, was attempting to make contact with Torus, a company specializing in network solutions. But the hardware manufacturer mistakenly contacted Taurus, a minor start-up who was working on a database program. The company's founder Peter Molyneux took the call, and despite Commodore's error, went along with it, setting up a meeting during which he secured the use of free Amiga hardware for his studio.

With access to Commodore's new hardware Molyneux shifted the company's direction into video games (a decision that brought about a change of company name to Bullfrog), and secured a contract to create a port of the Amiga title *Druid 2*. To help design the art for the game Bullfrog hired a young computer artist Glenn Corpes. Corpes, who had some coding ability, created a 3D landscape in which the height of the terrain could be adjusted in real time. Molyneux found the effect mesmerizing and, with no particular endgame in mind, the two men began to experiment.

Molyneux suggested they add 1,000 diminutive humans to the landscape in order to see what might happen when the player raised and lowered the ground. However, the single-player game only began to solidify with the involvement of Electronic Arts, the sole publisher to show an interest in the game at this early stage. EA proposed the pair introduce a level progression system and following this change, journalist Bob Wade articulated that *Populous* cast players as a divine entity in the game, and the term 'God Sim' was coined.

While the team at Bullfrog firmly believed in its creation, the lukewarm response from so many publishers prior to signing with EA meant that there was little hope for commercial success. Broke and penniless, it looked as though Bullfrog may have to wind down operations post-launch. Then the first royalty cheque arrived for £13,000. The team paid off their debts and pondered what to do with the remaining money. Then the second royalty cheque arrived. It was for £250,000.

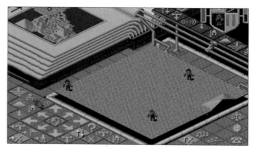

SIMCITY

Town planning, the preserve of civic suits, revealed its inherent thrills, drama and humanity through a PC game that gave us the power to engineer our environment.

In a world of shoot 'em ups, fighting games and driving simulators, Will Wright's concept for a game about city planning seemed not only out of place, but completely untenable. Cast as a city mayor, players are asked to manage the growth and planning of a simulated metropolis, a premise that, to many publishers at the time, seemed destined for failure or obscurity.

The idea for the game came to Wright following the release of his first development, the Commodore 64's *Raid on Bungling Bay*. The young designer found that he had more fun playing with the in-built level editor than he did with the main game and, as a result, began to cultivate an interest in the intricacies of urban planning. The concept of how he might turn a level editor into a stand-alone game was crystallized when Wright read *The Seventh Sally*, a short story by Stanislaw Lem in which an engineer creates a miniature city with artificial citizens for a deposed tyrant to oppress.

The first version of the game was created for the Commodore 64 in 1985, but it wasn't till four years later, after Wright had founded Maxis Software with entrepreneur

Year: 1989
Developer: Maxis
Publisher: Brøderbund
Original format: Amiga, Macintosh
Play today: iOS

Left: Following the *Newsweek* article Wright received calls from governmental agencies around the world wanting to adapt and use the technology, including the CIA and the US Defense Department.

> **"At the time of *SimCity*'s release there were no games that adults wouldn't feel embarrassed playing on the market. They were all arcade shoot 'em-up things."**
> Will Wright, creator of *SimCity*

Jeff Braun, that the game was published. Finding a backer for a game in which there was no formal success or failure state was a challenge and initially Brøderbund, the company that would eventually publish the game, declined to become involved. In 1988, Wright and Braun returned to Brøderbund with a near-complete version of the game. Now able to experience Wright's vision for themselves, the publisher's executives Gary Carlston and Don Daglow saw the game's infectious appeal and a deal was made.

Selling the game to the public, however, was difficult. Sales were so meagre to begin with, that Wright and Braun supplied all of the game's technical support themselves, working from Braun's apartment. But word of mouth resulted in the game being featured in *Newsweek* magazine, a feature that transformed the game's fortunes as 10,000 schools installed the game in classrooms as an educational tool for their students.

In *SimCity* Wright established a style of management game that would come to define his career, the starting point in a personal creative trajectory that would eventually lead to one of the most popular PC game series yet made, *The Sims*.

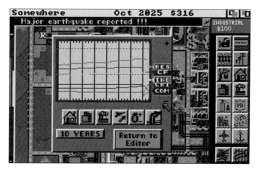

74

THE 1990s

> "Many people who have seen these so-called next generation machines have already said that they just can't see what the difference is..."
>
> Shigeru Miyamoto, creator of *Super Mario 64*

By the end of the 1980s the video game industry had settled into rhythms of hardware iteration and sequential software releases that have since defined the games business. Games that shared common characteristics were beginning to cluster beneath loose banners of genre, while Japan took the industry's driving seat from Atari and the other American pioneers who had fallen prey to greed, hubris and bad management.

At the start of 1990, the stage was set for what would become the most important decade in the development of the medium. In Nintendo's follow-up to its world-conquering Famicom and in the competition provided by Sega's Mega Drive, the first true console war resulted in a technological arms race that gave birth to innovation and invention. Mario and Sonic became poster boys for a new era of creative rivalry, vying to claim the hearts and minds of different territories around the globe and asking that young consumers, for the first time, pick sides.

The fall in the cost of processors caused a steep rise in the potential capabilities of home console machines, evolutions that would close the gap with arcade technology, thereby diminishing the potency of the very industry from which they derived. Meanwhile, the establishment of networked systems saw the development of mainstream multiplayer games, giving birth to the first widely available Massively Multiplayer Online (MMO) experiences and internet-based shooters such as *Quake*.

New game styles and types were still ripe for discovery, with *Alone in the Dark* popularizing survival horror, *Wolfenstein 3D* bringing together the primitive components of the first person shooter into its contemporary form, and *PaRappa the Rapper* establishing the Simon Says-esque music game without which we wouldn't have had *Guitar Hero* or *Rock Band*.

Perhaps the most significant development in the decade was in the addition of an entire new dimension to video games as they moved from 2D sprites to 3D polygons, a charge led by newcomer Sony and its pioneering PlayStation. Far from a mere

aesthetic development, 3D graphics opened up a new world of functional opportunities, bringing with them a slew of previously unknown challenges to game designers.

The advent of CD-ROM technology, first introduced to the mainstream by *Myst*, changed the way in which games were delivered to players, and, in their immeasurably increased capacity, allowed lengthy video sequences to be added to games, closing the gap between the video game and film in previously unimagined ways.

The 1990s was the decade in which the handheld console came of age, the formative Nintendo Game & Watch systems that inspired Gunpei Yokoi's Game Boy system and its legions of me-too imitators. When Nokia installed a rudimentary pellet collecting game *Snake* onto one of their mobile phone handsets in 1998, one of the first truly viable convergent platforms was established, sewing the seeds of today's iPhone and Android devices.

By the end of the 1990s the industry and the titles it produced would be virtually unrecognizable from those that defined its beginning. That the lavish in-game cinematics of *Metal Gear Solid* could have arrived within ten years of sprite-based fighters such as *Final Fight* boggles the mind. And yet, it's this very diversification that illustrates the maturing of the medium. The detailed 3D of Dreamcast's *Soul Calibur* is no 'better' than the cartoonish 2D of *Street Fighter II* in the same way that watercolour is not inherently better than oil for a painter. They are merely different tools for expression, albeit ones with interactive implications for the designer behind them.

By the close of the 1990s, players would have come to realize that the march of technology did not necessarily work in tandem with the development of 'fun' and that strong game design was only loosely related to artistic approach and technical prowess. Nevertheless, it was the drive to bigger and better graphics and sound that led to a great many innovations in the medium through the 1990s, and this obsession of hardware and software makers alike would stretch and redefine the industry in profound ways.

MUST PLAY:
Metal Slug
Viewpoint
The King of Fighters '98
The Last Blade 2
Garou: Mark of
the Wolves

Year: **January 1990**
Manufacturer: **SNK**
Original Cost: **$649**

JANUARY 1990

[AES]

NEO-GEO

77

NEO-GEO

Ostentatious, exclusive, powerful and prohibitively expensive, SNK's Neo-Geo brought the amusement arcade home with unprecedented accuracy.

It is the Rolls-Royce of video game systems, a status symbol, a console whose games started at $250 a piece in 1990, and whose rarest titles today can cost upward of $1,000 on the collector's market. An anomaly, the Neo-Geo was the first home games system to identically match the specifications of its arcade counterpart, an achievement that came with a slogan ('Pro Gear Spec') and price tag to match. Sleek, with a thin, black body and two huge robust, arcade-style joysticks, the Neo-Geo remains as desirable today, its library of 130-odd games as sharp and captivating as they ever were.

Shin Nihon Kikaku ('New Japan Project') began operations on 22 July 1978, releasing its debut, *Maikon Kit*, a *Breakout* clone, before making its name with shoot 'em ups such as 1981's *Vanguard* and 1985's *Arian Mission*. In 1986 the company formally changed its name to SNK Corporation and signed a third-party licence deal allowing it to develop games for Nintendo's home systems. While working as a Nintendo licensee proved lucrative thanks to hits such as the Famicom's *Ikari Warriors* and the Game Boy's *Funny Field*, SNK's management wanted to return to the company's arcade roots in order to reinvigorate an industry flagging in the face of Nintendo's success in the home.

The idea was inspired: manufacture an arcade board that used interchangeable cartridges, much like those employed by the home consoles of the time. Prior to this, arcade operators were required to physically replace fragile PCBs with new ones or, worse still, buy a brand-new dedicated machine. Based on SNK's new system, dubbed the Multi Videogame System (MVS), all operators needed to do to change the game in their arcade was to buy a new cartridge and slot it in.

In an unprecedented move, SNK then took the exact inner workings of its MVS technology and housed it in plastic casing, ready to release as ahome console. Initially,

the company marketed the systems as rental-only machines, thinking the high manufacturing cost of each unit meant the console would be too expensive to sell at retail. But after two months, after a torrent of requests, SNK opted to sell the Advanced Entertainment System in shops, positioning it as a deluxe console that rendered the term 'arcade conversion' obsolete.

Word of this magical system that could translate the arcade experience pixel-for-pixel spread quickly, especially in Japan where the thought of owning arcade-perfect games in the tight space of a Tokyo bedsit seemed too good to be true.

The company soon became synonymous with the fighting game genre, its *King of Fighters* series establishing itself as *Street Fighter*'s main rival in arcades. This emphasis was primarily thanks to Takashi Nishiyama, who had worked on the original *Street Fighter* at Capcom before SNK poached him. Nishiyama was the jewel in SNK's development staff, launching its flagship series, *Samurai Shodown*, *The King of Fighters* and *Metal Slug*.

But the system's exclusive prices worked against it in the long run. Few parents would pay $600 for a console and $250 per game for their child when they could buy Super Nintendo, a suite of games and still have enough change left over for a holiday. Then, by the mid-1990s, games were popping into 3D, and Yu Suzuki's *Virtua Fighter* series had made SNK's exquisite 2D sprite work appear antiquated. But while fashions shifted, SNK doggedly continued to develop games, releasing some of the company's finest work such as *Metal Slug 3*, *Last Blade 2* and *Garou: Mark of the Wolves*, well into the Sony PlayStation era.

On 22 October 2001 SNK finally collapsed, filing for bankruptcy and placing its intellectual property rights up for sale. Later that year SNK's founder, Eikichi Kawasaki, purchased SNK's rights through Playmore, a company he set up in anticipation of the company's collapse.

"SNK Japan did not share information with SNK US. We would often have to go out and purchase European imported products to find out what was in the pipeline."

Chad Odaka, SNK America's customer service manager

Below: The opportunity to learn the intricacies of these complex games at home before taking their skills to the public arcade gave birth to a new breed of professional arcade player.

[038]

JOHN MADDEN FOOTBALL

JOHN MADDEN FOOTBALL

After a tortuous few years' development and an abortive debut release, the Apple II version of *John Madden Football* was rebuilt from the turf up for the Mega Drive.

Year: 1990
Developer: In-House
Publisher: Electronic Arts
Original format: Sega Genesis
Play today: Emulation

"I reviewed NFL tapes of four NFL games to model the actual second by second behaviour of all 22 positions on the field."

Bing Gordan, EA's head of marketing and product development

Right: After the game's release Jerome Bettis, a back for the Pittsburgh Steelers, called EA and said: "I'm playing the game and, while I appreciate what you guys did, you made me too good."

Although *John Madden Football* wasn't the first video game interpretation of American Football, the sheer challenge of moving 22 players and a ball around a screen simultaneously on formative computer technology ensured that few attempted such an ambitious proposition throughout the 1980s. But this was the game to establish numerous conventions that are still used in games today, from the three-quarter top-down view of the playing field to the personality endorsements that adorn so many contemporary sports titles.

With the Apple II computer as the lead platform, the developers of *John Madden Football* faced numerous technical challenges. To help minimize the load on the processor, early prototypes featured seven-on-seven players. When Madden saw the restricted team sizes he baulked, threatening to remove his name from the product unless the team could manage to create a playable game of authentically balanced 11-on-11 football. The team returned to the chalkboard and, after two years of determined development, succeeded in creating a playable game that matched Madden's ambition.

However, the Apple II version of *John Madden Football* was poorly received. After the extended development period and in the light of the critical derision and commercial failure, the game became known at EA as 'Trip's folly'. The publisher's accountants insisted that the money invested into the project, including Madden's advance, be written off as non-recoupable. But Hawkins would not be deterred and commissioned the development of a new version of the game led by Rich Hilleman, who had recently finished producing the company's successful 3D racing simulation, *Indianapolis 500: The Simulation*, and veteran sports

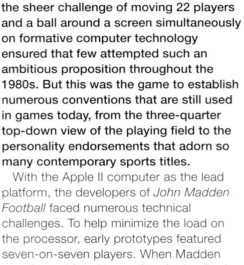

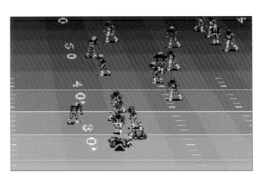

Above: Orr and Hilleman's reboot of the Apple II version of the game was significant: the Mega Drive release has little in common with its forebear.

game designer Scott Orr, who had worked on the Activision title *Gamestar Football*. The pair complemented one another: Hilleman was a stickler for simulation and realism, while Orr's arcade sensibilities kept the interface simple and intuitive. During development Hawkins received a call from Sega America's Michael Katz asking if he had any Madden games that could be ported to their new Mega Drive console. Impressed by the Mega Drive's specifications and, realizing that Katz was desperate for a football game, he negotiated a lower royalty rate to be paid to Sega for every game sold. The deal brought EA on board as a Sega partner, and in 1990 *John Madden Football*, now unrecognizable from the Apple II version, was released. The game changed the character of sports games forever in its unique blend of hardcore strategy and arcade presentation, establishing one of the medium's longest-running and highest-earning sports franchises.

FIRE EMBLEM: ANKOKU RYU TO HIKARI NO TSURUGI

Created on a "whim" as a means to keep three interns occupied, Nintendo's first tactical role-playing game took chess' raw strategy and overlaid a theatrical storyline.

All video games owe some aspect of their design to board games, but in Intelligent Systems' *Fire Emblem* series the debt is at its clearest. Played out on a series of gridded environments, the turn-based combat is chess-like in both its structure and complexity.

A clutch of fighters, each with their own range, efficiencies and weaknesses, are pressed into your hand; victory is won by successfully manoeuvring each around the play field, decimating the opposing forces while keeping as many units alive as possible. The ingenious twist on the idea in *Fire Emblem* is that, rather than using abstract pieces, each pawn is given a name and a backstory and, if he or she is lost in battle, their death is permanent.

The game's developer, Intelligent Systems, started life as a one-man outfit.

Toru Narihiro was hired by Nintendo to port games for the Japanese-only Famicom Disc software to the standard ROM-cartridge format used overseas. From these small beginnings, the company became an auxiliary program unit for Nintendo, helping out the dream team developers at Nintendo R&D1 and Nintendo EAD with creating system tools and bug fixing.

Late into the Famicom's life, Narihiro had his own idea for a game, a military tactics game loosely based on the tile-based combat seen in *Ultima III: Exodus. Famicom Wars* was the first entry to what would become the *Advance Wars* series, a sharp and tactical game whose keen ferocity belied its cutesy visuals. But it wasn't till another Intelligent Systems employee, designer Shouzou Kaga, took the idea and applied it to a fantasy world in *Fire Emblem: Ankoku Ryu to Hikari no Tsurugi* that an entire subgenre was born.

Kaga worked on the game with three student interns at the company, using rudimentary graphics and never thinking the game would make it to commercial release.

On launch the game defied these low expectations, its setting and rich characterization inspiring Sega's *Shining Force*, Konami's *Vandal Hearts* and Quest's seminal *Ogre Battle* series, games which later begat *Final Fantasy Tactics* and *Disgaea*. Variously known as the Simulation RPG, the Tactical RPG and, in the West, the Strategy RPG, *Fire Emblem* and *Advance Wars* spearheaded video gaming's own animated board game style of play, one in which every move can be critical to success.

Left: Game Boy creator Gunpei Yokoi had heavy involvement in the *Fire Emblem* series, producing three instalments between 1990 and 1996. *Fire Emblem: Seisen no Keifu* was the last game Yokoi worked on before his death in 1997.

Year: **1990**
Developer: **Intelligent Systems**
Publisher: **Nintendo**
Original format: **Famicom**
Play today: **Nintendo DS (Fire Emblem: Shadow Dragon)**

> **"The original *Fire Emblem* was made on a whim with the help of three students on an internship. So at the time we couldn't pour much energy into the graphics."**
>
> Shouzou Kaga, creator of *Fire Emblem*

[040]
THE SECRET OF MONKEY ISLAND

THE SECRET OF MONKEY ISLAND

A comedic triumph, Ron Gilbert's swashbuckling *The Secret of Monkey Island* is also notable for its expressive animation, creative puzzle design and a rapier wit.

Year: 1990
Developer: In-house
Publisher: LucasFilm Games
Original format: PC
Play today: Xbox Live Arcade, PC, iOS

Below: Tapping the full stop key will skip a single line of dialogue. When asked why he chose this key, Gilbert replied: "It seems obvious to me: a period ends a sentence."

R outinely labelled the funniest video game of all time (a well-deserved distinction albeit one without much in the way of competition), LucasArt's seminal point-and-click adventure also succeeds in delivering one of the medium's most affecting atmospheres.

If *Maniac Mansion* saw Ron Gilbert articulating a new genre with the raw materials of jokes and puzzles, *The Secret of Monkey Island* elevated the concept with the addition of sharp-minded hero Guybrush Threepwood and the inhabitants of the Island itself, each as memorable as the last. Threepwood arrives in the Caribbean hoping to break into the pirate trade, resulting in an irreverent, swashbuckling adventure game that combines inventive puzzles (that one can actually solve through deduction rather than trial and error) with delicious situational comedy and, in the game's insult-trading

Below top: Guybrush Threepwood, who dreams of becoming a pirate, standing on the deck of his ship.

Below bottom: Guy on the beach of Mêlée Island.

Above: In the game Guybrush Threepwood meets three old pirate captains, who set him three trials that he must complete before becoming a pirate: win a sword duel, find buried treasure, and rob the governor's mansion.

sword fight battles, some rapier wit. It's difficult to imagine a game with *The Secret of Monkey Island*'s leftfield premise passing concept stage today, but Ron Gilbert's employer LucasArts was immediately keen. The head of the games division, Steve Arnold, understood the importance of allowing creative people to be creative, and, following the success of *Maniac Mansion*, trusted Gilbert's eye and judgement. However, just as the young designer began to put pen to paper he was appropriated to create a tie-in game for LucasFilm's forthcoming movie, *Indiana Jones and the Last Crusade*. *The Secret of Monkey Island* was put on hold while Gilbert rushed to finish the movie tie-in.

Whatever frustration Gilbert may have experienced in being pulled off his pet project, with hindsight the delay was fortuitous. The additional experience Gilbert gained working on a high-profile movie tie-in game taught him the value of careful planning. Gilbert's first task on returning to the *Monkey Island* project was to pen a series of short stories that could form the basis of the *Island* narrative. One of these vignettes introduced ghosts to the island, and from this concept the ghost pirate LeChuck was born.

The invention of GuyBrush Threepwood was more circuitous. Originally Gilbert had planned that the central character be an

amnesia sufferer, therefore unaware of his own name. When he dropped this narrative device, Gilbert was forced to settle on a name. Steve Purcell (best known as the creator of Sam and Max) was drawing different potential lead characters using the editing program DPaint that refers to an object as a 'brush'. As the character didn't have a name yet, Gilbert referred to him as 'the guy', leading Purcell to save his brush files as guybrush.lbm. The name stuck.

One of Gilbert's frustrations with the point-and-click adventure template was the capacity for a player to become stuck on a particular puzzle and then be unable to progress any further. As a way to counteract this problem he designed the first chapter of the game with a non-linear structure, offering a trio of separate tasks to the player that could be switched between mid-play if he or she became stuck.

Thanks to the flexibility and power of SCUMM engine editor, built for *Maniac Mansion* Gilbert and his co-writers, Tim Schafer (who would go on to create *Grim Fandango*, *Psychonauts* and *Brutal Legend*) and Dave Grossman (*Day of the Tentacle*) were able to tweak puzzles with ease, moving scenes and dialogue around on the fly, without the need for final art assets or animation.

This flexibility allowed the designers to create a 'rough cut' of the game, like a movie director, and thereby to fine-tune their ideas before committing to them. As a result *The Secret of Monkey Island* was playable at a very early stage of development and the game's logic and puzzles were buffed and play-tested for months, perhaps a reason for the game's enduring appeal today.

Despite the rapid progress, *The Secret of Monkey Island* fell behind schedule and as a result, members of the development team, along with other LucasFilm staff, were asked to help assemble thousands of boxed copies in order to ship the game on time. Unbeknown to many players, their copy of the game may have come with an instruction manual hand-folded by its maker.

Above: Two screenshots from the game *The Secret of Monkey Island*. Using a point-and-click interface, the player progresses and solves puzzles by choosing one of 12 commands, including Push, Pull, Pick up, Open or Talk to.

The Secret of Monkey Island solidified LucasFilm's position at the forefront of adventure game development and its irreverent voice (that frequently mocked the conventions of the genre it helped establish), set the tone for the following decade of LucasArts releases while training a generation of players in the fine art of insult sword fighting.

"I based a lot of the look on the Disneyland [theme park] ride *Pirates of the Caribbean*. I wanted you to feel like you were in that world."
Ron Gilbert, creator of *The Secret of Monkey Island*

THE KNOWLEDGE
Gilbert originally intended that the *Monkey Island* series be a trilogy, but left after the second game in order to set up his own studio, Humongous Entertainment. While LucasArts created a third game without him, Gilbert still dreams that one day he will obtain the rights to the series, and be free to create the 'true' *Monkey Island 3* he always envisioned.

MUST PLAY:
Yoshi's Island
Chrono Trigger
Super Metroid
Final Fantasy VI
F-Zero

Nintendo SUPER Famicom

NINTENDO SUPER FAMICOM

Forced to launch the successor to the Famicom ahead of time thanks to Sega's successes in the US, the release of the Super Famicom brought Japan to a standstill.

Nintendo president Hiroshi Yamauchi began planning a 16-bit successor to the Famicom in the mid-1980s. He placed Masayuki Uemura, designer of the original Famicom, in charge of the secretive project, his only request that the R&D team be poised to enter the 'next generation' market by 1990. However, Nintendo's global dominance of the video game industry removed any sense of urgency from the project. Why hurry to make the Famicom obsolete while it continued to bolster company profits month after month?

By the start of the new decade the tectonic plates of the video game world had begun to shift and grind. Sega had sold more than 1 million consoles in the US. While these figures were dwarfed by Nintendo's 31.7 million sales, Sega was making inroads. Its suite of licensed games and advertising campaigns, emphasizing the 16-bit capabilities of its machine, made Nintendo's proclamation that it would only enter the 16-bit market when it was ready began to appear bullish.

Yamauchi applied pressure on Uemura and his team, still leaving the technical specifics to the engineers, but requesting that they attempt to make the Famicom's successor compatible with its predecessor's games. But the functionality added $75 to the system's estimated manufacturing cost and Yamauchi decided that the price increase was too significant to warrant backward compatibility.

The team had better luck elsewhere. The new machine, dubbed the Super Family Computer (Super NES in the West), could generate 32,000 colours, a far greater number than the Mega Drive's 512, providing a useful advertising hook. Likewise, its Super FX chip facilitated some of the earliest 3D effects – put to effective use in games such as *Star Fox* and *Secret of Mana*.

The excitement that preceded the Super Famicom's Japanese launch in 1991 was unprecedented in games. After seven years of market dominance in Japan, Nintendo and its mascot had come to define the medium. On 21 November 1990 the launch of Nintendo's second home video game system brought unparalleled disruption to Japan's streets. The company had kept the launch date a delayed secret, so pre-orders ran out as the nation panic-bought. Some stores required customers to pay the full ¥32,000 (£169) in advance to secure a system, while others opted for a lottery system to decide which would-be buyers would receive a console. Nintendo shipped 300,000 units the night of the console's launch in 'Operation Midnight'. 100 ten-ton trucks each carrying 3,000 machines were used to collect the stock from secret warehouses in an effort to outwit the Yakuza (gangsters), who were rumoured to be planning to hijack some of the trucks.

While high drama may have been part of Nintendo's launch plans, much of what happened next could not have been anticipated. With 1.5 million pre-orders and just 300,000 units in stock across the country, four out of five customers were to be disappointed. One toy shop near Shakujii Koen train station in Tokyo received just six units. Adults called in sick in order to go shopping and, as a result of traffic problems, the Japanese government requested that in future, console launches take place at weekends. Within a year 4 million Super Famicoms were in Japanese homes.

However, the US launch was less auspicious. Sega's system had taken root and despite a $25 million marketing plan, by the end of 1991 the system had only shifted 700,000 units. Nintendo's machine caught up with, then overtook, Sega's. The company encouraged quality third-party releases by limiting licensees to three games a year. Any game that earned 30 or more points in the Nintendo rating system didn't count toward the three and would be featured in the company's magazine, *Nintendo Power*. The incentive worked and the Super Famicom library of games is one of video gaming's strongest. When the system was discontinued, Nintendo had sold 49.10 million units worldwide, the best-selling console of its era.

Above: To counter the Super Nintendo's launch in the US, Sega reduced the cost of its Mega Drive to $149 and bundled a copy of *Sonic The Hedgehog* with every system.

"When Apple president Michael Spindler was asked in March 1991, which computer company Apple feared most, he quickly answered, 'Nintendo'."

Bill Gates, chief operating officer, Microsoft

[041]

Year: 1990
Developer: Nintendo EAD
Publisher: Nintendo
Original format: Super Famicom
Play today: Nintendo Wii (Virtual Console)

Above: Mario's antagonist Bowser was originally sketched as an ox by Miyamoto, but his drawings were misinterpreted by animator Yoichi Kotabe as a turtle.

SUPER MARIO WORLD

Enlarging, deepening and perfecting all of the invention and flourish of the previous 8-bit Mario titles, 'super' in the title was totally apt.

If the Famicom's *Super Mario Bros.* trilogy had established the side-scrolling platform game, *Super Mario World* perfected the design. The game presented the next generation Mario, and the roomy technical boundaries afforded by his leap on to the Super Famicom allowed Nintendo's mascot space to grow, evolve and soar like never before.

Features that creator Shigeru Miyamoto had longed to include in the previous entries to the series, such as Yoshi (a dinosaur companion to follow by Mario's side), were for the first time technologically possible. Meanwhile, the system's screen-rotating Mode 7 effects allowed the designers to create levels and boss characters in imaginative ways, intended to impede progress and upset expectations.

Giant sprites are overlaid on multitudinous layers of background, each scrolling in graceful parallax to add previously unseen depths to the world. Likewise, the opportunity to visit the game's stages in a non-linear order and utilize different exit

points to access yet more new secret lands invests the game with a sense of personal adventure that had only been alluded to by the series before. This is the player's journey of discovery, as much as it is Mario's.

A team of just 15 staff achieved all this, working under the direction of producer Shigeru Miyamoto and director Takashi Tezuka. After months of exhausting, strenuous work completing the Famicom's *Super Mario Bros. 3*, Miyamoto's Nintendo Entertainment Analysis & Development team had been given 15 months off to simply explore the limitations of Nintendo's forthcoming console, the Super Famicom.

It was in the midst of these technical experiments that Miyamoto was asked to begin work on *Super Mario Bros. 4*, using the knowledge gained during the team's downtime into creating a game that could launch alongside the Super Famicom and, crucially, inspire consumers tempted to switch allegiance to Sega's Mega Drive to wait patiently for the release of the new Nintendo system.

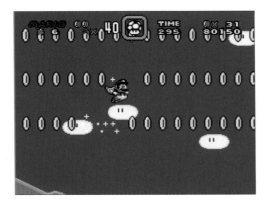

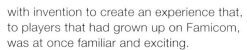

Development was onerous. Miyamoto's relatively small team was under unparalleled pressure to demonstrate the full potential of the new hardware, while simultaneously building upon the great many ideas and innovations they had already laid out in *Super Mario Bros. 3*.

But despite the pressures, Miyamoto and his team broke new ground with resourceful twists on formula to inspire and excite the player.

In one stage, to ease the player into the feel of flying in the game, all enemies were removed from a brilliant blue sky, and replaced with a sea of coins laid out in such a way to playfully teach the player how to navigate in the air.

The sheer expanse of the game dwarfed all that had gone before, offering a wealth of different continents, each characterized by diverse audio and visual themes for players to explore.

In Japan, a nation still in thrall of Nintendo, *Super Mario World* was the ideal launch title, elegantly combining nostalgia with invention to create an experience that, to players that had grown up on Famicom, was at once familiar and exciting.

In the US, however, Nintendo's late entry to 16-bit generation hardware had enabled Sega to gain significant ground. When *Super Mario World* launched alongside the new console on 9 September 1991 for $200, the Mega Drive (known as the Genesis in America) had already enjoyed a price cut, making Nintendo's system appear expensive by comparison.

For all *Super Mario World*'s advances, the very same sense of familiarity that had buoyed the game's success in Japan worked against it in America, where Sonic's speed and novelty felt like the future, and Mario's primary-colour environments and kindergarten enemies seemed childish by comparison. But history – that harshest of critics – has been kind to *Super Mario World* and today the game bears all of the hallmarks of a Nintendo classic, one that paved the way for even greater triumphs in the subsequent games that bore its hero's name.

"Wait, and I will learn more about the limits of this machine."
Shigeru Miyamoto, producer of *Super Mario World*

Below: The 1993 movie *Super Mario Bros.* was Hollywood's first attempt to create a video game tie-in. Starring Bob Hoskins and Dennis Hopper, the film was a critical and commercial failure.

THE KNOWLEDGE
The entirety of *Super Mario World*'s soundtrack, with the exception of the music played in the title and credits screen, on the over-world map and when battling Bowser, consists of variations on a single melody.

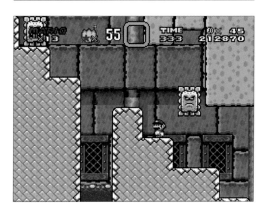

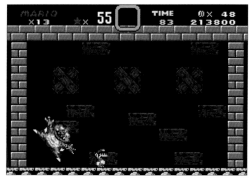

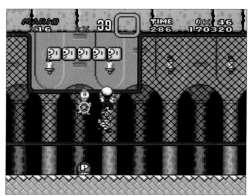

Year: 1990
Developer: In-house
Publisher: Hudson
Original format: PC Engine
Play today: Various

"One day I was flipping through a computer magazine in Japan and I saw a Hudson ad. I checked the address, and it was close to me, so one day I knocked on the door and got in."

Takahashi Meijin, a former programmer on *Bomberman*

BOMBERMAN

Originating in 1980 as a tech demo by a minor game developer based in Sapporo, Japan, it was a decade before *Bomberman* discovered its full explosive potential.

Some classic game series land fully-formed in their debut, each sequel merely trying to ape the original's success without dulling its brilliance. Others, like Hudson's *Bomberman*, require time to mature and technology to advance before they realize their full potential. *The Bomber Man*, as the game was originally known, originated in 1990, and was the result of an internal coding exercise to demonstrate the power of the BASIC compiler software.

The game enjoyed a small-scale release in Japan for the MSX in 1983 (and was ported to the Sinclair Spectrum as *Eric and the Floaters*, the following year), but was a pale imitation of what has now become one of the most established and recognizable series in video games. In the game you control the explosives expert, laying down timed explosives before retreating to a safe distance to wait for the fuses to expire, demolishing the partition walls separating Bomberman from the exit.

Bomberman's switch to Nintendo's Famicom (Hudson was Nintendo's first third-party software vendor for the system) saw the introduction of the vibrant colour scheme and bold, cutesy character design that's since grown familiar. But even at this point, the title was still primarily a repetitive series of find-the-exit single-player levels, without any of the frantic competitive multiplayer aspect with

which the game would later make its name. It was only after Hudson partnered with NEC to release the PC Engine and developed a multitap adapter for the console that the full potential of the idea was revealed. The effect whereby any enemies caught in the blast radius of a bomb were incinerated to ash had been in place since the first game. But by placing up to five human competitors in the same corridor maze, and asking that each attempt to be the last Bomberman standing, the game received an urgency and clarity of purpose that had previously been lacking. The need for tactical deliberation in the face of mounting blind panic intensified with this explosion of human competition, and a classic formed out of the resultant mushroom cloud.

Since the PC Engine remake of *Bomberman* there have been more than 30 different iterations of the game. Arguably, the Sega Saturn version of the game is the strongest, raising the number of players running about its mazes to a confounding 16 (albeit only for those with the correct controller-multiplying add-on hardware) before introducing a range of power-ups designed to provide additional complexity. But it was in the PC Engine game that Hudson grasped the pure jewel of the experience the team had been searching for since the first game. And it's one that the company's continued to grasp ever since.

Right: Hudson is named after an axel part of the C62 locomotive that used to pass near the childhood house of the company's founders, Yuji and Hiroshi Kudo. The company eventually bought the train and set it up as a tourist attraction.

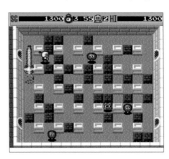

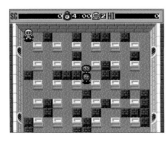

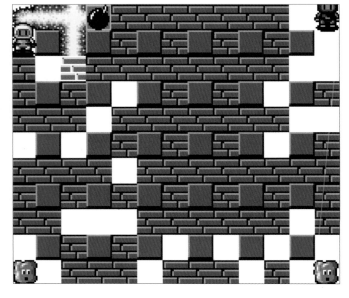

LEMMINGS

Despite their diminutive stature, the stakes are high in this puzzle platform game in which you must guide a colony of lemmings to safety across perilous cliffs.

A game in which you must guide a community of suicidal rodents to safety, saving as many as you can, *Lemmings* appears to have precious little to do with developer DMA Design's later *Grand Theft Auto* series. But the two creations share some traits. Initially *Lemmings* appears to be a run-of-the-mill early 1990s platform game, albeit one teeming with single-minded sprites as they incessantly trip and fall over terrain and hazards. But, just as *Grand Theft Auto* reveals itself as a masterpiece of sandbox (open-ended) design, so *Lemmings* also allows its player to complete each mission in a variety of creative ways, encouraging everyone to seek out their own solutions to its puzzles.

Across the game's expansive series of levels, you must guide the titular lemmings from an entrance to an exit point, influencing their behaviour in order to avoid traps and pitfalls. Rather than enjoying direct control over their movements, interaction is limited to assigning individual lemmings one of eight different behaviour types. For example, the 'miner' skill will cause a lemming to begin digging a hole through the soil below him, creating a tunnel into which the other lemmings behind him will fall. Conversely the builder skill will cause a lemming to build a staircase across a chasm, creating a pathway where before there was only a sheer drop.

Below: The mother of Scott Johnston, one of the designers on the game, provided the voice for the lemmings in the first version of the game.

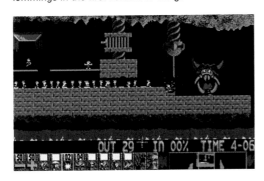

The idea for the game was conceived almost by accident when programmer Mike Dailly, DMA Design's first employee, ran some tests to create an animated character in an 8x8 pixel box as part of development for another game, *Walker*. Another team member Russell Kay said of the demo, "there's a game in that" and the idea for *Lemmings* was seeded.

Levels were designed in a Deluxe Paint interface allowing multiple designers to create levels and challenge one another internally – and each designer's character and personality is reflected in their creations. Dailly included clues as to how to solve his levels in their titles and was also responsible for creating a number of 'crossover' custom levels, featuring art and assets from other Psygnosis titles such as *Shadow of the Beast*, *Menace*, *Awesome* and *Shadow of the Beast II*.

Around 55,000 copies of the game sold on launch day, a large number for a British release at the time, while ensuing updates and ports shifted more than 15 million copies of *Lemmings* in subsequent years. But more than its financial success, *Lemmings* established the concept of indirect control, a feature of every Real Time Strategy game (in which all actions occur in real time) since.

Year: 1991
Developer: DMA Design
Publisher: Psygnosis
Original format: Commodore Amiga
Play today: PC

"Dave Jones used to try and beat us, and after proudly stabbing a finger at the screen and saying 'There! Beat that!', we'd calmly point out a totally new way of getting around all his traps, and doing it in a much simpler method. 'Oh...', he'd mutter, and scramble off to try and fix it."

Mike Dailly, programmer on *Lemmings*

Year: 1991
Developer: Capcom
Publisher: Capcom
Original format: Arcade
Play today: Xbox 360/PlayStation 3

STREET FIGHTER II

Street Fighter II's arcane commands redefined the arcade as an elitist fight club where only the most dedicated and willing pixel pugilists would prevail.

Iconic? Of course. *Street Fighter II*'s pixilated pugilists stick in the memory more readily than almost any other in video games. The hunch and poise of Ryu; Ken's scarlet Ki, his blond mop of hair a yellow tip to a searing flame; Chun Li's sea-blue dress and flowing hair ribbons; E Honda's bulk and wobble, his face all fierce eyes and war-paint, his hands a blur of slap. Yes, each fighter in Capcom's seminal game is as celebrated and recognizable as Bruce Lee or Muhammad Ali in both gait and costume.

But more surprising, more important is the fact that the very verbs of *Street Fighter II*'s inputs stick in the mind and muscle memory through the years. Down > down – forward > forward > punch. To anyone who has ever learned how to summon a *Street Fighter* fireball, the input string is as important and enduring a piece of vocabulary as any learned in an English class. *Street Fighter II* defined an entire genre, elevating the awkward jabs and jumps of fighting games to a competitive art form, establishing the rules and inputs used to this very day.

1989, and Capcom was looking for a fighting game hit for the US market. The genre was growing in popularity, buoyed by the success of *Yie Ar Kung-Fu* and *The Way of the Exploding Fist*, and the Japanese company's American office was eager to capitalize on that success. Capcom had just completed work on their CPS-1 arcade board and so settled upon two fighting game ideas: *Final Fight*, a scrolling beat 'em up in the style of *Double Dragon*, and a sequel to the company's lacklustre 1987 game, *Street Fighter*.

Noritaka Funamizu, appointed lead producer on both projects, was uneasy about the approach. *Street Fighter*'s debut had been a commercial failure and he doubted that *Final Fight* would connect with Western players. He was wrong. *Final Fight*

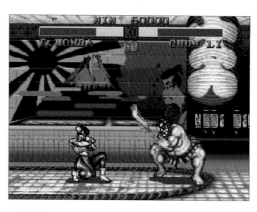

sold 80,000 arcade units in the US, turning Capcom's global fortunes around. In the light of his success, Funamizu was appointed a team of 40 developers, more than double the team size of any project in Capcom's history. The company was banking everything on the game, and internally word spread that if *Street Fighter II* was a failure it could bring the business down. Rather than

Below: **Of the 40 staff assigned to the project, 20 were assigned to work on the character art and code.**

Left: **The project lasted for two years, the longest in Capcom's history at the time.**

Above: The game had the most number of bugs (errors in the code that broke the game in some way) in Capcom's history. 26 final masters were created before the game was declared bug-free.

 starting with a storyline, or particular style of fighting, Funamizu began with eight characters, deciding what their core special moves would be, and from that, assigning each a different fight style. A huge amount of time was spent refining the moves, rendering them on-screen in exaggerated, visually bombastic terms, for example, turning Zangief's pile-driver move into a ten-foot high spinning pro-wrestling move with just as much basis in fantasy as reality.

Contrary to popular belief, the team spent far more time on character animations than they did on balancing the game, ensuring that every input had a unique and satisfying output. In order to introduce variety to the game, the series of one-on-one fight stages was interrupted by bonus stages, in which the player was charged with destroying an expensive car or a pile of bricks. It was while testing this section of the game and checking the animation cycles carefully that Funamizu noticed an anomaly.

He saw that it was possible to introduce a second punch before the animation of the first one had finished playing out. This technically allowed a player to link one animated move into another without interruption, stringing together attacks that were impossible to block if the first attack landed. However, the timing was so strict that the team decided to leave it in as a hidden feature. It was this feature that would come to define the very genre, as advanced players would attempt to string together combinations of hits, preventing their opponent from countering. Through this accident the 'combo' was invented.

Soon after the game's release into arcades, the team received word that a resourceful arcade operator had created a bespoke cabinet, in which two screens were hooked up to the same arcade board and placed back to back, allowing shy Japanese players to challenge one another while being spared the social confrontation of physically meeting. Capcom released its own version of the VS. cabinet and the fighting game boom spread throughout the country like a wild fireball. Capcom sold around 140,000 cabinets, an unprecedented number for the company. Following Street Fighter II's success, the company began to release updated versions with new features and characters, kicking off the yearly iterations that have since defined Capcom's fighting oeuvre (much to the chagrin of the fans).

Below: Street Fighter II was released for the Super Famicom on 10 June 1992 in Japan and was the first 16-Megabit cartridge for the system.

"Of course we were naïve, and we got low salaries thanks to the company head, but we had this incredible sense of adventure you don't find today."
Noritaka Funamizu, lead producer of Street Fighter II

Year: 1991
Developer: Sonic Team
Publisher: Sega
Original format: Sega MegaDrive
Play today: Xbox Live Arcade

"I would not have thought for a single minute it would be so successful. I think this success is one of the reasons Sega became a major player."

Yuji Naka, designer of *Sonic The Hedgehog*

Below: *Sonic The Hedgehog*'s soundtrack was composed by Masato Nakamura, a member of Japanese pop band *Dreams Come True*.

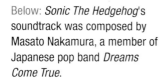

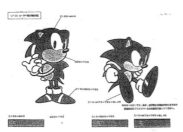

SONIC THE HEDGEHOG

Speed-freak hedgehog Sonic, a notorious acrobat and vivacious treasure hunter (despite his unlikely species) finally provided Sega with its missing mascot.

In life, the spiny hedgehog has it rough. He spends the year either quaking in bushes hidden from ravenous predators, skittering across main roads between the oily traffic or sleep-dead in the cosy grip of hibernation. And yet, as Sega's bright blue mammal streaks through Green Hill stage, eyes determined, feet a blur of red trainers, no other creature has ever seemed more comfortable performing high-speed jumps and dizzying loop-de-loops.

Sonic's high-energy verbs of play – spin, roll, streak and ricochet – made Mario's clutch of moves seem sedentary by comparison. Leave the character unattended for a few seconds and he turns to glare out of the screen, tapping an impatient foot, as if you're wasting his time, keeping him from his mission. Indeed, the moment Sonic first dropped into a ball before spinning at two hundred fierce rotations per minute around a 360-degree ramp, your eyes racing to keep up with the shuddering screen, the landscape of gaming was forever changed.

In 1990, Sega's plans to wrestle ownership of the space beneath our television sets from Nintendo seemed doomed to failure. It's not that the Mega Drive was necessarily less powerful than Nintendo's machine. Rather, Sega was lacking one crucial element to drive sales: a mascot. Recognizing the need for a 'Mario', CEO Hayao Nakayama set his employees a challenge to design a character to represent Sega's personality, citing Disney's Mickey Mouse as an example of the kind of personality he was after. Then, he said, he wanted a killer video game for the creation to feature in.

Nakayama's only stipulation was that the character be able to jump, a request that led the company to consider rabbits and kangaroos as potential animals upon which to base the character. Eventually the designers settled on two possible contenders: an armadillo and a hedgehog, on the basis that both creatures roll into a ball, a move that could offer interesting interactive potential in a game. It was a sketch from Sega artist Masato Oshima that led the studio to settle upon a stylized blue hedgehog, an idea that Sega's American office thought was nothing short of ridiculous.

Yuji Naka was a young game designer at Sega whose previous work included *Phantasy Star*, one of the formative Japanese RPGs, and *Ghouls 'N Ghosts*, a notoriously challenging action game featuring a knight in silver armour who battles hordes of cutesy undead. With Sonic's character design decided, Naka and his team were tasked with designing the game that he would inhabit, one that

Below: In America the Sega Mega Drive outsold the Super Nintendo at a ratio of two-to-one during the 1991 holiday season, in part thanks to Sonic's cultural appeal.

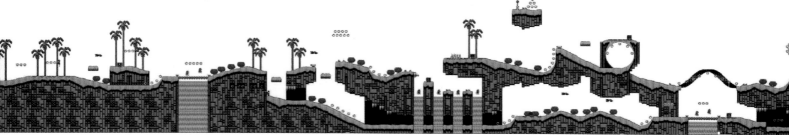

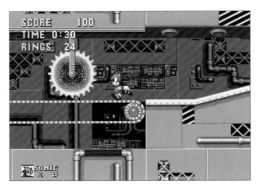

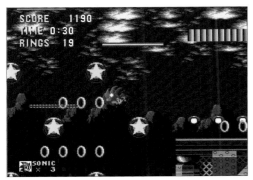

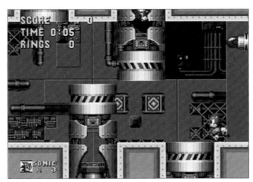

Above: Akira Watanabe was the illustrator of the character art featured on the packaging and was told by the developer to create a design 'similar to pop art'.

Above: *Sonic The Hedgehog* inspired a subsequent wave of similar mascot-based platform games such as *Bubsy*, *Ristar*, and *Earthworm Jim*.

Above: Immediately after choosing a hedgehog for the lead character, the 5-person AM-8 team at Sega changed its name to Sonic Team.

would both establish Sonic as the company's symbol, as well as help the Mega Drive claim some of Nintendo's market share.

Naka wanted to mirror Mario's simplicity of control and so decided to restrict the *Sonic* game's controls to the d-pad and a single button (one less than is used in Miyamoto's game). Secondly, Sonic Team wanted to realize the Mega Drive hardware's potential, creating a tension in which gameplay and technical achievement vied for their attention.

The team spent no fewer than six months feeling out the Mega Drive's technological boundaries. Naka, who was a programmer himself, drove an obsession in his team to see how fast they could move Sonic through the game's environment, finding ways to turn technical tricks, such as being

able to rotate the screen 360 degrees, into playable stages. The results were astonishing, making the racing games of the time seem dull and slow by comparison.

In America the game replaced *Altered Beast* as the bundle-in title for the console, a decision that Sega Japan was initially averse to. It was a masterstroke, giving the Mega Drive an overnight identity and mascot character to set against Mario.

Thanks to the quality of the game, Sega America's reservations about the character were silenced and huge numbers of consumers who had been holding out for the Super Nintendo decided to buy a Mega Drive in the interim, setting the stage for what would become the first major two-console rivalry in the medium's history.

THE KNOWLEDGE
The 'T' in *Sonic The Hedgehog* is capitalized. Al Nielson, Sega's marketing manager, registered 'The' as Sonic's middle name.

©1991,1992 Nintendo

Year: 1991
Developer: Nintendo EAD
Publisher: Nintendo
Original format: Super Famicom
Play today: Nintendo Wii (Virtual Console)

"At the time it didn't seem like they'd really figured out what most of the game elements meant. So it was up to me to come up with that story while I worked on the manual."
Yoshiaki Koizumi, author of *A Link to the Past*'s manual

Below: The game's script was written by Kensuke Tanabe, a graduate of the Visual Concept Planning Department at Osaka University of Arts.

THE LEGEND OF ZELDA: A LINK TO THE PAST

Another Super Famicom update for a treasured Nintendo series; another stand-out release that remains one of protagonist Link's strongest and most affecting.

Shigeru Miyamoto once famously said that the Nintendo 64's *The Legend of Zelda: Ocarina of Time*, released seven years after this, its immediate predecessor, was how the designer had always intended the Zelda series to appear. The 2D titles presented mere floor plans in anticipation of the arrival of the third dimension to video games. If that's true, then *A Link to the Past* was the game that not only perfected the 2D games that had gone before, but also established the rhythm and tone that would characterize the series arrival to

3D. On its foundations *Ocarina of Time* was built and therefore, for the player who prefers a certain dramatic and visual succinctness, this is the game that best expresses the series' essence, its taut design and rude abundance of ideas.

Development of the new Zelda game reportedly commenced on the Famicom in 1988. Dubbed *Zelda III*, the game's platform of choice switched to the Famicom's successor when Sega's Mega Drive forced Nintendo to make the jump to the 16-bit generation. With *Super Mario World* planned as a launch title, Nintendo

Above: *A Link to the Past* contains 12 dungeons, more than any other official Zelda game.

afforded the team generous time to perfect their ideas. Not only that, but the developer offered the designers a generous 8Mbit of storage memory on the game cartridge, double that of other Super Famicom games in development at the time.

The extra space was put to good use. While this is a 2D game, by introducing tiered dungeons across multiple floors, its puzzles took on a 3D quality, as Miyamoto and director Takashi Tezuka began to play with spatial conundrums, turning each dungeon into a giant, layered puzzle that must be picked apart component by component. Not content with this invention, the developers then took the game to the fourth dimension, exploring the nature of time itself with a cross-dimensional meta-puzzle.

Midway through the game, protagonist Link is unexpectedly transported to a parallel dark realm, in which you, the player, are taunted with visions of what will happen to the world of Hyrule should you fail in your mission. The device is one of gaming's most ingenious, and has been subsequently copied both within the Zelda series itself by way of *Ocarina of Time* and *Twilight Princess*' future and shadow realms, and in entirely unrelated,

acclaimed games, such as Squaresoft's *Chrono Cross* and Konami's *Symphony of the Night*. The ingenuity lies in the relationship between the dark and light worlds and the way in which actions in one affect the other, allowing the designers to create puzzles that stretch the mind of its would-be solver. Interestingly, the design choice to make both light and dark world structurally identical in this game was forced by technical limitations, allowing both dimensions to share the same graphical assets. To have two worlds with different layouts would have required a 16Mbit cartridge.

A young Yoshiaki Koizumi, who would go on to become director of the Nintendo Wii's *Super Mario Galaxy* was a member of the development team, charged with creating the art, layout and eventually the writing for the game's manual. At the time Koizumi started work on the manual, the story was still so loose that he was tasked with drawing the game's various elements into a cohesive narrative, demonstrating the extent to which Nintendo focuses on systems over story, even in its adventure games.

While the game underwent numerous narrative changes for the West, principally in the removal of religious imagery and terminology, the mechanics remained resolute in the face of localization. The game went on to become one of the best-selling games on the Super Famicom, shifting more than 4.6 million copies worldwide and, more importantly, inspiring a new generation of designers to explore one of the chief, unique opportunities presented by video games: the interrelation of separate dimensions tied together by virtue of their systems.

A Link to the Past not only provided the template for the later Zelda games, but it also laid the foundations upon which all the great adventure games would build thereafter.

Above: The Japanese version is dubbed *Zelda no Densetsu: Kamigami no Triforce* (*The Legend of Zelda: Triforce of the Gods*).

Below: The game made use of the Super Famicom hardware to add visual effects.

THE KNOWLEDGE
Every month throughout 1992 a comic book adaptation of *A Link to the Past* was published in *Nintendo Power*. Illustrated by Shotaro Ishinomori over 12 issues, the comic is a loose adaptation of the original game's story, featuring several plot changes and new characters.

Year: 1991
Developer: Eric Chahi
Publisher: Interplay
Original format: Amiga
Play today: PC

> **"Right from the beginning I wanted to create *Another World* by myself. It was something I was used to doing ever since I started to create computer games; I'm an autodidact."**
>
> Eric Chahi, creator of
> *Another World*

ANOTHER WORLD

A one-man creation at a time when most games were designed by teams of coders, artists and musicians, Eric Chahi transported us to *Another World*.

The greatest strength of video games is their capacity to transport us to otherworldly places, to experience the contours of the human imagination not through mere words as in the novel, nor remote visuals as in cinema, but touch. Eric Chahi's *Another World* provides a gateway into another such dimension. One stormy night physicist Lester Knight Chaykin arrives at his underground laboratory, home to a particle accelerator. In an understated cutscene, we see Chaykin sit down at his computer and initiate an experiment, the result of which sends him spiralling off into a barren alien world of shadow dangers.

Devoid of any of the usual screen clutter and featuring little dialogue, the game instead frames its story with cutscenes, roto-scoped character animation and a pacing more evocative of cinema than a video game. Chahi's inspiration came from the Amiga version of LaserDisc title *Dragon's Lair*. Astonished by the game's style, but disheartened by the fact that to achieve this level of animation *Dragon's Lair* was spread across no fewer than eight floppy discs, Chahi wondered if he could use vector outlines to create a similar graphical effect with less storage cost. The results of Chahi's initial tests were encouraging and he immediately began

Above: The game was released in North America under the title *Out of this World* to avoid confusion with a popular soap opera of the time *Another World*.

work on a science fiction story that fell somewhere between his two favourite computer games at the time, Jordan Mechner's *Karateka* and Dennis Caswell's *Impossible Mission*. Chahi worked for two years on the game, importing recordings of himself from a video camera to use for roto-scoping animations and using a tape recorder to record the sound effects for the game. A true one-man operation, Chahi even designed the game's box art himself. The title was the first 2D title to use polygons for the entirety of its graphics, a technical decision that led to the game's distinctive aesthetic and, arguably, its enduring appeal.

WOLFENSTEIN 3D

Juxtaposing stylized, cartoonish visuals with a divisive, controversial theme, *Wolfenstein 3D* appalled critics of the medium even as it laid its future foundations.

The game *Wolfenstein 3D* was designed to shock. Opening with the Nazi Party anthem 'Horst Wessel Lied', players are charged with working their way through a maze-like bunker, whose walls are adorned with swastika flags, while fending off attacking dogs and gunning down German soldiers in the hunt for Adolf Hitler. But more than its divisive theme (which saw the game banned in Germany and subject to high-profile objections from the American pressure group, the Anti-Defamation League), here was a video game that shook the medium into further evolution through its striking technical proficiency.

The 3D technology that allowed wallpaper-like textures to be applied to each polygon was created by Chris Green, a young programmer at Looking Glass, who would go on to develop the *Thief* games. It allowed rudimentary blocks to be painted with hand-drawn art, a technique that is still used to add colour and detail to 3D computer-generated worlds today. When John Carmack, co-founder of id Software heard about the invention, he worked out how to achieve the same effect using the company's own 3D engine and released the first texture-mapped game, *Catacomb 3-D*.

Encouraged by the response to *Catacomb 3-D*, id Software halted work on its console-style games in order to solely focus on a new texture-mapped 3D shooting game. Carmack's business partner, John Romero suggested the team base the new game on *Castle Wolfenstein*, a 1981 Apple II game in which players sneaked around a Nazi castle looking for

Above: Due to its use of Nazi symbolism and the Nazi Party anthem, 'Horst Wessel Lied', the PC version of the game was withdrawn from circulation in Germany in 1994.

secret war plans. As work progressed, the developer soon realized that it was far more fun to simply gun down Nazi soldiers with a machine gun than sneak around them, and the brutal first person shooter style of *Wolfenstein 3D* was settled upon.

Despite the shift in emphasis, designers Tom Hall and John Romero wanted to keep secret walls in the design which the player could push against in order to access hidden areas. Carmack resisted the idea for most of the game's development, before finally implementing the feature close to release.

While the rudimentary art may fail to inspire passions today, in 1992 the rich colours added a novel vividness that only accentuated the game's controversial appeal. Originally it was designed to use the same 16-colour palette as prior id Software 3D titles such as *Hovertank 3D* and *Catacomb 3-D*, but at the suggestion of the game's funder Scott Miller the team moved to the 256-colour VGA graphics palette and artist Adrian Carmack (no relation to John) drew each sprite frame by hand.

By the end of 1993 the controversy had done nothing to mute the game's success and *Wolfenstein 3D* had sold in excess of 100,000 copies, popularizing a style of first person shooting game that is still recognizable in today's blockbuster FPS titles.

Year: 1992
Developer: id Software
Publisher: Apogee Software
Original format: DOS
Play today: XBLA/ PSN

"Putting in more high-speed gameplay elements would have been great but, hey, we made the entire game and shipped it in 6 months."

John Carmack, designer of *Wolfenstein 3D*

Below: The initial concept for the game focused more on stealth than action with the ability to drag dead bodies and swap uniforms with fallen guards in silent attacks. These features were dropped when they slowed the game down.

[049]

SUPER MARIO KART

©1992 Nintendo

Year: 1992
Developer: Nintendo EAD
Publisher: Nintendo
Original format: Super Famicom
Play today: Nintendo DS

"We decided to see what it would look like with Mario in one of the karts, and everyone thought that looked even better. Who knows, maybe the designer who drew overalls on the earlier guy intended that it be changed to Mario all along!"

Shigeru Miyamoto, producer of
Super Mario Kart

Below: *Super Mario Kart* features eight playable characters from the Mario series – Mario, Luigi, Princess Peach, Yoshi, Bowser, Donkey Kong Jr., Koopa Troopa and Toad.

SUPER MARIO KART

Designed to plug a hole in Nintendo's line-up of game types, this bright racing game was appropriated by Mario and his bright cohorts during development.

Prior to *Super Mario Kart*'s release, Nintendo's titular, mustachioed mascot had featured in a variety of games in various guises. But each had been threaded together by a common theme – jumping – and the plumber had hitherto limited his transport to a diminutive dinosaur. In pressing Mario into a car's driving seat, Nintendo started the engines on true franchising, demonstrating that its hero was fit for more than just leaping through the Mushroom Kingdom on a mission to rescue a princess. In fact, he was equally at home sending her into a spinout courtesy of a well-placed banana peel.

That the game conjured a subgenre from thin air is notable but far from unique. However, its primary-colour take on the kart racer has never been bettered, even by Nintendo's own efforts, and is miraculous. It's a template that has been endlessly copied. IP holders such as Square-Enix and Sega have since aped the kart racer's nippy charms for their own respective line-ups of colourful characters, but, while *Super Mario Kart* is easy to mimic, it's evidently impossible to improve upon.

Characterization was low on the list of priorities for the team initially tasked with creating a racing game for the Super Famicom. When development started, overseen by Shigeru Miyamoto, Tadashi Sugiyama and Hideki Konno (the map director for *Super Mario World*), Mario had nothing to do with the game. Instead, the team placed a generic racing car driver in overalls in the driving seat of a kart for the prototype, making him three 'heads' tall (in

Above: In the Japanese version of Super Mario Kart, every character has a winning animation that involves a bottle of champagne. In the Western version none of the characters drink from the bottle.

contrast to space-racer *F-Zero*'s seven heads-tall size) in order to match the proportions of the vehicle.

Having already mastered the Mode 7 techniques needed to give the player a sense of moving through a 3D environment,

Super Mario Kart was explicitly designed to see if the Super Famicom could handle displaying two players simultaneously on the screen using the same techniques. This goal led to the game's use of 'split screen' in which the television is divided into two halves with each player's progress in the race displayed in a different section.

Three months into the project, one of the artists placed a model of Mario into a kart in place of the generic driver they had been using up to that point and in that moment, the idea for a Mario-themed racing game was born. Far from merely importing the key characters in the Mario universe into the game, Nintendo EAD imported the very essence of his universe. Pea green hills undulate under mellow yellow skies while the game's eight kindergarten power-ups and weapons are pick-ups stolen from so many '?' blocks.

The beauty of the game rests in its trim simplicity. Eight characters are divided into four handling types and presented with 20 themed tracks so memorable that players can map each course in the mind years after racing them. Although the disparate components are few, the chaos born from their interaction is infinite. While most game designers work hard to eliminate the random from their rule sets and worlds, here Nintendo EAD treasured such capriciousness. Power-ups are weighted to favour the weaker player, teleporting those in last place to pole position in the blink of an eye, leading to a moment-by-moment churn in placings that makes the game at once infuriating and deliciously captivating.

Above: All tracks in *Super Mario Kart* bar Rainbow Road in the Special Cup are based on locations found in *Super Mario World*.

The list of small miracles *Super Mario Kart* gifted to the medium is long. The physics of the various karts, the influenced collisions and handling, the boost start (for players who hit the throttle at the perfect moment during the timer countdown), the short hop allowing you to skid into corners, and the clutch of items so finely tuned to balance the offensive with the defensive. With 8 million copies sold, *Super Mario Kart* became the third best-selling game on the Super Famicom worldwide, behind *Super Mario World* and *Donkey Kong Country*. But its influence runs deeper and wider than mere sales figures, writing the blueprint for both a subgenre and, perhaps more importantly, the care, attention and love with which all spin-offs, whatever their theme, are subsequently measured.

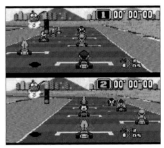

Above: Lakitu owns the *Super Mario Kart* track and oversees all races, holding up the starting signal and using a fishing rod to lift any fallen drivers back onto the racetrack.

THE KNOWLEDGE
The banana peel item, used to hold up a rival kart behind you, was originally a tiny oilcan, which would leave an oil spill on the tarmac when dropped.

Year: October 1992
Developer: NetherRealm Studios
Publisher: Midway
Original format: Arcade
Play today: iOS

"It was a snowball thing. It was a game that a lot of players really loved to play, and then it became a game that people said, 'Don't play this.' To me, it just added fuel to the fire."

Ed Boon, creator of
Mortal Kombat

Below: The 1995 movie *Mortal Kombat* is the most successful film based on a fighting game property, grossing $70,454,098 at the US Box Office and more than $122 million worldwide.

MORTAL KOMBAT

One of the first 'video game nasties', *Mortal Kombat* moved games closer to a sort of photorealistic violence, and attracted widespread outrage as a result.

For all its enduring popularity – and the series remains the best-selling fighting game franchise – *Mortal Kombat* was always a game fuelled by notoriety more than superiority. The infamous 'Fatality' finishing moves, in which, for example, a character freezes their opponent before landing an upper-cut that explodes them into a thousand shards of blue-tint flesh, had the playground appeal of a smuggled soft porn mag. Kids who had seen these supposedly gruesome finishing moves bragged insufferably over those who had not.

The game's mechanical simplicity and inherent controversy were both the result of its technical approach. By using digitized actors for its combatants, the game moved the medium closer to the 'photorealism' many game makers still chase to this day. But at the same time, the technique meant that each of the game's seven characters moved and attacked in similar ways, with none of the physics-bending abilities of *Street Fighter II's* fantastical pugilists.

The game's development began in 1991, with a team of just four men: one programmer, Ed Boon; two artists, John Tobias and John Vogel; and a sound designer, Dan Forden. The original plan was to create a fighting game featuring a digitized approximation of the action movie star Jean-Claude Van Damme. However,

the actor declined to lend his likeness to the game, so the developers focused on a one-on-one fighting game using the same techniques but with fictitious characters.

Mortal Kombat was the first fighting game to introduce 'juggling' in which an opposing character could be kept in the air by stringing together repeated strikes when knocked back, as well as the first to feature an unlockable secret character in the guise of Reptile. But despite these innovations, the game's character designs endure in a way that its style of play does not.

Nevertheless, the game has a long-lasting legacy. Thanks to the combination of its pixelated realism with gory (if comic book) violence, US government senators Joseph Lieberman and Herb Kohl launched an inquiry into 'video game violence and the corruption of society' in response to its release.

FINAL FANTASY V

In a genre typified by prescribed plotlines and inflexible characterization, *Final Fantasy V*'s job system allowed players to express themselves in powerful ways.

Year: 1992
Developer: In-house
Publisher: Squaresoft
Original format: Super Famicom
Play today: Nintendo DS

Prior to the release of *Final Fantasy V* – a game that remains creator Hironobu Sakaguchi's favourite 2D entry to the series – the Japanese RPG prized story over mechanics. *Dragon Quest* and its legions of imitators had been content to spin different yarns using the same basic building blocks of combat and development that defined the genre since the beginning.

Final Fantasy V featured a more simplistic storyline than its immediate predecessor and successors, instead offering a functional tale designed to drive players into its best assets: the battle system and flexible capacity for character development. The former introduced the Active Battle System (a feature seen in almost all subsequent Final Fantasy titles, including the thirteenth title), which made the amount of time players took to input a command a factor in deciding the order of moves. In this single invention the dry menu-based combat of the earliest computerized RPG titles was transformed into a pressured test of reaction and judgment, demanding players employ speed as well as strategy in overcoming their foes.

Meanwhile, the 'job' system – which allowed players to allocate different vocations with different skills and benefits to each of their characters, a design first seen in *Final Fantasy III* and later further expanded in the series' first true spin-off, *Final Fantasy Tactics* – was expanded and overhauled for *Final Fantasy V*. With no fewer than 22 different job classes to master, each with its own strengths and weaknesses, players were able to customize their four-man party with unprecedented flexibility. Choices could reflect a player's preferred play-style, greatly affecting the rhythm and speed of battles. In a genre known for its prescribed narratives and characterization, *Final Fantasy V*'s job system allowed players to inject some of their own temperament or preference into the experience.

Final Fantasy V launched the career of Tetsuya Nomura, Square-Enix's prized artist who, having designed the monsters for the fifth game, went on to create some of the company's most iconic characters, from *Final*

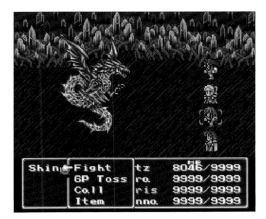

Above: The cover of *Final Fantasy V* shows the character Bartz Klauser, one of the crystal warriors, with his chocobo, Boco.

"While more experienced gamers loved the complex character building – Final Fantasy V's just not accessible enough to the average gamer."

Ted Woolsey, translator
at Squaresoft

Fantasy VII's Cloud, to Sora, the protagonist from *Kingdom Hearts*, a multi-million yen collaboration between Square-Enix and Disney.

Following the game's Japanese release, work began on an English-language version for America. However, close to completion, Square-Enix decided the game was too complex for Western tastes, instead releasing the American-developed *Secret of Evermore* in its place. It was ten years before the fifth *Final Fantasy* received an official English release, although fans painstakingly did the work of translating the game's thousands of lines of dialogue themselves a few years earlier, releasing their work onto the internet in a downloadable patch.

Right: Squaresoft planned to bring *Final Fantasy V* to America under the name *Final Fantasy Extreme*.

[052]

FIFA INTERNATIONAL SOCCER

Year: 1993
Developer: EA Sports
Publisher: Electronic Arts
Original format: Sega Mega Drive
Play today: Various

> "Until FIFA is indistinguishable from football in real life and plays exactly like football we'll always have more to do."
>
> Matt Prior, FIFA's current creative director.

FIFA INTERNATIONAL SOCCER

The first game to secure endorsement from the football world governing body, EA's soccer game still offered substance beneath the style and heavyweight licensing.

The significance of a powerful license for a sports game's commercial success had been clear since Don Daglow and Eddie Dombrower's endorsement of the 1983 Intellivision game *World Series Baseball*. By 1993 Electronic Arts had established itself as the industry leader in securing first-rate licences for its sporting games. Nevertheless, while the publisher's *John Madden Football* and *NHL* launched without much competition, soccer was already an oversubscribed, competitive field with *Sensible Soccer*, *Kick Off* and *Match of the Day* all offering exhilarating approximations of the sport for gamers.

However, by acquiring a licence from FIFA, the world governing body of football, Electronic Arts bought its way into unprecedented legitimacy, the intimation that their game, above all of the others, offered players the official video game of the sport. But *FIFA International Soccer* bore substance beneath the air of officialdom that the FIFA licence brought. This was also the first football game to break with convention by presenting an isometric view of the field, in contrast to *Kick Off*'s top-down view,

Above: The PlayStation release of *FIFA '06* came bundled with a fully playable version of the first game in the series.

European Club Soccer's side view, or *Sensible Soccer*'s bird's eye view of the action. *FIFA International Soccer*, or '*FIFA '94*' as the first title in the long-running series would come to be known as following the establishment of EA's yearly updates, played a pacey, gratifying game of football. However, when players discovered a bug in which it was possible to score by placing an attacker in front of the opposing team's goalkeeper, and having the ball rebound into the net for an easy goal, some of that keen sense of legitimacy was lost.

The FIFA series has subsequently become EA's best-selling and most profitable franchise. For some years during the PlayStation era, the game struggled to find its feet, losing out to Japanese rival Konami's *International Star Soccer* (latterly *Pro Evolution*) in terms of critical accolades, and attracting criticism for what were seen as minimal improvements in each successive release. But more recently, EA's careful investment in the property, and the team that designs it, has seen the critical acclaim begin to match the looming heights of its sales.

Below: The game's direct sequel, *FIFA 95*, was exclusive to the Sega Mega Drive.

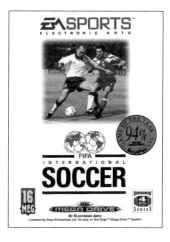

Below: A deluxe edition of the game was released for Mega CD, including new features such as a player name editor and commentary by Tony Gubba.

GUNSTAR HEROES

Treasure's debut set the tone for this diminutive Japanese studio's subsequent creative output: colourful and humorous yet built on the finest arcade foundations.

Gunstar Red and Gunstar Blue, the twin stars of Treasure's debut release, embody much of the spirit and attitude that would go on to define Japan's premier boutique developer's subsequent output. Slanting forward, all eager poise and wound energy, the flop-haired heroes almost tumble through this side-scrolling sucker punch of a Mega Drive game, one that, in its expressive and characterful animations, pressed against the boundaries of what was possible on the system early into its existence.

The game's core invention, whereby the various effects of four different types of bullet can be combined to create 14 different variations, each with its own inherent strengths and weaknesses, allowed players to adjust their in-game tools to suit a preferred play-style. But the game's true jewels are to be found in its boss battles, which delight with their spectacle and originality. In particular, the hulking bipedal robot that runs into and out of the screen – a motif revisited by the developer in 1998's Radiant Silvergun – pushed their host hardware far beyond what it had been before.

Masato Maegawa, who, along with a clutch of colleagues, left his position at Konami to go independent, formed Treasure on 19 June 1992. The company's first development was a licensed game for McDonalds, the development money for which helped fund the company's first in-house originated game, Gunstar Heroes (which released two weeks before McDonalds Treasure Land Adventure). This set-up, taking on commercially successful work-for-hire while self-funding internal projects that become critically acclaimed, has continued throughout the studio's journey.

Likewise, the endearing animated vignettes that punctuate the Gunstar Heroes experience, adding character and humour, have reappeared throughout the company's body of work. Technically accomplished, creatively inventive and best played with a supportive friend, Gunstar Heroes marked a high point that all small Japanese development studios have since attempted to imitate.

Year: 1993
Developer: **In-house**
Publisher: **Treasure**
Original format: Sega Mega Drive
Play today: XBLA/ PSN

"Lately all I see are sequels, or translations of popular arcade games. It is really sad. We are going to develop original games only!"
Masato Maegawa, co-founder of Treasure

Below: In Japan the game was later ported to Sega's handheld system the Game Gear, albeit with some decrease in size and scope in order to fit the hardware.

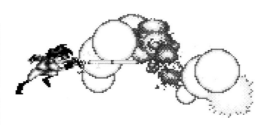

Below: Almost all of Treasure's initial 18 staff came from Konami, where they had worked together on Qix, The Simpsons, Castlevania 4, Contra 3 and Axelay among others.

MYST

Myst's unqualified commercial success appeared to redirect video gaming's future towards the unflinching pursuit of photorealism, but its true legacy lay elsewhere.

PHILIPS   COMPACT DISC INTERACTIVE

Year: 1993
Developer: Cyan Worlds
Publisher: Brøderbund
Original format: PC
Play today: Sony PSP/Nintendo DS

"We started work and realized we would need to have even more story and history than would be revealed in the game itself. It seemed having that depth was just as important as what the explorer would actually see."

Myst designer Rand Miller

Above: The non-human natives of the *Myst* universe were originally called 'Dunny', changed to 'D'Ni' when the designers discovered the term was an Australian slang term for 'toilet'.

S
urrounded by bleeping arcade games, happy-go-lucky platformers and furious shoot 'em ups, *Myst* offered an unusual pond of calm in an ocean of neon and noise. But don't mistake its ponderous pace and lack of bombast for tranquillity. This is a world without inhabitants and conflict, but its silence is one of eeriness rather than calm.

Designed by brothers Robyn and Rand Miller, who were inspired by Jules Verne's *The Mysterious Island*, *Myst* came to typify some of the emerging differences between PC and console video games and their respective ambitions. If consoles were home to hyper-speed twitch challenges, the home computer technology, upon which one organized finances or wrote project plans, seemed more suited to thoughtful, unhurried puzzles.

Certainly without the PC's CD-ROM drive, *Myst* could never have existed. The series of 2,500 exquisitely rendered vistas, through which the player clicks to progress the interactive slideshow, required the size of

Below: *Myst*'s title derives from a shortening of *The Mysterious Island*, a Jules Verne novel and prequel to *20,000 Leagues Under the Sea* which the Miller brothers' father read to them as boys.

memory space that consoles' cartridges could not provide, sending the developers into CD-ROM territory, with its polycarbonate expanse. The team, who only had experience creating children's games, spent months formulating its puzzles, whose obscure nature frustrated just as many players as they enthralled.

Upon its release, *Myst*'s visuals convinced many that the game offered an early vision of the future, the highly detailed textures and serene animations seemingly indicating the pursuit of slavish realism lay on the medium's horizon. But while *Myst* remained the best-selling PC game, until 2002 when *The Sims* stole the accolade, its curious brand of interactivity failed to define the future of game design. For all its beguiling power, and the strange sense of esoteric nostalgia one still feels when revisiting its sterile scenery, game designers have mostly continued to prize thrills over thoughtfulness.

In demonstrating the potential of CD-ROM-based gaming, *Myst* inspired Western developers to follow suit, making the switch to developing for Sony's PlayStation two years later a simple one, determining the future of games, albeit in ways its designers never quite envisioned.

RIDGE RACER

A hyper-realistic recreation of how it feels to drive a sports car, in every eight-year-old boy's imagination, *Ridge Racer* went on to legitimize Sony's fledgling PlayStation.

As a holiday destination, *Ridge Racer* is nothing short of idyllic. A Sonic-blue sea gives way to miles of warm yellow sand, punctuated by leafy palm trees and sunbaked white villas. Not that many players had much of a chance to daydream in Namco's brochure-like vision. *Ridge Racer*'s coastline is one underscored by undulating tarmac, around which players throw cars in graceful, white-knuckle skids.

Ridge Racer, or 'Riiiidge Raaaacerrrrr', as anyone who has heard the riotous introduction of the game's announcer will forever mentally pronounce the title, was not the first racing game to feature texture-mapped polygons, beaten to that accolade by *Daytona USA* by some months. But in its slip-slide handling, which made taking corners at a high-speed angle an art form, the game succeeded in twisting the realities

Below: Namco a secured a US patent on the use of a 'minigame' as a game's loading screen following its use of *Galaxian* in *Ridge Racer*, one that remains in force today.

Above: In the PlayStation version of the game, players were given the ability to choose to switch in their own music CD to the disc drive, and choose from the first six tracks as the game's soundtrack.

of motorcar racing into something as exaggerated and brilliant as its environmental hues. Where *Hard Drivin'* and *Virtua Racing* strived for realism, *Ridge Racer* aspired to hyper-realism and a simulation of the thrill of driving a sports car at high speed.

The game was unorthodox in its use of a first person perspective, but its place in history was established not in its original arcade iteration, but in its arrival to Sony's PlayStation a year later, as the strongest and most vibrant title in the launch line-up for this unknown, unanticipated machine. Namco's decision to back Sony's entry to the video game industry sent a strong signal to other Japanese developers, encouraging many to defect from Nintendo to work on the new system.

It was with the near-arcade-perfect version of the game that the developer demonstrated the unrivalled 3D power of Sony's PlayStation, all previous cynicism withering in the light of its fashionable lens flare. Namco's gall in including the entirety of *Galaxian*, its 1979 arcade shoot 'em up, as a part of the game's loading screen, spoke volumes about the power of PlayStation, and the game's role in legitimizing the console cannot be underestimated.

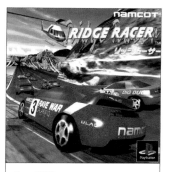

Year: 1993
Developer: In-house
Publisher: Namco
Original format: Arcade
Play today: PSN

"We're hoping to sell one copy of *Ridge Racer* for every PlayStation sold. Well, if it's at all possible."
Namco's Youchi Haraguchi

Below: *Ridge Racer* was a launch title for the Sony PlayStation in Japan, US and Europe.

[JAG]
ATARI JAGUAR

Year: **1993**
Manufacturer: **Atari**
Original Cost: **US $249.99**

ATARI JAGUAR

Atari's final console was a tragedy, an embarrassment to the company whose work once defined the industry and a disappointment to all who believed in the name.

> **"Many Jaguar buyers complained that the system's controller was over-complex, its 15 buttons lacking intuitiveness, and its bulk feeling uncomfortable and unwieldy in the hands."**
>
> Sam Tramiel, president of Atari

Do The Math. The Atari Jaguar's marketing slogan encouraged potential buyers to compare the console's 64-bit specification to that of its rivals, the Super Nintendo and Sega Mega Drive, both 16-bit machines. In reality, it was a poor choice of words, many disputing the company's claim that this was the first 64-bit system.

Regardless of the numbers, Atari's return to the console manufacturing business was disastrous. Launching in the US in November 1993, neither the hefty price tag nor hefty controller made the system appealing to buyers still smitten with

Mario and Sonic's latest outings. Likewise, a dearth of launch games was followed by yet more paucity of product over the course of the console's first year, developers either struggling with buggy hardware or with simply finding games that suited the system's idiosyncrasies.

The release of the Jaguar CD add-on did nothing to reverse these fortunes, its lacklustre titles giving consumers too few reasons to invest in what was a cumbersome upgrade. Eventually, the marketing slogan proved to be self-instructional, as Atari's executives were forced to weigh sales of the system against the high investment required to continue its development and support. The Jaguar's specifications and library of games looked pitiable by comparison to those of the Sega Saturn and Sony PlayStation, and sales, which had already slowed to just 25,000 units in 1994 and 1995, dried up almost completely in the face of such boisterous competition.

By December 1995, Atari had sold just 125,000 units, with 100,000 units unsold in warehouses. Atari's revenues declined by more than half, from US$38.7 million in 1994 to $14.6 million in 1995, and the company pulled out of the hardware manufacturing business completed shortly after, the Jaguar a heartbreaking conclusion to a company that had once sold 30 million consoles.

The Jaguar's story doesn't end there. In the late 1990s toy manufacturer Hasbro Interactive acquired Atari's properties and declared the console an open platform, opening the doors to homebrew development and feeding the machine's small but industrious cult following.

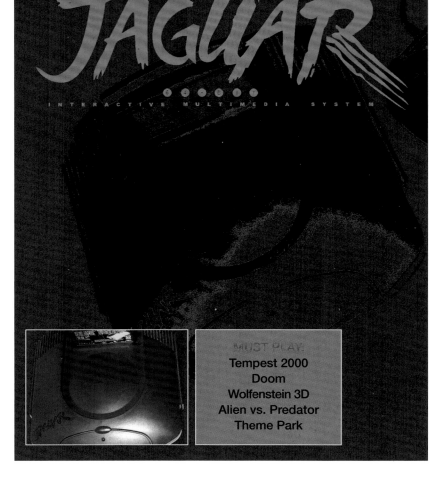

MUST PLAY:
Tempest 2000
Doom
Wolfenstein 3D
Alien vs. Predator
Theme Park

Right: Many Jaguar buyers complained that the system's controller was awkward and difficult to manage.

VIRTUA FIGHTER

Yu Suzuki's 3D fighting game brought temperance and visual restraint, while emphasizing the technicality of unarmed combat on the screen.

The fighting game's transition to 3D brought with it a newfound sobriety for a style of video game that had, for some years, exaggerated the physics of reality for visceral effect. Screen-filling fireballs and blur-effect hurricane kicks are nowhere to be found in AM2's distinguished fighting simulator, a game which redacted *Street Fighter*'s six-button configuration to just three basic building block moves: kick, punch and defend. The result is a game that prizes timing and reflex over manual dexterity, whose interactive components can be picked up by anyone, but whose complexities are mastered over months, not moments, of practice.

Virtua Fighter's approach, like so many titles seeded in the seismic shift between 2D and 3D gaming, was led by technology. Sega's star designer, Yu Suzuki, creator of arcade sensations *After Burner II*, *OutRun*, *Space Harrier* and *Super Hang-On*, had first explored 3D polygonal graphics with his F1 racing title, *Virtua Racing*, in 1992. Developed for the company's powerful Model 1 hardware (an arcade board designed in conjunction with a team that would later become the aerospace manufacturer, Lockheed Martin), *Virtua Racing* had grown from a tech demo designed to show off the hardware into a fully fledged racing simulator. Following the vast success of the game in arcades, Suzuki wanted to apply the techniques used to replicate boxy cars in 3D, to recreate the human form. *Virtua Fighter*

Below: While researching the game in China, Yu Suzuki met with a master of Hakkyokuken, the technique used by Akira in the game.

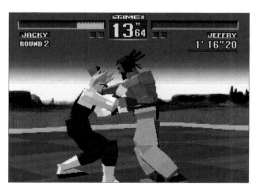

SEGA video game images - under licence by SEGA Corporation

Above: A graphically-enhanced version of the game, *Virtua Fighter Remix*, was sent as a free gift in the mail to registered Sega Saturn owners in 1995.

was the direct result of the team's tests. The blocky humanoid characters may appear outdated today, but in November 1993 they appeared as men and women from the future. While their bodies, each comprised of fewer than 1,200 polygons, were primitive, the striking animations were anything but, bringing the ebb and flow of hand-to-hand combat to vivid life.

Significantly, each of the game's eight combatants is distinctive in exhibiting a different fighting style, differences that lent the game a realistic, varied feel in the hand. *Virtua Fighter* laid the blueprint of the modern 3D fighting game, its template borrowed by countless multi-million-selling franchises including *Tekken* and *Soul Calibur*. Yet Suzuki's series remains the most technical of the crop, its thrills to be found in the split-second drama of counterattacks and parries, rather than theatrical special moves.

Year: 1993
Developer: AM2
Publisher: Sega
Original format: Arcade
Play today: MAME

"The difference between Miyamoto-san and I is that he takes the same game and takes it deeper and deeper, like with the Mario series. I like to work on different games and concepts. I don't like doing the same thing. The same goes for the hardware. I like to change the hardware I work with."

Yu Suzuki, creator of *Virtua Fighter*

Left: Unlike other fighting games of the time, *Virtua Fighter* relies on a control stick and three input buttons: 'Punch', 'Kick', and 'Block'.

[057]

DOOM

Year: 1993
Developer: In-house
Publisher: id Software
Original format: PC
Play today: Xbox 360

DOOM

Another technical triumph from wunderkind programmer John Carmack, *Doom*'s development became a philosophical battleground over the role of story in games.

Primitive and obvious, *Doom* is a celebration of dark juvenile fantasy, of giant guns and glistening guts and of roaring demons in space. And yet, in its refined balance of speed and power, it's an experience that popularized the enduring 'first person shooter', whose legacy runs far deeper than its premise.

Following the tremendous success of *Wolfenstein 3D*, most of iD Software's staff began work on a direct sequel, *Spear of Destiny*. Meanwhile, John Carmack was hard at work creating a new, improved 3D engine to power the studio's next big release. Originally planned as a licensed game based on James Cameron's *Aliens* movie, the team ultimately decided to eschew the licence in order to secure greater creative freedom. Inspired by a recent *Dungeons and Dragons* campaign the team had played which ended with demons overtaking a planet, John Carmack suggested

Below: *Doom*'s graphic violence and demonic imagery have drawn criticism since the game's debut.

"There is a scene in *The Color of Money* where Tom Cruse [sic] shows up at a pool hall with a custom pool cue in a case. "What do you have in there?" asks someone. 'Doom,' replied Cruse with a cocky grin. That, and the resulting carnage, was how I viewed us springing the game on the industry."

John Carmack, creator of *Doom*

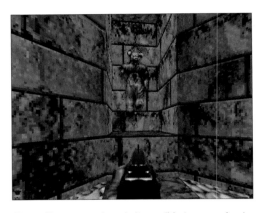

Above: Stereo sound made it possible to approximate the direction and distance of a sound effect, allowing players to use sound as a clue to peril.

the theme of demons vs. technology, and so a science fiction world in which a space marine must overcome the forces of hell was born.

A core controversy defined the development of *Doom*, one that, in many ways, typifies an ongoing creative battle in the medium. The game's creative director, Tom Hall, wanted the game to feature an intricate storyline, viewing narrative as the main way in which the plotless shooter *Wolfenstein 3D* could be progressed. As a result Hall set about writing the Doom Bible, an expansive document featuring an elaborate mythology and backstory to the world.

Hall originally planned for the game to have six episodes, but the game's programmer, John Carmack, disapproved of the convoluted storyline, believing that Hall's emphasis on realism would come at the cost of gameplay. Carmack famously quipped: "story in a game is like story in a porn movie. It's expected to be there, but it's not that important," a difference in creative viewpoint that forced Hall's resignation from iD in the summer of 1993.

This demotion of narrative may not have limited the game's commercial success (even if one reviewer bemoaned the fact you couldn't talk to the monsters), and the masterwork of the underlying interactive design assured it a pivotal place. But the game's success didn't necessarily prove Carmack's point as the list of games influenced by *Doom* includes just as many story-rich titles such as *BioShock* and *Far Cry* as it does unadorned shooting galleries.

SENSIBLE WORLD OF SOCCER

Dedication to transporting the detail and trivia of international football leagues into the game made *Sensible World of Soccer* as engaging off the pitch as it was on.

Sensible Software's second soccer game is to the world of football management what *Gran Turismo* is to the world of motorsport – an obsessive work of tribute and fanaticism. Featuring 1,500 teams composed of over 24,000 professional international footballers, the British developer's commitment to integrate every obscure league they could into the game made this not only the most comprehensive football management title, but also a zealous celebration of the beautiful game in every corner of the world in which it is played.

By 1994, football management games had been a feature of the gaming landscape for over a decade. Addictive Games' *Football Manager*, widely regarded as the first, had debuted on the ZX Spectrum in 1982, with imitators revising the formula each subsequent year. But it was *Sensible World of Soccer*, sequel to the top-down Commodore Amiga football game, that married the world of sheepskin coat-wearing management with the distinguished match play of its predecessor.

The first *Sensible Soccer*, a twitchy, fast-paced football game, had won a multitude of fans with its simple, yet nuanced play style. The game's artist and designer, Jon Hare, intended the game to have a management meta-game, but had to remove this element due to time constraints. For the sequel, the team implemented their original vision, hiring two staff to do nothing but research teams and players for inclusion in the game.

The core engine was left largely unmodified from the first game, Hare and developer Chris Chapman fearing that tampering with the code could spoil its fine-tuned balance. Instead, they set their attention on providing a boundless range of tactical options for virtual managers to deploy, offering players the chance to either sit by the sidelines and direct the players, or get stuck in directly controlling the team.

Despite the rudimentary visuals, the effective, economical use of animation and the subtle ways in which weather and physics affect the ball make *Sensible World of Soccer* more convincing than its 12-pixel high characters would suggest. In the keen thrill of moment-by-moment match play, and the questing excitement of taking a club up the leagues over the course of a 20-year career, *Sensible World of Soccer* delights and inspires both on the pixel pitch and off.

Year: **1994**
Developer: **Sensible Software**
Publisher: **Renegade**
Original format: **Amiga**
Play today: **Xbox 360**

"Sometimes, the best part of creative work can be like magic, and that's true of games. Something just works and it's perfect, but it's not premeditated or planned – it just happens."

Jon Hare, co-founder of
Sensible Software

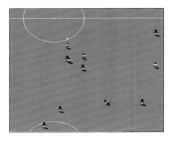

Left: Despite the simplicity of the controls (just eight directional inputs and a shoot button), a wide variety of context-sensitive moves are available to the player.

[059]

SUPER METROID

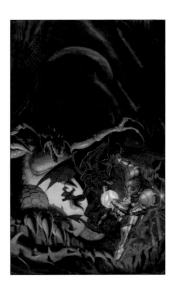

Year: 1994
Developer: Intelligent Systems
Publisher: Nintendo
Original format: Super Famicom
Play today: Nintendo Wii (Virtual
Console)

"When they discovered something new – a new item or new location – we wanted the player to feel that he/she had made that discovery independently, without help from the game."

Yoshio Sakamoto, director of
Super Metroid

SUPER METROID

Revealing the darker side of Nintendo's creative psyche, *Super Metroid* gave birth to a new style of 2D game, where the thrill of exploration is the vital motivation.

If Mario is Nintendo's daytime TV platform game franchise, *Metroid* fills the studio's post-watershed schedule. The cold alien landscape of the planet Zebes is home to twilight monstrosities, sprawling platform puzzles viewed in the half light and an armoured protagonist, Samus, one of the only Nintendo leads to wield a gun.

As with many Nintendo classics, *Super Metroid* built upon the successes of the Famicom era. The series' debut, originally a Famicom Disc System release, established many of the core systems discernible in this second sequel (after the Game Boy's *Metroid II*), commissioned by Nintendo thanks to its success in North America. Director and designer Yoshio Sakamoto's initial focus was on using the Super Famicom's extra power to improve the graphics of the previous two Metroid games, leaving their systems untouched.

As with many game designers of the time, Sakamoto and his team were deeply influenced by Ridley Scott's film *Alien*, and, in particular, the design work of concept artist H.R. Giger. With the move to the Super Famicom, the team felt they finally had the graphical power to create a world that could replicate some of the eeriness and loneliness of Scott's work and the result is, even today, a masterpiece of mood.

Initially Sakamoto worked on a prototype with a small team of programming staff from Intelligent Systems, only three of whom had worked on the original game. It was in this phase that Sakamoto and his co-designer Tomomi Yamane began to explore what new ideas and abilities could be introduced to increase the mechanical complexity, in the same way that the visuals were being updated. A game that was more fully focused upon exploration began to emerge, one that encouraged the player to backtrack in order to visit previously inaccessible areas as Samus learned new abilities. In this concoction a new style of 2D video game was articulated, one later joined upon by *Castlevania: Symphony of the Night* – leading to the neologism:

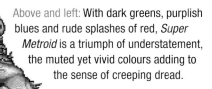

Above and left: With dark greens, purplish blues and rude splashes of red, *Super Metroid* is a triumph of understatement, the muted yet vivid colours adding to the sense of creeping dread.

'Metroidvania'. In this type of game players form a mental map of the world, returning to previously encountered areas when they've gained the required ability 'key' to unlock the secret, changing the feel of the game as they progress. The team of young Nintendo programmers eschewed the storytelling techniques used in RPGs, instead creating gameplay riddles that had to be solved by experimentation and careful thinking. With seemingly endless secrets, *Super Metroid*'s world balances the joy of discovery with the threat of adversity, the game's final twist more than justifying the challenge in reaching it. A masterpiece, as timeless and mysterious as the planet on which it's set.

Below: Ridley Scott's influence is made clear at the start of the game as Samus pursues the leader of the Space Pirates, named Ridley, to the planet Zebes.

THEME PARK

Bullfrog's attempt to capitalize on the success of *SimCity* placed players in the numerous roles of amusement planner, park director and drinks stall attendant.

I n the five years following the release of Will Wright's *SimCity*, developers across the world tried their hand at turning ostensibly dry, managerial vocations into video games. *Theme Park* was British developer Bullfrog's attempt, with the added benefit that its theme of choice was nothing short of thrilling. Originally conceived as a marketing game for Disneyland, *Theme Park* offers players the chance to plan and design an amusement park, laying down rollercasters, haunted houses, shooting galleries, Ferris wheels and as many cotton candy stalls as you can squeeze into your plot of land as you attempt to satisfy visitors while turning a profit.

The game's ingenuity lies in the inherent tension in its theme. The tourist destination you create must offer enough thrills and excitement to attract customers, who waddle around your grounds expectantly. But fail to maintain your rides, or push your profit margins on refreshments too far, and disgruntled customers will flee your business. Visitors' enjoyment matches your own, as the game taps into the keen sense of fulfilment to be found in meeting and

exceeding the expectations of your patrons when running a business. Likewise, disappointed customers lead to feelings of guilt and frustration, as problems spiral out of control and your funfair turns into a nightmare.

Conceived by Peter and Demi Habassis who worked alongside Peter Molyneux, developer Bullfrog ensured the management heart of the experience was representative, with the hiring and firing of staff a key component to running a successful park. But the developer took an altogether more lighthearted approach with the visuals. Indeed, it's the little touches that make *Theme Park* stand out, the 30 core attractions in the game supported by a slew of incidental animations and smaller rides and stalls that bring the park to hypnotic life.

In *Theme Park*, Bullfrog established a style of game that would go on to define the studio's subsequent work, which had players managing hospitals and rollercoasters, as well as influencing the strategic side of programmer Peter Molyneux's later work, such as *Black and White* and *Fable*.

Year: 1994
Developer: Bullfrog Productions
Publisher: Electronic Arts
Original format: PC
Play today: Nintendo DS

"I always found characters in costumes at theme parks scary and wanted to recreate this feeling in the game. They are not meant to be cuddly and friendly but more – as I remember them – a bit sinister and spooky."

Peter Molyneux, designer of *Theme Park*

Left and below: *Theme Park* is an amusement park that the player must build by adding rides, shops and attractions. The idea is to make a profit, sell up, then build a new theme park in another part of the world.

Left: *Theme Park* was Mark Healey's first game. The designer would later go on to co-found Media Molecule, creators of *LittleBigPlanet*.

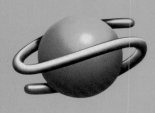

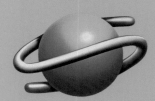

MUST PLAY:
Radiant Silver Gun
Panzer Dragoon Saga
Street Fighter Alpha 3
Nights
Guardian Heroes
Virtua Fighter

Year: **1994**
Manufacturer: **Sega**
Original Cost: **¥44,800**

NOVEMBER 1994

[SAT]

SEGA SATURN

111

SEGA SATURN

Sega's entry to the 3D era was characterized by misfortune and poor decision-making – but in Japan a fascinating library of games began to emerge.

The story of Sega's Saturn is often told as a tragedy: the tale of a console born too late, a 2D powerhouse released just as the gaming world popped into 3D. In the West, Sega's follow-up to the Mega Drive was without doubt a wretched failure, losing the company much of the ground and goodwill its 16-bit machine had clawed from Nintendo.

In a reversal of the Mega Drive's fortunes, in Japan, where 2D shoot 'em ups and fighting games were still fashionable, the Saturn enjoyed far greater success than its forebear. While the seeds of Sega's retreat from the game hardware business were sowed here, a clutch of important and enduring classics also grew from its fertile creative soil.

Sega's plans for the Saturn were drawn up in 1992, under the codename Giga Drive. The decision was made to use CD-ROM technology for its games, and the machine was specifically designed to better the 3DO, the only other 32-bit console available at the time. The internal architecture was based on Sega's Model 1 arcade hardware, adapted by its creator Hideki Sato and his team. A number of prototypes were built in 1993 and, as the team approached a design they were happy with, the name was changed from Giga Drive to Aurora and, finally, Saturn.

However, this machine was very different to the one that would launch almost two years later. In December 1993, almost a year before the Saturn's planned launch, Sony revealed the system specifications of Ken Kutaragi's PlayStation project. These alluded to 3D graphical capabilities that matched Sega's cutting edge arcade hardware, and the capacity to handle complex 2D processing, too.

When Sega CEO Hayao Nakayama obtained a copy of the PlayStation system specs and compared them to those of his company's Saturn prototype he called an emergency meeting with his R&D department. One staff member reportedly said of the meeting that his boss was "the maddest I've ever seen him". Nakayama was furious at the way in which Sony had bettered his own machine. Sato was charged by Nakayama to 'fix' the Saturn so it could compete with the

PlayStation. With less than a year till launch, Sato handpicked a team of 27 Sega engineers to start work. There was no time to commission a new chip for the machine, so Sega was forced to look to existing components. The team opted for a dual-processor architecture, despite the fact that Sega's US head Tom Kalinske had contacted Silicon Graphics, one of the companies behind the PlayStation's 3D capabilities, to research a simpler single chip design. Allegedly, Nakayama opted for the dual-processor design as a favour to an old golfing buddy at Hitachi.

The use of dual processors was key to the Saturn's effectiveness at 2D graphics and relative failure at 3D graphics. Polygonal generation could only be handled through manipulation of the sprite engine, and as a result struggled with texture transparency and playfield rotation, effects that the PlayStation excelled in. While teams familiar with parallel programming could produce surprising results, few developers had this sort of experience.

Despite the troubles in the months leading up to November 1994, the system's Japanese launch was a success, thanks largely to the release of *Virtua Fighter*, Sega's arcade fighting game hit. By Christmas day 500,000 units had been sold, 60 per cent more than Sony had managed with its PlayStation. But the US launch in May 2005 was a disaster. The day Sega announced the price point of $399 (£249); Sony announced the PlayStation would cost $100 less.

Released into just four retail chains, before the dry summer period for the games industry, the Saturn's lack of a strong launch line-up was clear. The machine's challenging internal architecture was causing developers huge delays, allowing Sony to take a clear lead.

A year later, the members of Sega's US marketing team were fired, with Sega of America's president, Tom Kalinske, handing in his resignation more than a month later. The collapse of Sega in the West meant that many of the system's best games were never released outside Japan. In a 3D world, Sega's 2D powerhouse seemed anachronistic at launch.

> **"You can have the best games in the world. You can have the best machine on the market. But unless you roll the two together with solid marketing you won't succeed."**
>
> Mark Hartley, former marketing director of Sega Europe

Below: A fictional character, Segata Sanshiro – a Judo master who tracks down and punishes those who do not play the Sega Saturn – promoted the system in Japan.

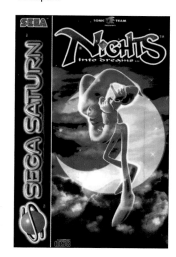

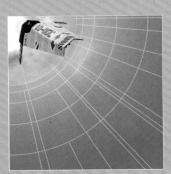

MUST PLAY:
Castlevania Symphony
of the Night
Final Fantasy VII
Gran Turismo
Wipeout 2097
Metal Gear Solid

PLAYSTATION

Sony's system would revolutionize the Japanese video game market, but it owed its existence to a corporate desire for revenge rather than creative questing.

Never underestimate the force of revenge. Without it, Sony's PlayStation would never have made it from designer Ken Kutaragi's wild imagination into 102 million homes around the world. Neither would games have popped into 3D with the forceful brilliance facilitated by Sony's debut without that most ancient of creative incentives: a business vendetta.

At the Consumer Electronics Show in June 1991 Sony unveiled its first video game console, a joint creation from the Japanese electronics giant and Nintendo. A Super Famicom with an in-built CD-ROM drive, the system was designed to be Nintendo's route into the emerging world of multimedia entertainment, as well as Sony's first tentative step into a market that, to date, it had watched from afar.

The next day, Nintendo announced it would be breaking its deal with Sony, instead partnering with its rival, Philips, on the project. Few snubs in Japanese business have been played out so publically, and the turnabout was humiliating to Sony, despite the fact that the relations had been deteriorating for months over how revenue would be shared and collected by the two companies.

The next month Sony president Norio Ohga called a meeting to plan litigation against Nintendo. But financial recompense through the courts would not be enough to sate his appetite for revenge. Ohga stood to his feet and declared to the room: 'We will never withdraw from this business. Keep going.'

Kutaragi, buoyed by this support from the most senior level of the company, pulled together a team of engineers that had been working on a 3D graphics engine designed to augment live television broadcasts with 3D images in real time. The technology, dubbed System-G, shared technological similarities with the way video games work, even if, as a high-end workstation, the thought of introducing this sort of technology to the home seemed impossible.

By June 1992 all relations with Nintendo had been severed and Kutaragi was called to present his work to Ohga and other Sony executives. It was here the designer revealed his plans for a proprietary CD-ROM based system capable of rendering 3D graphics for use in a video game. Ohga asked what sort of chip the machine would require and Kutaragi replied it would need one million gate arrays. Ohga laughed at the figure: the maximum Sony made at the time was 100,000. Kutaragi, in a moment of shrewd understanding, replied: "Are you going to sit back and accept what Nintendo did to us?"

Ohga, wanting to protect Kutaragi from Sony's board, who viewed video games as toys and feared entering the market would dilute the company brand name, moved the designer to Sony Music, a separate subsidiary. The move was significant as Sony Music understood that creative talent needs nurturing in a way that the drier, tech-focused core part of the company didn't. Likewise, their expertise in manufacturing huge amounts of discs would prove invaluable.

Attracting developers to the new system proved straightforward. Without an internal development studio at Sony, the lack of competition to many potential developers was an advantage. In Japan, Nintendo's huge royalty rates made development for the machine a huge risk for publishers, so Sony's more reasonable rates proved attractive.

When PlayStation launched in Japan on 3 December, 1994 a huge number of developers across the world were busy creating software for the machine. Namco's launch title, *Ridge Racer*, was a startling port of the arcade game, one that demonstrated the power of the system in no uncertain terms. All 100,000 launch units sold out, with another 200,000 units shifted in the following 30 days. Pricing was key to its success, and, even though Sony lost money on each unit sold until 1995, the fact the PlayStation was ¥5,000 cheaper than Sega's Saturn helped Sony gain crucial ground in the 32-bit race.

By March 2007, Sony had sold 102 million systems across the world, success born in a perfect storm of technology, pricing, marketing and, perhaps most importantly, old-fashioned rivalry and honour.

> "I remember thinking: 'Oh my God, the name is bombing and everyone is going to hate it.' I shared the information with Tokunaka-san [president of SCEI], and he said: 'Oh, that's nothing. You should have heard what people said about Walkman."
>
> Phil Harrison, president of Sony Computer Entertainment Worldwide Studios

Below: Various PlayStation logos, ending in the latest 'PS' logo.

[061]

COMMAND AND CONQUER

Year: 1995
Developer: Westwood Studios
Publisher: Virgin Interactive
Original format: PC (MS-DOS)
Play today: PSN

"At the time, Brett [Sperry] said that it seemed to him that the next wars won't be fought nation-to-nation, but fought between Western society and a kind of anarchistic terror organization that doesn't have a centralized government. It turned out to be very prophetic."

Louis Castle, co-founder of
Westwood Studios

Right: The live action cutscenes feature Westwood team members as the cast and were filmed in spare rooms and warehouses near the studio's offices.

COMMAND AND CONQUER

A Real Time Strategy game, *Command and Conquer* appeared to predict that a Western society would be fighting against a terrorist network.

Best exemplified by *Command and Conquer*, the Real Time Strategy genre, or RTS as it would come to be known, has its roots in an obscure Japanese Mega Drive game, *Herzog Zwei*. TechnoSoft's fast-paced two-player game requires each player to establish a base, then mine resources in order to fund the manufacture of military units that must be sent out in an effort to overcome one's opponent. One of the strongest Mega Drive titles, it nevertheless remained relatively unknown until three years later, when the Las Vegas-based Westwood Studios borrowed its ideas and created a similar game styled on the 1984 David Lynch film, *Dune*.

The *Dune* games laid many of the foundations upon which *Command and Conquer* would build, being the first game to allow players to use the mouse to direct units. But despite the game's huge success, Westwood had a list of features it wanted to add, and it was eager to do so away from Lynch's name. Brett Sperry, co-founder of Westwood Studios and executive producer on *Command and Conquer,* wanted to create the company's next game without a "leg-up" from a licence, proving that the game style was strong enough to stand on its own two feet.

Originally the team intended *Command and Conquer* to have a high-fantasy setting, with wizards and warriors, but with the shockwaves of the Gulf War echoing around them, the team decided a contemporary war environment would be more relevant and accessible to players. Westwood envisioned an alternate universe set in 1995 where the the Global Defense Initiative – the game's version of the United Nations – squared off against a bizarre cult, the Brotherhood of Nod led by the charismatic terrorist Kane.

Noteworthy for its camp, live action cutscenes that intersperse the action, the story provides the set-up for the true jewel of the experience: strategy. Battles see each side racing to gather Tiberium, the planet's valuable resource, inspired by the 1957 B-movie *The Monolith Monsters*, building an army before sending them out in an attempt to conquer the opposition. Additional missions, in which the player controls a single special-ops unit, interrupt the basic rhythm of play. Thanks to some delicate balancing, one of the most compelling two-player competitive experiences in video games emerged, establishing a franchise and popularizing a new genre in the process.

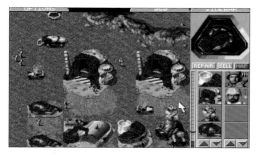

WIPEOUT

Instrumental in moving games from the bedroom to the club in the cultural perception, *Wipeout* demonstrated that games had appeal beyond teenagers.

In *Wipeout*, video games shifted from childish diversion to a crucial part of the cultural zeitgeist. Much of this transformation can be attributed to its fashioning rather than its qualities as a hovership racing game. With futuristic, Japanese-esque packaging, menus devised by the now-defunct Designers Republic and a soundtrack from mid-90s club cool artists such as the Chemical Brothers, Leftfield, Orbital and The Prodigy, the game is often remembered more for its style than its substance. But *Wipeout*'s brilliance runs deeper than its presentation, even if its legacy is one of legitimacy, rather than influence.

But for all its aura of slick cool, *Wipeout*'s origin is geekish. The game's designer-to-be Nick Burscombe glanced over a colleague's shoulder and saw a Softimage animation of two vehicles from grid-based

Below: Tim Wright composed *Wipeout*'s soundtrack under the alias CoLD SToRAGE. Songs by Leftfield, the Chemical Brothers, and Orbital were included in the European version of the PlayStation game.

Above: Set in 2052, there are four different racing teams to choose between, each with its own line-up of ships offering differing acceleration, top speed, mass, and turning radius.

strategy game *Matrix Marauders* racing one another. In that moment Burscombe, who had been spending the previous few weeks playing through Nintendo's *Super Mario Kart*, visualized a kart-style game using these futuristic hoverships.

Burscombe discussed the idea with *Matrix Marauder*'s designer, Jim Bowers, and came up with the name *Wipeout*. Both men were listening to British dance act The Prodigy at the time, and joked about commissioning the band to create a remix of the classic Beach Boys surf track, *Wipeout*, for the game's soundtrack. The idea stuck, and The Prodigy became one of the first artists signed up to feature on the game's soundtrack.

Just as crucial to *Wipeout*'s success with the style press was the involvement of The Designers Republic. Initially commissioned to create the packaging design, the company's involvement escalated when artist Lee Carus applied the header from a fax from the agency as a decal to one of the game's hoverships.

R&D time on the game was short as Psygnosis wanted to time the release to coincide with the PlayStation's UK launch. Nevertheless, the team was able to squeeze a great deal of performance from the hardware at such an early point in its life. The rough edges were smoothed for its sequel, however, and with more refined weapon balance and handling, it is the better game. But *Wipeout*'s impact is unrivalled.

Year: 1995
Developer: In-house
Publisher: Psygnosis
Original format: PlayStation
Play today: PSN

"At the time I didn't feel like licensed music was any great achievement. We had a CD and a CD player – it made sense to play CD quality music. It's only in retrospect that I suppose it was a big leap for the industry."

Nick Burscombe, designer of *Wipeout*

Below: The icons of the various companies who helped to make *Wipeout*.

Year: 1995
Developer: AM5
Publisher: Sega
Original format: Arcade
Play today: PlayStation 2

"We asked Toyota and [Lancia owner] Fiat for help with testing but they turned us away several times. We kept trying and after they saw what we had they relented."

Tetsuya Mizuguchi, creator of
Sega Rally

Right: Designer Tetsuya Mizuguchi spent three weeks driving down the American west coast to Mexico photographing textures for use in the game.

SEGA RALLY CHAMPIONSHIP

A young Tetsuya Mizuguchi paired with *Ridge Racer* designer Kenji Sasaki to create an arcade game that would take Sega off-road with elegance and style.

There's a cleanness to *Sega Rally Championship* that, in these days of complex simulation racers with their innumerable options and rambling structures, has an invigorating appeal. A choice of just two cars greets the player: the Toyota Celica or Lancia Delta, each of which must be steered through the three stages that comprise the titular championship. Dubbed with a childlike plainness 'Desert', 'Forest' and 'Mountain', the straightforwardness of the game's presentation bespeaks its creator's confidence – here is a game fit enough to shine without embellishment.

Nevertheless, in the hands, the game is anything but artless. The cars strain against their driver. They roll and bump along the grit with joyful abandon, growling around corners, kicking up clouds of mud and earth like headstrong stallions. As with *Ridge Racer*, drifting is the key to success; twitch corrections to inertia necessary to ease the

Above: Mizuguchi provided the in-game engine sound effect for the Lancia Delta by recording his own car.

car into and through corners in what remains some of the most potent racing on offer in video games. The similarities to Namco's arcade racer are more than superficial. Kenji Sasaki, director of *Sega Rally*, was one of the key members of the original *Ridge Racer* team, and chose the rally theme simply because, with *Ridge Racer* and *Daytona USA* already on the market, it offered a motorsport niche relatively untapped in the arcade scene.

As with any development team attempting to break new ground, it was difficult to know whether or not their innovation was likely to be successful. At one point Sasaki became so burned out developing the game he feared he'd forgotten what made racing cars so enjoyable, so took his own sports car high up into the Japanese mountains in search of a reminder. In those peaks he found what he was looking for, returning to AM5's studio with a demand that the team make the third track in the game a mountainside. The result was the first 3D rally game, one that would go on to inspire copycat designs around the globe.

SEGA video game' images - under licence by SEGA Corporation

VIRTUAL BOY

Nintendo's first video game hardware failure was released before it was ready, much to the dismay of its designer, Gunpei Yokoi. And yet its legacy lived on.

Not only was it the first blemish on Nintendo's unspoiled track record in the video game hardware business, but the Virtual Boy was also the handheld that helped end the illustrious career of its inventor, Gunpei Yokoi. And yet, its innovations in stereoscopic 3D pioneered technology that would reappear 16 years later in the guise of Nintendo 3DS. Whatever the Virtual Boy's failings, the concept of a 3D game system was not among them.

In some ways, the Virtual Boy came to Nintendo. US firm Reflection Technologies approached the Japanese technology giant seeking a buyer for its new screen technology which used twin mirror-scanning LED displays to deliver separate images to each of the player's eyes. By arranging each image to match the disparity humans see in real life, the sensation of depth was achieved. In 1992 Nintendo acquired the exclusive worldwide rights to the technology and Yokoi's Research & Development 1 team began working on a system to employ it.

Codenamed the VR-32, the Virtual Boy went through a number of different design stages, one of which even saw the unit mounted on the users' head like a VR unit. However, as soon as the decision was made to shun head tracking, the team settled upon a table-mounted design. The delicate internal mirrors meant that any jolt could render the device entirely inoperable, and so what at first glance appeared to be a battery-powered portable successor to the Game Boy, was in fact a stationary, tripod-supported machine.

While the system housed a 32-bit processor, the need to power two screens meant that the additional clout wasn't immediately apparent. On the system's launch in July 1995, there were none of the crowds that had greeted the Super Famicom's arrival. The lack of any top-tier Nintendo-brand software certainly contributed to the lack of consumer interest, but as reports of players suffering

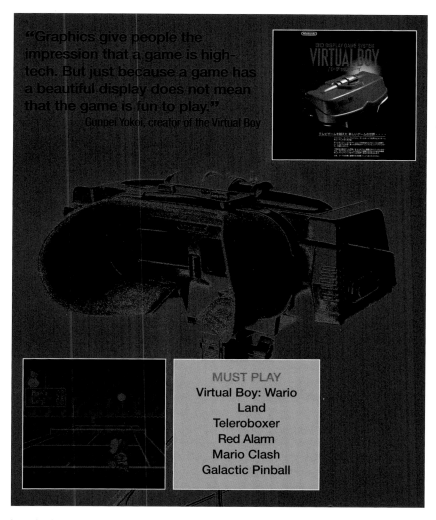

"Graphics give people the impression that a game is high-tech. But just because a game has a beautiful display does not mean that the game is fun to play."
Gunpei Yokoi, creator of the Virtual Boy

MUST PLAY
Virtual Boy: Wario Land
Teleroboxer
Red Alarm
Mario Clash
Galactic Pinball

headaches during play sessions began to circulate (the red LEDs were chosen for their power-saving properties, but caused considerable eye-strain), the console's fortunes faded.

Only 22 titles were released for the *Virtual Boy* over its short lifespan, with only 800,000 systems sold in Japan and the US (the European launch was cancelled). Yokoi, who had expressed dismay at Nintendo's eagerness to ship the console before it was ready, was blamed for its failure. He left Nintendo under a cloud, the Virtual Boy's lack of success overshadowing, at least in the short-term, his vital work in taking Nintendo into the video game business.

Below: The Virtual Boy was the last system Gunpei Yokoi designed for Nintendo.

Year: 1996
Developer: GameFreak
Publisher: Nintendo
Original format: Game Boy
Play today: Nintendo DS

Above and below: **Characters from Satoshi Tajiri's** Pokémon.

POKÉMON

Satoshi Tajiri's modest experiences collecting and documenting insects in the countryside as a child inspired what has gone on to become a game phenomenon.

Satoshi Tajiri's childish obsession was to influence the creation of a video game. In the summer holidays he would head out from his family home just outside of Tokyo to search the surrounding undergrowth for mini-beasts, carefully studying each one he caught, before cataloguing it in a notepad bought for him by his parents.

His family saw him as a quiet, unassuming boy with a healthy outdoors obsession. No one could have imagined that, as an adult, he would turn his hobby into a video game, casting himself in the lead role (in Japan, protagonist Ash is called Satoshi). Nor might anyone have guessed that this game, a game about collecting creatures, naming them, training and trading them, would go on to become the second most successful video game franchise around the world.

Second only to Nintendo's *Mario*, *Pokémon*'s game sales are in excess of 200 million across the globe, its influence stretching far beyond the confines of the video game medium. This is a game that has spawned countless animated television series and feature films, hundreds of thousands of children's rucksacks and lunchboxes (Hasbro paid $325 million to market the toys) and attracted criticism from a number of the world's major religions. Children everywhere have absorbed Pokéarcana, learning the intricacies of the game world and the secrets and techniques necessary to find the most rare creatures, and grow them into the most efficient battlers. Still, for Tajiri, it was always just a game about collecting insects.

Tajiri was always something of an outcast. He had no desire to study in college and, when his father tried to secure him a job as an electrical engineer, he refused. He wanted to be an

Above: As of the release of *Pokémon Black 2* and *White 2*, 649 fictional species have made appearances in *Pokémon* media.

entomologist, as a way to formalize his fascination with insects, especially beetles. But Tajiri's obsessive personality was easily distracted, and as soon as he discovered video games, his focus was drawn. In 1982 Tajiri launched a video game magazine called *GameFreak* with his friend Ken Sugimori, the artist who would eventually draw the Pokémon. Writing about games inspired Tajiri to think about making them, and he bought and took apart a Famicom to see if he could work out how to develop for it.

When Nintendo released the Game Boy an idea hit the burgeoning designer, who imagined digital insects being transferred along the link cable that connected two systems. He took the idea to Nintendo who, impressed at Tajiri's previous efforts, offered him a contract. But while Tajiri was placed under the tutelage of master designer Shigeru Miyamoto, development was far from smooth.

In the six years it took to finish the game *GameFreak* nearly went bankrupt on multiple occasions. Five staff quit when Tajiri admitted the severity of his company's financial situation and, by the time *Pokémon* was ready for release (in two editions, Red and Blue, each with Pokémon unique to the version), the Game Boy was nearing the end of its life cycle. Indeed, the handheld was so outdated by this

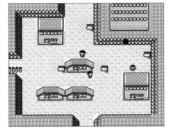

Above: Released in 2016, *Pokémon Go,* an Augmented Reality game for smartphones, allowed players to venture outside to collect monsters in real streets and fields. Within six months it was downloaded more than 500 million times.

point, that no magazines would cover the game, and, initially, no toy manufacturer would consider marketing spin-off toys. But, as with so many of Nintendo's greatest successes, sales continued at a consistent rate, building over a period of months as word of mouth spread. When Tajiri leaked the fact that he had hidden a secret 151st Pokémon in the game, Mew, a character one could only acquire through trading, rumours began flying around playgrounds and sales doubled.

As *Pokémon* began climbing the charts Nintendo took the decision to commission an animated television series and, almost overnight, the game turned into a

phenomenon. Children would be introduced to the franchise through cartoons, before progressing to trading cards when they were a little older, before, finally, arriving at the video games, which are deep and compelling enough to attract not only the young but also the young at heart, for whom the appeal of collection and completism remains.

Tajiri's great accomplishment was in celebrating the joy of discovery, of offering children born into urban environments the opportunity to experience the thrill of finding and cataloguing creatures, and sharing their experiences with their peers. The visual simplicity belies the game's overarching complexity, whereby a strong *Pokémon* team consists of tens of thousands of thoughtful decisions, each unique to the player. Herein lies the secret to how Tajiri managed to catch, if not everyone, then certainly 200 million of 'em.

"Every new insect was a wonderful mystery. And as I searched for more, I would find more. If I put my hand in a river, I would get a crayfish. Put a stick underwater and make a hole, look for bubbles and there were more creatures."

Satoshi Tajiri, creator of *Pokémon*

Below left: In 2001, Saudi Arabia banned *Pokémon* games and cards, alleging that the franchise promoted Zionism by displaying the Star of David in the trading cards.

THE KNOWLEDGE
Before creating *Pokémon*, Tajiri was an obsessive gamer. He spent so much money at one arcade that the owner gave him a Space Invaders machine to take home.

PRESS ANY BUTTON

©CAPCOM CO.,LTD. 1996,1997 ALL RIGHTS RESERVED

Year: 1996
Developer: In-house (Capcom Production Studio 4)
Publisher: Capcom
Original format: PlayStation
Play today: PSN

"I loved the film *Dawn Of The Dead*. I realized that in a game it would be possible for players to use their own techniques and thinking in order to survive the experience. I thought that this difference between horror games and horror movies could be something wonderful."

Shinji Mikami, creator of
Resident Evil

RESIDENT EVIL

The creaking mansion is, at first glance, home to little more than a misery of clichés. Giant tarantulas that bristle from the ceiling, cobras that rise open-mouthed from behind crates in the cellar and zombies that toe a delicate line between terror and farce, *Resident Evil*'s hackneyed plot and amateurish voice acting is B-movie fodder. And yet it was in these corridors that the survival horror subgenre was popularized.

As with many Japanese classics, *Resident Evil* was born of corporate mandate. Tokuro Fujiwara, Capcom's general manager, approached Mikami, a young designer who had worked on only a handful of licensed Disney games, with a brief: create a horror game similar to Capcom's Famicom title, *Sweet Home*, a movie tie-in that had been a minor hit for the developer in 1989.

Sweet Home was the first to combine the frights of cinematic horror with a type of fear-mongering unique to video games: the limiting of player resources, curtailing one's reach and effectiveness in the fiction.

Resident Evil, which lifted *Sweet Home*'s ponderous door opening animations when loading new areas, took the premise further, providing only infrequent boxes of ammunition and limiting access to its typewriter save points. As a result every dash down a corridor is fraught with danger, not least because you never quite know when doing so will trigger a rabid dog to burst through the window.

Originally Mikami planned for the game to be a straight ghost story, settling on zombies when he realized a tangible foe would make for more fun. For six months he was the sole team member on the project, Capcom

Above: Mikami planned for the game to become a comedy after the third 'week' of game time, an idea discarded because of the time it would take.

eventually allocating another game designer for three months thereafter. The game was viewed with some scepticism internally, Capcom's outside consulting company even recommending that the developer discontinue the project, a memo that only steeled Mikami's resolve. Mikami originally intended that the game feature fully 3D game environments, but it appeared that PlayStation could not render as many assets as Mikami wanted. The team made the shift to pre-rendered backgrounds to accommodate the limitations, one that caused no small amount of issues with regard to the control scheme, in which the left and right buttons swivel the character on the spot awkwardly. The cumbersome controls only add to the sense of panic when lining up a shot while under attack by a zombie.

The designer's skill was in providing sufficiently engaging context for the player to overlook the shortcomings. He achieved this by borrowing a slew of techniques from cinema to heighten tension, and using zombie groans and footsteps to tighten anticipation long before enemies arrived on screen. Thanks to the pre-rendered backgrounds, the team was able to use static cameras, placing them strategically to create blind spots in order to disorientate the player.

In total, the game sold just shy of 3 million copies worldwide. Dated and camp today, *Resident Evil*'s influence is no less diminished, its schlock ambience and gurning zombies infecting so many contemporary game designers with their appeal.

SUPER MARIO RPG

The final collaboration between Nintendo and Squaresoft, the game saw Mario drawn into a world of hit points and magic.

Despite his role as producer on the game, it seems likely that *Super Mario RPG* was a mash-up of genres forced upon *Super Mario* creator Shigeru Miyamoto, a man who once professed a "fundamental dislike" for the Japanese role-playing game. And for many, while *Final Fantasy* developer Squaresoft had published its stat-crunching story games for many years on Nintendo hardware, the idea of the two companies working together in a creative capacity seemed destined to failure. After all, here were two styles of game with fundamentally different approaches and philosophies of interactive design: the bright, cutesy immediacy of the platform game at total odds with the often dark, lengthy dialogue-heavy trajectory of the Japanese RPG.

In reality, the union worked startlingly well. For one thing, the kidnapped princess narrative premise of all Mario games transposes well to the RPG template and Square's shrewd idea to make the over-world game play out like an isometric platform game, and the battles play out like a simplified RPG, allowed each company's tradition to meet in the middle and settle upon something wholly new and exciting.

Of course, with Nintendo's bank of assets, Squaresoft's fantasy approach was tempered and coloured by Mario and his supporting

Below: *Super Mario RPG* was the final Mario game released for the Super Famicom and one of the last that Square released before the company switched allegiance to Sony.

Above: *Super Mario RPG*'s lineage was continued in the *Paper Mario* series, developed by *Advance Wars* creator Intelligent Systems.

cast, the only aesthetic issue today perhaps being the creative decision to opt for the waxy-effect sprites used by SNES-era *Donkey Kong Country*, which have aged poorly in subsequent years.

The last game that Squaresoft and Nintendo would work on together following the former company's defection to Sony's hardware, *Super Mario RPG* acted as a bright sign-off on a creative era that had given rise to some of the greatest 2D RPGs yet made. Moreover, in the game's infusing of the JRPG with an altogether brighter, more joyous temperament, *Super Mario RPG* laid the foundations for Nintendo's subsequent diversions into the genre by way of the *Paper Mario* series and, more recently, the *Mario & Luigi* adventures, which owe the Super Famicom game their soul, if not their style.

Year: 1996
Developer: Squaresoft
Publisher: Nintendo
Original format: Super Famicom
Play today: Virtual Console (Wii)

"Mr Miyamoto wanted to do an RPG using Mario and Square had the programming ability. There was a chance for both companies to talk and it went well.**"**
Yoshio Hongo, staff member on *Super Mario RPG*

Below: Squaresoft's Keisuke Matsuhara was event planner on *Super Mario RPG*, a designer who worked in a similar role on many of the company's best-loved titles, from *Chrono Trigger* to *Final Fantasy VII*.

Year: **1996**
Developer: **id Software**
Publisher: **GT Interactive**
Original format: **PC**
Play today: **PC**

> **"As soon as I was given a chance to build levels I started absorbing books on architecture and design. Ancient Middle Eastern style buildings were of special interest to me and I'd apply their proportions to many of the levels I built."**
>
> American McGee, level designer on *Quake*

QUAKE

id Software's follow up to *Doom* may not have been the game John Romero wanted, but its role in popularizing online multiplayer was critical and enduring.

Wolfenstein 3D begat *Doom* begat *Quake*. The breeding is impeccable, even if its boisterous, metal-head designers were hardly the kind of boys that girls would take home for tea – although they do drive Ferraris. The industrial shooter lineage brought with it refinement with each new release and *Quake*'s level design was among id Software's most accomplished, the corridor environments revealing an eerie sense of otherworldly place, sticking in the memory like scenes from a recurring dream. Not only that but *Quake*'s multiplayer propelled competitive gaming from hobby to sport, where entire prize fortunes – not just names – could be won and lost in the heat of twitch battle.

The *Quake* project originated in 1991, when the team conceived the idea to create a top-down RPG using the 2D engine used in the company's *Commander Keen* game, which was dubbed *The Fight For Justice*. Preliminary work yielded poor results and the idea was shelved while the company worked on other

titles. But following the release of *Doom II*, id Software co-founder John Romero returned to the *Quake* concept and set about writing a design document for a first person exploration game in which combat would be viewed from a sideways-on perspective.

Meanwhile, Romero's business partner John Carmack was busy writing a new 3D engine for the project, one that would advance 3D gaming perhaps more than any other commercial game development in the mid-1990s. But Carmack's reticence to hire new staff meant that prototypes were slow coming, and after a year in development it became clear that it was going to take far longer to realize Romero's vision for the game than had been anticipated.

A meeting was held and the company decided to scrap the design document, and instead create a new first person shooter in the vein of *Doom*. Reluctantly, Romero wrote a new design, one that could be executed within seven short months, a creative U-turn that led to his immediate departure following *Quake*'s release.

Right: To embellish *Quake*'s nightmarish visions, id Software asked the industrial band *Nine Inch Nails* to create a rasping soundtrack for the game, which became as much a part of the game's texture as its brown corridors.

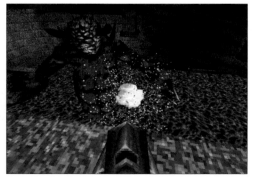

Left: The *Quake* game engine provided several major advances: polygonal models instead of pre-rendered sprites, full 3D level design, pre-rendered light-maps and the option for players to modify the game files themselves.

But the game's treasure lay in its multiplayer component, written by Romero himself, and playable over networked computers. In this area *Quake* is about split-second predictions. That's not unusual for a first person shooter – rounding any corner in an FPS and lumbering into the arms of a foe becomes a quick draw game to see who can squeeze the trigger first – but here, thanks to the speed at which characters move, the reactions required are more about anticipation than fight/flight reaction. It's a game about firing a rocket ten metres to the left of an opponent who is travelling at breakneck speed, in the hope that it will hit the target mid-sprint.

While *Modern Warfare* and *Battlefield* are about making opportunities and then taking shots, *Quake* is about the science

of expectation, a machine gun volley of estimation challenges designed to test your foresight. Here accuracy is only the second most important skill after twitch prophecy, and as a result, the thrills the game offers are of a different character to most modern-day first person shooters.

Following the game's release a lively community grew up around the game, both in terms of players looking to perfect their competitive tricks with descriptive names such as 'rocket-jumping' or 'bunny-hopping', to those looking to redesign its world through home-made modifications.

Quake's widespread popularity led to numerous sponsored tournaments across America, one of which saw John Carmack lose his Ferrari 308 in a wager to one Dennis Fong.

THE KNOWLEDGE
The first major fan-made *Quake* mod released to the public was *Team Fortress*, a sequel to which was released by *Half-Life* creator Valve in October 2007.

MUST PLAY:
Super Mario 64
The Legend of Zelda:
Ocarina of Time
Sin and Punishment
The Legend of Zelda:
Majora's Mask

Year: 1996
Manufacturer: Nintendo
Original Cost: ¥25,000 (£249.97)

JUNE 1996

[N64]

NINTENDO 64

125

NINTENDO 64

The N64's power and poise offered huge potential to developers – but Nintendo's unfavourable commercial deals meant few were willing to explore this.

For 13 years Nintendo consoles had dominated the video game landscape. The Famicom hoisted the industry from the pit into which it had been cast by Atari's calamitous business decisions in the early 1980s, while its successor had allowed developers around the world to make their fortunes – and swollen Nintendo's coffers through steep licensing cuts. In creative terms the company's internal teams, particularly Shigeru Miyamoto's EAD division, had helped perfect the art of 2D video game design, maturing those styles of play stumbled upon by the medium's American pioneers and embellishing them into ever more complex, expressive permutations.

But familiarity breeds contempt and Nintendo's ongoing market dominance meant that crucial mistakes were made in approaching its next generation of video game hardware. For one, a high-profile snub to Japanese electronics giant Sony in 1991, whom Nintendo was supposed to be partnering with in creating a CD-ROM drive for the Super Famicom, sowed a seed of revenge from which the PlayStation, the system that would eventually usurp Nintendo's position as market leader in the 1990s, would grow.

Moreover, Nintendo's confidence in its Super Famicom deadened any sense of urgency for a successor, which, combined with delays to launch title Super Mario 64, ensured the system's launch lagged behind that of its rivals. The decision to opt for cartridge-based games instead of CD-ROM-based media would prove costly, both in terms of manufacturing, and the way in which Sony was able to step in with its vastly cheaper disc-based games. Finally, Nintendo's high percentage cuts from other companies' games released for its systems had driven a slew of Japanese developers fed up with the Kyoto-based publisher's tall demands into Sony's arms – factors that combined to muffle the success of a console that was host to some of its era's strongest games. Development of the console began in 1993, when Nintendo partnered with Silicon Graphics, a California-based maker

of computer hardware and software whose workstations had been used to generate CGI animations in films such as *Terminator 2* and *Jurassic Park*. 'Project Reality', as it was then known, saw the two companies partner to create a low-cost real-time 3D graphics system, its name a statement of intent to create a console whose visuals were indistinguishable from reality.

Two years later at the Shoshinkai Software Exhibition in Japan, Nintendo unveiled the fruits of its partnership, a console now dubbed the Nintendo Ultra 64. Eleven games were shown; two were in playable form. The demos were enough to convince most attendees that the delays had been justified. In particular, the system's controller, designed by Genyo Takeda, appeared to represent a paradigm shift for the bridge between player action and on-screen reaction. The controller's primary novelty was in the introduction of an analogue stick positioned on its centre prong, an invention that would change the way in which console games were played in crucial ways.

In the next six months, the planned April 2006 release date was missed, reportedly so Shigeru Miyamoto could spend additional time perfecting launch title *Super Mario 64*, while pressure from game developer Konami saw the console's name changed to, simply, Nintendo 64. When the system finally launched in June, Sony's PlayStation had been on the market for 18 months. The launch line-up was eerily similar to that of its predecessor, with one Mario title, a Pilotwings title and a Shogi game, giving the launch a sense of familiarity that perhaps translated to consumer ennui. Until the US launch of the system, not a single other title was released for the Nintendo 64. For all *Super Mario 64*'s startling brilliance, one title cannot carry a system, and this paucity of releases would come to define the N64's life.

By the end of the system's life just 387 games had been released. Conversely, more than 1,000 games were available for Sony's PlayStation, revealing how Sony had convinced third-party developers to defect from Nintendo with its open-publishing model.

> **"If you rely too much on the hardware and not enough on ideas, you won't make games: you'll have demonstration software. New technology can make things more interesting, but if that's all we emphasize, the game will be boring."**
> Takashi Tezuka, assistant director of *Super Mario 64*

[068]

SUPER MARIO 64

Year: 1996
Developer: In-house (Nintendo EAD)
Publisher: Nintendo
Original format: Nintendo 64
Play today: Nintendo Wii (Virtual Console)

Above: One of the Lakitu Bros, who help Mario in the game. American Charles Martinet was the voice of Mario in *Super Mario 64*, and has been ever since.

"Mr. Tezuka's [SM64's assistant director] wife is very quiet normally, but one day she exploded, maddened by all the time he spent at work. In the game, there is now a character who shrinks when Mario looks at it, but when Mario turns away, grows large and menacing. This is the image Tezuka presented of his wife and we thought it would be great in the game."

Shigeru Miyamoto explains the inspiration behind the Boo enemies

SUPER MARIO 64

Mario's venture into 3D could easily have been timid and exploratory, but instead was fully formed and accomplished, defining the new system and the new era.

Video gaming's tentative steps into 3D saw the medium's most recognizable mascot arrive at a critical crossroads. Mario had, in no uncertain terms, established much of the vernacular of 2D gaming, arranging the nouns and verbs of video play to structure a language that almost all the world's designers would subsequently use to converse with players. But in gaming's embrace of the third dimension, it appeared that the diminutive plumber was set to be dragged into obsolescence by the side-scrolling world in which he had made his name and popularized his medium. The world was no longer flat.

After years of creating masterpiece after masterpiece, an unbroken hot-streak of excellence that had swollen Nintendo's fortunes and inspired at least two generations of game designers, Shigeru Miyamoto and his team at Nintendo EAD were presented with a blank sheet of paper.

Left and above: *Super Mario 64* was re-released in Japan on 18 July 1997 in a new version that supported the Rumble Pack, an add-on that introduced haptic (based on the sense of touch) feedback to the game.

Previous hard-earned lessons were of limited value: their flat worlds needed to be burst into 3D, ensuring Mario's continued relevance in this brave new reality. But even more than that, here was a team responsible for writing an entirely new language for their character and his players to speak, one that would dictate both the fortunes of Nintendo's new console, and articulate many of the early rules of 3D video games and interactivity. Get it wrong and few would continue to sing from Nintendo's hymn-sheet.

Nintendo EAD aim in this regard was simple: the pure act of controlling Mario must be nothing short of joyous. Before creating any of the world, its objectives or peril, Nintendo created a golden rabbit, named MIPS after the Silicon Graphic subsidiary. MIPS worked on the Nintendo 64's architecture and was dropped in a virtual field. In the subsequent tech demo, MIPS would run away from Mario, drawing the player after him.

Like the child of a primeval hunter play-chasing prey, the instinct to chase and copy the rabbit's bounding jumps acted as a means to teach the player how to reach into in this brave new multidirectional world. In this way, Miyamoto finalized his character's movement before any of the surrounding game was built, tweaking motion and momentum till the act of

running, springing over terrain, triple jumping on to a tree or into a moat and even throwing Mario into a pointless breakdance animation was playfully instinctive and smile-inducing; play for play's sake.

Next, the developer set about defining the structure into which Mario's latest adventure could slot. The travelogue quest, heading from West to East across sequential levels, was discarded, replaced instead by series of themed 360-degree worlds accessed via the central hub of Prince Peach's Disney-esque castle. New levels would become accessible one by one, allowing the player to literally dive through paintings on the castle's walls into new lands, in much the same way that players had been jumping through television screens into Mario's colourful dimensions for the previous decade. This structure would become the de facto standard for 3D platform games in subsequent years.

But the game's true abstract innovation was in the currency of progress. 120 stars regulate the speed of advancement through *Super Mario 64*, new paintings offering windows into themed stages unlocking at set thresholds through the experience. In this innovation the aims of play shifted: stars could be awarded for anything, allowing the designers to sprinkle micro and meta challenges throughout the world, which could be tackled by the player in any order, and whose completion all fed into

the same forward push towards the game's end. That conclusion, a face-off with arch-kidnapper Bowser, can be tackled when your collection of stars is just halfway complete, allowing players who simply want to tie up the story to feel just as satisfied as the completist, who cannot rest happy till they have wrung every star from every challenge on offer. The star system is now so commonplace in games that it's easy to forget quite how freeform and unexpected it was at the time. And yet, here was just one trailblazing feature of a game that did so much more than simply transport the 2D platform game into a new dimension – whether in its use of analogue control to push Mario from a saunter to a sprint, or in its dynamic camera system that appointed a full-time virtual cameraman to track your every input.

A game far more than its constituent parts, *Super Mario 64* offered a journey into the unknown that was wholly pioneered by its makers, then replicated by its players and finally copied by the game's legions of imitators. The world of video games had changed forever and *Super Mario 64* was the big bang that heralded this new dawn.

Above: A sequel titled *Super Mario 64 2* was planned for the Nintendo 64DD and, by 1999, was some way towards completion. But the commercial failure of the Disc Drive add-on saw the game sink without trace.

THE KNOWLEDGE
While working for the Nintendo *Power* magazine, editor Leslie Swan suggested to the development team that they hire a writer to work on the game's dialogue for the English version. 'Eventually one of the team heads asked if I would consider coming over and doing the job for them,' she says. 'While I was there they asked me if I would record the voice for Princess Peach.'

[069]

NIGHTS INTO DREAMS

Year: 1996
Developer: Sonic Team
Publisher: Sega
Original format: Sega Saturn
Play today: PlayStation2

"I remember crying when checking the in-game movies. I have developed many games, but this was the first and last time I was moved by my own game."

Yuji Naka, creator of
NiGHTS into Dreams

Right: Naka and his team researched the relationship between colours and meanings using different methods including dream diagnosis in order to align the game's theme and aesthetic.

NIGHTS INTO DREAMS

Sonic's distant cousin takes to the skies in an allegorical game about night terrors born of bullying, and finds a way straight to the joyful dreams of flying.

Released just 12 days after the Nintendo 64's radical new control pad debuted in Japan, Sega's first analogue controller could so easily have led the revolution had the schedules fallen differently. If *Super Mario 64* was designed to show off this new world of analogue control with gentle tilts of the stick to propel Mario into a run, Yuji Naka's *NiGHTS into Dreams* encouraged sweeping arcs to throw its airborne jester protagonist into dizzying loop-de-loops.

Not even Mario had replicated the freewheeling sensation of flight with the casual grace Sonic-creator Yuji Naka and his team achieved in *NiGHTS*. Here, traditional video game player checklists and objectives were pushed to the background, the focus being instead on the immediate, joyous thrill of flight, with a player's performance in each dream stage graded on style and speed as much as how many orbs one managed to collect. Challenge derived, not from progressing from stage to stage or defeating the game's ingenious bosses, but from attempting to achieve

A-rankings, a score attack emphasis usually absent from platform games. The sense of dream-like flight was compounded by the game's premise. Elliot and Claris are two teenagers who, having been bullied at school, drift into the troubled dreams in which the game takes place. Here they must overcome their fears and low self-esteem. After the somewhat heavy-handed set-up, Naka's aim was to speak to players without using words, instead using colour, music and animation. In this way *NiGHTS* remains an artistically affecting game.

Naka programmed the final game himself before stepping into producer roles. The designer famously created a free demo of the game that, thanks to the Saturn's internal clock, would theme its levels in tinsel and snow when played at Christmas. A piece of loving fan service (inspired by Naka stumbling across a Christmas-themed version of *Lemmings* when visiting the US) *Christmas NiGHTS* was perhaps the most creative and generous marketing tool yet seen in games.

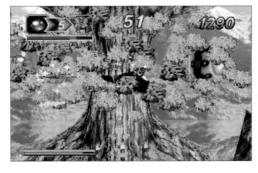

SEGA video game images - under licence by SEGA Corporation

MERIDIAN 59

The first 3D virtual online world, the game brought together players over the emerging internet, allowing players to live second lives on the other side of the screen.

Year: 1996
Developer: **Archetype Interactive**
Publisher: **The 3DO Company**
Original format: **PC**
Play today: **PC**

The online role-playing game predates the internet by some margin. The niche, text-only multi-user dungeons (MUDs) played on American university campuses in the late 1970s and early 1980s, first allowed multiple players to quest together. It was during these formative years that brothers Andrew and Chris Kirmse, computer science students at MIT and Virginia Tech respectively, spent countless hours playing one such game, *Scepter of Goth*, a multiplayer fantasy RPG that ran on an IBM PC XT powered by a bank of 16, 300-baud modems.

In the summer of 1993 both young men secured internships at Microsoft, where they were introduced to a pre-release copy of Windows 95, Microsoft's forthcoming operating system. It was here the pair saw the potential for a graphical version of *Scepter of Goth* that could theoretically allow players to quest together over the emerging World Wide Web.

They spent their life savings on two top-of-the-line computers – Pentium 66s with 16 megs of memory and 500 megabyte hard drives – and set them up in the windowless basement of their parents' house in Virginia. Here they began to construct *Meridian 59*, a virtual world that would go on to become the first commercial, 3D massively multiplayer online game. Originally planned as a 2D game, the brothers decided to write a 3D engine after reading a book that outlined the processes used in id Software's *Wolfenstein 3D*. Despite the primitive visuals of their first attempt, the thrill of walking up to another player in 3D was intoxicating, and both men knew that in this prototype the seeds of a revolution had been sown.

Following the brothers' graduation *Meridian 59* turned into a more serious commercial venture, the pair founding Archetype Interactive and hiring staff to aid creation of the game. A playable build was released at midnight on 15 December 1995. Kevin Hester, a programmer at 3DO played this early version of the game and brought it to the attention of his CEO, Trip Hawkins, who promptly agreed to acquire Archetype for $5 million in stock.

It was poor timing as 3DO's stock tumbled in value over the next few months, the company's financial difficulties damaging *Meridian 59*'s marketing ahead of the game's official launch in September 1996. Nevertheless, *Meridian 59* has proved the most enduring MMORPG for the 1990s, its servers still active today, and its design popularizing many of the traits seen in *World of Warcraft* and its ilk, from character gesturing to feature-enhancing patches and monthly subscriptions.

> **"We were proud of the fact that we were first, especially that such a small, young team had beat out the rest of the industry. It was a once-in-a-lifetime opportunity to take a new idea from concept all the way to a commercial product."**
>
> Andrew Kirmse, creator of *Meridian 59*

Shabado

Queen Venya'cyr damages you with her attack.

Left: More than 25,000 players joined *Meridian 59*'s public beta. The game's launch on 27 September 1996 predated its next major rival, *Ultima Online*, by a year.

Year: 1996
Developer: Core Design
Publisher: Eidos Interactive
Original format: Sega Saturn
Play today: PlayStation 3 (PSN)

> "There was resistance from marketing quarters saying that female characters never sold."

Toby Gard, creator of *Tomb Raider*

TOMB RAIDER

Lara Croft may not have been video gaming's first cultural icon, but she was the first to grace the covers of the style press, legitimizing the medium in the eyes of some.

Lara Croft, the 27-year-old archaeologist daughter of Lord and Lady Henshingly-Croft, was the character to step from the confines of a video game into the brittle arena of mainstream media. Mario and Sonic may have invaded the cultural landscape, but they did so as poster mascots for pre-teens. Croft, meanwhile, found herself on the cover of *Face* magazine, *Newsweek*, *Rolling Stone* and *Time*, her smooth polygonal face and fulsome bust doing more to move gaming from its position as nerdish niche to aspirational pastime than anything before.

Of course, sex can only go so far in selling creativity. The true secret of Croft's success lay not in her improbable physical proportions but in the poise and grace of the game she fronts. *Tomb Raider*, still one of the strongest entries to the series, was a puzzle platform game with a taut, imaginative sense of adventure. The game opens with a plane crash in the Himalayan mountains with Croft as the sole survivor of a twist of fate that would see her propelled from private school-educated aristocrat to Indiana Jones-esque explorer.

Toby Gard, a young designer in his early twenties working for British developer Core Design, originally conceived two characters for the game, one male and one female,

Above: Six different women have served as the official Lara Croft publicity model, including model Nell McAndrew, actress Rhona Mitra, and, most recently, gymnast Alison Carroll.

Left: American film star Angelina Jolie portrayed Lara Croft in two feature-length *Tomb Raider* films, which together grossed nearly US$500 million worldwide.

opting to drop the male protagonist when the team realized that fully implementing a story with two protagonists was too ambitious for the game. The backstory that Croft's writers invented was intricate, but it was the diversity in the game's locations, the ingenuity of its huge environmental puzzles and the assured, precise controls that secured her fame and the game's fortunes.

If *Wipeout* made gaming acceptable to a generation of clubbers, *Tomb Raider* made the medium respectable in both the eyes of the style press and middle England. What other game has had its heroine turned into a backing dancer for U2, and a model for the bastion of British propriety, Marks and Spencer? As a result, Lara Croft did just as much for her medium outside the confines of her game as she did inside it, an inexhaustible icon both in terms of her athleticism and marketing clout.

Left: A 2013 reboot of the series was also dubbed *Tomb Raider*, although this was set before the events of the first game in the series.

SEGA video game images - under licence by SEGA Corporation

DIABLO

By switching the ponderous turn-based dungeon exploration of *Rogue* to real time, *Diablo* turned the traditionally sedentary RPG into an all-action fantasy.

Year: 1996
Developer: Condor Games
Publisher: Blizzard Entertainment
Original format: Mac, PC
Play today: Mac, PC

By 1996, PC-based RPGs had become so bogged down in statistics and number crunching that the audience had shrunk to a fraction of the size it once enjoyed. Into this stagnant creative environment *Diablo* arrived, to slim down the bulk and complexity of computerized *Dungeons and Dragons*, and instead focus on the more immediate and primitive thrills of hitting monsters and hoovering up the resultant loot. While the experience that then occurs could ungenerously be described as somewhat brainless, the trek through its gloomy, procedurally generated isometric caverns remains obstinately captivating.

The game originated with programmer Dave Brevik, who had worked on a prototype of the idea while he was still at high school in 1985. When the team at Condor Games was asked to pitch a PC project to Blizzard Entertainment, Brevik's idea seemed a good match. The publisher agreed and the pair signed a contract. *Diablo* began life as a turn-based game, each monster taking a step after the player had inputted their move, as in *Rogue*. But Blizzard suggested the team

switch to real-time combat and, once the change was made, the modern action RPG was born.

Six months prior to the game shipping Condor Games ran into financial difficulties, and with low operating funds, Blizzard stepped in with an offer to buy the studio, turning it into Blizzard North in the process. Now, with considerably deeper pockets to draw from (while independent, the budget for *Diablo* had been a meagre $500,000) the team was able to add a multitude of features, principal among which was the incorporation of the newly finished Battle.net, an online service created by Blizzard South that allowed players to quest together over the internet. At the time, online PC gaming still required users to type in IP addresses manually to connect with other players, so the ease of Battle.net use was a boon to *Diablo*'s success. Soon over a million players were connecting online.

Many of the game's features were duly imitated, from the randomly generated dungeons to the exclamation marks over the heads of quest givers. Yet *Diablo*'s classes, characters and endless rewards have rarely been surpassed in the action RPG field.

> **"We wanted to create an RPG to reflect how we'd played *Dungeons and Dragons* as kids: hit monsters and gain loot. Our mission was to ensure the minimum amount of time between when you started the game up and when you were clubbing a skeleton."**
> Max Schaefer, co-founder of Condor Games

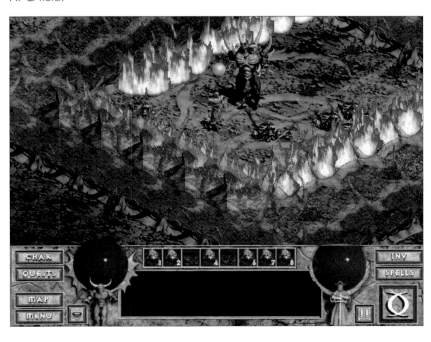

START MENU

THE HIP HOP HERO

©1997 Sony Computer Entertainment Inc. ©Rodney A. Greenblat / Interlink
Trademark of Sony Computer Entertainment America Inc.

Year: 1996
Developer: NanaOn-Sha
Publisher: Sony Computer
Entertainment
Original format: PlayStation
Play today: Sony PSP

PARAPPA THE RAPPER

The creative partnership between a New York artist and Tokyo musician transformed the role of music in games from soundtrack to become a core component of play.

The holder of numerous distinctions in gaming, *PaRappa the Rapper* is the first and only game to feature a rapping dog; the first and only game in which a chicken teaches you how to bake; and the first and only game to offer karate tips from a bipedal onion, who barks staccato commands: 'Kick! Punch! It's all in the mind'. But more than any of this, *PaRappa the Rapper* was the first determined effort to treat music not merely as an embellishment to the on-screen action, but as a fundamental component of the game. In its assured and timeless design, here was a game that laid the foundations upon which *Guitar Hero*, *Rock Band* and every other title that make up the rhythm-action landscape, would later build.

Combining the talent of Tokyo-based musician Masaya Matsuura with those of New York-based artist Rodney Greenblat, the game is a simple love story (albeit one focused on the blossoming relationship between a dog and a sunflower) that combines Sesame Street hip-hop with kindergarten absurdism. Its design and narrative are idiosyncratic, to the extent that *PaRappa the Rapper* has no imitators today, but in the *Pong*-like simplicity of its instructions – 'Tap buttons in time with the beat to make the dog rap' – a revolution was seeded.

As with every creative endeavour without a precedent, inspiration for *PaRappa the Rapper* lay outside its chosen medium. The Paul Hardcastle dance record '19', released in 1985, was recorded by mapping audio samples to keys on a keyboard so that, when one was pressed, a sample would play. Matsuura replicated the sampling technique in his own studio, triggering various

instrument samples before deciding that the human voice was by far the most fun to play with. It was an experiment that the musician would return to when thinking about how to create a video game that didn't merely feature music, but rather focused upon it.

PaRappa the Rapper was Matsuura's second interactive project, his first a simple piece of music sequencing software called 'Tunin' Glue' released for the Bandai Pippin, a Macintosh-based CD-ROM multimedia computer. 'Tunin' Glue' was released after the Pippin was discontinued, a disastrous development debut for NanaOn-Sha in scheduling terms, but a project which nevertheless taught Matsuura lessons that would prove invaluable in creating his next game. For Matsuura, the relationship between games and music appeared quite natural, both mediums sharing an essential

Above: *PaRappa the Rapper*'s story was written by Gabin Ito, who in addition to being a video game writer is also a well-known Japanese conceptual artist.

Below: Matsuura's influences were far and away from video games, instead looking to the tone of Western animations such as *The Snowman* and *Pingu* for inspiration.

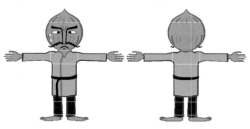

Left: The game's freestyle sections allow players to inject their own personality and performance into a song, a freedom few subsequent music games have successfully allowed their players.

verb in 'play', both dormant without the interaction of a 'player', but, as an outsider to the games industry, few appeared to share his vision.

Sony's entry to the video game industry brought with it a new perspective, not least because this was a company with far more trust and experience in the music industry than the games industry. Sony executives saw something in the kooky visionary Matsuura that was appealing – in many ways he was a more familiar sort of creative mind to the company than the game designers and interactive artists.

In early 1994 they put him in contact with a New York artist, Rodney Greenblat, who had been working for Sony Creative Products designing cartoon characters for lunch boxes, t-shirts, stationery and keychains, and asked the pair to work together on creating a story and characters for Matsuura's game idea. Greenblat faxed designs from New York to Tokyo, marking his favourites with a star. From the bright charm of *Sunny Funny* to the inimitable gait of *Chop Chop Onion Master*, Greenblat's bold, childlike designs came to define the game just as keenly as its like-styled soundtrack.

Matsuura developed the game with a small team of six artists, four programmers, a writer and biculturalist, whose role was, at the insistence of Sony, to make the game appeal

to a global audience. The team was crammed into a single apartment room where there was only one power source which was used to alternately power the air conditioning or supply the Silicon Graphics machine used for creating art. However, when the project slipped and the summer heat descended and the team was unable to simultaneously use the computer and the air conditioning, they resorted to working in their underwear. It was a never-say-die attitude that defined the project.

PaRappa the Rapper's debut in 1996 was inauspicious. Sony's initial shipment to retailers was only around 30,000 units, a relatively small number for a first-party published game at the time. But the game sold at a steady rate of around 20,000 copies a week till, one year in, it had broken a million sales. At a cost of around 80–90 million yen (around £550,000) to create, the game's success was unprecedented. Greenblat's designs propelled the game's characters to marketable stars, while its beat-matching mechanic introduced one of the most significant game design innovations of the decade, one that Matsuura and his team at NanaOn-Sha continued to explore and develop with games such as *UmJammer Lammy*, *Vibribbon*, *Musika* and *Major Minor's Majestic March*.

"I found that there were walls between the music and games industries that I constantly had to break through. I'm very grateful that the modern industry is much more welcoming to outsiders like me."
Masaya Matsuura, creator of *PaRappa the Rapper*

THE KNOWLEDGE
PaRappa the Rapper won the awards for Outstanding Achievement in Interactive Design and Outstanding Achievement in Sound and Music, and was nominated for Interactive Title of the Year at the 1998 Interactive Achievement Awards.

Year: 1997
Developer: In-house
Publisher: Squaresoft
Original format: PlayStation
Play today: PSN

"I was frustrated with the perennial dramatic cliché where the protagonist loves someone very much and so has to sacrifice himself and die in a dramatic fashion in order to express that love. I mean is it even right to set such an example to people?"

Yoshinori Kitase, director of *Final Fantasy VII*

FINAL FANTASY VII

The shift to disc-based media finally afforded the *Final Fantasy* team the room it required to allow its artistic ambition to match that of its storytelling ambition.

The camera is aimed upward, or inward, pressed against a sheet of blackness pitted with buckshot stars. It's the heralding of a big bang, a birth not only of a new virtual world but also of a new way of making and presenting video games.

From this vast expanse of space a jump cut to a wide-eyed girl, a flower seller clutching a bouquet. Our view pulls back to reveal her surroundings: a grimy steampunk city through which the camera reverses till it is high up above the smoking towers and crisscross scrawl of streets below. There's a trumpet fanfare and the game's logo, backed by a flaring comet of intent, stamps on to the screen – *Final Fantasy VII*. It holds position for a few seconds, before making way for the camera to, once again, lurch into motion, retracing its path downward towards a steam locomotive as it pulls into a station and the game's protagonist Cloud disembarks.

Final Fantasy VII's cinematic opening not only unveils the game's universe with mesmerizing efficiency, but in 1997 also acted as a trailer for a new brand of storytelling in video games, one closer to that of film than any seen before. Arresting in its level of technical accomplishment, the game caused yet another paradigm shift, as its player guides Cloud through an act of political terrorism before retreating to the city's slums, where he joins his co-conspirators in their squalid headquarters.

Below: The lyrics to *One-Winged Angel*, the song that plays during the game's final confrontation, are taken from *Carmina Burana*, a 1930s cantata written by Carl Orff.

Above: The game's antagonist Sephiroth Sephiroth wields the sword, Masamune. Named after a famous Japanese swordsmith, the Masamune has appeared in numerous Square games including *Chrono Trigger* and *Vagrant Story*.

The Japanese RPG had toyed with mature themes in the past, particularly in Square's own *Final Fantasy* series, but the shift to 3D, which swapped the squat, almost cute 2D characters of the series' past for humanoid models, running through exquisitely detailed backgrounds, lent the drama a keener edge. Today its characters are strange balloon animals, all bulges and weird protractions, but at the time they were the most expressive actors ever pushed on to a video game stage.

Reaching this point was an epic journey of its own. Until *Final Fantasy VII*, Square had enjoyed a monogamous relationship with Nintendo, every one of its games following the first *Final Fantasy* appearing on the Japanese giant's hardware. And the original plan was for the seventh entry to the series to follow suit, the developer even releasing some early 3D character shots supposedly running on Nintendo's next generation of hardware. But Square's Hironobu Sakaguchi reneged on the deal, causing a falling out with Nintendo president Hiroshi Yamauchi that wouldn't be reconciled till both men left their respective companies years later.

Although the combination of animated cutscenes, random battles and a traditional JRPG battle system alienated some players – anecdotally, *Final Fantasy VII* is the most returned game of all time in the West – for

Above: Series creator Hironobu Sakaguchi originally planned for the story to take place in New York in the year 1999. Elements of the original script were later used in *Parasite Eve* and *Final Fantasy VIII*.

many more, the concoction proved irresistible, and almost overnight the Japanese RPG was propelled from a niche import to one of the most popular styles of games on the PlayStation.

As the gaming world marvelled at a new 3D dawn, *Final Fantasy VII*'s stentorian soundtrack, expressive spells and soaring storyline seemed to draw itself up to the huge potential of disc-based games and 3D worlds. The geography of the place, from the undulating peaks that can be circumvented in an airship to underwater caverns, explorable only via submarine, *Final Fantasy VII*'s universe is as deep as it is broad.

It was also the game to launch the career of artist Tetsuya Nomura, whose designs remain iconic today. Amnesiac protagonist Cloud, with his large sword and nuclear-grade hair gel, brought the anime Japanese hero to the mainstream. Love interest Aerith, in her rose dress, plaited hair, and 'sudden death' made perhaps more of an impact on the world of games than any other female character to grace a game for less than a third of its length. Developed at a huge cost of $45 million, *Final*

Above: The team consisted of 120 artists and programmers, using PowerAnimator and Softimage 3D software. It was the most expensive video game of its time, with a budget of around $45 million.

Fantasy VII is comprised of 330 CG maps and an unprecedented for the time 40 minutes of full motion video, the creation of which used the talent of more than 100 team members. While today the game looks dated, at the time this was game development on a Hollywood scale. But while *Final Fantasy VII* speaks in the language of its genre's tropes, it does so in an inimitable, affecting manner, with a cast of memorable characters that have outlasted many of those from its successors. *Final Fantasy VII* tempered its tragedy with comedy, scenes in which the player must cross-dress as a desirable woman and gain entry into a salubrious establishment, or engage in dinner dates with other characters that go woefully wrong. Irreverence underpins the game like a sub-bass note, a key component in its success and lasting appeal. Not only did the game sell the Japanese RPG to the West, it also legitimized Sony's PlayStation in Japan to those who doubted it could be any more than a platform for small scale curios casting an emotional spell over its players that is still yet to fully wear off.

"We felt a wind of change inside the company during the development process. There was this incredible feeling I'll never forget: we were making a new thing… making history. Imagine."
Yoshinori Kitase, director of *Final Fantasy VII*

Below: In 2005 Square Enix released a full-length CG animated feature film called *Final Fantasy VII: Advent Children* (2005) set several years after the events of the game.

Year: 1997
Developer: LightWeight
Publisher: Squaresoft
Original format: PlayStation
Play today: PlayStation 3 (PSN)

BUSHIDO BLADE

This realistic sword fighting game in which every attack can finish an opponent raised the tension even as it lowered the rate of on-screen action.

With the advent of 3D, video games had headed down an artistic path away from the stylized, cartoon visuals of their adolescence towards a kind of uneasy realism. The graphical journey mirrored one that was happening beneath the surface of games too, as the exaggerated physics of *Super Mario* and *Sonic* made way for a more sombre approach to gravity and biology, and games began to attempt to replicate real-world activities with some measure of accuracy.

Bushido Blade took the hyperactive feudal Japan fighting of SNK's *Samurai Shodown* series and slowed it to the tempo of reality. Its grand innovation was to make fighting more like fighting – its violence unlike Hollywood's screen violence, being less dramatic, less graceful and quicker in character. The game dispensed with the health bars that had long been a visual shorthand in games to indicate a fighter's well-being or closeness to defeat and instead rendered damage as a drooping, broken arm or limp, useless leg. The game faced up to the truth that, in a sword fight, few walk away from a piercing lunge to the torso and, as such, it's a game that can be lost with a well-timed Katana strike to the stomach.

What was interesting in play was that the increased stakes forced players to read their opponent, blocking by default and only venturing an attack at the most opportune moment. When a battle can be lost in the blur of a split-second thrust, there's an in-built disincentive away from recklessness or thoughtless 'button mashing', and *Bushido Blade*'s enduring triumph was in creating a fighting game in which trepidation trumps showboating.

The first game from Lightweight, a developer part-owned by RPG creator Squaresoft, *Bushido Blade* fathered a curious offshoot of feudal-era Japanese fighting games, from its somewhat lacklustre sequel to the *Kengo* series of fighters. However, none of Lightweight's subsequent games managed to capture the taut atmosphere of this first game, where the lazy chirrup of crickets is only occasionally interrupted by the twang of a shamisen and the hissing whisper of lifeblood spraying in a tubular spout from a mortally wounded samurai.

Below: *Bushido Blade*'s score was created by Namco and Arika composer Shinji Hosoe with additional contributions by Ayako Saso and Takayuki Aihara.

Below: *Bushido Blade* was the 25th best selling game of 1997 in Japan, shifting just shy of 388,000 copies in the country.

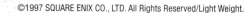

CASTLEVANIA: SYMPHONY OF THE NIGHT

Drawing upon *Super Metroid*'s tremendous example, Konami's 2D reinvention of its vampire series is filled with secrets, and saves its greatest trick till last.

Year: 1997
Developer: KCET
Publisher: Konami
Original format: PlayStation
Play today: Xbox 360 (XBLA)

Despite the intricate detail and exquisite animation, *Castlevania: Symphony of the Night* was a visual anachronism even in 1997. Game magazines in the West dismissed it as a relic from a bygone time, and shopkeepers were obliged to discount many of the 15,000 copies reportedly manufactured for the UK before the run sold out. There appeared to be no place in the bright new polygonal world of PlayStation for Konami's muted sprites, the game viewed as an archaic curio released five years too late.

But beneath the visuals one of the greatest 2D action-adventure games stands as tall and resolute in the face of the winds of fashion as the gothic castle in which it takes place. Director Toru Hagihara and his team may not have broken new ground with its mechanics, instead borrowing heavily from *Super Metroid* in constructing a castle that opens up with the acquisition of new abilities, but from the watery cellars in the castle's belly to its moonlit ramparts, they perfected them.

Playing as Alucard, the conflicted son of Dracula, you are charged with uncovering the castle's chambers and secrets in search of the arch vampire. As you collect new abilities, so your reach into the castle extends, providing a breadcrumb trail to follow backward and forward through its themed corridors and wings.

Two notable female creatives left their imprint on this world: Ayami Kojima, whose architectural and sprite designs are in equal parts beautiful and monstrous, and Michiru Yamane whose orchestral soundtrack is routinely held up as one of the medium's strongest. Likewise, the game's final twist reward, unlocked after what is presented as the final

boss, turning the entire castle on its head so every floor becomes a ceiling and doorway becomes a ledge, has never been more generously bettered.

Koji 'IGA' Igarashi, who acted as both scenario writer and programmer on the game, always saw it as an offshoot to the main series, using the 'X' in its Japanese title, *Akumajo Dracula X*, to denote the fact. But it's testament to the strength of the design that *Symphony of the Night*'s template has been adopted by the mainline series, and that this game more than any has come to define gaming's leading vampire fiction.

Below: The decision to create a longer, deeper game was inspired when Igarashi saw dozens of *Castlevania* games in the used bargain bin in Japanese stores shortly after release.

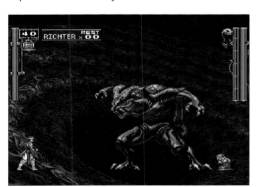

"Action games could be cleared in a short time, but I wanted to create a game that could be enjoyed for a much longer period."
Koji 'IGA' Igarashi, assistant director of *Castlevania: Symphony of the Night*

INTERNATIONAL SUPERSTAR SOCCER PRO

Konami's breezy, deft attempt to create a soccer series to rival EA's *FIFA* series found its target at the first strike, even if it's struggled to maintain a lead.

Year: 1997
Developer: In-house
Publisher: Konami
Original format: PlayStation
Play today: n/a

Below: The Japanese release featured narration by Jon Kabira and commentary by Yasutaro Matsuki, a former international football player and manager.

"When I first started working on *Winning Eleven* I just thought I was creating a game – I never really compared it with real football. But these days it's not rival football games with which we compete so much as the real game itself."

Shingo 'Seabass' Takatsuka, producer of the *Winning Eleven* series

Plotting the history of video gaming's other great soccer franchise is no simple task. Japan's premier league football game debuted in 1994 on the Super Famicom with *International Superstar Soccer*, a game developed by Konami's Osaka studio, KCEO, as a direct rival to *FIFA Football*. As with EA's game, *ISS*, as it was to become affectionately known, leaned towards arcade thrills and immediate accessibility rather than attempting to recreate a realistic simulation of the beautiful game in pixels.

A year later, however, Konami decided to create a second football series, known in Japan as *Winning Eleven*, to run alongside *ISS*, but which attempted a truer-to-life approximation of the sport. Developed by Konami's Tokyo studio, KCET, *Winning Eleven* emphasized tactical passing play over spectacle and improbably high score-lines. For Westerners, however it was hard to distinguish between the two series as they were marketed as cross-breeds sharing the same brand name.

International Superstar Soccer Pro, (known in Japan as *Winning Eleven '97*), was the first game in the ISS Pro series to be released in the West for the PlayStation, and its arrival shook the world of football video games. Presenting a more measured, challenging recreation of football, it outstripped EA's *FIFA* series on almost every count bar marketing budget and Konami's underdog fast became the

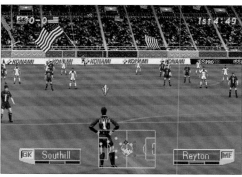

Above: Despite coming a distant second to EA's *FIFA* series in terms of sales, most football and game aficionados considered Konami's to be the superior game.

discerning football fan's choice. What the game lacked in licensed real-life player names (famous players were renamed with comical puns, David Beckham, for example, becoming 'Duckham') it made up for with its distinguished pacing, realistic ball physics and outstanding multiplayer.

ISS Pro kicked off a development war between Konami and EA, whose competitive annual updates to their respective soccer series continue today in the lead-up to Christmas each year. Today, EA's concerted investment in its *FIFA* series has closed the gap in quality between the two series, with each yearly release finding its own defenders and detractors. But throughout the late 1990s, Konami's *ISS Pro* games remained untouchable.

FINAL FANTASY TACTICS

Yasumi Matsuno turned to European dark fantasy for his chess-like masterpiece, a tale of knights and political intrigue quite unlike the series with which it shares a name.

Year: June 1997
Developer: In-house
Publisher: Squaresoft
Original format: PlayStation
Play today: Sony PSP, iOS

The series *Final Fantasy* has always been built from reinvention. The fundamental building blocks may remain constant, but by arranging them differently from game to game, developer Squaresoft has kept the series perennially fresh, while still managing to retain threads of identity and personality that tether each title to its branding. But *Final Fantasy Tactics* represented the first radical departure, both from the hero-sent-to-save-the-world narrative, and the familiar rhythms of exploration and battle.

Instead, this, the first *Final Fantasy* spin-off game, is a chess-like tactical RPG. There is no traditional exploration to be done in the world of Ivalice, as you instead move from point to point on a map, recruiting teammates and, through turn-based battles, developing a squad to reflect your strategic predilections. The story focuses on the upper echelons of royalty and government, as you expose an evil that runs to the heart of both church and state, themes far more mature and controversial than those normally found in Squaresoft's flagship fairy-tale series.

The first game to be designed and directed by Yasumi Matsuno, who would go on to produce other challenging classics such as *Vagrant Story* and *Final Fantasy XII*,

Below: One of gaming's most interesting fantasy stories was somewhat lost in translation in the original American release of the game. This was entirely reworked for the 2007 Sony PSP re-release.

the medieval tone and aesthetic followed that of the young designer's previous games. Prior to working on *Final Fantasy Tactics*, Matsuno worked at Quest, a small developer specializing in feudal tactical RPGs. Hirónobu Sakaguchi, creator of *Final Fantasy*, was so impressed by Matsuno's work that he offered the designer and Hiroshi Minagawa, and Akihiko Yoshida, jobs with his company, specifically to develop a *Final Fantasy*-themed tactical RPG.

The result is one of the most thoughtful and challenging experiences of the 32-bit era, a game that challenges its player with not merely with completing the game, but doing so with style and pizzazz. The depth of the battle and team management system dizzies the mind, and with the strategy couched in such an unusual and affecting story, you come to view each unit as far more than a pawn, a relationship between player and avatar rarely matched by the mainline series from which *Final Fantasy Tactics* sprouts.

"It's incredible how well the game stacks up after all these years – it really is a masterpiece of game design."

Shingo Kosuge, co-producer of the 2007 *Final Fantasy Tactics* re-release

Below: Some of the characters designed by Yasumi Matsuno, whose creations battle in a medieval kingdom.

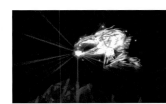

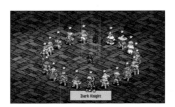

[079]

GOLDENEYE 007

Year: 1997
Developer: **Rare**
Publisher: **Nintendo**
Original format: **Nintendo 64**
Play today: **n/a**

"I heard a rumour that a couple of the guys from the *Donkey Kong* team had gone to a party for the new Bond film and had been offered a game. Tim Stamper wasn't too interested, I surmised, so I said: 'I'd like to make this. I'm a Bond fan.' And he said: 'Yeah, okay. Write a document and I'll take a look.'"

Martin Hollis, creator of *GoldenEye 007*.

GOLDENEYE 007

Proving that the first person shooter wasn't the sole preserve of the PC, with its keyboard and mouse control, the first console shooter came with a licence to kill for.

The first line on the first page of *GoldenEye*'s original 7-page design document is surprising: 'The game will be similar to *Virtua Cop* in terms of gameplay.' After all, this was the game that would trigger a paradigm shift in how console-based First Person Shooters were viewed, a genre previously considered incompatible with anything but PC hardware. With hindsight it seems impossible that a game whose shadow looms so persistently over the console FPS landscape could be inspired by a simple on-rails light-gun game. But for all its genre-defining success, *GoldenEye 007*, like the films from which it owes its world, is built from simple blocks. It just so happened that, in the shadow of their arrangement, history changed.

The game's core design owed a great deal to its Hollywood licence. The cyclical Bond narrative of the films has a game-like quality, all death-defying escapes, thrilling gadgetry and high-speed explosions, while the canvas of author Ian Fleming's universe is broad and diverse enough to fill a hundred games. Likewise, Bond himself, while a simple, stereotypical cipher, is so well-defined in the cultural consciousness

Below: Most of the guns in the game were modelled on real weapons, the Walther PPK, Kalashnikov AK-47 and FN P90, but had their names changed since Nintendo did not want to license from arms manufacturers.

Above: The videotape that the player must steal from the Severnaya bunker during Bond's escape with Natalya is a copy of the movie *GoldenEye*.

that Rare felt it didn't even need to display the character on screen. For the game's designer, Martin Hollis, these world-building and world-characterizing factors, all delivered without effort via the licence, proved invaluable. But they are also factors shared by all Bond games, and yet this is the only one that really matters. The world, it turns out, is not enough.

In truth *GoldenEye 007*'s keen brilliance rests beneath the theme and setting – it is a game built on classic and timeless principles. *Super Mario World* inspired the mission structure, in which each level had multiple objectives, scaling in complexity as the difficulty setting is notched up. In aping *Doom*'s control scheme Hollis found the requisite accessibility he wanted for his game, while the position-dependent hit animations (enemies recoiling from a shot

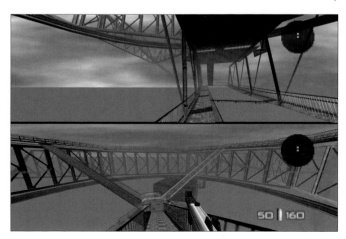

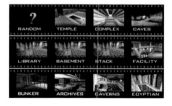

to the shoulder, or doubling over from a blast to the groin), the introduction of innocents you shouldn't kill, and the aiming mode, were all pulled from that first unlikely point of reference: *Virtua Cop*.

GoldenEye 007's brilliance is, in part, dependent on context. Hollis and his team skilfully turned technological limitation into strengths. The slow pace of early 3D and the challenging design of the Nintendo 64's controller became assets in Rare's hands, while the convenience offered by the game's easily navigated, exceptional split-screen multiplayer modes raised the FPS bar higher than even the strongest PC titles had yet managed. But the game's core and enduring brilliance is in the moment-to-moment combat, a repetitious reward found in the flailing of every Soviet soldier that's taken a bullet. Beyond that, it's the details

that delight: the powerful recoil of the sniper rifle, the thwup satisfaction of a silenced PP7, the roaring ineptitude of two dual-wielded Klobbs, the joy of a takedown from a concealed proximity mine, the riotous cast of playable villains, the unapologetic straying from the film's structure in order to facilitate a stronger game and the perfectly pitched rise in complexity and challenge with each higher level of difficulty.

Yet these were all assets that revealed their worth to a gamer slowly. As with many of Nintendo's biggest triumphs, *GoldenEye 007* sold at a slow but steady rate. Released two years after the film with which it shares a name debuted, many saw it as an out-of-date proposition at launch, while the reputation of games licensed from films still hadn't repaired since Atari's industry-crippling *E.T. The Extra-Terrestrial*. But word of mouth prevailed and the game continued selling at a steady rate throughout the late nineties and into the next century, outperforming its spiritual sequel *Perfect Dark* to become the best-selling Nintendo 64 game in the US, ahead of first-party classics *Super Mario World* and *Zelda: Ocarina of Time*. And beyond the confines of its system's history, here was a game that legitimized first person shooting on console systems, breaking new ground from which *Halo* and *Call of Duty* would later grow. And as for Bond games since? Nobody's done it better.

Above: The face of Bond in the game is that of the actor Pierce Brosnan; he made his Bond debut in the film *GoldenEye*, 1995. The textures used on the faces of standard enemies in the game were all created from photographs of Rare staff.

Below: Every character in *GoldenEye 007* was motion-captured, with around 200 different enemy actions that could be spliced into one another.

THE KNOWLEDGE
The eight single-controller and double-controller button schemes offered in the game's options are named after various Bond girls in the 007 movie series: Honey, Solitaire, Kissy, Goodnight, Plenty, Galore, Domino and Goodhead.

[080]

ULTIMA ONLINE

Bridging *Meridian 59*'s quiet invention and the success of *World of Warcraft*'s later popularity, *Ultima Online* popularized the internet-based role-playing game.

Year: 1997
Developer: Origin Systems
Publisher: Electronic Arts
Original format: PC
Play today: PC

"It took us years to convince anyone to let us do *Ultima Online*... for the last 10 years, non-online gaming has been financially insignificant compared to online gaming."

Richard Garriot,
creator of *Ultima Online*

Below: With few earlier online world examples to learn from, *Ultima Online*'s developers faced novel issues requiring an understanding of psychology, social interaction, economy, and other concerns unique to virtual worlds.

It was a long and winding seven years following the release of *Ultima Online* before the Massively Multiplayer Online RPG – an awkward mouthful of a genre classification originated by the game's creator, Richard Garriot – found mainstream global appeal in Blizzard's *World of Warcraft*. But during this time *Ultima Online* busied itself with establishing and refining the rules of the online RPG, laying the foundations of persistent online worlds that allowed players to quest with – and compete against – one another that would be both copied and built upon in years to come. For many, it's a world yet to be superseded. *Ultima Online*'s population remains large and committed enough that publisher EA still maintains the game's servers, continuing to update the game's faithful clients long after other virtual worlds have vanished into the virtual ether.

Ultima Online was not the first persistent 3D online RPG, that distinction belonging to Archetype Interactive's *Meridian 59*. But it was the first such world to find success in the early days of the internet, benefiting from a dedicated following from the offline *Ultima* PC games to attract a far greater number of world immigrants than its immediate competitors. It was this competition that hurried the world's creation. Following the appearance of *Meridian 59*'s Alpha test in late 1995, Origin Systems allocated resources away from *Ultima IX* to speed up completion of *Ultima Online*, inviting thousands of players to participate in its own test of the game in 1996 in what was the largest internet gaming environment to date.

Word of the game's existence spread quickly, with more than 50,000 players paying the $2 entry fee to join the game's beta-testing phase in summer 1997. Three months later, the full game went live, its various technical bugs and issues inspiring impassioned debate on the game's forums as to whether it was in fact ready for release. Nevertheless, *Ultima Online*'s core innovations, such as in-game events that affected the entire lore of the world, and progressive features such as item crafting and persistent player housing, established mechanics used in almost all MMOs that followed.

While the game has a lingering contingent of players who continue to log on each day, it's now one of the least accessible MMOs on the market. But for those who can ingratiate themselves to the existing community, and work around the arcane interface, here is an online world that's both historically significant and curiously enduring in relevance.

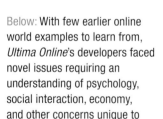

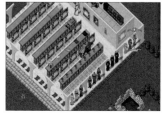

FALLOUT

The ruined city, scarred by nuclear holocaust, offers a clutch of fascinating adventures and meaningful choices for those brave enough to exit the vault.

Video games allow us to act as tourists to destinations that few people would choose to visit from outside a virtual dimension. In Black Isle Studios' post-apocalyptic RPG *Fallout*, we're invited to tour the ruins of southern California, a city buffeted by a mineral wind and stinging sleet, laid low by a devastating nuclear attack. From the moment you exit the relative safety of your character's home, Vault 13 – an eviction forced upon the player character as the safe house has lost its 'GECK', a chip that makes water drinkable and life sustainable in the wasteland – and take your first lungful of radioactive breeze, it's clear this is a wasteland of grim authenticity. If any player harbours any sort of attraction to the idea of settling into an anarchic, rubble-strewn, radiation-soaked America, *Fallout* soon smothers the allure.

Below: 'I Don't Want to Set the World on Fire' by the Ink Spots was planned as *Fallout*'s theme tune but Black Isle couldn't obtain the rights. 11 years 'later the song was used in *Fallout 3*.

Above: *Fallout* drew upon the branding and imagery featured in 1950s pulp magazines, science fiction and superhero comic books.

And yet, in these ruins, video games found one of their most nonsensically captivating locales. With anarchy there comes a giddy, perilous sort of liberty and despite the enmity of *Fallout*'s geography and inhabitants, and the barrenness of its land, its world is rich with opportunity. The pseudo-sequel to the 1988 post-apocalyptic RPG *Wasteland*, designer and producer Tim Cain and his team sought to increase the player's agency in an RPG world by offering multiple ways to complete the objectives uncovered in the barren landscape. Likewise, character development is a game of problematic trade-offs. Invest your skill points into science and diplomacy and the game you subsequently play will have a very different timbre to the one you experience if you simply master ballistics. This lends each choice a weight and importance, one that many modern games seek to replicate in their similar systems.

The game's unique ambience and style proves as memorable as the role-playing, drawing upon the iconography and sounds of 1950s America, lending the experience a warped nostalgic feel despite the fact the story is set in 2161. With outstanding voice acting, including narration from Ron Perlman, *Fallout* set new standards in game development. 'War. War never changes', claims the game's catchphrase adage. True, perhaps, but rarely has its ruined aftermath been such an intriguing place to visit.

Year: 1997
Developer: Black Isle Studios
Publisher: Interplay Entertainment
Original format: PC
Play today: PC

"How you behave in the game really matters. Be a jerk, and people won't barter with you. Save a town and become a hero in their eyes. This is a true role-playing game: you are responsible for your own actions."

Tim Cain, designer of *Fallout*

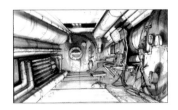

GRAN TURISMO

Choosing realism over exaggeration, *Gran Turismo* replicates the look and feel of cars of all styles and prices in an experience that's as much encyclopedic as ludic.

Year: 1997
Developer: Polyphony Digital
Publisher: Sony
Original format: PlayStation
Play today: Sony PSP

"I've always liked racing games. When I was around 15 years old it just came to me as an idea of a race game I wanted to play. A game in which there would be an accurate physics simulation and, of course, real-world cars."

Kazunori Yamauchi, creator of *Gran Turismo*

Below: The opening song used for the North American and European versions of the game is a Chemical Brothers remix of the *Manic Street Preachers* song 'Everything Must Go'.

Not only a video game, *Gran Turismo* is also a grand and exhaustive resource. Its creator, professional racing driver and CEO of developer Polyphony Digital, Kazunori Yamauchi's self-professed mandate to create a complete digital document on the modern motorcar is unflinching and inexorable, each new release in the series adding further breadth and detail to the vehicles it presents. By placing family saloons and curvy hatchbacks next to the planet's most fearsome speed kings, the game presents a more rounded picture of its chosen theme, one not seen in the medium before its debut release in 1997. If it's possible for a video game to also act as an encyclopedic document, *Gran Turismo* offers not only a replication of the world's cars through the ages, but also presents us with the opportunity to virtually drive them, experiencing their various thrills and idiosyncrasies at first hand.

Prior to *Gran Turismo*, all racing games were fundamentally aspirational, giving players a chance to live out childhood fantasies of driving gleaming Ferraris and F1 torpedoes. Those delights are present in Polyphony's game, but there's also the chance to seek out that 1988 Volvo estate your family used to drive; to celebrate the mundane in motorsport, as well as the marvellous. Indeed, in a hundred years time, when many of the production cars we drive today are artefacts from the past, *Gran Turismo* will act as an interactive historical piece, a vertical slice of motorcar racing from the turn of the 20th century that gives future generations a chance to play with outdated technology with immediacy and realism.

Gran Turismo's development began in 1992, prior to the release of its host platform, Sony's PlayStation. But the idea was much older. In 1982, a 15-year-old Yamauchi, enamoured with the simplistic racing games to be found in the arcades near his home, conceived of a car-based video game that, rather than accentuating

the laws of gravity and physics for on-screen thrills, instead sought to replicate them. Instead of inventing new car designs for games, the teenage Yamauchi decided that, should he ever have the chance to design a racing video game, he would use production cars. While he didn't have a word to describe his idea, in this moment Yamauchi conceived the 'simulation racing game', a concept that would be tentatively explored in Atari's *Hard Drivin'* (page 67), but that wouldn't come close to resembling this original vision until he was given the chance to create his own driving simulator.

However, *Gran Turismo* wasn't Yamauchi's first driving game. *Motor Toon Grand Prix*, a cartoon racing game in the tradition of *Super Mario Kart* was where the designer earned his virtual licence. Its bubbly vehicles, with headlamps for eyes and grills for teeth perhaps offered an outlet to expunge the designer's more playful design sensibilities. Three years later, when *Gran Turismo* debuted after half a decade in development time (employing the talents of a core team of seven designers, developers and artists), there was no trace of comedy or lighthearted mischievousness on its virtual tarmac. Instead, here was a purist's celebration of realism. This game may be an exuberant love letter to motorsport, but it's one penned in the tone and language of a scientist or engineer.

Below: Creator Kazunori Yamauchi estimated that *Gran Turismo* utilized around 75 per cent of the PlayStation's maximum performance.

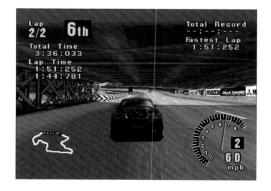

Above: The *Gran Turismo* series is the best-selling Sony PlayStation-exclusive franchise yet, with over 56 million units sold.

Above: *Gran Turismo* features 140 cars and 11 tracks. Two 1995 Honda del Sol were included in the Japanese version, but were removed from the North American and European versions.

The most immediate impact the game made was in its visuals, which appeared to utilize the PlayStation hardware more effectively than any other game on the market. While the game may lack the boisterous exuberance of Ridge Racer, *Gran Turismo*'s minutely detailed game world has been designed to communicate the forces and frictions of racing cars, offering a barrage of feedback, visually, aurally and haptically – through the introduction of the Dual Shock rumble controller, released at the same time as the game. In particular, *Gran Turismo*'s replays, which artfully approximate the camera pans and zooms of motorsport television, wowed onlookers with their reflective detail. The only weakness in the creation – and it's one that persists today – was that the obsessive attention to detail and slavishness to realism crumbles in the force of an impact. Sony was unable to convince the car manufacturers from whom the company licensed the vehicle's likenesses to allow them to crumple bumpers or bodywork in a crash. That two cars can tear away unscathed or blemished from a head-on collision breaks the illusion of reality that's so carefully built and maintained elsewhere, and moves the game an inch closer to an advertising brochure than it perhaps should.

On release, Yamauchi's expectations were modest. But what he supposed would turn out to be little more than a niche title for petrol-heads came to define a new style

of console-based video games, one that prized obsessive attention to detail and showed how other industries could work with video game developers to promote their products – not through mere placement, but through true collaboration and engagement.

In subsequent years the *Gran Turismo* series has continued to gather and grow, and 2013's *Gran Turismo 6* features 1,200 cars with 33 tracks. The game's effect extends beyond the small screen. The Nissan-sponsored GT Academy uses the game to discover the next generation of driver talent, winning a place on Nissan's real life racing team. Many of the GT Academy's graduates have gone on to glittering careers in professional racing, one of the few examples where a talent honed in a video game has proved valuable in a real world setting.

Today, the series has sold in excess of 60 million copies, but it was in this debut that the face of racing video games was forever altered.

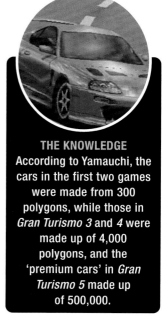

THE KNOWLEDGE
According to Yamauchi, the cars in the first two games were made from 300 polygons, while those in *Gran Turismo 3* and *4* were made up of 4,000 polygons, and the 'premium cars' in *Gran Turismo 5* made up of 500,000.

[083]

Year: 1998
Developer: Entertainment Japan
Publisher: Konami
Original format: PlayStation
Play today: PSN

"I think the first time the game's success struck me was when I came to London in 1999 to promote the game. I walked into a shop and the staff knew about me. I couldn't believe it. It was the most surprising moment in my life."

Hideo Kojima, creator of *Metal Gear Solid*

METAL GEAR SOLID

The first 3D title in Hideo Kojima's stealth series allowed the aspiring film director to ape cinematic technique – but without diminishing the game's interactive appeal.

We call them stealth games, the creeping and khaki, silencers and sneaking building the illusion of military gravitas and martial solemnity. But at its heart, *Metal Gear Solid* and its imitators are lavishly dressed children's games of hide-and-seek. There's no shame in that. The thrill of holding your breath while hiding in a locker, or tensing your muscles while crouched beneath a roomy cardboard box in a bid to avoid detection is a surefire way for any living creature to mainline fight-or-flight adrenaline. Game designers are in the business of eliciting real-life thrills through systems, so the idea that hide-and-seek, a game perpetually played in playgrounds across the globe, should make for a powerful experience is logical.

Creator Hideo Kojima's brilliance, however, lies in the packaging of the idea, couching the act of creeping through the shadows in a carefully orchestrated Bond-esque scenario in which one man must infiltrate a radioactive waste facility armed with little more than a radio, a bandana and a packet of cigarettes. Despite the one-man army set-up, *Metal Gear Solid*'s narrative offers more layers of complexity than Ian Fleming's novels, and Kojima rarely shies away for a chance to allow a character to soliloquize on the nature of warfare, or the role of solider pawn – those very same figures controlled by the player – on the battlefield. It's a game about 20th-century dread: the fear of

Above: Hideo Kojima hired *Metal Gear Solid*'s concept artist Yoji Shinkawa straight out of college in 1994. 'Shinkawa was born to be a video game artist,' he later said.

annihilation in the white-out of an apocalyptic blast and the night terror notions of your enemies lying hidden under your beds.

But *Metal Gear Solid*'s era-defining brilliance was in the verisimilitude of the world and the sheer range of interactive possibilities it offered its player. Often the goal is little more than 'get from A to B without being detected' but the way in which you move, picking routes through the snow blanket that covers the game's memorable location, Shadow Moses island (a part of Alaska's Fox Archipelago), choking out guards or distracting them with thrown cigarettes, makes the adventure feel peculiarly personal. It's a heady achievement for a game that wears its cinematic influence on its sleeve, Kojima employing filmic techniques such as reaction shots, choreographed camera

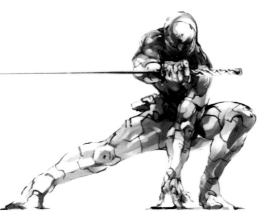

THIS WAY UP

angles and cutscenes but never in such a way that restricts the player's own imagination.

While *Metal Gear Solid* was the game to both formalize and popularize 'Stealth' as a kind of genre, it was far from the first game to make sneaking around undetected a mechanic, with two 8-bit predecessors in the series released for the MSX establishing both the *Metal Gear* characters and universe and its core interactive conceit. Likewise, Sony Japan's ninja sneaking game, *Tenchu*, preceded *Metal Gear Solid* by some seven months. But it was Konami's game that became the focal point for the skulking movement, its ultimate challenge that players finish the game without being detected offering the tight focus around which the rest of the experience pivots. The game – originally titled *Metal Gear 3* till Kojima reasoned that not enough people

Below: Shadow Moses is a remote Alaskan island so icy that the soldiers stationed here must be injected with peptides to prevent their blood from freezing beneath their white furs.

were aware of the first two games in the series to present it as a trilogy – was designed for the 3DO Interactive Multiplayer system. However, following the commercial failure of the system in Japan, development switched to Sony's PlayStation in 1995. While the story retains a lighthearted edge, characters frequently breaking the fourth wall and referring to the PlayStation hardware itself, or referencing clues to be found in the instruction booklet, elsewhere the game prizes realism. The development team spent time with the Huntington Beach SWAT team, filming live demonstrations of the vehicles, weapons and explosives they use, while weapons expert Motosada Mori provided technical advice in the research, which included visits to Fort Irwin Military Reservation in California.

As a result the game walks a delicate line between military sim and Hollywood action flick, a combination made yet more interesting by the non-confrontational heart of the game that rewards evasion and subtlety over brute force. The resulting nuance offered something not yet seen in games: a brand of interaction that encouraged thoughtfulness yet was broad enough to allow for impulsiveness. The recipe proved irresistible and the game became the sixth best-selling title for PlayStation with 7 million sales. Its themes, narrative and interactive have since expanded in a slew of sequels, but none exhibit the tight restraint of this 3D debut, a game of hide-and-seek with nuclear-grade stakes.

Above: Jeremy Blaustein, who also localized the Sega CD version of Hideo Kojima's earlier game, *Snatcher*, translated the English version of *Metal Gear Solid*.

THE KNOWLEDGE
A Japanese radio drama version of *Metal Gear Solid* was produced after the release of the original PlayStation game. 12 episodes were aired from 1998 to 1999 with all characters portrayed by their original Japanese voice actors.

Year: 1998
Developer: **Valve Corporation**
Publisher: **Sierra Studios**
Original format: PC
Play today: PC

"We set up a small group of people to take every silly idea, every cool trick, everything interesting that existed in any kind of working state somewhere in the game and put them into a single prototype level. When the level started to get fun, they added more variations of the fun things. If an idea wasn't fun, we cut it."

Ken Birdwell, senior developer at Valve Corporation

Below: *Half-Life* features numerous licensed weapons such as the Glock 17 pistol, Franchi SPAS-12 shotgun and MP5 submachine gun, yet some of the characters are unarmed white-coated scientists.

HALF-LIFE

As a first person shooter featuring a weedy scientist rather than a muscled marine, *Half-Life* looked and played quite unlike any of its competitors.

First person shooters had always featured meathead protagonists, Rambo-esque embodiments of boyhood power fantasies, all rippling biceps and improbably weighty guns. Into this testosterone-drenched landscape stepped Gordon Freeman, a physicist, more scientist than soldier, more thinker than thug. As a result, in 1998, Freeman and the world he inhabited were far more alien to players than the hellish Martian landscapes of *Doom*: here was a gun game grown in a laboratory, its characters dressed in white coats, not flak jackets.

Half-Life's introductory sequence has the player ride a tram deep into the heart of the Black Mesa research facility, a ponderous yet exhilarating journey through clinical corridors of normality. The subsequent disaster – an experiment gone wrong that rips a hole in time and space through which face-hugging aliens crawl – may be closer to the nightmarish visions of first person shooters gone by, but the surrounding setting remains distinct and fascinating.

The first game from Valve Corporation, founded in 1996 by former Microsoft employees Mike Harrington and Gabe Newell, *Half-Life* was originally titled *Quiver*, after the Arrowhead military base from Stephen King's novella *The Mist*, which provided inspiration for the story. Valve built the game using the *Quake* engine as licensed by id Software, modifying the codebase by around 70 per cent to incorporate skeletal animation and Direct3D support. As newcomers to the industry, Harrington and Newell found it hard to

secure a publisher, many put off by the pair's seemingly unharnessed ambition for the game. Eventually Sierra, who had been looking for a 3D action game using the *Quake* engine, signed the team for a one-game deal.

Despite significant delays (in September 2007 Valve decided to redesign every level in the game), *Half-Life* shipped in November 1998, wowing audiences with its unique approach to storytelling. Rather than wresting control of the action for the player in order to present cinematic cutscenes, Freeman is instead free to eavesdrop on conversations as an active participant rather than a detached viewer. The technique revolutionized how developers approach storytelling in games, just as Freeman himself showed that often strength is to be found in the relinquishment of control.

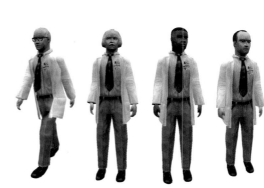

DANCE DANCE REVOLUTION

The first mainstream game controlled with one's feet, Konami's *Dance Dance Revolution* series turned the music game into a performance opportunity.

Music games may have been born in the kindergarten rhymes of *PaRappa the Rapper*, but it was Konami that took the principle of beat-matching out of this abstract, cartoonish wrapper and planted its feet in reality. *Beatmania* was the Japanese company's first rhythm action game, a curious amalgam of mixing and one-handed piano playing that discarded joysticks and buttons in favour of a plastic DJ's turntable. But it wasn't till the company's second 'Bemani' title, *Dance Dance Revolution*, released 11 months later, that the rhythm action genre found universal appeal.

In part that's down to the simplicity of the premise. Few games manage to reduce their interaction to the four points of a compass: up, down, left and right. But then few games are played with one's feet, and the act of stepping in time with the music, and being scored on your timing in doing so, is so universally understood, that *DDR* is arguably the most accessible video game yet made. But while understanding comes easily, true mastery is hard won. Everyone's

first time with the game descends into an awkward tussle of limbs – equal parts hilarious and humiliating, the muscle memory required to conquer the streams of directional inputs extending across one's whole body, not merely the fingers and thumbs.

As a result, *DDR*, when played by a competent player, is one of the most spectacular video games to watch, and soon after release videos of Japanese players' best performances shared across the web. While the game can be played as a pure score attack game, players steadying themselves on the aluminum rest bar attached to the rear of the dance platform while sight-reading the flurry of arrows descending on screen, many saw the potential for genuine performance, designing dance routines and competing at events around the world. The *DDR* bubble may have burst in recent years with the decline of the arcade, but Konami's dance game remains one of gaming's most fascinating and inimitable activities.

Year: 1991
Developer: DMA Design
Publisher: Psygnosis
Original format: Commodore Amiga
Play today: PC

Below: In 2006, Konami announced that the *DDR* games would be used as part of a fitness programme across West Virginia's 765 state schools.

"The fact is that the most important part of *Dance Dance Revolution* and music games in general is the music itself."

Naoki Maeda, sound producer of *Dance Dance Revolution*

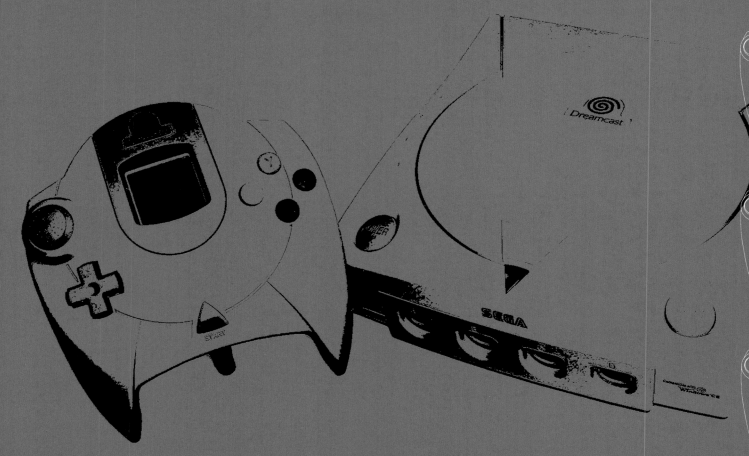

MUST PLAY:
Rez
Shenmue
Jet Set Radio
Bangai-O
Samba de Amigo

SEGA DREAMCAST

Viewed by many as little more than a stop-gap machine, Sega's final console was years ahead of its time, introducing features that have become industry standard.

On the 21 May 1998, Japanese salarymen opened their newspapers to find a full-page advertisement showing a picture of a battlefield littered with the bodies of samurai. Overlaid on to the gruesome scene was the text: "Has Sega been defeated for good?"

To most onlookers, the answer was a resounding 'Yes'. Following a triplet of high-profile hardware disappointments in the Mega CD, the 32X and, to a lesser extent, the Saturn, Sega's console successes had been few and far between in recent years. Moreover, despite some strong creative software, the Saturn's crushing worldwide defeat at the hands of Sony's PlayStation and the Nintendo 64 had left Sega with losses of $242 million for the financial year ending March 1998. Could there really be a way forward for the beleaguered company?

But the advertisement was one of a pair taken out by Sega itself, the follow-up published the next day in the same papers, now showing the samurai rising to the feet in readiness to fight once again. Six months later Sega would launch the Dreamcast, the company's final foray into the hardware manufacturing business, a console on whose shoulders the fortunes of Nintendo's one-time main rival rested, and in whose innovative design the very future of video games could be perceived.

Two rival R&D teams competed against each other to design a machine capable of placing Sega ahead of its rivals, one based in America and one based in Japan. This unusual gestation period came about when the newly appointed Sega of Japan president Shoichiro Irimajiri enlisted the services of Tatsuo Yamamoto from IBM to work on a design in the United States. However, when Hideki Sato, head of hardware development at Sega of Japan, caught wind of the plan he instructed his own team to produce a design for a new console, challenging his boss to choose whichever console came out stronger.

At first, Irimajiri opted to go for the IBM design that used graphics processors from the company 3Dfx. But when 3Dfx leaked details and specifications of the then-secret Dreamcast project when declaring their IPO, Sega immediately pulled the plug on the project, and instead opted for Sato's design.

The specifications were impressive. As well as offering four controller ports for multiplayer, and memory cards with LCD screens that could be removed and used as rudimentary handheld systems away from the console, the Dreamcast was the first system to come with a built-in modem for online gaming. Despite a somewhat tepid Japanese launch, the Dreamcast's innovative features secured 300,000 pre-orders and 500,000 unit sales in the first two weeks following its US launch.

EA decided not to support the machine, but the similarities in internal architecture between the Dreamcast and Sega's cutting-edge Naomi arcade hardware meant that the console became home to some of the best arcade-to-home conversions such as *Soul Calibur* and *Crazy Taxi*. The Dreamcast exclusive titles maintained the bright, primary-colour aesthetic of Sega's arcade output with games such as *Sonic Adventure* and *Power Stone* while the SEGA Sports label plugged the gap left by EA's shunning of the machine with NFL 2K1, marketed as the first football game with online play, outselling the official Madden game during its first weeks on the market.

But the announcement of Sony's successor to the PlayStation dealt a shuddering blow to the Dreamcast's fortunes, Sony's marketing promise of a mysterious 'Emotion Engine' that would elevate video games to a new art form slackened interest in Sega's machine, which was soon seen as a stop-gap. In truth, the Dreamcast was years ahead of its time. Its pioneering work in introducing the first console MMORPG and allowing players to play against one another across the world, established concepts that define video games today. In March 2001, two years after the system's US launch, Sega announced it was not only discounting the Dreamcast, but retreating from the console hardware business altogether.

> **"We believe that Dreamcast will be the best games machine in the world for between three and five years."**
>
> Shoichiro Irimajiri, president of Sega

Above: A representation of the Dreamcast logo. After the discontinuation of the Dreamcast, Sega released the Japanese-only title *Segagaga*, a game in which players have to turn around the fortunes of a console maker.

[086]

LEGEND OF ZELDA:
OCARINA OF TIME

© 1998 Nintendo

Year: **1998**
Developer: **Nintendo EAD**
Publisher: **Nintendo**
Original format: **Nintendo 64**
Play today: **Nintendo 3DS**

Below: **Ganondorf is the main antagonist of the Zelda universe and appears in most of the games in the series.**

LEGEND OF ZELDA: OCARINA OF TIME

The first 3D Zelda game, *Ocarina of Time* is a bona fide masterpiece whose legacy is still influencing the way games are designed many years after its release.

Developed concurrently with *Super Mario 64*, *Zelda: Ocarina of Time* missed its intended launch date by two years. While extended delays in video game development are often a sign of incoherent vision, or a developer whose ambition has outstripped its skill, for the first 3D Zelda title this wait was a pause for perfection, proving designer Shigeru Miyamoto's oft-repeated maxim that 'a delayed game is eventually good; a bad game is bad forever.'

That said, it's hard to believe that *Ocarina of Time* was ever 'bad', even if Miyamoto stepped into a more hands-on directorial role during development when the schedule began to slip. Cracks can usually be seen in any game that endures a shift in purpose or vision midway through development but in this regard, *Ocarina of Time* is without blemish. Perhaps it's because the Zelda blueprint had been so perfected over the course of its 2D iterations, that building this world in 3D was simply a case of following the lines of foresight laid down in previous years.

Zelda games are recurring myths that have you, very often, re-treading old familiar ground. You start off a small, defenceless boy and, by overcoming a series of challenges, gain access to tools and weapons that extend your reach into the game world. You have to try to forget you ever played a Zelda game before you start a new one because each new title in the series is an echo of the last: the detail changes, but the rhythm and structure stay largely the same. And yet *Ocarina of Time* succeeds in bringing enough novel ideas of its own to the world of Hyrule that it's impossible to view the game in such derivative terms. No, this world is inspired, selecting themes from its lineage like strains of simple melody and reworking and expanding them into bold new symphonies. The core conceit is one such

example, borrowing the triumphant idea of a co-existent light and dark world from its Super Famicom predecessor, and twisting and developing it in captivating ways.

Not that the division between *Ocarina of Time*'s two worlds is necessarily complex: rather, here are two dimensions divided by nothing more than time. In one you exist as the child Link, a frolicking green-suited elf boy who, like David facing Goliath, draws himself up to his full height in an attempt to take down the adult antagonist, Ganondorf. The second world is the same as the first, except viewed seven years later, the child now a man and able to perceive the darker edges of existence that are hidden from adolescence.

In this later world, Ganondorf has already won, your task then is to to face up to him for a second time in a bid to grasp success where your younger self found failure. As with *Chrono Trigger*, interest comes from the relationship between the two temporal dimensions; the most minor detail, such as

Below: **Link is guided through the game's many quests by his fairy, Navi, who is always on hand to remind him what his next objective should be.**

"At the beginning of the project, [Miyamoto's] attitude was: 'Okay, guys, I will let you go ahead and make this game.' At some point, he said, 'No, no. I've got to get in here.' I think maybe we were moving a bit slow for him. He could not hold back anymore. "

Eiji Aonuma, dungeon designer for *Legend of Zelda: Ocarina of Time*

a lone tree stump in a sacred meadow, assuming peculiar gravity as the older Link reminisces with a lingering look on something that happened years before.

The world's details enthrall, the experience of first heading out from the training village across the central field, the sky above changing hue from noonday sun to burnished red in step with your sprint reveals Nintendo's understanding of aesthetic wonder. Bold invention is to be found in the Rubik's Cube dungeons, designed by series veteran Eiji Aonuma, the interlocking puzzles a mesmerizing kind of clockwork, whose cogs, when correctly turned, unlock doors to ever more inventive bosses. Played today, the game is a marvel of technical and

creative engineering and, in the context of 15 years of subsequent 3D action games, it can be difficult to appreciate how much new ground *Ocarina of Time* broke. But this was the game that invented left-trigger targeting, a mode of interaction later used by everything from *Modern Warfare* to *Mass Effect*. This was also the game to shrink what had become a vast and unwieldy world with equine transportation; Link's relationship with his horse, Epona, one of the most humane and gentle of any game before it. Again, Nintendo's EAD was establishing a new kind of vocabulary for the coming of a new technology, one which many subsequent games would come to converse in, but few would employ to such poetic effect.

THE KNOWLEDGE
The game's development team numbered over 120, including stuntmen motion captured for Link's movement and sword fighting. Despite the motion capture work elsewhere in the game, cutscene director Takumi Kawagoe hand-animated all of the cutscenes in the game to give a more personable, stylized effect.

Below: Nintendo has re-released *Ocarina of Time* on every console since the Nintendo 64, most recently converting the game to 3D for their 3DS.

Below: In *Ocarina of Time*, Link must travel between the past and the future, using the titular instrument in order to stop Ganondorf's takeover of Hyrule.

[087]

Year: 1999
Developer: Sega AM-3
Publisher: Sega
Original format: Arcade
Play today: Xbox Live Arcade

Below: Creative director Kenji Kanno Kanno wanted the game to explore the "daily life and routine" of a taxi driver.

CRAZY TAXI

Designed to reward skilled players with a longer experience than is usually found in arcades, *Crazy Taxi* took a mundane vocation and made it hyperactively cool.

O stensibly a strange profession on which to base an arcade game, in reality, the task of delivering demanding customers to destinations against strict time limits has a keen sense of the video game about it. *Crazy Taxi* is the inverse of an RPG's fetch quest, one in which you must deliver the quest-giver themselves to their goal before scanning the streets for another assignment.

The idea for the game came to director Kenji Kanno when stuck in traffic one day. From this seed of an idea, Sega's AM-3 division assigned a team of 12 programmers and artists to work with Kanno, all of whom objected to the idea of basing a game on taxi driving.

But the team persisted with the idea and 18 months later the game was released into arcades, a bright spark of originality in what

had become a graveyard of identikit experiences. Despite the bold visuals and contemporary soundtrack, *Crazy Taxi*'s arcade heritage ensured a pure, focused score attack game that, when played by a skilled driver, could deliver up to an hour's worth of play on a single credit.

A port from the NAOMI arcade hardware to the Dreamcast signalled the beginning of numerous flawless conversions from the arcade to the home, securing Sega's console's reputation in the process.

[088]

Year: 1999
Developer: Sega AM-3
Publisher: Sega
Original format: Arcade
Play today: Xbox 360, PS3

VIRTUA TENNIS

Standing midway between dour realism and outlandish fantasy, Sega's virtual take on tennis remains one of the strongest and most graceful in the medium.

W hile most video game replications of sports aim for increasingly weighty realism, Sega AM-3's *Virtua Tennis* (*Power Smash* in Japan) has been content to revel in a exaggerated, boisterous take on tennis simulation. Eschewing the 'big-headed' graphical style of Namco's *Smash Court Tennis* series, Sega opted for realistic visuals and real-world licensed tennis star players. But, despite the TV-style presentation, the embellished physics and fast-paced movement make this an interpretation of real-world tennis viewed through the lens of arcade sensibilities, and it's the most thrilling virtual version of the sport to date for it.

At the game's core is a refined control system, just three button inputs – lob, slice and top spin – offering a vast array of context sensitive shots. The emphasis is on positioning the player character behind the ball early to maximize power and control.

The result of endless testing and refining, the control scheme works well owing to the poise and fluidity of character animations. Players slip from a jog to a sprint and back again with seamless grace, launching themselves in a flailing dive on to the grass or clay when almost out of reach of a shot, or powering up with a deep forehand when in a fortuitous position. The core brilliance of play has evolved very little over the course of the series, Sega once again demonstrating that often the best video game replications of real-life activities owe less to realism than the imagination.

SUPER SMASH BROS.

The idea of taking Nintendo's family-friendly mascots and pitting them against one another in a battle was so illicit that *Super Smash Bros.* development began in secret.

PRESS START

Year: 1999
Developer: HAL Laboratory
Publisher: Nintendo
Original format: Nintendo 64
Play today: Nintendo Wii (Virtual Console)

Masahiro Sakurai created the cute pink marshmallow character Kirby at the age of 19 soon after joining HAL Laboratory, an independent Japanese development studio that exclusively makes games for Nintendo. But by 1998, with no less than five Kirby titles under his belt, Sakurai wanted to diversify and work on a different kind of project to the soft-edge platformers with which he had made his name.

What better way to confound expectations than with a fighting game, he reasoned? However, Sakurai, aware that many fighting games bred for consoles rather than the mean streets of the arcade floundered, knew that he needed a unique angle if he was to convince his bosses of the viability of the project. He knew he wanted the game to be a multiplayer proposition for up to four players but with Capcom's *Power Stone* offering the same feature, this was hardly a headline-grabbing novelty.

So Sakurai settled on a more controversial idea: to pluck characters from Nintendo's rich, child-friendly lineage and throw them into the ring to battle it out against one another. Knowing that the chances of gaining permission to pitch Princess Peach against Luigi in a one-on-one bare-knuckle battle were slim, Sakurai made a prototype in secret. He chose four characters for the prototype – Mario, Donkey Kong, Samus and Fox – and, when he was satisfied that the game was enjoyable and successfully trod the fine line between happy-go-lucky scuffling and all-out brutality, he presented his project to Nintendo.

Against his expectations, Nintendo agreed to fund the project, but belief in *Super Smash Bros.* was low and the company warned Sakurai that the game was unlikely to secure an overseas release. In reality, the unlikely pairing of Nintendo's mascots with tag-team sumo wrestling-style gameplay offered an enthralling slice of cartoon violence, and *Super Smash Bros.* sold 1.97 million copies in Japan, securing it a US release, where it sold a further 2.93 million. While sometimes criticized for its simplicity, *Super Smash Bros.* managed to sell the fighting game to a demographic for whom *Street Fighter*'s showboating combos had grown inaccessible, a populist move perfectly in keeping with its line-up of universally liked pugilists.

Below: *Super Smash Bros.* was inspired by *The Outfoxies*, a 1994 arcade game by Namco.

> **"I actually think it's a miracle that we got *Smash Bros.* and all the Nintendo characters to work together in the first place."**
>
> Masahiro Sakurai, creator of *Super Smash Bros.*

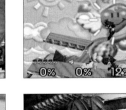

Year: 1999
Developer: Neversoft
Publisher: Activision
Original format: PlayStation
Play today: XBLA/PSN

" I had always wanted to help create a video game that represented the reality and excitement of professional skateboarding."

Tony Hawk, professional skateboarder

Below: Big drops must be landed by holding down the Ollie button till wheel meets concrete.

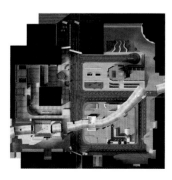

TONY HAWK'S PRO SKATER

Arriving just as skateboarding was undergoing a resurgence around the world, *Tony Hawk's Pro Skater* helped drive Sony's console yet further into the mainstream.

Thanks to extensive motion-capturing, *Tony Hawk's Pro Skater* caught the likeness of one of skating's most famous practitioners in thorough detail. But when it came to replicating the activity itself, developer Neversoft took a more loose approach, instead attempting to capture skating's essence rather than its exact detail. It was a smart move, the game stretching the boundaries of physics to allow players to execute flips, spins and tricks that were impossible to recreate in real life, but which somehow made players feel that they should be achievable, if only one were as skilled and dexterous as Tony Hawk.

In truth, the game benefited from fortuitous timing, arriving at the height of PlayStation's success just as skateboarding was undergoing its own resurgence around the world. In turn, it fast became part of the success story, helping to drive Sony's console yet further into the mainstream consciousness, while popularizing skateboarding among a new generation of players, who were led to believe they, with practice, may be able to replicate the on-screen acrobatics at the local skate park.

The tension in the game's focus between technical skating and outrageous acrobatics originated with Tony Hawk himself, who took a more hands-on approach to development than most sportsmen who lend their name to a video game. Neversoft's skill was allowing a vast array of tricks to be executed with the eight-button, dual stick layout of the

Above: A meter fills as you execute tricks, allowing you to trigger specials when filled. New specials are available for purchase.

PlayStation controller, making the technically impossible intuitive and accessible.

Underneath the spectacle, the game is a fairly straightforward score attack proposition, the aim of the game being to link together aerials, flips, and grinds around the game's environments, in order to multiply the chain's total score. Each of the game's nine levels has five additional objectives, adding an extra layer of diverse focus to each excursion and maintaining interest through a variety of goals.

Despite the unique requirements of a skating game, the engine for the game wasn't built from the ground up, but instead modified from that used to build Capcom's *Resident Evil*. The defining skateboarding series of its generation, the Tony Hawk games have more recently been superseded by EA's more realistic *Skate* series, but its unashamedly arcade-like sensibilities make the PlayStation entries still influential today.

SHENMUE

Developed at unprecedented expense, Yu Suzuki's *Shenmue* was a commercial flop but a creative success, revealing wonder hidden in the monotony of daily routine.

Many video games pursue realism, but few actively pursue reality. The daily grind of modern living is often too uneventful, mundane and repetitious to provide absorbing escapism. We play video games to evade the monotony of daily existence, not to rehearse it. That the most expensive video game yet made in 1999 should seek to replicate in meticulous detail life within the Japanese city of Yokosuke in the mid-1980s was confounding. Eventually Yu Suzuki's grandest project to date would sink under the weight of its own ambition (in the end, just two instalments of the intended six-part series were released) and yet there remains modest beauty to be found within *Shenmue*'s routine.

There is, of course, a bigger picture at play in the game. You play as Ryo Hazuki, a young man living to avenge the murder of his father – but here is a game in which the

Below: *Shenmue II* followed a 2001 sequel, with a third game planned. However, production ended with the second game, leaving the trilogy unresolved.

Above: In 1999 *Shenmue* was the most expensive video game yet made: production cost $47 million.

journey is as important as the destination. The lines that link the drama are filled with a detailed interactive snapshot of a Japanese city at a cultural crossroads, caught between centuries-old tradition and the future's bright, neon lights. You are free to roam the city, taking on part-time jobs, conversing with residents, gambling (the game's hungry slot machines were tested to meet Las Vegas standards) and even to sit down at the local arcade to play Suzuki's own arcade games of the era.

Originally conceived as a traditional RPG based on the *Virtua Fighter* series, development started on Sega's Saturn, moving to Dreamcast in 1998. Sega allocated an unprecedented amount of resources for the game, spending $20 million on a minor army of artists, animators and coders. Clay models of every character, no matter how insignificant, were created for reference, while *Shenmue* was the first game in which every character in its world had its own-recorded dialogue.

Despite becoming the fourth best-selling Dreamcast title, sales failed to match Sega's expectations. When the game's sequel also failed to perform as hoped, Suzuki's vision was smothered ahead of time. Nevertheless, this is a game that offers an extraordinary snapshot of a developer struggling to break free of gaming's previous constraints and in doing so, helping to define new creative boundaries.

Year: 1999
Developer: Sega AM2
Publisher: Sega
Original format: Dreamcast
Play today: Dreamcast

"I did not pursue realism. I pursued reality. It's different."
Yu Suzuki, creator of *Shenmue*

Year: **2000**
Developer: **Maxis**
Publisher: **Electronic Arts**
Original format: **PC**
Play today: **PC**

"You can play *The Sims* as a straight game, and very goal-orientated. You can play with it as a modeling system, and just use it to design houses. You can use it for telling stories. Meta-games that live on top of the Sims themselves."

Will Wright, creator of *The Sims*

THE SIMS

It is natural that, following the success of Will Wright's *SimCity*, the designer would want to zoom into a city's homes to capture a simulation of domestic living.

It seems perverse that, having perfected the grand city-building game with *SimCity* in 1989, it would be 11 years before Will Wright would be able to create a modest home-building game with which he was happy. But then, the bird's eye view of town planning, all regimented roads, straight-lined sewage pipes and vertical taxation scales, has an air of spreadsheet straightforwardness to it. By contrast, at ground level, inside the houses that make up a city, people are unpredictable, changing their behaviour on a whim often with little rhyme or reason. Modelling human behaviour, in all its domestic capriciousness is a far harder task than modelling city behaviour, a challenge which Will Wright and his team at Maxis were only too aware.

Work on *The Sims* started as early as 1993. Wright had recently finished work on *Sim Ant*, a game that simulates an ant colony with notable realism. After this microcosmic success, Wright wondered if it might yet be possible to simulate human behaviour in a similar, organized way to how he had designed ant behaviour. That thought collided with another influence, that of Austrian architect Christopher Alexander, who posited that environment design influenced human behaviour. Wright contemplated whether it might be possible to create a game that, rather than merely featuring architecture, was essentially about architecture, in which players are scored on their designs depending on how efficiently people live within its confines.

In this unlikely clash of ideas, the best-selling PC game yet made was conceived. But few other than Wright could see the merit in the concept. A focus group established in 1993 scored the idea the lowest of all the game concepts they were shown and *The Sims* was shelved while

Wright moved to work on *SimCity 2000*. However, the tenacious designer maintained a quiet, urgent belief in the concept and three years later he managed to secure a small team with which to create a prototype. Internally at Maxis, the game was viewed with some scorn, referred to as 'the toilet game', a reference to a minigame task in which characters must clean the lavatory. Its portrayal of domestic life was viewed as too mundane and uninteresting by many to make for convincing subject matter for a video game, and Wright's constant referral to the premise as an 'interactive doll's house' did little to broaden the concept's potential audience wider than that of young girls.

In 1998 an executive at Maxis cancelled the project, unhappy at the plodding progress the team was making on the game. But still Wright refused to lay the concept to rest, recruiting a tools programmer at the developer who was between projects, and directing him to

Left: In 2002, *The Sims* became the best-selling PC game yet made, with in excess of 6.3 million copies sold, displacing the previous record-holder, *Myst*.

work on *The Sims* in secret. The greatest challenge in building the game was in creating the AI verbs with which to interact with the objects in the world. In most games, AI has very specific, defined behaviours (shoot the player, aim for the goal and so on) but in *The Sims*, the computer characters' behaviour needed to be procedural and generalized, able to inspire a character to sit down on a couch to watch TV before deciding to take a shower, or to make out with a girl. The tools coder worked on this aspect of the game and, when it was functioning at a basic level, he and Wright realized they had created something extraordinary within its apparent ordinariness.

In the game you don't direct the Sims' every move. You can encourage your characters to take jobs or engage in relationships, but their decisions are largely their own. The virtual humans can die from starvation, electrocution, viruses and fire and, if left to their own vices, can grow depressed through sitting for too long in front of the TV. Far from terrorizing these tiny people, most players develop a fierce attachment to them and a forceful concern for their well-being.

The expandability of *The Sims*, whereby add-on packs could bolt on new features to the experience, added a year to the

development time, but was key to the game's on-going success following release. Add-ons kept the game relevant the lives of the Sims interesting and dynamic, and exponentially grew the creative opportunities in the game for dynamic storytelling, thereby swelling the community.

In 2002 *The Sims* overtook *Myst* as the best-selling PC game, having sold 6.2 million copies worldwide. By 2005 that number had risen to 16 million and, by 2010, more than 125 million titles had been sold. As a game that nobody but its creator believed in at almost every stage of its development, *The Sims* represents perhaps the greatest success story in gaming, its own narrative just as fascinating as the emergent tales to be found within its virtual walls.

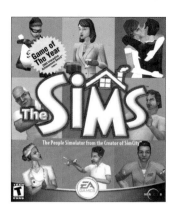

Above: Arguably *The Sims* is more of a toy than a game, as there is no way to 'win' and the player can play indefinitely.

Below: The need to nurture your Sims' emotional well-being as well as their physical well-being was a crucial evolutionary novelty.

THE KNOWLEDGE
The Sims speak Simlish, a made up but emotionally charged language. The development team experimented with fractured Ukrainian and Tagalog, the language of the Philippines, to create Simlish. Inspired by the code talkers of World War II, creator Will Wright also suggested Navajo.

THE 2000s

The 1990s had changed the face of video games with the introduction of a new dimension to our screens. To think that a 3D epic like *Shenmue* could have closed a decade that opened at a time when games could only speak exclusively in the language of sprites and flat textures was inconceivable in 1990.

And while the introduction of true 3D technology into the home in the latter part of the 2000s touched the world of video games – at least for those who could afford a 3D television set and who were prepared to wear the necessary glasses – the visual development of games slowed dramatically in the subsequent decade. *Red Dead Redemption* and *Uncharted 2: Among Thieves*, for all their exquisite detail and refined animation, are mere inches on from *Shenmue*'s accomplishments on the grand scale of game graphics' evolution.

So the 2000s was a decade less about changes in the way that we view games but more about changes in the way in which we play games. *Diablo* and its accessible Battle.net online multiplayer technology had pointed to a future in which gaming over the internet could be a mainstream proposal, while Sega's pioneering work with Dreamcast in setting up persistent servers laid the foundations upon which Microsoft's Xbox Live was built.

This was the decade in which high-speed internet connections became ubiquitous for much of the Western world, an advance in society's technology that facilitated the rise of online gaming, allowing players from around the world to compete at precision e-sports titles such as *Quake 3 Arena*, *StarCraft 2* and *Street Fighter IV*. Internet technology also allowed the online RPG, pioneered by *Meridian 59*, *Ultima Online* and *EverQuest* to blossom, while *World of Warcraft* repackaged their anachronistic designs into something compelling for all-comers.

The rise of social media platforms and the ubiquity of the Flash plugin for computer browsers opened the world of video games up to broader audiences. Facebook games such as *FarmVille* drew in web users who initially visited the site simply to connect with friends and family, but ended up staying for the play. Meanwhile, 100,000 Flash games drew the attention of office workers around the world, wanting a two-minute distraction in their coffee breaks from spreadsheets and meetings.

Nintendo, in choosing to sidestep the graphical arms race that had defined gaming for its first 30 years, began to focus on targeting non-gamers with a precision and success not seen before. The Nintendo Wii's joystick-less controller sought to remove the alien physical obstacle that kept so many older people from trying games, while Sony's Eyetoy and Microsoft's motion-sensing Kinect eliminated the interface entirely, allowing humans to 'be the controller', kicking footballs and swatting at flies directly with their feet and hands, rather than through the plastic conduit of a controller.

This was also the era of meta-gaming, Microsoft's introduction of Achievements with the launch of the Xbox 360 giving each console player their own ongoing account to which medals awarded for setting certain records in games were stored. In doing do, high-score competition, that oldest of all video game features, broke out from the confines of individual titles, becoming instead a meta-pursuit, with every virtual accomplishment recorded for posterity.

And just as the industry's biggest releases began to dwarf Hollywood's output both in terms of the budgets required to build them and the profits they subsequently hauled in, so a grassroots development community blossomed at the other end of the scale, an indie development community able to release their creations to the world using low entry new platforms such as Apple's App Store, Microsoft's Indie Games Channel or, of course, the internet itself.

For the first time game development became a feasible enterprise for the masses, and the rags-to-riches one-man development stories behind games such as *Minecraft* have served as an inspiration to many to create their own games. From Ralf Baer's jottings on a New York stoop in 1966 through to the release of *Call of Duty: Black Ops* in 2010 and its $360 million worth of sales in its first 24 hours of release – the 'largest entertainment launch in history' – video games have grown from nerdish curio to the world's most vibrant creative entertainment medium.

MUST PLAY:
Ico
Grand Theft Auto:
San Andreas
God of War II
Shadow of the Colossus
Dragon Quest VIII:
Journey of the
Cursed King

PLAYSTATION 2

With more than 150 million sales, Sony's PlayStation 2 is one of the best-selling games consoles yet made, a machine that remained in mass production for no fewer than 13 years.

For a video game system that scraped its way into existence by way of a simple grudge, the original PlayStation exceeded the meagre expectations of Sony's management who had once viewed the idea with such disdain. By 1999, Sony's Computer Entertainment division was responsible for a sizeable 40 percent of the company's revenues, establishing itself as a key pillar in the business. Not only that, but the system had reshaped the way in which developers and publishers worked with console platform holders, reigniting an industry that was lagging in the mid-nineties, much as its rival, Nintendo, had done a decade earlier.

Expectations for the PlayStation 2 contrasted to those of its predecessor. Consumer excitement played a key factor in burying Sega's Dreamcast, as people held off subscribing to the 'next generation' of game hardware in anticipation of Sony's next creation. Behind the company's closed doors Ken Kutaragi, the man who had so doggedly believed in the original PlayStation project, was hard at work, now with the benefit of a huge R&D team and the full support and confidence of the Sony board.

The PlayStation 2 was unveiled in March 1999, a year ahead of its release, and exceeded expectations. At the core of both Sony's marketing plan and the machine itself was the 'Emotion Engine', a CPU chip that contained 10.5 million transistors on a die measuring 240mm^2, power that would, Sony claimed, allow video games to communicate emotion like never before.

Out of context, and with the hindsight of the PS2's lacklustre launch line-up, the claims were pretentious. But there was science behind Kutaragi's spiel: he wanted to create a CPU capable not just of number-crunching, but of delivering the mathematical capability required to simulate emotion. When Sony staff first unveiled their academic plans for the Emotion Engine at a silicon chip conference in San Francisco in 1999, few in attendance believed the company could manufacture such a thing, let alone in the volume required for a global console launch.

The system's other specifications impressed with DVD-playback, backward compatibility, and an extension of the analogue functionality of the Dual Shock controller to its face buttons. But not everyone remained convinced. At a special showing at the start of 2000, the PS2's first batch of titles did little to communicate the great potential of this black slab: *Fantavision*, a firework-exploding puzzle game, and *Dark Cloud*, a routine Japanese RPG, appearing as if they'd been developed for the original PlayStation, not this brave new world of digitized emotion.

An even greater problem for Sony was manufacturing sufficient numbers of consoles to meet initial demand. On the system's Japanese launch, on Sunday 4 March 2000, the allocated 600,000 consoles sold out immediately, one empty-handed customer even throwing himself off a roof in Tokyo's electronics district, Akihabara. The US launch on October 26 was mixed too, the initial shipment of 1 million consoles revised down to 500,000 at the last minute, while the UK launch on November 24, 2000 offered a mere 80,000 consoles, brought into the country by four chartered Russian jets who flew to Japan to pick them up, aircraft procured by Sony Europe when they heard Europe wasn't to receive its PS2 allocation in time for Christmas. Meanwhile, BBC TV show *Watchdog* targeted the system as part of a 'Rip-off Britain' exposé thanks to its £300 price point.

In the system's first year there were many developer gripes with the system's architecture, which, according to Capcom's Shinji Mikami, lacked adequate development tools. However, by the system's second year, Rockstar's vast and original *Grand Theft Auto III* illustrated PS2's tightly wound potential. As developers mastered the hardware, and games began to match the machine's promise, the PS2 gained huge momentum. In 2010 it became the best-selling console ever, with 148 million units sold around the globe, success that took video games into more homes than any other system, the emotion engine, in part at least, living up to its lofty name.

> **"I don't think, looking at the launch line-up, you would have extrapolated 148 million sales. It was a mixed bag. There was nothing there that you would have said was completely changing the way games were played."**
>
> Phil Harrison, ex-head of Sony Worldwide Studios

Above: 'Did you see the movie *The Matrix*? Same interface. Same concept. Starting from next year, you can jack into *The Matrix!*' Ken Kutaragi, creator of the PlayStation 2 allows hyperbole to run away with him.

[093]

Year: 2000
Developer: Ion Storm Austin
Publisher: Eidos
Original format: PC
Play today: PC

"The idea was to give players lots of tools so the core ideas of choice, consequence and player freedom would naturally follow."

Warren Spector, creator of
Deus Ex

DEUS EX

A diverse blend of role-playing, shooting, adventuring and immersive simulation, *Deus Ex* left the means of completing the game's challenges to the player's discretion.

On numerous counts, *Deus Ex* was prophetic. While developer Ion Storm Austin may have removed the World Trade Centre from the New York skyline to save on texture memory, the narrative justification – that the twin towers were destroyed in a terrorist attack in the near future – proved miserably prescient. So too did the incorporation of role-playing game character development into a first person action game. Following *Deus Ex*, player choice in tackling in-game problems in a variety of different ways was to become of prime importance to all games in the next decade, from *BioShock* to *Fallout 3,* regardless of ever less relevant genre classifications.

With references to a worldwide avian flu epidemic that breaks out shortly after the turn of the millennium, it's perhaps fitting that *Deus Ex* is essentially a melting pot for conspiracy fiction. Dastardly corporations are tied to the illuminati, who are tied to the Templars, who in turn have something to do with alien landings, which are tangentially related to genetic experimentation, forming a cat's cradle of paranoid conspiracy threads. Small wonder the developer managed to settle upon one or two predicative truths within the huge web of fiction.

You play as JC Denton, a cipher into which you pour your own choices and decisions as the avatar slowly comes to resemble yourself. You work for a terrorist group responsible for decapitating the Statue of Liberty, the husk of which acts as the offices for the anti-terrorist group you later betray. The benefit of the imperfect ideologies that tussle for your loyalty, setting the moral compass spinning, is that you are allowed to draw your own conclusions and act accordingly; there's no coherent narrative voice guiding your actions or, when there is, it's usually immediately conflicted by an opposing murmur.

Above: First published for Windows PCs, *Deus Ex* was later ported to Mac and PlayStation 2.

Likewise, JC's relative incompetence with a firearm and comparatively weak resilience (in contrast to the health-regenerating titanium-skinned protagonists of most shooting games) turned weakness into a strength. By making JC an imperfect avatar, the player was forced to take more responsibility for their actions. Success in combat is hard-won and the player must count the potential cost of every skirmish. Without a maxed-out pistol skill, the point-

Below: The robots were inspired by the ED-209 from the 1987 movie *RoboCop*.

Above: Skill points are used to enhance a character's abilities in eleven different areas, allowing the player to favour a particular style of play.

Above: *Deus Ex* features 24 lethal and non-lethal weapons including crowbars, electroshock weapons, laser guided anti-tank rockets and assault rifles.

multiple methods to complete a task was present from the start. The shape of the game changed dramatically over the course of its development, both in terms of locations (the White House and a visit to a moon base were both culled during the planning stages) and mechanics, which saw the skill and augmentation systems overhauled following some testing by other studios. Soon the hard work began to pay off, as the development team saw testers devising emergent solutions to the problems thrown at them, some of them not yet discovered by the designers themselves.

Nevertheless, the complexities of creating a game with so much raw possibility and so many branching narrative tendrils was a devastating challenge for the team, and in-fighting and tensions routinely threatened to bring the project to a standstill. *Deus Ex* was born of these conflicts of approach, and Warren Spector's skill in creating a vessel dynamic and broad enough to accommodate them all. The one truth that stands resolute out of the conspiracy theories that muddy the game's narrative is the cliché that with freedom comes responsibility. In *Deus Ex*, it's always very clear that the full weight of responsibility rests, not on JC's shoulders, but your own.

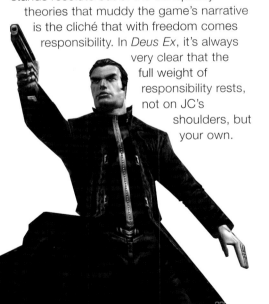

blank range required to score an instant kill means that the environment must be carefully rigged to tip the odds in your favour.

The germ of the idea arrived to creator Warren Spector while he was working at Origin in 1994. Tired of fantasy and science fiction, Spector wanted to make a game grounded in the frustrations of reality, a plan that was moved into production when John Romero offered him a job at Ion Storm to work on whatever he wanted to a few years later. In September 1997 Spector and half a dozen ex-Looking Glass colleagues drafted the first *Deus Ex* design document, and Eidos then agreed to fund the project.

While the original plan for 25 sprawling missions was soon discarded, the core theme of allowing a player

THE KNOWLEDGE
Deus Ex co-creator Warren Spector disliked the game's opening music and planned to request the composer rewrite the melody until he found he couldn't stop humming it. The original theme remained in the game.

COUNTER STRIKE

A fan-made mod for Valve's 1998 science first person shooter, *Half-Life*, *Counter Strike*'s success encouraged PC developers to open their games up to modification.

Year: 2000
Developer: **Minh Le/ Valve**
Publisher: **Vivendi Universal**
Original format: **PC**
Play today: **PC**

"*Counter Strike* is probably the most popular multiplayer first person shooter in the world. It's flattering, yet at the same time we know that any day now it's bound to go away."

Minh Le, creator of *Counter Strike*, March 2000

When id Software first released the tools they used to create *Quake* alongside the game in order to allow the fan community to modify the game to their own ends, developers began to see the value of the video game remix culture. Mods offer players the chance to place the stamp of their own creativity on the game world on a purely graphical level. But when a skilful amateur takes the component parts of a game and creates an entirely new version before sharing it with the rest of the community, a game's popularity can be vastly extended.

The power of this sort of novelty wasn't fully seen till the release of *Counter Strike*, a modification for Valve's 1998 science first person shooter, *Half-Life* (itself a game created from a licensed version of the *Quake* engine). Created by Minh Le, a 21-year-old computer studies major at Simon Fraser University in Burnaby, Canada, *Counter Strike* is an online game for multiple players, featuring one team in the role of terrorists and another in the role of counter-terrorists.

The mod fast gained momentum among the internet community and, by the time Minh and co-creator Jess Cliffe were ready to release a fourth beta of the game, Valve stepped in to help the pair with the coding. In 2000, Valve bought the rights to *Counter Strike*, coordinated a deal with Sierra to have the mod released as a boxed product and promptly hired Le and Cliffe.

Counter Strike's success and the subsequent revenue the game generated proved inspirational for other PC game publishers, who began to provide widespread community tools and support to their games, counting on the community to maintain interest in a game, sometimes for years after its release.

Counter Strike has remained the most popular PC multiplayer FPS thanks to numerous updates over the years, while the release of *Counter Strike Source*, an update that saw the game take on the *Half-Life 2* engine, was the event that Valve used to push its Steam publishing platform.

Right: In recent years Valve has implemented an anti-cheat system designed to stem the rise in players using modifications to cheat their way to success in the game.

PHANTASY STAR ONLINE

With *PSO* Sega not only sent its aged RPG series into space, but also used the game as a vehicle to demonstrate the power and potential of online console games.

Year: 2000
Developer: Sonic Team
Publisher: Sega
Original format: Dreamcast
Play today: n/a

Visually, *Phantasy Star Online* is *Dungeons and Dragons* made over with neon-pink hair and set in outer space. It was also a machine gun volley of records: the first console-based MMORPG; the first Dreamcast title to show off the capacity of its emergent online service; and the first international software to successfully implement a bilingual text mechanism that allowed Americans, Europeans and Japanese to communicate with one another in their own language.

Here was an online RPG that borrowed heavily from the now ubiquitous PC MMORPGs (Massively Multiplayer Online Role-Playing Game) on the market, then twisted their conventions and ideas into something wholly unique. A game precision-designed for its hardware, *PSO* was the first online multiplayer game to feel as though it only could have existed on a console, its action RPG design sensibility owing as much to Sega's arcade pedigree as to multi-sided dice rolls of Western tabletop games.

In stark contrast to Nintendo, whose experiences with the Satellaview had turned the company away from online gaming, Sega's president at the time, Isao Okawa, was vocal in his belief that the future of games was to be found in networked play. Okawa tasked Sonic Team's Yuji Naka with choosing one of Sega's flagship series to turn into a persistent online game, Naka settling upon *Phantasy Star*, Sega's

Above: Communication between players happens via direct text entry, Symbol Chat, Word Select, and/or by keyboard.

formative RPG, which had enjoyed three further iterations since its debut on the Master System.

Set on the bright coloured science fiction world of Ragor, *PSO* looked nothing like the muted fantasy worlds of *EverQuest* and *Ultima Online*. Neither did it play much like them, its heavy emphasis on cooperation, allowing four players to quest together with customized characters, healing and supporting one another while sharing loot, exemplifying online gaming at its best: people working together and helping each other for fun.

Although the cheats and hackers moved in, souring the experience, for many *PSO* remains their most enjoyable and cooperative formative MMO experience, long after the servers were shut down and the world was left to sink like archaeological remains in the memory.

> **"I thought that in an online environment people would enjoy cooperating rather than competing."**
> Yuji Naka, creator of *Phantasy Star Online*

Left: The game was initially known as *The Third World*.

SEGA video game images - under licence by SEGA Corporation

BEJEWELED DELUXE

The first poster game in the so called 'casual' movement, *Bejeweled Deluxe*'s visual simplicity betrays its fundamental complexity and stiffness of challenge.

Year: 2001
Developer: PopCap Games
Publisher: PopCap Games
Original format: Web
Play today: Web

"PopCap players are 65% female and 70% of them are over the age of 30. It's a demographic that's been completely and utterly written off as gamers."

James Gwertzman, director
of business development
at PopCap Games

Initially released as a free-to-play Flash game titled *Diamond Mine*, when a premium version of the game was finally put up for sale, its developer rigged a buzzer up in the office to sound every time a copy was sold. They soon had to turn it off. At the height of this simple puzzle game's success, one copy of *Bejeweled Deluxe* was sold somewhere in the world every ten seconds.

In *Bejeweled* the objective is to swap one gem with an adjacent gem to form a horizontal or vertical chain of three or more like-coloured jewels. Bonus points are given when more than three identical gems are formed or forms two lines of identical gems in one swap.

Designed by the founder of Seattle-based developer PopCap Games, Jason Kapalka, the game leapt from obscurity when the developer went in search of a partner to help with promotion. When PopCap approached Microsoft hoping to have *Diamond Mine* hosted on its Microsoft Zone web-game portal, the Redmond Company agreed on the basis it change the name to *Bejeweled*. The endearingly straightforward match-three game soon was attracting unprecedented

Above: In 2011 PopCap released an HTML5 version of the game, available on the Google Chrome Web Store for free.

numbers of players and, as soon as a downloadable version was made available it was downloaded in excess of 150 million times, proving for the first time that little games can, in the right hands, become exceptionally big business.

Bejeweled soon became the poster boy for a new brand of video games and players dubbed (often in a derogatory sense) 'casual gamers'. In mechanical terms, the game is no more casual than *Tetris* or *Columns*, its bright, colourful looks masking an engaging, smart game that, as in keeping with the worn arcade adage, is easy to pick up but difficult to master.

However, via its accessibility to anyone with a computer and an internet connection, *Bejeweled* caused a new influx of people to become interested in the hobby, those who would not consider themselves to be 'gamers'. These players were uninterested in graphics or a developer's reputation, but shared that desire common to all who play games: to learn and master the challenges presented by a designer. PopCap continues to serve this so-called casual audience, but in crafting compact, enjoyable games, has in recent years won over more traditional players too, breaking down walls and disintegrating the divisive terminology that was to characterize the late 2000s.

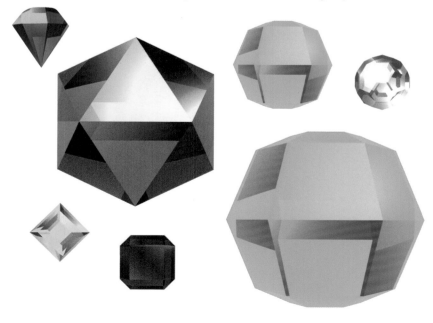

DEVIL MAY CRY

Planned as a *Resident Evil* title, Hideki Kamiya's action classic has little in common with Shinji Mikami's horror series, save the need to survive against great odds.

Devil May Cry started life as the fourth instalment of *Resident Evil*, an origin almost impossible to discern in the final product, the only similarities between the games being the B-movie acting and the dingy corridors. Elsewhere, this is a hyperactive explosion of action and reaction, all survival, no horror. A kinetic, martial rush, *Devil May Cry* has the rockstar-cum-acrobat protagonist Dante firing pistols at demons mid-cartwheel one moment, and hacking at their ankles with a flurry of katana swipes the next.

The game's triumph was in making dynamic fight scenes previously only seen in pre-rendered cutscenes in real-time play, Dante's signature underarm swipe lifting enemies into the sky, before a reverse hail of bullets keeps them aloft, the score ticker flipping upward with each juggle.

Below: The player's performance in each mission is given a letter grade of A, B, C, or D, with an additional top grade of S.

Above: Secret Missions, located in hidden or out-of-the-way areas, provide permanent power-ups for protagonist Dante.

Creator Hideki Kamiya joined Capcom to work on the original *Resident Evil*, soon striking up a friendship with series producer Shinji Mikami. Kamiya was promoted to director for the second instalment of the series, charged by his bosses with creating a title that would sell "in excess of 2 million copies". When *Resident Evil 2* achieved the target, Kamiya's role as a creative force within the studio was secured. But Kamiya's plan to make the next game in the series a purely action-based title was too risky for Capcom, who instead encouraged the designer to continue working on the idea, but as a new IP (intellectual property).

Kamiya drafted the help of *Resident Evil* series writer Noboru Sugimura, who penned the skeleton of a story that would become *Devil May Cry*. The action-led focus allowed Kamiya to explore score attack mechanics in a way that the *Resident Evil* template had never allowed. While at college, Kamiya completed Nintendo's *Star Fox* once a day, an obsession with the perfection of skill reflected in *Devil May Cry*'s fixation with grading the player and encouraging 'S-rank' faultlessness. The result is one of the greatest arcade titles to be found outside of the arcade, a game of singular style that encourages both mastery and showboating, and whose unfettered imagination gave game designers permission to dream big and dream strange in daring ways.

Year: 2001
Developer: in-house (Team Little Devils)
Publisher: Capcom
Original format: PlayStation 2
Play today: PlayStation 2

"A while into development we realized we could hold both guns and swords in system memory. So, we decided to put a sword on Dante's back and put different buttons for both weapons, so the users can change between them in a split second."

Hideki Kamiya, creator of *Devil May Cry*

Below: *Devil May Cry* introduced the 'style!' meter and ranking, to get players to attack, while avoiding damage.

[098]

Year: 2001
Developer: Intelligent Systems
Publisher: Nintendo
Original format: Game Boy Advance
Play today: Game Boy Advance

"We were aiming at the GBA's target audience – relatively young children – and at that time I thought they would like the pop design – the bright colours and rounded characters – and the comedy elements. When we got feedback from the game we discovered that it had sold mostly to teenage boys, so..."

Makoto Shimojo, director of
Advance Wars

ADVANCE WARS

This breezy, almost saccharine representation of military operations offers players one of the strongest strategy games yet seen, a marvel of diminutive tactical play.

For 13 years Nintendo and Intelligent Designs had quietly refined its *Famicom Wars* series of turn-based military strategy games in Japan. And for 13 years the Japanese publisher had considered the games too complex for Western tastes. Patronizing, perhaps, but the benefit for Western players was that, when *Advance Wars* finally trundled out of Japan in 2001, it did so with the benefit of over a decade's spit, polish and iteration behind it. Small wonder it was perfect.

The game's great appeal rests in the board-game-like rigidity of its rules, a breezy approximation of modern warfare in which you move tanks, planes and infantry around a 10x15 grid in an effort to overwhelm your opponent. The heart of modern warfare is retained, both in the unit types, the behaviour of weapons and even the tactics that player generals must employ to gain the upper hand, but the chummy stylization allows the game to appeal to the broadest possible audience, without alienating those who can see through its super-deformed clothing.

Director Makoto Shimojo assembled a diverse team for the project, many of whom didn't specialize in 'Simulation Game' development. This diversity of sensibilities infuses *Advance Wars* with flavours rarely found in the genre, the precision of unit movement more akin to a shoot 'em up, the rhythms of attack and defence rendered in animations that enjoy a musical quality.

Below: **Designer Kentaro Nishimura claims that** *Advance Wars*' success changed Nintendo's understanding of Western tastes.

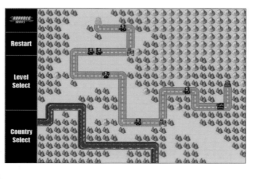

Despite the care and attention, when the game was finished, Shimojo presumed this game, like the previous five entries to the series, would be for Eastern eyes only. But when staff as Nintendo's American office played the game, working through the accessible yet exhaustive tutorial Shimojo included in the game, they insisted on a US release, a decision that paved the way for the *Fire Emblem* games to leave Japan.

The synergy between hardware and software makes *Advance Wars* the best in series, its subsequent sequel hoping to improve on its formula, but finding no room to do so. A masterclass in refined, waste-less design, the game's relentless ability to deliver concise, dramatic and even humorous scenarios make it accessible and timeless.

SUPER MONKEY BALL

The absurdist premise and warmly hysterical presentation may imply this is a children's game. But at its heart lies a series of fiendish spatial puzzles.

Year: 2001
Developer: Amusement Vision
Publisher: Sega
Original format: Arcade
Play today: Nintendo Wii (backward compatibility, i.e. can work with older technology)

The only video game to be played with a plastic banana is *Super Monkey Ball*. The arcade version of the game has you manoeuvring the titular monkey-in-a-ball around its series of devilish mazes using, not a joystick, but a plastic banana, protruding from the machine's control panel.

Created by Toshihiro Nagoshi's newly created Amusement Vision, the game has a childlike simplicity: tilt a maze to steer a ball around it, and make it from the start to the finish within the time limit. There are no enemies – a pacifist design even the venerable *Marble Madness* hadn't quite managed to commit to – save for your own shaky nerves. Sega's inimitable spin on the concept elevated it from a dry, Victorian-era premise to an absurdist, drug-tinged journey in which you manoeuvre a capsule ball containing one of four squealing monkeys around a maze suspended in a bright sky with sheer drops into nothingness all around.

The home version of the game was a GameCube launch title and it acted as a statement of intent for its host console, encapsulating the inclusive philosophy that Nintendo would continue to curve toward over the next decade. The physics engine worked perfectly with the GameCube controller's analogue stick, which could be locked into its diamond-shaped plastic housing in order to send the monkey ball in a straight line. The console version saw Nagoshi and his team embellish the theme – already a sizeable proposition with 118 mazes – with a clutch of riotous minigames. *Monkey Target*, arguably the strongest of the set, is a gliding simulator, asking the player to consider wind speed and direction while guiding a monkey ball with skill and finesse onto distant targets in the ocean. *Monkey Billiards*, *Monkey Race*, *Monkey Golf* and *Monkey Fight* added their banana-themed spin but it's the mix of cutesy visuals and hardcore appeal in the main game that made *Super Monkey Ball* one of the best-selling GameCube games.

Left: The player can collect bananas by rolling the ball over them. The fruit awards extra points, and extra lives.

"We wanted something that would catch people's eyes in the arcades, and make the game feel fun when you played it."
Toshihiro Nagoshi, creator of *Super Monkey Ball* on the game's banana controller

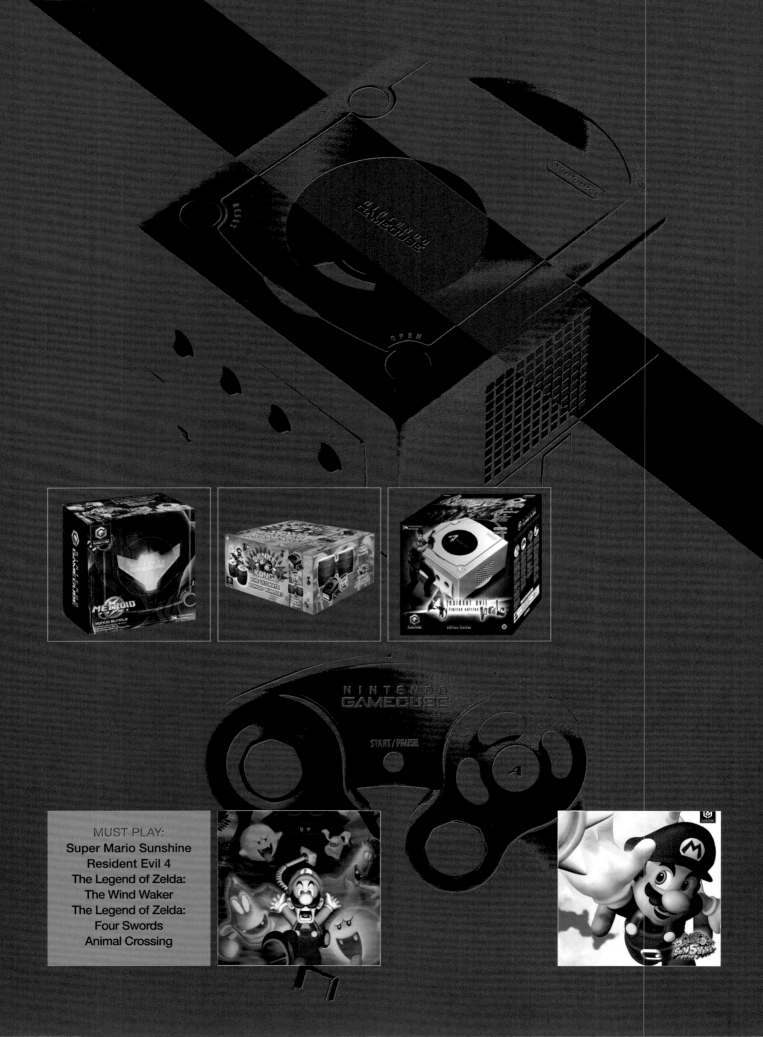

MUST PLAY:
Super Mario Sunshine
Resident Evil 4
The Legend of Zelda:
The Wind Waker
The Legend of Zelda:
Four Swords
Animal Crossing

NINTENDO GAMECUBE

Nintendo's follow-up to the N64, codenamed Dolphin, boasted a competent design that never managed to prove inspirational, in neither hardware nor software terms.

The mighty had fallen. Nintendo, the saviour of the video game in the mid-1980s and its definer for the next decade had, by the time of Nintendo 64's decline, lost its place at the heart of the industry it had established and sustained. While *Super Mario 64* and *The Legend of Zelda: Ocarina of Time* had helped describe the formative language of 3D gaming, Nintendo's reluctance to abandon cartridge-based games in favour of disc storage had cost the company dearly.

Not only that, but Nintendo's image continued to primarily be one of a toymaker, while the video game audience was now advancing into its twenties and thirties, a stage of life for which Sony's PlayStation seemed more tailored, in the marketing, if not the reality. Sega's early entry to the so-called 'next generation' had made the Nintendo 64's fuzzy 3D look positively archaic. Had Japan's leading console manufacturer become irrelevant?

Nintendo's answer to the creative and business conundrum in which it found itself surfaced in 1999, with leaked details of a project codenamed 'Dolphin', a new console rumoured to use a 128-bit custom processor and optical disc media. At the company's SpaceWorld event the following year the GameCube, as it had come to be known, was officially unveiled (despite the name change, references to 'Dolphin' remained in the system's model number, DOL-001 and the name of its CPU, 'Flipper').

The boxy console appeared to have taken its design cues from Apple's desirable desktop computers, prizing compactness over bulk and power, but it was the proposed price point, which at ¥25,000 (around £125) was far cheaper than its rivals, that was most arresting. Along with the game casing, a slew of titles were shown. While many of were never released, *Meowth's Party, Perfect Dark* and a 'realistic' Zelda game all discarded before reaching the market, Nintendo appeared to have answered its critics by altering its business approach on a fundamental level in order to adapt to a changing market.

The system was created by numerous Nintendo teams and affiliates, Western designers such as *Goldeneye* creator Martin Hollis even pitching into the development of the machine. In anticipation of Sony's PlayStation 2, Nintendo focused on graphical capabilities, dumping NEC, developer of the Nintendo 64's MPU in favour of IBM due to the company's advances in copper chip technology. Following criticism that the Nintendo 64 had been a difficult console to develop for, Nintendo worked to make the GameCube accessible, allowing developers to concentrate their energies on artistry instead of working around the hardware. In testament to this, Sega claimed in 2001 that it was able to create a playable version of *Phantasy Star Online Version 2* for the system in less than a month.

Despite the sensible approach to development of the system, the GameCube would flounder following release. Even with strong third-party support and the lowest hardware price of all consoles on the market, Nintendo fast slipped into 'third' place, halting GameCube production for a brief period in 2003 to reduce surplus units. The company sold just 22 million units by the end of its life cycle compared to PS2's 100 million consoles, and the Xbox's 24 million by the same point.

In part the lacklustre performance was thanks to the 1.5 GB proprietary disc format, which offered developers far less memory space than PlayStation 2 and Xbox's 8.5 GB Dual-Layer DVDs. Meanwhile, the lack of DVD playback forced consumers wanting a cheap DVD player to opt for Sony's machine. Most problematically, the system lacked a must-have exclusive too, *Super Mario Sunshine* and *The Legend of Zelda: The Wind Waker* falling short of the novel greatness of their predecessors. Indeed, the GameCube proved that Nintendo is a company at its best when trailblazing and that flounders when following trends instead of establishing them. In its competent unimaginativeness, Nintendo almost lost its identity, a mistake the company would not make again.

"No matter how good the hardware, it is no good if there is no interesting software."
Atsushi Asada, executive vice president of Nintendo in 2001.

Below: The music that plays while accessing the GameCube system menu is a slowed version of the Famicom Disc System start-up theme.

[100]

ICO

TM/ ©2001 Sony Computer Entertainment Inc.

Year: 2001
Developer: **Team Ico**
Publisher: **Sony**
Original format: **PlayStation 2**
Play today: **PlayStation 2**

"It's no exaggeration to say that Yorda is the main character in the game. Giving life to Yorda, giving her appeal and presence, was the key to *Ico*'s success."

Fumito Ueda, creator of *Ico*

ICO

Fumito Ueda's otherworldly debut explores the relationship between a boy and a waif-like girl in a game that achieves elegance without becoming ostentatious.

Sparse, misty, and painted in thin watercolour tones and second-hand nostalgia, *Ico* doesn't look very much like a video game at all. Nor indeed does it sound like one, the virtual air in games so often rammed with gunfire, screams or the heavy might of an orchestra, here left to breathe with the sighs of the wind and the clip clop of a child's footsteps on stone. Neither does the protagonist, a skinny young boy with an oversized Viking helmet and a wooden sword, look very much like the game heroes we have grown accustomed to, those burly men whose power is writ in their biceps, or the athletic women whose adolescent appeal is found in their moans and curves.

But more than all of this, what sets *Ico* apart is that it does not play very much like a video game. In Fumito Ueda's debut masterpiece you lead the waif-like girl-child Yorda by the hand along a castle's craggy ramparts, crying out to her to follow your footsteps, catching her by her wrist when she falls, and batting away the black ghouls that tug at her bright white dress, trying to

pull her back towards her captor, the castle's queen. It is a game about custody, about caring for someone weaker than yourself at the expense of the speed of your progress – a rare theme in a medium obsessed with the relentless exertion of power and dominance over others in search of the quickest route to a goal.

It's not that the premise itself is in any way bold and new. 'Escape the castle and save the girl' has been the set-up to countless video games just as it was the set-up to countless stories in film and literature before it. Neither are the building blocks of interaction especially inventive: running, jumping, climbing and swinging are all familiar virtual actions. Rather, in this curious relationship between a small boy and a tall girl something revolutionary occurred. It was perhaps the first time that the PlayStation 2's much-touted Emotion Engine delivered a murmur of what its bold name had promised, not in the delicately weighted hybrid of puzzle game and platformer that *Ico* represented, but in the way it made you, the participant observer, emote.

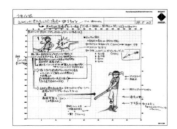

Right: *Ico*'s minimal dialogue is spoken in a fictional language. Kazuhiro Shindÿ plays the role of Ico, the voice of Rieko Takahashi appears as Yorda, and Misa Watanabe is the Queen.

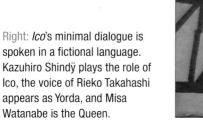

Ueda, *Ico*'s creator and lead developer originated the game concept in 1997, envisioning a boy meets girl story in which the only communication between the two main characters would be through hand-holding. Drawing inspiration from the absence of any on-screen dials or gauges in Eric Chahi's *Another World*, Ueda created an animation to convey his vision, and his team used this animatic as a reference point to ensure development never strayed too far from the original concept.

The director began working with producer Kenji Kaido, lead designer of Sony's *Ape Escape!* in 1998, together with a close-knit team of artists from outside of the games industry, creating the game for the original PlayStation. After two years of development it was clear that the system's straining technical capacity was unable to deliver the team's vision. They would either need to halt production, alter their vision or explore new hardware options. Ueda opted for the latter, switching development to PlayStation 2, using key frame animation to give the artistic feel to the character's movement and subtracting superfluous design ideas in order to create a clutter-free experience.

In truth, much of the game's power is found in the girl, Yorda, the beguiling combination of her fragility and strength. Her tentative steps contrast with Ico's

Above: A novelization of the game titled *Ico: Kiri no Shiro* (*Ico: Castle of Mist*) was released in Japan in 2004. It was written by author Miyuki Miyabe.

youthful, gangly movements, giving the effect of a dance that somehow communicates both the innocence and awkwardness of adolescence.

So often Yorda impedes progress, cutting off the easy solution, but never in such a way to irritate. Despite attracting critical acclaim, often confounding writers who tried to pin down the game's ethereal appeal, *Ico* found only modest commercial success. A high-definition re-release in 2012 sought to bring the game to a wider audience, along with Ueda's subsequent game, *Shadow of the Colossus*, but *Ico*'s idiosyncratic charm kept it from mainstream acclaim. Nevertheless, this remains one of the medium's most haunting journeys, an experience that's difficult to recall in firm details, but whose ambience returns at the smallest of triggers: a fleck of sunshine on some cobblestones, the flicker of a ghoulish shadow, the sight of two hands clasped.

THE KNOWLEDGE
The cover used for the Japanese and European versions of the game was drawn by Ueda himself, inspired by the surrealist artist Giorgio de Chirico and his work, *The Nostalgia of the Infinite*.

[101]
GRAND THEFT AUTO III

Year: 2001
Developer: DMA Design
Publisher: Rockstar Games
Original format: PlayStation 2
Play today: PlayStation 2

"There was something about *GTAIII* that drew a line in the sand between games and movies, and it felt like: this is us taking over now."

Sam Houser, creator of *Grand Theft Auto III*

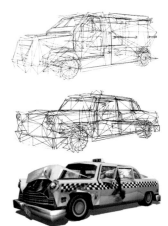

Below: Following the 9/11 terrorist attacks on the World Trade Center, Rockstar delayed the game by three weeks to make a number of small changes.

GRAND THEFT AUTO III

Grand Theft Auto's pop into 3D brought with it a shift in tone, moving the game away from the violent farce of earlier titles and closer to Hollywood crime thrillers.

More than any other, *Grand Theft Auto III* is often cited as the game that closed the gap between video game and film. In the 3D streets of Liberty City – New York through a glass darkly – the influence of cinema's classics from *Taxi Driver* to *Goodfellas* can be heard bold and clear in every gunshot and tyre screech, the mob movie atmosphere heightened by voice actors pulled from *The Sopranos* and a soundtrack licensed from *Scarface*. Many games had aspired to a Hollywood-esque delivery, but it was only in the power of PlayStation 2 and the ambition of Edinburgh-based DMA Design that the hope became a possibility.

But *Grand Theft Auto III*'s legacy is more than merely making a game look like a film, even if its advances in structuring missions around storytelling broke ground that 1000 imitators would seek to plough. Rather, it's in the non-prescribed stories generated by its world and the player's reach into it that Rockstar's (then DMA Design) magic is primarily conjured. It's in hijacking a vehicle from an obese Manhattan-ite, before

reversing it over her and screeching away into a head-on collision with a fire engine. It's in the incredulity of seeing the ensuing mayhem as an ambulance, alerted to the carnage, tears around the corner bowling through the crowd, raising the very body count it sought to lower. And it's in the retelling of these stories on countless forums and around innumerable water-coolers the world over that propelled the game to household name and helped establish a new genre, the 'sandbox'.

Prior to this third instalment, *Grand Theft Auto* was known as a pair of cult violent crime games whose murderous reputation was somewhat at odds with their rudimentary, top-down graphics. But even in these early games, the shoots of Rockstar's vision were apparent, the boxy, pinball-esque view of Liberty City even then a cartoon playground in which you could run over cops and terrorize 5-pixel-wide Hare Krishnas. But in the move to 3D, the somewhat abstract overarching mission ('earn a million points!') was dropped, and the boundless

potential of this heaving city harnessed into more structured tasks bookended by filmic cutscenes.

The move to 3D may have been a logical step, but it wasn't a straightforward one. This huge, complex, heaving world had to stream in constantly from the PlayStation 2 disc, a technique that other developers had been using, but nowhere near to the extent that *Grand Theft Auto III* required. Streets in front of the player had to be rendered on the fly, while those behind the camera were fast discarded from memory in order to maintain the frame rate. Meanwhile, the full range of the game's soundtrack, streamed in via the radio in each vehicle, had to be poised and ready to play depending on whichever station the player switched to.

DMA Design worked wonders with its relatively limited budget, hiring character actors such as Kyle MacLachlan and Joe Pantoliano to elevate the voice acting and character performances in the game far higher than anything heard before in games. Despite the rudimentary lip-synching and basic character models, these performances stand time's unforgiving criticism and *Grand Theft Auto III*'s story, while undoubtedly derivative of cinema, stands not only as a pioneer but also as a high point.

Nevertheless, when the game was shown at the video game conference E3 in the summer of 2001, expectations were low. Sam Houser, president of Rockstar Games and Les Benzies, the game's producer, showed the game to a muted consumer reaction, its scope impossible to communicate via a 5-minute demo on a show floor. The reaction only made the team more eager to realize its vision and

five months later *Grand Theft Auto III* released to widespread critical acclaim. Critics, now offered days to explore Liberty City and absorb its detail and breadth of possibility, were able to catch what Houser and his team were aiming for, and the mature cinematic influences captured the imagination of an older demographic of players whose tastes and sensibilities had so far been largely ignored in games. Following its release *Grand Theft Auto III* remained at the top of the charts for a year, leading up to the release of its follow-up, *Grand Theft Auto: Vice City*, Rockstar cementing both their own reputation and, in Mafiosi style, the fate of their lacklustre imitators forevermore.

"From a pure game mechanic point of view, the fact that you could go with a hooker, and then whack her and take your money back, just the game mechanics of that – looking at it completely isolated from the fact it involves a hooker – were brilliant."

Sam Houser, creator of *Grand Theft Auto III*

Above: Set in a fictional city in the US, *GTAIII* is an action-adventure game in 3D, reminiscent of a Hollywood thriller.

THE KNOWLEDGE
The American DJ, Lazlow Jones made his debut in *GTAIII* on the game's virtual radio station Chatterbox radio. Jones has written dialogue and acted as host of a radio station in every *GTA* game since.

MUST PLAY:
Halo: Combat Evolved
Fable
Knights of the Old Republic
Jet Set Radio Future
Ninja Gaiden

XBOX

Deep pockets and a core team of visionaries helped the publisher of routine PC software to make the switch from work to play with its hefty black Xbox.

When Bill Gates, founder of Microsoft, took to the main stage at the Game Developers Conference in San Jose, California on 10 March 2000 to announce the company's long-rumoured entry to the home video game console market, he was full of hyperbolic promise. The X-box (as it was written at the time) was to be a system three times as powerful as Sony's PlayStation 2, transforming the way in which we consume media in the living rooms of our homes.

It was bullish enthusiasm that few industry watchers shared. Sony was at the height of its success, having clambered over rivals Nintendo and Sega to lead the video game industry into the new century. Each of these three console makers had its own niche on the gaming landscape: Nintendo as purveyor of primary-colour game worlds that fired our childhood imaginations; Sega as the creator of adrenaline-rich arcade thrills; and Sony as the mainstream giant in whose slipstream the others were pulled. There appeared to be no room for another to muscle in on the bright-lit frisson of home video games, let alone a developer of routine office software.

The idea for the system came not from the top, but from the middle of the corporation. In the run-up to the launch of Sony's PlayStation 2, a number of Microsoft engineers became concerned at the Japanese company's claims that their new console was set to wipe the PC from the home. Ted Hase, Otto Berkes, Seamus Blackley and Kevin Bachus came together to design a home games machine, one based on PC architecture, but that could compete with the traditional games consoles in the living room. Originally known as the DirectX-box, the project took off when James 'J' Allard joined the group. An avid game player Allard was sceptical that an 'eMachines for games' device, with a custom version of Windows would be able to compete in the console market. He argued that the console shouldn't run Windows, the company's ubiquitous operating system, but instead something tailored to the machine's strengths. Likewise, it was Allard who maintained that the systems should ship with broadband-only

Ethernet connections, sidestepping the dial-up modem users to ensure that online multiplayer gaming was fast enough to allow for competitive play.

While Allard is often cited as being the 'father' of Xbox, in truth, there were many creative minds responsible. It was Ed Fries who managed the team that would design and build the system over a course of 24 months, while it was Seamus Blackley's experience in game development that convinced game makers of the system's potential. A video game console is only as good as its games, and without Bungie's exclusive launch title *Halo: Combat Evolved*, a game that brought about a sea-change in console-based first person shooters and added legitimacy to Microsoft's bulky box, the story may have been very different. But even with a skilled team of visionaries behind it, Xbox's place at the console gaming table was, to a large extent, paid for. Following the system's launch Microsoft fast muscled into second place in the console arms race, but at a cost to the wider company of $6 billion in losses, a financial punch that few corporations could take.

In part, the long haul success of the machine was down to Xbox Live, an online service that allowed subscribers to play online games with others around the world and to download new content directly to the system's hard drive. While Sega's online Dreamcast service predated Xbox Live by some margin, Microsoft benefited from a proliferation of faster internet speeds, enabling games such as *Halo 2* to be played at a competitive level remotely.

The system suffered in its later years at the hands of modders, who circumvented Microsoft's system protections to install their own operating systems and run pirated games. But arguably modding helped build grassroots support for the machine, which by the time of its discontinuation in late 2006 had sold 24 million units worldwide. In five short years Microsoft established itself as a leading developer of console hardware, finding success through a combination of deep pockets, tall luck and a clutch of strong games.

> **"In focus testing, the marketing team left the name 'Xbox' on the shortlist of names simply as a control, to demonstrate to everyone why it was a horrible name for a console. Of course, it outscored everything they came up with."**
>
> Ed Fries, Microsoft VP of game publishing

Below: The original Xbox Live servers were finally shut down on 15 April 2010.

Year: 2001
Developer: Bungie
Publisher: Microsoft
Original format: Xbox
Play today: Xbox 360

Below: *Halo*'s multiplayer mode was playable just five weeks prior to the game's release.

HALO: COMBAT EVOLVED

A first person shooter that redefined a genre, demonstrated the potential of Microsoft's new Xbox and has influenced video game design since its release.

It is one of those rare entertainment releases whose influence looms so large over the cultural landscape that it is almost difficult to imagine a time before its arrival. There are the now ubiquitous evolutions the game brought to the first person shooter. The two-weapon limit gave its firearms a strategic meaning, ensuring that every twin combination of guns chosen changes the fundamental way in which players must approach a battle. Enter a skirmish with a sniper rifle and a pistol and the *Halo* you experience will be different to the one you run into with a shotgun and a needler, the reduction in choice a simplification that, in turn, brought newfound complexity and nuance.

Then there was the rechargeable shield, an ingenious piece of design that makes ducking for cover not only a way to dodge bullets but also a respite in which to recuperate. Ten seconds spent cowering behind a rock or tucked in a doorway is an evasive manoeuvre to rebuild your shield defences, a simple yet profound tweak that infuses battles with a rhythm of assault and cover that would subsequently permeate the video game landscape beyond.

But more than that, there are the ways in which *Halo: Combat Evolved* changed the balance of power among the console-makers, earning Microsoft and its new venture into video game hardware a respect that

Above: The Elite shout "Wort, wort, wort!" as a battle cry, an audio file created by slowing and reversing another character's phrase: "Go, go, go!"

would have taken far longer to build had the game not been part of the Xbox launch line-up. It made a company known as a spreadsheet publisher become known, almost overnight, as a shrewd game publisher. *Halo* had a legitimizing effect on Xbox, a system that prior to release had been viewed as a ridiculous, bulky folly from a mistrusted outsider.

It wasn't planned this way. When Bungie began work on *Halo: Combat Evolved* the title was a real time strategy game designed for Microsoft's archrival Apple, a science fiction successor of one of the company's earlier titles, *Myth*. On 21 July 1999, during the Macworld Conference & Expo, Steve Jobs announced that *Halo* – as it was simply known, *sans* subtitle at the time – would be released for Mac OS and Windows simultaneously. Even at E3 2000, the following year, *Halo* did not resemble its final form, but was instead a third person action-adventure, a far cry from *Ringworld* that players would experience the following year.

The change in direction was inspired by Microsoft itself, who brokered a deal with Bungie, acquiring the studio in June 2000 before moving the entire company to Redmond, Washington. *Halo* became a Microsoft exclusive as Bungie rewrote the game engine specifically for the forthcoming Xbox, turning the game into a first person shooter and, unbeknown to

Above: Master Chief was the first video game character to have a waxwork at Madame Tussauds.

Above: *Halo* contains 3,000 lines of dialogue, a number that rose to 21,000 in its sequel.

them, laying out the most significant design in console shooters since Rare's *GoldenEye*.

As inseparable from Xbox as Mario is from a NES, *Halo* only came together in the final weeks of development, a "perfect storm" as technical lead Chris Butcher described it, when the Xbox hardware settled into its final form, drawing itself up to the height of Bungie's ambition for the project. And what ambition it was. It's not that the various components of *Halo* are complex or myriad. In fact, the concrete elements of the design can be distilled to a few core factors: the enemy designs and behaviour, the recharging shield, the limited arsenal of weapons and the sharp AI of your marine teammates. But these elements combine in a magical way, encased in a wider science fiction story that, by its conclusion, had drawn four

factions on to the battlefield. Never before had a game developer given the lone wolf player a sense of being caught up in a war that they were neither inspiring nor orchestrating, their role as much one of spectator as catalyst and solution.

While Bungie were forced to drop Xbox Live support, as Microsoft's online infrastructure was not ready for the console's launch, the game's release was tremendously successful. Buoyed by gushing reviews, the game sold a million units in five months and three million by the summer of 2003. But the game's significance extends far beyond its sales records, both in terms of the influence of its mechanics, its enemy design, its vehicles, its organic AI, its exaggerated physics and its silent space marine protagonist, a video game icon that is as recognizable today as Mario or Sonic.

"At the time, Microsoft marketing didn't think *Halo* was a good name for a video game brand. It wasn't descriptive like all the military games we were competing with. We told them *Halo* was the name. The compromise was they could add a subtitle. Everyone at Bungie hated it. But it turned out to be a very sticky label… so in hindsight it was a good compromise."

Jaime Griesemer, designer on *Halo: Combat Evolved*

Below: Drawings of weaponry and armour for the video game.

Below: A flamethrower was one of the original weapons planned for *Halo*.

2001

[103]

REZ

REZ

Year: 2001
Developer: **United Game Artists**
Publisher: **Sega**
Original format: **Dreamcast**
Play today: **Xbox Live Arcade**

Rez's futuristic aesthetic and electronic soundtrack combine to propel the player along the rails of an abstract sensory journey inspired by the artist Kandinsky.

It is difficult to cut through the artifice to the core of the *Rez* experience. Just as this shooting game has its player fly questingly through scenes of digital hyperbole in search of the truth, so the bluster that surrounds one of the most idiosyncratic video game experiences shrouds its essence. And it is, in essence, a simple core.

Designer Tetsuya Mizuguchi's has pinned *Rez*'s influence on the works of Kandinsky, one of the founding members of the Bauhaus art movement of the early 20th century. Then there are the links Mizuguchi has made between the game and synaesthesia, a neurological condition in which sufferers see music as colour.

At its heart, *Rez* is an old-fashioned shooting gallery arcade game, the likes of which you might find at a holiday camp amusement arcade – albeit one stationed on Alpha Centuri. Indeed, this on-rails shooter – backed by a storyline lifted wholesale from the Disney movie *Tron* – adds little more to the video game landscape than *Space Harrier* or *Afterburner* had offered years earlier in terms of its raw systems.

Situated inside an unnamed cyberspace, the player must break through a series of firewalls in order to save the central

Below: *Rez* is set in a futuristic computer network called the K-project, controlled by a malicious AI named Eden.

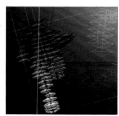

AI, Eden, from a computer virus. Your character moves through the game space on invisible rollercoaster rails and players must shoot enemies before they shoot you, using a targeting system that locks on to multiple adversaries, and an overdrive counter that can destroy everything on screen.

There are no 'lives'. Rather, the player's character moves through seven distinct phases of evolution, with each new mutation activated by collecting power-ups. Receive a hit and you drop a step back down the evolutionary ladder, till you fail in the most basic form and land in the Game Over screen.

The game's joy is found in the aesthetic, rather than the systemic. This sound and light show is a video game rendering of a trance voyage. You swoop and dive through living abstract spaces filled with mind-piquing pyrotechnics in which the highbrow talk of Russian abstract painters and neurological foibles or the lowbrow hand-muffled giggling about a third-party sex toy peripheral and its rhythmic pulsing (*Rez*'s trance vibrator add-on remains the most ludicrous video game peripheral) fades to background noise.

For creator Tetsuya Mizuguchi, the journey began behind the wheel of a car. The designer's early work at Sega was with arcade driving games, *Sega Rally Super Stage* and *Manx TT*, titles that slavishly attempted to

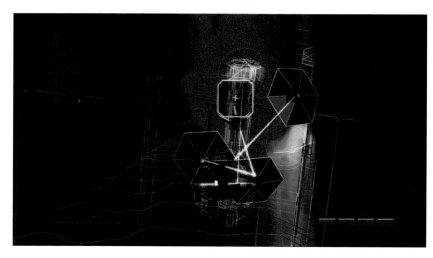

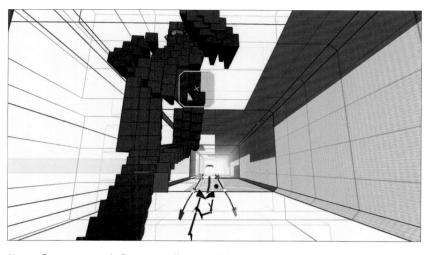

> **"Kandinsky dedicated his life to painting pictures while listening to music. He felt that all sounds have colour, movement, even smell and taste. This is crossing over different senses – synaesthesia. We wondered if he lived in the 21st century and worked with a game console instead of a canvas, what might he have created?"**
>
> Tetsuya Mizuguchi, creator of *Rez*

recreate the realities of driving with sit-on cabinets. By the time he began work on *Sega Rally 2*, Mizuguchi was disillusioned with the medium, feeling little interest in the prevailing creative curve towards realism.

In 1997 a designer at Sega came to Mizuguchi with an animation he had created of a long-legged woman fighting robots in a space station. In this demo, Mizuguchi perceived a type of video game he wanted to make, one that combined music, drama, and a story to create a holistic experience that stimulates all of the senses. The resulting rhythm game, *Space Channel 5*, offered the designer a chance to break free from the constraints of realism, and set him on a path to abstract game making, one whose next stop was *Rez*.

Below: Completing all five of *Rez*'s levels unlocks alternative modes, colour schemes and secret areas.

SEGA video game images - under licence by SEGA Corporation

Above: *Rez* was named after a non-album track by the band Underworld. The track was originally released in 1993 in the UK, a club anthem that influenced Mizuguchi.

For a game with such a futuristic, science fiction exterior, its creative team at United Game Artists began work in a curiously low-fi manner, taking a trip to Kenya to watch tribal musicians sing and improvise over simple beats established by handclaps. This influence can be seen right at the start of the final game, where each explosion triggers a lone, computerized handclap effect, a robotic rhythm from which the music grows and develops. This world music starting point was then combined with Mizuguchi's love of rave culture, especially the way in which sound, lighting and colours synchronize to overwhelm the senses. Art director Katsumi Yokota took these principles and worked them into abstract, wireframe landscapes that heave and shape-shift with the music's ebb and flow.

As with Mizuguchi's earliest arcade games, *Rez* exhibits a sense of journey, from the musical progression through Adam Freeland, Keiichi Sugiyama and Ken Ishii to the evolution of the player character from amoebic blob to pulsing sphere of energy. The result is a game of hypnotic progression and regression, an unprecedented feat of abstract imagination and a creative achievement that transcends its commercial performance (just 200,000 copies sold in Japan, and a fraction of that elsewhere in the world) just as it transcends its basic, shooting gallery heart.

THE KNOWLEDGE
2011's motion-controlled *Child of Eden*, a pseudo-sequel to *Rez*, cast the player as conductor to a blip orchestra, each sweep of the hand directing the music even as the screen explodes with light and colour.

Year: 2001
Developer: Nintendo EAD
Publisher: Nintendo
Original format: Nintendo 64/
  GameCube
Play today: Nintendo Wii (backward
  compatibility)

"While I was working at Nintendo there would be many, many late nights when I would come home after my children had gone to bed. So, I imagined a game we could do together, even if we weren't there at the same time."

Katsuya Eguchi, creator of
Animal Crossing

Below: *Animal Crossing* runs to the GameCube's internal clock and calendar, including popular seasons and holidays in the game.

ANIMAL CROSSING

A game that operates in real time and is never 'won', where neglected relationships disintegrate, neighbours leave, and mortgages have to be paid.

With its unrelenting charm – the high-pitched twittering language of its squat, animal inhabitants; the wholesomeness of catching fish and bugs, delivering presents and messages; of digging for fossils and weeding in order to keep the town presentable – it's easy to accuse *Animal Crossing* of being childishly mundane. But while this unhurried game appears to be a simple social simulator, a doll's house sprung to life, there is a darker undercurrent to the commentary.

Tom Nook, the monopolistic businessman with whom you first interact when you disembark the in-bound train to your new life within your destination town (unique to each player), has the gentle yet firm tone of a mafia Godfather. He houses you in a rundown abode and offers the employment you require to begin to pay off its mortgage. But it's more than a magnanimous gesture, as his shop in which you work stocks desirable furnishings with which to decorate your apartment, and, when the house is paid for, Nook is only too pleased to extend the property, drawing you back into the cycle of consumerism that swirls beneath this pastoral village.

It's a wry commentary on 21st-century first-world living, perhaps, but it doesn't sully *Animal Crossing*'s beguiling atmosphere. As wage slave treadmills go, the one to be found within this game has a lazy, out-of-town sense of straightforwardness, far diminished from the hyperactive urgency that fires our own urban realities. It's a tone that derives, in part, from the impetus behind its creation, a desire to escape the rat race of modern video game development, a desire to reconnect.

Katsuya Eguchi joined Nintendo in 1986, working as a designer on *Super Mario Bros. 3* before assuming a director role on *Star Fox* in 1993 and becoming an increasingly key member of Nintendo's trailblazing EAD division. As Eguchi was subsumed by work at Nintendo, working on *Wave Race 64* and as a lead designer for *Yoshi's Story*, so his home life began to suffer as late nights saw him arriving home after his children had already gone to bed.

It was in the midst of the frustration of work/life balance that Eguchi began to think of ways in which he could better connect with his children, to find out what they were up to each day and to somehow enjoy a shared experience – even when he had to work late and wasn't physically present.

Dobutsu no Mori (*Animal Forest*) was a result of this thinking, a game in which multiple players could inhabit a town alongside a set of characterful animals, posting each other messages in virtual letters and on message boards to connect asynchronously.

Released for the Nintendo 64's ill-fated 64DD add-on in April 2001, a GameCube version followed in December, the name changed to *Animal Crossing*, a port that made use of the system's internal clock to dictate the passage of time in the game, giving the sense of a virtual existence that moves in step with our own.

The game's ponderous pace was almost entirely unique at the time. Here was a Nintendo game in which there was no

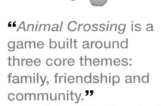

"*Animal Crossing* is a game built around three core themes: family, friendship and community."

Katsuya Eguchi, creator of *Animal Crossing*

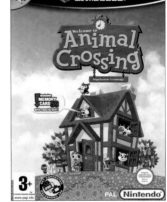

princess to rescue, no time limit to beat, no puzzle to solve or set goal to chase. Rather, it was a game that prized social interaction with its inhabitants; your set of townsfolk randomly selected by the game from a few stock personality types.

Despite this randomness, each character's appearance, set of stock phrases, the position of their house in the town and their taste in clothes and decorations, somehow meld together to create a cat's cradle of relationships, creating local heroes and villains painted in the ordinary tone of village living.

Much of the compulsion to return to the town daily lies in the gentle simulation of real world events: the first snowfall, the annual arrival of the cherry blossom between April 5 and April 7, the

Christmas reindeer, and the New Year fireworks. These in-game highlights are matched by the routine wonder of striking up a virtual friendship, or catching a rare bug to add to your collection. Devoid of a win state, *Animal Crossing* demonstrated that a game that cannot be 'beaten' can still manage to captivate and communicate a deep sense of accomplishment.

Its virtual relationships may often be fuelled by empty pleasantries – the fickle townsfolk likely to shower you with presents one minute and up and emigrate the next – but this only serves to make the moments of true connection all the richer.

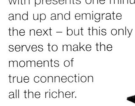

[105]

Year: **2002**
Developer: **Squaresoft**
Publisher: **Squaresoft**
Original format: **PlayStation 2**
Play today: **PlayStation 2**

"I wanted to make a game that gives space for your imagination. That's why I don't like revealing everything and saying: 'This is the answer.' Just like when I was a kid, I want to make something that can allow people to let loose their imagination."

Tetsuya Nomura, director of
Kingdom Hearts

KINGDOM HEARTS

Inspired by a meeting in a lift, *Kingdom Hearts* the game married the Disney and Square-Enix empires in a charming, if uneven, story.

It seemed, at the time, an unlikely marriage. Square-Enix, a purveyor of grand, sometimes overblown role-playing games featuring spiky-haired protagonists and philosophical affectation appeared to have little in common with America's venerable animation company. But it soon proved to be a union of crowd-pleasing foresight, merging Disney's invaluable cast of princes, princesses and talkative animals with characters and worlds plucked from Square-Enix's RPG catalogue. In creative approach too, the Japanese and American companies had much in common, each having attained long-term success in crafting modern fairy tales filled with vibrant, marketable characters for younger audiences.

Yet, for a series filled with such auspicious characters, *Kingdom Hearts'* beginnings were decidedly inauspicious. Producer Shinji Hashimoto was caught with a Disney executive in an elevator (the two companies shared offices in the Pfizer building in Tokyo at the time), striking up a conversation that would lead to work starting on the creative coalition in February 2000.

Kingdom Hearts was the directorial debut of Tetsuya Nomura, Squaresoft's most valued character artist and the designer of many of the company's most recognizable characters such as *Final Fantasy VII*'s Cloud and Sephiroth. Nomura oversaw a team of

Below: **Protagonist Sora is joined by Donald Duck, Goofy and others in a battle against nefarious evil forces.**

Above: *Kingdom Hearts* features well-known actors for both the Japanese and English versions including Haley Joel Osment as the voice of Sora.

100 Squaresoft staff, crafting an action RPG with a simple story designed to appeal to Disney and *Final Fantasy* fans alike. But when company president Hironobu Sakaguchi saw how the project was progressing, he pushed Nomura to develop the storyline further, arguing that it was *Final Fantasy* fans more than Disney fans who would drive sales, and therefore the game should primarily appeal to this audience.

The result is a game that deals with curiously un-Disney-like themes of betrayal, loss and death, a sombre tone that is offset by an upbeat parade of Disney and *Final Fantasy* cameos. But if it was the Disney faces that sold the game to audiences, it was Squaresoft's flair for beguiling RPG systems that maintained interest and, after the debut titles sold just shy of six million copies, the franchise ballooned to take in numerous sequels, spin-offs and, of course, a whole new world of merchandise.

FINAL FANTASY XI

The 11th game in the *Final Fantasy* series risked alienating series fans by moving from a solitary adventure to an online multiplayer game played over the internet.

Year: 2002
Developer: Square-Enix
Publisher: Square-Enix
Original format: PlayStation 2
Play today: Xbox 360/PC

While online role-playing games continued to ascend in popularity and profitability in the West, Japanese uptake had been sluggish. Sonic Team's pioneering *Phantasy Star Online* allowed Eastern and Western players to co-operate for the first time over the internet via its innovative inter-lingual communication technology. But for many Japanese, ruled by strict social codes of conduct in real life, the prospect of dealing with more transient virtual niceties kept them within the safe borders of the offline RPG.

Final Fantasy was the company's most valuable property. To risk alienating the fanbase with a game in such a fundamentally different style was risky, but to do so in a genre with which the developer had no previous experience seemed reckless. But the idea for the game came about during a particularly enterprising period in the company's history. Company director Hironobu Sakaguchi, eager to expand Square-Enix's business into new areas, had embarked upon a film venture with the animated feature *Final Fantasy: The Spirits Within*. Buoyed by the success of the PlayStation *Final Fantasy* games it seemed as though the company could do no wrong. It was while in Hawaii working on the motion picture that Sakaguchi saw the giant popularity of MMOs such as *EverQuest* in the West and decided to take the gamble, appointing Hiromichi Tanaka, who had joined Square in 1983 at the same time as Sakaguchi, to lead the project.

The result was the vibrant, exhilarating world of Vana'diel, filled with much of the creative furniture of the *Final Fantasy* series, yet maintaining a tone and direction uniquely its own. With its Japanese presentation and rich heritage, the game succeeded in selling the online RPG to Japan, securing its place as the dominant MMO in the region by 2006 with nearly 300,000 subscribers logging on a day. Now one of the longest-running Japanese MMOs, the *Final Fantasy XI* gambit paid off, proving Sakaguchi's instinct correct, even as Square Pictures' failure proved his other ideas flawed.

Below: *Final Fantasy XI* cost between two and three billion yen, a price tag that included the creation of the PlayOnline Network Service.

> **"*Final Fantasy XI* has many aspects of the first three games [in the series]. Our approach was to ask ourselves the question: what would we have made back then if we'd had the technology of today?"**
>
> Hiromichi Tanaka,
> producer of *Final Fantasy XI*

Year: **2002**
Developer: **BioWare**
Publisher: **Infogrames**
Original format: **PC**
Play today: **PC/Mac**

Below: *Star Wars: Knights of the Old Republic*, a role-playing game based in the Star Wars universe, used a modified version of the *Neverwinter Nights'* Aurora engine.

NEVERWINTER NIGHTS

The first computer role-playing game that was limited not by the narrative constraints of its story, but by the human imagination of its creator.

Video games owe one of their greatest debts to the pen-and-paper role-playing games that rose to prominence in the 1970s via *Dungeons and Dragons*. These Tolkien-esque adventures, driven by dice throws and brought to life by the collective imagination of their players, provided a great seam of creativity and inspiration from which game designers have long drawn.

Their influence has seeped into almost every style of video game, be it in their grandiose stories, or via their more functional mechanisms of progress, such as experience points and character levelling. But despite the genre's prominence in this digital medium, proponents of pen-and-paper RPGs had long argued that video game RPGs were a poor cousin to their inspiration. The argument went that no computer programme could replicate the flexible ingenuity of a human dungeon master (a sort of game director, in the table-top game), who is able to modify rules, characters and subplots on the fly in order to ensure his or her players remain interested and invested.

Neverwinter Nights' grand innovation was to replicate the structure of pen-and-paper RPGs far more faithfully than any video game before it, offering human dungeon masters complete control over the game. The advance (while the feature had been seen in previous titles such as *Vampire: The Masquerade – Redemption*, never before with such complexity and flexibility) came at the cost of the single-player

game, which scaled back in size from BioWare's previous title, *Baldur's Gate II*. *Neverwinter Nights* instead promoted its multiplayer heart, which through the dungeon master client allowed a creative player to define their own game world, story and campaign. For the first time a computer RPG was limited not by the narrative constraints of its story, but by the imagination of its creator.

To encourage different adventures, BioWare set up a series of persistent online servers, each of which could hold up to 96 players. Soon would-be dungeon masters were creating worlds based on separate genres and themes, from traditional *Dungeons and Dragons*, combat arenas, chat rooms and even whole servers dedicated to sexually-oriented roleplay. Attracting near-universal acclaim from critics, much of the technology developed for *Neverwinter Nights* was subsequently used in blockbuster single-player RPGs such as *Knights of the Old Republic*, *The Witcher* and *Dragon Age: Origins*. Nevertheless, its enduring legacy is in rediscovering many of the features lost in the RPG's epic journey from board to screen.

"There was a bug a long time ago where sometimes your character would turn into another object in the game, such as a door or chest. That was pretty funny, although incredibly hard to track down."

Senior Live Team programmer, Craig Welburn

TOM CLANCY'S SPLINTER CELL

Written and designed in conjunction with US author Tom Clancy, Sam Fisher's talent for sneaking espionage added variety and focus to *Metal Gear Solid*'s vision.

Year: 2002
Developer: Ubisoft Montreal
Publisher:Ubisoft
Original format: Xbox
Play today: Xbox 360, PC

Japan's *Metal Gear Solid* and America's *Thief* had made skulking in games fashionable. Throughout the early 2000s, a bevy of releases across various genres began introducing 'stealth' levels, imitating these now classic digital games of hide-and-seek in the hope of borrowing some of their raw intensity. But 'stealth' was primarily being used by developers as a seasoning, a loan game mechanic useful for introducing variety, not necessarily definition.

Ubisoft Montreal, however, had the ideal licence with which to make an entirely stealth-focused game. Having worked on titles such as *Rainbow Six* and *Ghost Recon*, games based on the works of military-themed fiction author Tom Clancy, the studio was well aware of the myriad ways in which the writer's brand of military storytelling suited the video game medium. Often set in the near future, allowing designers to fabricate exciting gadgetry yet still grounded in present realities, most Clancy novels centre around geopolitical conflict, sending their protagonists around the world to various exotic locations while clutching and depending upon the latest technology.

For *Splinter Cell* author Clancy and the game's producer, Mathieu Ferland, originated the character of Sam Fisher, a lone NSA operative whose talent was for stealth not

Above: The game's soundtrack was composed by British composer Michael Richard Plowman.

battle, with players able to creep through the shadows to the game's conclusion without making a single kill. With more emphasis on gadgetry than Kojima's *Metal Gear Solid*, *Splinter Cell* presents players with a virtual toolbox and allows them to pick their own route to accomplishing any given objective in the game. Adhesive-backed cameras can be attached to walls to provide information; snake cameras can be pushed under doors to spy while the night vision goggles give the game its characteristic green wash.

A technical marvel, *Tom Clancy's Splinter Cell* pushed the Xbox hardware further than ever, Ubisoft Montreal creating a soft-body physics programme to allow light to filter through curtains and sheets to billow in the wind, technical advancements imitated by many subsequent 3D action games. For a game overseen by an author, *Splinter Cell* succeeds in limiting the amount of narrative interruption more than *Metal Gear Solid*, allowing the player freedom to tell their story through the stacking choices made in their journey.

"*Splinter Cell* is more an action-adventure game than a shooter. Because the character needs to interact more often with the environment, it was more obvious to develop the game in a third-person view.**"**
Mathieu Ferland, producer of *Tom Clancy's Splinter Cell*

Below: While Fisher is usually equipped with a firearm, he carries limited ammunition. The emphasis is fully on stealth.

Year: 2003
Developer: Nippon Ichi
Publisher: Nippon Ichi Software/
Atlus USA, inc./Koei Limited
Original format: PlayStation 2
Play today: Sony PSP

"When I heard that they were going to make a version of *Disgaea* for America, I didn't think it was going to sell at all, because it's a game with a very Japanese feel and jokes I thought that only Japanese people would understand."

Souhei Niikawa, producer of
Disgaea: Hour of Darkness

DISGAEA: HOUR OF DARKNESS

Nippon Ichi's dark comedy took the character of *Advance Wars* and the depth of *Final Fantasy Tactics* before introducing unprecedented freedom to their rules.

The odds were stacked against *Disgaea*. It arrived without fanfare, the creation of an obscure Japanese developer, Nippon Ichi, a tiny game studio operating from the heart of the Gifu Prefecture in Japan, far away from the bright lights of Tokyo. Until *Disgaea*'s arrival the tactical (or 'simulation') RPG was deeply entrenched in tradition, the grid-based mechanics – where games play out like two generals moving toy soldiers across a tactical map in a battle for domination – solid and immovable, nobody willing to venture far from their strict guidelines.

Following 1997's *Final Fantasy Tactics*, a near-perfect expression of ten years of preceding tradition, almost no developer tried their hand at the genre. That *Disgaea* arrived without display demonstrates how quickly its reputation grew as an exciting, deep and complex game concerned not so much with the renovation of an aging tradition as with its bold reinvention.

Rather than trying to compete with the strait-laced storyline of its predecessors, *Disgaea* instead opts for an irreverent art style and storyline in the style of a television comedy show. Set in the esoteric Netherworld, the game draws back the curtain on the prissy but endearing anti-hero Laharl as he awakens from a two-year sleep in the belly of a hellish castle. The cast of supporting characters are memorable, the dialogue fresh and

Above: The game can be completed many times in order to discover its multiple endings. Each time the player's party – all characters, items, and abilities – is carried over.

irreverent, poking fun at stereotypes and playing with video game tropes and convention.

But the premise is only there to push players into the jewel of the experience: its strategic underbelly. *Disgaea* instead heaps flexibility onto the genre's fundamentals. You're left to create your own team, picking each member's class, name and equipment. Characters can take on protégés and even learn abilities from them if they fight side by side for long enough, fostering micro-alliances between your squad. In battle, units can be picked up, stacked and thrown across maps while enemies can be lobbed into one another to create more powerful hybrids and even captured and conscripted to your side.

You can enter esoteric world representations of your weapons and equipment, manually upgrading your swords and armour, the game offering a statistical pool in which to splash about in, creating a team that is the sum of 10,000 choices. After *Disgaea*, the tactical RPG would never be the same again.

WARIOWARE, INC.: MEGA MICROGAMES!

This rudely creative reduction of the medium's core mechanics to five-second microgames offered a pointed alternative to the fashionable video game epic.

Year: 2003
Developer: Nintendo R&D1
Publisher: Nintendo
Original format: Game Boy Advance
Play today: n/a

It is, in essence, a video game tour of the history of video games, a rudely creative reduction of the medium's core mechanics to first principle microgames, each one 5 seconds long and with a single word barked instruction. For players less wowed than wearied by gaming's grand narratives and expansive worlds, *WarioWare, Inc.* cleanses the palate with its irresistible minimalism, cutting away the indulgence of gaming in favour of brevity; a machine gun volley of microgame tasks requiring high speed comprehension skills and taut reactions.

But don't mistake brevity for a scarcity of ideas; this game is brimming with creativity. In part, the game's display of imagination is thanks to its unique development. *WarioWare*'s debut began as a secret project run by a team of programmers at Nintendo's R&D1, led by Goro Abe. Without seeking the permission of their superiors, the group began to design a set of quick-fire minigames, inspired by similar games that were offered as a bonus in the Nintendo 64 DD game, *Mario Artist: Polygon Studio*. The programmers believed this style of concentrated gameplay was strong and different enough to warrant further investigation

and so began to jot down ideas for 5-second microgames on yellow post-it notes, a single game per sheet of paper.

When the team had collected enough workable ideas, Abe approached Hirofumi Matsuoka, one-time game designer on Metroid, now a producer at Nintendo R&D1 who agreed to lead the project, and told the team to stick their post-it note microgame ideas to his desk. Word spread throughout Nintendo R&D1 and programmers and designers from other teams began adding their ideas on the desk. These were whittled down to those that Matsuoka believed could sit comfortably alongside one another in a game. Microgames that were considered lewd or too Japanese were discarded, while those whose objective could be immediately understood were put to the top of the pile.

A game of boisterous ingenuity emerged from this unique approach to design, one unafraid to parody Nintendo's own back catalogue (Mario becomes a 5-second game about jumping on stuff, while Zelda ducks into a cave to complete his micro-mission), or to throw obscure or abstract of tasks at its player. Each microgame is as unlikely as the last, involving tests of timing, dexterity or reaction. Following the game's release, minigame collections became ubiquitous, but none could top Nintendo's own exuberant debut, a game venerating the past while pointing to the future.

"When everyone was coming up with their own ideas, each of the programmers also started working on their own graphics for the game, which is why the style is very different with each minigame."

Goro Abe, programmer and designer on *WarioWare Inc.: Mega Microgames!*

Below: Each stage is a collection of themed 'microgames' programmed by one of Wario's friends.

Below: Many of the game's sound effects originated in the 2001 Game Boy Advance title *Wario Land 4*.

Year: 2003
Developer: CCP Games
Publisher: CCP Games
Original format: PC
  (Windows/Linux)
Play today: PC

"*EVE* will never be a mainstream game. We're complex, we're open ended and you can lose six months work in a second. But we believe this is what makes *EVE* so unique and we're trying to follow this vision and principles as well as we can."

Nathan Richardsson, former
senior producer of *EVE Online*

EVE ONLINE

This Icelandic-made online universe is a playpen for social creativity, allowing players to come together in peace or in aggression and to set their own goals.

The concept is straightforward: take the classic space trading/combat computer game *Elite* and make it a persistent online game in which the plotting and dealing occurs between real people. The reality is overwhelming in its complexity. This virtual galaxy is home to 250,000 players, spread between 7,500 star systems, all linked by warp points. The geography is only the first aspect of the game's awe-inspiring grandeur, in which dynamic, player-authored plotlines, vast conspiracies and intergalactic heists add drama and sparkle to the basic game.

In *EVE Online* player-created corporations vie for control of space; hierarchies of players emerging in what is one of medium's only true persistent and evolving worlds. As a paying subscriber you are free to take a lone wolf approach and maintain a low profile as you work to earn money with which to improve your ship or weapons. Alternatively, you can throw yourself into a Machiavellian world of intrigue, working in a group, amassing wealth, building hulking spacecraft and seeking to rule the galaxy.

Perhaps the most famous story to emerge from *EVE Online*'s fertile moon rock was when members of a mercenary group, the Guiding Hand Social Club, worked for 12 months to infiltrate a powerful corporation, taking on jobs

Above: *EVE Online*'s developer CCP was founded in June 1997 by Beck, Kristjánsson and Hardarson.

and ingratiating themselves with its staff at all levels. Then, in one orchestrated attack, the group seized its assets, ambushed its female CEO, blew up her ship and delivered her frozen corpse to the client that bought the assassination. Not only was this an act of astounding coordination, untouched by the game's developers, but it had real world value too: the virtual assets seized amounted to tens of thousands of US dollars.

Many other games inspire devotion, but arguably none offers a world that can truly accommodate the unpredictability of human interaction. While it is not the easiest game, *EVE*'s boundaries are so vast and freeform that sociologists and economists view the game as a microcosmic experiment revealing the same social forces that drive our own reality.

KNIGHTS OF THE OLD REPUBLIC

Set four millennia prior to the events of the original trilogy, *Knights of the Old Republic* nevertheless captured the *Star Wars* spirit better than any game before.

Year: 2003
Developer: BioWare
Publisher: LucasArts
Original format: Xbox
Play today: Xbox 360/PC/Mac

I t took a pen-and-paper role-playing game and a digital time machine to produce the first great *Star Wars* game. With a battle system entirely based on *Wizards of the Coast*'s classic tabletop RPG, Canadian developer BioWare was free to focus its full attention on recreating the character, world and essence of the licence. In setting the game four millennia prior to the events of George Lucas' movies, to a place where the galaxy was familiar enough to feel part of the canon and yet distant enough to afford the developer control and autonomy over the world, here was a *Star Wars* title to wipe away the memory of so many feeble movie tie-ins, as if to say: those were not the games you were looking for.

Star Wars keeper LucasArts and BioWare's marriage came following the latter's success with the *Baldur's Gate* RPGs, a series of fantasy adventures that held storytelling in equally high regard as loot-gathering and monster-battling. While previous *Star Wars* games had usually focused upon the action from the films, with X-wing and lightsabre battles, LucasArts decided to approach

a storyteller for their next title hoping that some of the films' broader themes of galactic ethics could be touched upon by a video game.

LucasArts gave BioWare the choice of setting the game during the time of Episode II, or 4,000 years prior to the movies, a period of fictional mythology barely covered in the *Star Wars* universe. BioWare chose the early setting for the freedom it would afford them. But by placing the player in the role of a young Jedi and allowing them to guide their character towards the light or dark side of the Force via a string of ethical dilemmas, the game retained the moral essence of the movies.

BioWare's skill is in providing nuance to the missions, presenting player choices rarely painted in black and white but instead shades of grey. With lightsabres and a thunderous soundtrack, *Knights of the Old Republic* enjoys all of the trappings of its licence. But it's in its deft use of morality and player freedom that the game feels like a bona fide part of the universe, rather than a flimsy tribute to a famous scene, as was the case with so many other *Star Wars* games.

"We wanted to create something that combined the strategic aspects of our *Baldur's Gate* series and *Neverwinter Nights* but which presented it through fast, cinematic 3D action. That required us to make something that hadn't really been done before."

Knights of the Old Republic
director Casey Hudson

Above: The player's dialogue options vary based on the gender and skills of the main character.

Year: 2003
Developer: Ubisoft Montreal
Publisher: Ubisoft
Original format: Xbox/PlayStation 2/
GameCube
Play today: PlayStation 3

"Sands of Time was one of those creative collaborations when everything meshes. The game was a career milestone for many members of the team, including me."
Jordan Mechner, creator of
Prince of Persia

PRINCE OF PERSIA: SANDS OF TIME

The first blockbuster reboot of a long dormant series, *Sands of Time* remains its finest, a game of rewriting the world's wrongs.

Thirty years in and the video game medium was ready to mimic Hollywood in revisiting their formative hits for contemporary make-overs. While sequels had come to define many of gaming's blockbuster series through the 1990s, *Prince of Persia: Sands of Time* was the first full-scale reimagining of a long-idle series. And few reboots have been executed with such finesse, *Sands of Time* not only capturing the tone and spirit of Jordan Mechner's 1989 2D classic, *Prince of Persia*, but also building upon its ideas in thoughtful, creative ways and popularizing a novel ideal: the ability to dynamically rewind time in the process.

In part the success was down to a combination of the correct ingredients. Ubisoft Montreal invited Mechner himself, now 36 years old, to work on the project. Initially hired as a consultant, Mechner soon found himself overseeing elements of the scriptwriting before, finally, joining the team full-time as a game designer on the project. The Ubisoft Montreal team, by contrast, was unusually youthful (the average age of the team was 22), pairing their naïve enthusiasm and raw talent with Mechner's assured experience and vision.

The product of the collaboration was one of the finest 3D action games of the early

Above: 2010 saw the release of a film loosely based on the game, directed by Mike Newell starring Jake Gyllenhaal, Gemma Arterton, Ben Kingsley, and Alfred Molina.

millennium. Framed as a story being recounted by the titular prince himself, the sands of time allow players to rewind their immediate mistakes, picking themselves off the floor when knocked down, or undoing a mistimed jump. More than a gimmick, the ability to undo missteps in the game is a crucial tool in the player's arsenal, and mixed with the refined platforming, puzzles and fighting, made for a hypnotic concoction.

Prince of Persia: Sands of Time was the game that propelled Ubisoft Montreal to the position of one of the world's leading studios, introducing the series to a new generation of players with over 14 million sales and kick-starting Mechner's career, which led to a professional screenwriting contract with Disney and Jerry Bruckheimer working on the *Prince of Persia* movie. But even more than the professional milestones, *Sands of Time* explored with unprecedented success a magic that only exists within the confines of a video game, the capacity to undo one's mistakes, to try again, right one's wrongs with a squeeze of the rewind button and thereby rewrite the story.

MANHUNT

Rockstar's darkest video game, *Manhunt* presents a bleak and relentless parade of screen violence, asking the player to face up to and question their actions.

Year: 2003
Developer: Rockstar North
Publisher: Rockstar Games
Original format: PlayStation 2
Play today: PC

Manhunt will explore the depths of human depravity in a vicious, sadistic tale of urban horror. Rockstar's announcement, made at the E3 gaming expo in 2003, laid out the game's broad aim, even if it revealed scant few details. Ask most developers why they make games and their answer will usually include the word 'fun'. But *Manhunt* is uninterested in such esoteric, feel-good notions, instead following a path towards a vicious kind of entertainment and voluntary discomfort, one sometimes found in other media, but almost never in video games.

Cast as death row convict James Earl Cash, roused from a mock lethal-injection procedure in the belly of a snuff movie set run by Lionel Starkweather, the player is in a game about dog-eat-dog survival. As you make your way through the Director's gruesome maze, leaping suddenly and brutally from the shadows to take down his bloodthirsty, mentally ill hunters, there is nowhere to retreat from the acts of sadism replicated on screen – no comic relief, no downtime in which to recuperate.

Each grisly takedown, from suffocating an enemy with a taut plastic bag to staving in a skull with a lead pipe, is rendered in cutaway scenes. So many games revel in the entertainment power of violence, but almost none force the player to face up to their acts of virtual (and victimless) crime. The game's encouragement of the very

worst type of virtual violence is found in its systems as well as its story, awarding star ratings at the end of each chapter based upon how many brutal executions were carried out to appease the virtual director. Mere face-to-face fighting is not rewarded.

Rockstar North borrows not only an aesthetic but also a tone from literature such as Richard Connell's *The Most Dangerous Game* and Stephen King's *The Running Man* and films such as *8MM*, and *Jacob's Ladder*. But there is no Hollywood moral justification to hide behind here: just the plain and repetitive act of virtual violence (something common to almost all games, from *Chess* to *Risk*) albeit rendered as never before.

The quality of execution intensifies the keenness of the brutality, little touches building the near-debilitating sense of peril and further tightening the atmosphere. From the CCTV cutaways to the use of the Xbox headset through which Starkweather goads and encourages, *Manhunt* hurls itself against creative boundaries as well as thematic ones. Nevertheless, the brutality ensured that Rockstar's darkest hour soon became the new millennium poster boy for video game violence, the outlandish style of the virtual killing making the game an obvious target for those distrustful of games. Perhaps for the first time it was a game worthy of the criticism as the relentless bleakness and dread of this world forces its player to consider their own relationship between entertainment and violence.

" *Manhunt* just made us all feel icky. It was all about the violence, and it was realistic violence. There was no way to rationalize it. We were crossing a line.**"**

Former Rockstar employee Jeff Williams explains how *Manhunt* caused controversy even within the company

Below: *Manhunt* used the console's microphone by allowing the player to use the sound of their own voice to distract in-game enemies.

Year: 2004
Developer: Namco/NOW Production
Publisher: Namco
Original format: PlayStation 2
Play today: PlayStation 2

KATAMARI DAMACY

Surreal, abstract and wildly eccentric, Keita Takahashi's *Katamari Damacy* is nevertheless set among the familiar detritus of contemporary living.

The PlayStation 2's most unconventional release, *Katamari Damacy* is an experience without precedent or imitator. Yet, it is also a game with a premise of almost childlike simplicity: roll an adhesive ball around the world. As you stick small objects to its surface, so its size increases and so you are able to collect larger objects. Repeat until your ball is large enough to become a star.

But to reduce the game to its raw components is to miss its absurdist wonder, the detail of the joyfulness that comes from tidying up the mess and detritus of humanity rolling up a sachet of soy sauce, a handful of drawing pins, a cat, a cell-phone, a salmon and a tree into a giant sticky ball. It's also a journey of rare completeness, designed to preclude a sequel (although its publisher would later demand one) as you move through the game's stages from the start point of a tiny Tokyo bedsit and work your way up in scale till you are rolling up the countries of the world for the magnificent endgame.

From its a capella soundtrack, to its diminutive hero, a green alien prince, this is a game of bold silliness, yet one that manages to offer one of gaming's most gripping pursuits, offering a world in which every object is a collectible waiting to be gathered up for nothing more than the sheer joy of collection.

The world's first stick 'em up started life in the idiosyncratic imagination of Kieta Takahashi, an ex-architecture student who wrote down the idea while studying at the Namco Digital Hollywood Game Laboratory, a

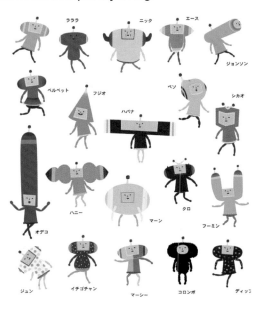

Above: The Prince's cousins are scattered through the world. When located they can be used as playable characters.

sponsored institute for game development education. Takahashi, one of the medium's true auteurs, wanted to create an experience that was new, easily understood, humorous and that could only be expressed through video game.

Together with a group of other students at the institute he created a demo that Namco pushed through into full production with a team of ten, and a relatively small sub-$1 million budget. Surreal yet wholly committed to its vision, *Katamari Damacy* remains one of gaming's freshest propositions, a cluster of ephemera that's difficult to put down both on screen and off.

"**I've always wanted to make things that would enable people to enjoy their lives. That's one reason I first looked to video games, to be able to make things that people could enjoy around the world.**"

Keita Takahashi, creator of
Katamari Damacy

Right: Each level features a hidden royal present that contains an object that the Prince can wear.

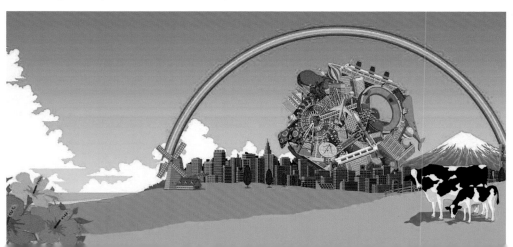

HALF-LIFE 2

Half-Life 2's gravity gun, a tool that allows players to overcome puzzle and foes using physics rather than bullets, fired the first person shooter into new territory.

Every video game needs a world to inhabit, be it the rectangle of blackness that frames *Space Invaders* or the looping ring world of *Halo*. But rare is the world that extends much beyond the confines of the game that runs through it. *Half-Life 2*, sequel to Valve Software's genre-evolving first person shooter, does just that, expanding beyond the space and time of Gordon Freeman's immediate journey to offer an environment far more robust that the polygons it's painted in.

The architecture in the suburbs of City 17, for example, predates the game's events by generations as concept designer Viktor Antonov stands old and new buildings shoulder to shoulder in the typical un-curated disarray of any long-established capital. Likewise, ambient events occur all around the player and, without a *Gears of War*-esque 'objects-of-interest' button to lock the camera on to them, each one is easy to miss, and therefore all the more powerful when caught in the eye of your camera. This is a world indifferent to your presence.

It was a game not without birth pains, and recurring endless delays pushed its release date back toward the brink of players' high expectations. Perhaps if *Half-Life 2* had emerged as a mere shooting game, those expectations would have been dashed on the rocks of familiarity. But in the introduction of the gravity gun, more a tool than a weapon that gave players the power to pluck objects from the world and launch them back into it, the wait appeared justified.

Above: Most of *Half-Life 2*'s puzzles are built around the game's detailed physics simulation.

Combined with the Havok physics engine, the inherent limitations of the first person shooter (in which almost every interaction with the world must be expressed in bullets) were wiped away. Now you could grasp a barrel from its standing place and fire it through a wooden door; solutions to the game's physical puzzles transcended its designers' imaginations by allowing the player to exert their own will into the world.

Plagued by pre-launch difficulties, including a potentially devastating pre-release leak of the game obtained by a young German hacker, neither the game's critical reception nor its commercial success were dampened, and *Half-Life 2* has continued to maintain its position at the pinnacle of video games' most over-subscribed genre.

Year: 2004
Developer: Valve Corporation
Publisher: Valve Corporation
Original format: PC (Windows)
Play today: PC/Mac/Xbox 360/
    PlayStation 3

"With *Half-Life* we were trying to build the company at the same time as we were building the game. It was not a whole lot of fun to try to do both of those things at the same time. With *Half-Life 2*, we have a much stronger team. People had a lot more confidence in terms of taking risks and that those risks would pay off."

Gabe Newell,
creator of *Half-Life 2*

Year: 2004
Developer: Blizzard Entertainment
Publisher: Blizzard Entertainment
Original format: PC/Mac
Play today: PC/Mac

Right: *World of Warcraft* takes place in Azeroth four years after the concluding events of the previous game in the series, *Warcraft III: The Frozen Throne*.

WORLD OF WARCRAFT

With a population to match that of a small country, Blizzard's *World of Warcraft* remains the most successful online role-playing game, years after its debut.

This is indisputably the game that took the online multiplayer RPG from a nerdish tributary of gaming to the rushing mainstream. In the years following *World of Warcraft*'s launch subscriber numbers have breezed past the 12 million mark, making Azeroth's a population to rival a small country from our own world. This is despite Blizzard requiring users of its forums to display their real names in an effort to reduce negative behaviour.

Was success owing to the chance to step fully into the world laid out by *Warcraft*'s previous strategy game incarnations? Doubtful, as for all their strengths, Blizzard's earlier titles in the franchise were never as popular. Perhaps it was the way in which the game opens primarily as a single-player experience, allowing newcomers to grow accustomed to the world and its rules before asking them to pair up with a stranger to embark on a quest? Possibly, but for every player for whom the game is at its best

Below: Development of *WOW* began in 1999.

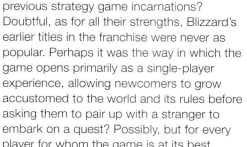

Above: The game uses elements of the graphics engine used in *Warcraft III*.

played as a solo venture, there are 20 more for whom the community provides the draw back into its virtual hills and fields.

The chance to role-play as blue elf or a buxom dwarf, to trace the arc of a story that reaches across this most vivid of worlds, or maybe the combat, with all of its foibles and arcane terminology, could be the appeal. The success may be of a more practical nature, found in the low PC requirements needed to get the game up and running, or the hybrid PC/Mac install disc that allows users of either operating system to quest together. The developer's fortuitous timing may have played a part, in launching a sprawling MMORPG just as broadband take-up became widespread across the world, or perhaps it has been Blizzard's expansions that inflate and also overhaul the world, adding new features and removing old ones, like a change of government that brings with it a brave new world to citizens willing to embrace change.

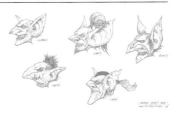

Above: The soundtrack was composed by Jason Hayes, Tracy W. Bush, Derek Duke and Glenn Stafford.

In truth, the alchemy behind *World of Warcraft*'s success cannot be reverse engineered. There are too many factors involved, many of them designed by human hand, many of them happy accidents of timing and market forces. It's difficult to talk about the game without referring to its statistical successes: that unimaginable large population, all of whom lay down $15 a month for a passport into the game, or the fact that by 2008, the game held 62 per cent of the global subscription-based MMO market.

But while few games changed the landscape of video games with such altering force in the first decade of the new millennium, to talk purely in terms of its external victories is to ignore its many internal triumphs. Even before the original game launched, *World of Warcraft* had undergone five years of development and rigorous play testing, time that allowed designers Rob Pardo, Jeff Kaplan and Tom Chilton the chance to see that players valued the power of choice more than anything else in their virtual worlds. A relaxed, welcoming approach allows players to pick and choose what elements they want to invest in in the world, focusing on the activities that excite each individual, while offering enough flexibility to ignore those areas that do not.

And since launch, the subsequent years of tweaking have only made Azeroth a better, more welcoming place. For all the copious quests and friction of combat, this is a kingdom of comfort, an amusement park of exhilarating attractions that allow players to pick and obsess over a particular area, or familiarize themselves with all of them.

It's not without its critics. Some say the game design fails to enrich, instead providing players with little more than a giant set of cogs to turn and grind while watching the numbers go up. Certainly for those Chinese sweatshop workers employed to develop and grow Westerners' avatars, taking the grind of advancement away from those rich or lazy enough to not want to do it, *World of Warcraft* is both a problem and a solution. Yet any game can inspire obsession, and while the reward for dedicating a lifetime to *Tetris* is that one becomes better at playing *Tetris*, the reward for playing *World of Warcraft* can be any one of a number of things. Whether it's worth the investment is a personal question. But it's one that at least 12 million people agree on.

Below: Blizzard requires the users of its forums to display their real names in an effort to reduce negative behaviour.

"You couldn't find the game at launch because we didn't think we'd sell that many up front. We knew that there would be growth and we'd add users over time, but I think it caught us off guard how quickly that growth happened. We just didn't have any idea just how big it would become."

Cory Stockton, lead content designer on *World of Warcraft*

THE KNOWLEDGE
The lyrics used for the song that backs *World of Warcraft*'s intro are in Latin. Composer Jason Hayes chose a collection of words he thought were thematically appropriate such as battle, struggle, loyalty and honour and pieced them together for the composition.

MUST PLAY:
Mario and Luigi:
Partners in Time
The Legend of Zelda:
Phantom Hourglass
The World Ends with You
Professor Layton and the
Curious Village
New Super Mario Bros.

[NDS]

NINTENDO DS

NINTENDO DS

After years of evolving the Game Boy in tiny increments, Nintendo's DS arrived as a dual-screened mutation, one few believed could compete with Sony's slick PSP.

For a while it appeared as though Japan's booming video game business was immune to the country's drawn-out economic bust. As Japan slumped into a deep recession, the industry flew an inverse trajectory, reaching a dizzying peak in 1997 thanks to the invigorating success of Sony's PlayStation. But soon enough the long winding lines of consumers that greeted each new high-profile game release in Akihabara also began to shrink as the nation's previously insatiable appetite for electronic entertainment waned. In 2002, America overtook Japan as the world's biggest consumer of video games and in 2003 Europe nudged into second place.

Of all the video game console manufacturers, Nintendo had the most to fear from this decline. Just as game sales were in dramatic regression in the company's key home territory, so Sony's PlayStation 2 had cast a long shadow over the GameCube, with Microsoft's newcomer selling 2 million more units of its Xbox than the one-time Japanese leader of the home console market. Moreover, for both Sony and Microsoft, video games were just one component of a sprawling empire. If their respective game divisions performed poorly for a time, other areas of the business could take up the slack. For Nintendo, as with Sega before it, there was no fallback. If the company couldn't turn its speeding decline around, it would have little choice but to follow Sega in turning its back on the console hardware business to focus exclusively on publishing.

It was into this tumultuous landscape that Nintendo's new president, Satoru Iwata stepped in 2002, replacing Hiroshi Yamauchi at the helm of a company headed for disaster. In November 2003, for the first time in the company's history, Nintendo announced a loss for the beginning half of the fiscal year. In the same breath, Iwata-san proclaimed that the company was developing a new system, neither a successor to the GameCube nor the Game Boy Advance, but a system that would "go back to basics" in the hope of attracting gamers of all ages, and players with no prior experience of games.

With the growing success of adult-focused games and online connectivity, the direction made little sense. While the desire to widen the boundaries of the games industry to encompass a broader mass market appeared logical, Iwata's statement that "you can't open up a new market of customers if you can't surprise them" seemed cavalier in Nintendo's immediate context.

A year later, when the Nintendo DS was unveiled, method still seemed to have been overtaken by madness. The silvery, rather somewhat bulky handheld system – decidedly not, as Nintendo was only too keen to emphasize, a successor to the GBA – opened like a book to reveal two screens, one of which was a touch screen that could be interacted with using a stylus. Despite the in-built microphone and wireless connectivity there seemed no way that this Game & Watch style throwback could be anything other than a side-project for the company. Sony dismissed the system as a gimmick, 'a knee-jerk reaction' to its futuristic, widescreen PSP handheld system, while many developers seemed equally sceptical and confused as to how to employ the system's idiosyncratic capabilities.

Within 12 months, Nintendo had not only proven its detractors wrong, but had turned around the company's fortunes. In the space of just one year the Nintendo DS sold 13 million units while the handheld accounted for 45 per cent of all software sold in Japan in 2005, enabling Nintendo to leapfrog Sony's control of the software market. As with the Game Boy, Nintendo began to iterate on the hardware, releasing the DS Lite and then the DSi in various incarnations, and by 2010 over 135 million units had been sold globally.

Most significantly, the Nintendo DS had proven Iwata's assertion that chasing innovation rather than technological superiority was the key to Nintendo's future, a simple ideological shift that would have a profound effect.

"The Nintendo DS will change the future of hand-held gaming."
Satoru Iwata, president of Nintendo

Below: Built-in PictoChat software allows users to communicate with other Nintendo DS users within local wireless range.

[PSP]

SONY PSP

Year: 2004
Manufacturer: Sony
Original Cost: ¥19,800

SONY PSP

Sony's debut handheld was the antithesis of Nintendo DS – presenting a sprawling high-resolution screen and a power comparable to that of its console cousins.

> **"This is the Walkman of the 21st century."**
>
> Ken Kutaragi, creator of the Sony PSP

Much of the PlayStation 2's ubiquitous success could be attributed, not to its games or graphics, but to the fact that the machine doubled as an inexpensive and stylish DVD player. In 2004 convergence was the new slogan in video game hardware manufacturing and marketing. Games? Games were no longer enough, so the story went. As such, Ken Kutaragi's focus when developing the PlayStation Portable was primarily on what the system could do when it wasn't playing video games.

It was this focus that drove the decision to use an optical media disc as the system's storage media, Sony devising the Universal Media Disc as a kind of mini-DVD on which both games and movies could be stored and viewed. To emphasize the cinematic ideology behind the system, the company placed a lavish 4.3 inch widescreen display at the centre of the handheld, one that, with 16,770,000 colours, appeared to have skipped several steps ahead on the evolutionary scale to any handheld games technology on the market.

When Sony revealed the handheld's design at E3 2004 and attendees had the chance to see the machine while running, the curious hardware innovations of Nintendo's rival DS seemed irrelevant. The PSP was a cinema in your palm.

The feverish excitement surrounding the machine's Japanese launch on December 12, 2004 seemed at odds with Japan's plunge into recession. Chinese importers employed the services of Akihabara's homeless to buy up units to sell back home for astonishing profit. 171,963 units were sold on launch day with nearly 500,000 units shifted by the New Year.

But the PSP's initial signs of success did not bear out in the long run. At the time few would have bet against Sony's decision to pack the most advanced technology into their first handheld in favour of Nintendo's decision to eschew power in favour of what were ostensibly seen as gimmicks. But in commercial terms Nintendo's courting of non-traditional game audiences paid off as the DS comfortably overtook the PSP in sales.

The final boot in the PSP's prospects (in commercial terms, at least) came on June 15, 2005 when hackers disassembled the PSP's firmware and released a hacked version for download on the internet. When installed the new software allowed PSP owners to run homebrew software and pirated games from the memory stick – with a clutch of emulators available for playing out-of-print games as well as titles currently on the market. The homebrew scene's gain was Sony's loss, as rampant piracy eroded game sales and disheartened developers abandoned the system en masse.

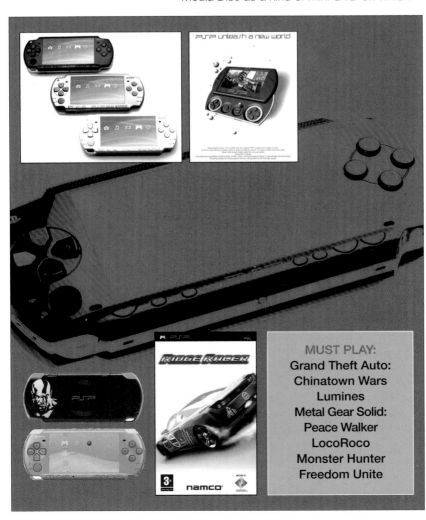

MUST PLAY:
Grand Theft Auto:
Chinatown Wars
Lumines
Metal Gear Solid:
Peace Walker
LocoRoco
Monster Hunter
Freedom Unite

RESIDENT EVIL 4

After three costly false starts, Capcom's Shinji Mikami inspired his team to redefine not only the *Resident Evil* series, but also action video game.

A far cry from the lumbering, predictable zombies that infested Raccoon City since the series' inception, *Resident Evil 4*'s red-eye glaring, pitchfork-wielding Los Ganados gave weight to its marketing slogan: 'A new kind of evil.' In these European woods, rural tranquility has given way to wild-eyed barbarism, mantraps hidden under ferns, and ramshackle huts home to staring peasants, hungry to burn heretics in the town square.

While the earlier *Resident Evil* titles had engendered fear through locked-off camera angles, tight corridors and limited resources, the fourth game induces panic through a mob of unpredictability, all sporadic bursts of speed and lunging sidestep dodges. For once Leon S. Kennedy must fully assume his role of police officer, learning how to control crowds, avoiding being flanked while preserving enough ammunition to cut a path through to safety as he heads into the cold stone castle of Ramon Salazar.

Resident Evil 4's bold overhaul was not limited to its series, its innovations changing the face of the action game forever. The over-the-shoulder viewpoint was subsequently adopted by games as diverse as *Gears of War* and *Batman: Arkham Asylum*, while its precision aim system, that snaps the camera inward to focus on targets, is now an industry standard. Yet its path to release was a tortuous one, the first prototype morphing into *Devil May Cry*, with three subsequent iterations being discarded by Capcom, one of them while 40 percent complete.

In the end it was series originator Shinji Mikami who wrestled the game back on track, somehow inspiring his beleaguered, disillusioned team to turn in some of Capcom's best work. Perhaps it was the huge amount of pressure the publisher applied to Mikami to make the game a success, threatening the series with cancellation if it didn't perform well commercially. Or maybe it was just personal weariness over a series that had fallen into a pattern of miniscule, largely uninspiring, formulaic tweaks. Whatever the reason, Mikami's bold reinvention of the series swept away any sense of series ennui, reinvigorating the survival horror genre while inspiring a new generation of action-adventure titles to follow its lead into uncharted territory.

Year: **2005**
Developer: **Production Studio 4**
Publisher: **Capcom**
Original format: **Nintendo GameCube**
Play today: **Nintendo Wii**

> **"We wanted to change the image of the franchise. [Our first attempts at the game] would probably be totally acceptable with other software companies. But it was not acceptable for R&D4 at Capcom."**
> Hiroyuki Kobayashi, producer of *Resident Evil 4*

Below: The protagonist faces red-eyed zombies and unpredictable mobs.

Right: The game's English voice actors recorded their parts in four sessions over four months.

[119]

Year: 2005
Developer: SCE Studios Santa Monica
Publisher: Entertainment
Original format: PlayStation 2
Play today: PlayStation 2

"I took one of the artists aside. I told him I wanted to see what would happen if Terry Gilliam made a pop-up book for kids: over-the-top, bombastic, operatic."

David Jaffe, creator of
God of War

Below: *God of War*'s creator David Jaffe drew inspiration from Capcom's *Onimusha*, telling his team: "Let's do that with Greek Mythology."

GOD OF WAR

Like the Greek myths that inspired the game, *God of War* is in no way delicate or refined.

The story of the first 30 years of video games is largely one of the scramble for spectacle, as game makers perfected the basics early on, then sought to express them in ever more exuberant ways on screen. In choosing the vivid and visceral world of Greek mythology for its theme, Sony's Santa Monica studios enjoyed a leg up in this regard, ancient Homeric visions of gods and monsters offering inexhaustible inspiration for its set pieces.

Kratos, the muscular Spartan protagonist, his heart full of vengeance, his head full of gruff expletives, hacks and slashes through a brutal storyline. Prizing spectacular presentation over interactive fussiness or complexity, *God of War* shrouds its simple systems in screen-filling Homeric visions that excite the heart with exhilarating fear, in much the same way they did for the Grecians three thousand years ago.

There's a cinematic tone to the game's presentation that has its roots in creator David Jaffe's childhood dreams of becoming a movie director. Whereas many game makers shy away from comparisons to film directors, preferring to celebrate the medium's distinctiveness, Jaffe embraced the similarities between game and film, and his intention with

God of War was to elicit the same feelings in a player as a viewer experience watching an action-adventure movie.

In 2002, after his lucrative success with the car-battling games, *Twisted Metal*, Jaffe was given carte blanche by Sony to make whatever game he wanted. Inspired by the *Onimusha* series, Capcom's liberal video game take on Japanese history, Jaffe settled on the idea of reworking the Greek myths in a similar manner. The work of American classicist Edith Hamilton provided a mine of inspiration, Jaffe marking "great mechanic" in the margins of one of her book's pages.

Jaffe kept *God of War*'s core mechanics superficial, so as not to overpower or distract from the visual aspect to the experience. Perhaps for that reason, the game is criticized for its underlying straightforwardness, critics arguing it's a game whose success is largely dependent on its tall budget and slick animation more than its inherent game-ness. Perhaps, but the video game is as much a visual medium as it is an interactive one. That some creations emphasize one aspect over the other is inevitable, and few come painted in such arresting colour and shape as *God of War*.

Below: Jaffe hoped players would feel like he'd felt as a child watching the 1981 film *Raiders of the Lost Ark*.

LEGO STAR WARS: THE VIDEO GAME

LEGO Star Wars may not afford players the sort of creative freedom that defines the plastic toy, but there's a no less compelling force at work in this hybrid.

Year: 2005
Developer: Traveller's Tales
Publisher: LucasArts
Original format: PlayStation 2
Play today: Xbox 360, PlayStation 3

The idea was straightforward but nevertheless unexpected: combine the abstract, creative logic of Denmark's most enduring toy bricks with the imaginative storylines and characters of George Lucas' beloved science fiction films. And yet, how easy it would have been to get wrong. The game succeeds because of a delicate balance of irreverence and respect toward the source material, reducing the films' narrative down to a series of un-voiced pantomime scenes, while swapping out the fire and fury of its climactic battles with a shower of plastic bricks and coins.

For British developer Traveller's Tales, the bricks came first. The team was working closely with the LEGO Company, attempting to find a way to turn the abstract joy of building with plastic into a video game. Inspiration came from a new range of LEGO toys, introduced in 1999, pairing the Danish toymaker's plastic with the first of the *Star Wars* prequels, *The Phantom Menace*. The team identified those elements to the *Star Wars* mythology that could work well as as game systems –

the esoteric Force, a magic that could be used to construct objects from piles of bricks, and the lightsabres and blasters, that could be used to do battle – and clicked them together with a logic that reflects that of its building block components. The developer opted for static backgrounds, to allow for faithful recreations of the films' locations, but filled each with LEGO block furniture, that could be broken apart and put back together again.

Much of the initial appeal comes from squeezing a button as the loose collection of bricks at your character's feet assembles itself in a magical micro-hurricane into a bridge or a ladder or whatever object is needed to facilitate minifigure Luke Skywalker's pre-laid story. Critics argue that there is no capacity for the personalization and invention that defines the plastic toy. Nevertheless, warm, stylish and occasionally frustrating, this is a secret-rich world that plunders the best of its two sources, inspiring a new generation to fall for each, and establishing a brickwork framework since used to rebuild colossi of contemporary family cinema franchises from *Harry Potter* to *The Lord of the Rings*.

"We were working to see if we could fulfill our belief as game players, that a lot of qualities in our favourite games had something in common with our feelings for LEGO."

Jonathan Smith, creator
of *LEGO Star Wars*

Left: Several levels were cut from the final game, such as Anakin's Flight and Bounty Hunter Pursuit.

[121]

NINTENDOGS

Year: 2005
Developer: Nintendo EAD
Publisher: Nintendo
Original format: Nintendo DS
Play today: Nintendo DS

Above: Puppies can compete in three contests: the Disc Competition, the Agility Trial, and the Obedience Trial.

NINTENDOGS

Nintendo's pet care game demonstrated the Nintendo DS' hardware capabilities as well as the company's shift in focus toward the mainstream.

No game better exemplifies Nintendo's shift in focus following the launch of the Nintendo DS. The simple addition of the letters 'g' and 's' to the company name indicate a shift from keen games to a gentler breed of play for play's sake. In this Tamagotchi-evolved, there are no levels, achievements or scores, the only goal to choose a pet and care for it.

Nintendogs began as a tech demo for the GameCube system designed by Shigeru Miyamoto, who was inspired to create a pet care game after his family bought a puppy. Nintendo EAD's Hideki Konno, director of *Super Mario Kart* and *Luigi*'s *Mansion*, returned to the prototype when searching for a suitable project to demonstrate the Nintendo DS hardware's new features. The touchscreen, he reasoned, would allow players to stroke, wash and play with their pet, while the microphone meant the virtual dog could learn the sound of its name. Finally, the wireless networking capabilities would allow two players (owners?) to bring their puppies together, a creative use of the hardware that fitted with Nintendo's mainstream focus and demonstrated exactly what the system could be in the right hands.

Originally titled *Puppy Times*, Nintendo president Satoru Iwata suggested the company release 15 versions of the game, one for each breed of dog, to allow players to feel as though they were picking out a pet from a kennel. Eventually, just three versions were sold, each with six breeds of dog, but the sense of ownership and affinity with the animal no less diminished.

[122]

BRAIN TRAINING

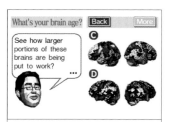

Year: 2005
Developer: Nintendo Software Development D
Publisher: Nintendo
Original format: Nintendo DS
Play today: Nintendo DS

BRAIN TRAINING

In converting Dr Kawashima's best-selling mental-exercise book into a video game Nintendo sought to convince that video games' effects were positive.

It's difficult to imagine any other console manufacturer than Nintendo focusing on the decidedly school homework-esque pursuits of mathematics, reading and memory tests when searching for a hit to sell its latest hardware. Yet in Dr Kawashima's bespectacled, disembodied head, and his ten-minutes-a-day worth of puzzles, Nintendo found a new mascot, and perhaps more importantly, a new audience.

It was no accident. One of Nintendo's more senior directors complained to Satoru Iwata that his peers did not play video games and encouraged the president to investigate a title that might appeal to over-50s. At the time, Professor Ryuta Kawashima of Tohoku University book *Train Your Brain* was a bestseller in Japan. Iwata, who also used the book, organized an hour's meeting with the author on the day of the Nintendo DS launch. The meeting turned into a three hour-long creative session in which both men discussed how they could turn the book, which provides daily mental exercises to keep the brain young, into software.

Iwata left the meeting and assigned nine developers to the project, giving them just 90 days in which to develop the game. Once complete, Iwata play-tested with staff throughout the company, everyone from those who worked in sales to cleaning, trying to gauge interest. Just 70,000 pre-orders were placed with retailers. But by 2009 the game and its sequel had sold nearly 18 million copies worldwide, introducing video games to the so-called 'grey' gamer.

KILLER7

Undertaker-turned-game designer Goichi Suda's psychological thriller places its player in the mind of a schizophrenic in a caustic, unrepeatable original.

The first worldwide release from Goichi Suda: *Killer7*, is a game about psychosis. Far from a detached study of mental disorder, this is a game that invites its player into the landscape of a broken-down mind, presenting a disorientating dementia that seeps from the multiple personalities of the lead character into the very fabric of the experience.

A schizophrenic game, *Killer7* darts from on-rails shooter to puzzle game, to light-gun shooting gallery to film noir mystery, never happier than when upsetting expectations, except perhaps when upsetting its player with tutorials delivered by severed horse heads and silhouetted gimps.

Harman Smith, the role (or rather roles) into which you step is host to seven personalities, each one changing his appearance and offering a different set of abilities with which to unravel the mystery. The eclectic team is pushed on to a narrative stage of geopolitical wrangling and suicide bombing, soundtracked by Trent Reznor-esque nightmares and non-sequitur profanity.

For creator Suda (or Suda51) the game offered the chance to explore new places in video games. The designer was drawn to the absurd and disturbing, writing a controversial ending to his second game, *Super Fire Pro Wrestling Special*, in which a world champion wrestler commits suicide. But in *Killer7*, the designer settled upon a more attractive kind of madness, one that adheres to its own off-kilter rules, a caustic original without any precedent or imitator.

Year: **2005**
Developer: **Grasshopper Manufacture**
Publisher: **Capcom**
Original format: **GameCube**
Play today: **PlayStation 2**

Left: *Killer7*'s cult appeal led to remakes of Suda51's older works and the creation of *No More Heroes*.

CIVILIZATION IV

Civilization IV allows players to dictate history's sweep (or at least attempt to) in a game in which success is measured in time and marked in geography.

In 1991's *Civilization* players assume the role of an ancient ruler and guide their primitive people through the centuries, finding victory either through absolute domination of rival rulers or the feat of landing a spaceship on Alpha Centuri. It was, arguably, a near-perfect game, exploring its outrageous scope with a deft touch that ensured the experience never got bogged down in details.

'A game is a series of interesting decisions,' creator Sid Meier once said, and rarely has that sequence of decisions been as consequential as in *Civilization*, each choice leading to a shift in power and dominion, rewriting events in a unique, personal way that makes the world and its tapestry of history your playthings.

Over the years, however, the series' influence and support waned, lacklustre sequels failing to add anything meaningful to the original's template, while rival strategy games came along and inspired an exodus from its world. And then, in 2005, *Civilization* was born again. In part it was the introduction of religion to the game mechanics, a topic previously seen as too offensive and esoteric to include, yet here elegantly introduced into the game systems as different faiths spread across the world and shifted the balance of power in subtle ways. The multiplayer reignited an asynchronous pursuit that could last hours to months, with a stripping out of the drudgery that had infected the series, resulting in a more enjoyable journey of empire building. The series was restored to its former glory and its players were granted the chance of future glory.

Year: **2005**
Developer: **Firaxis Games**
Publisher: **2K Games/Aspyr**
Original format: **PC**
Play today: **PC, Mac**

Above: 'Baba Yetu' was the first video game theme song nominated for a Grammy Award.

[125]

GUITAR HERO

Year: 2005
Developer: Harmonix
Publisher: RedOctane, MTV Games
Original format: PlayStation 2
Play today: PlayStation 2

"No one had any notions about it being a massive success; we all just thought it would be fun to do."

Rob Kay, game designer on *Guitar Hero*

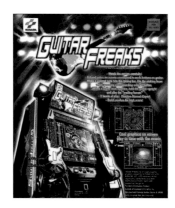

Above: The popular game *Guitar Freaks* was the forerunner and inspiration for *Guitar Hero*.

GUITAR HERO

Games have always enabled players to assume on-screen roles but *Guitar Hero*, with its plastic guitar peripheral, moved the make-believe to our side of the screen.

Since *PaRappa the Rapper* first turned rhythm-making into a game of Simon Says, music and video games had been engaged in an increasingly close dance. *Guitar Hero* wasn't the first video game to ask its player to strap on a plastic guitar and strum along with a rock soundtrack, Konami's *Guitar Freaks* having got there six years earlier. But Harmonix's peripheral-based debut did to music games what Elvis did for rock 'n' roll, repackaging the soul of its originators into something palatable to everyone.

Guitar Hero has you reading primary-colour musical notation as it scrolls down a stave before holding down the corresponding button on the guitar and strumming in time with the music. Hit the note correctly and a riff plays out in perfect harmony with the backing track. Miss, and the awkward splang of off-key strings will embarrass the virtual band. The experience may only be tangentially related to the act of playing guitar (although the game's strict appraisal of rhythm gives it bona fide musical worth) but the rock pastiche aesthetic, all big hair and amps that go to eleven, allows you to role play a rock god. It's air guitar evolved.

Unusually, the concept came from the publisher, not the developer. RedOctane's Kai and Charles Huang had noticed the popularity of *Guitar Freaks* in Japan and

raised $1.75 million of venture capital with the aim of designing their own guitar controllers to bring the game to the West. Meanwhile, Harmonix was busy creating its own music games. When the developer's president Alex Rigopulos approached Microsoft, vice-president of game publishing Ed Fries told him that no rhythm game would succeed without a peripheral. So when the Huangs later approached Harmonix to see if the company would be interested in developing a game to use its plastic guitar, Rigopulos jumped at the opportunity.

The music industry was initially sceptical of the idea, insisting that Harmonix use cover versions for the soundtrack. Their cynicism was short-lived as the game generated $45 million in the two months following its release, kick-starting a cultural zeitgeist and taking music games to the mainstream. Today, record companies soon campaigned to get their artists into Harmonix games, recognizing that video games have the power to kill the radio star.

Below: Later games in the series feature caricatures of celebrity musicians including Slash, Tom Morello, Jimi Hendrix and Kurt Cobain.

GEOMETRY WARS: RETRO EVOLVED

A tech demo created by a bored programmer, *Geometry Wars* would later define Xbox Live Arcade, reigniting a movement for new games in an old style.

Year: 2005
Developer: Bizarre Creations
Publisher: Microsoft Game Studios
Original format: Xbox 360
Play today: Xbox 360

It's a game whose simplicity of rules somehow leads to an overwhelming complexity of outcomes. The first analogue twin-stick shooter, *Geometry Wars: Retro Evolved* takes the raw principles of *Robotron* (one stick to direct movement, one stick to direct bullets) and pares the venerable arcade shooter back even further. In this locked-off area of space there is no one else to save bar yourself, no need to scan the screen before every level.

Indeed, in *Geometry Wars* there are no levels. Just an interminable cycle of waves of neon-block enemies, colour-coded to indicate their behaviour (be it meandering around your ship or streaking from corner to corner or any of a number of other movements). Likewise, there's no set level structure, each play-through gently different from the one before in terms of the sequence of ships that appear on screen. And yet, from this gonzo approach to game design, a rare kind of procedural complexity blossoms, one that rewards players with one of the most concentrated buzzes in video games.

Geometry Wars was an unplanned birth. The game started life as code used to test the analogue sticks on the original Xbox, programmed by Bizarre Creations' Stephen Cakebread while he worked on *Project*

Below: Chris Chudley from Audioantics, a game audio production company, composed the soundtrack.

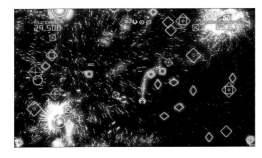

Above: A sequel, *Geometry Wars: Retro Evolved 2*, was released for Xbox Live Arcade in July 2008.

Gotham Racing. Toward the end of the project there was a code lockdown as the racing game entered its testing period. Bored of playing through the racing game, Cakebread returned to his test code and began turning it into a rudimentary shoot 'em up. When he showed the game to his colleagues the team was so impressed it decided to include the game as a hidden bonus in *Project Gotham*.

Two years later Microsoft approached Bizarre Creations to see if they'd be interested in updating the shooter for the publisher's soon to be released Xbox Live Arcade service. The team embellished the art and added leaderboards, and *Geometry Wars: Retro Evolved* launched alongside XBLA. In its delicate balance of simplicity and depth, the game defined Microsoft's contemporary arcade with pitch perfection, inspiring high-score rivalries among friends who hadn't been seen since the arcade's heyday.

> "We did talk about developing the visual style, but I was like, I have a week to put it into the game! And then it sort of set the style. We made the right choice because there was an interest in old school games – vector graphics, arcade machines, all that sort of stuff."
>
> Stephen Cakebread, creator of *Geometry Wars*

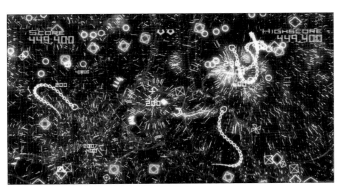

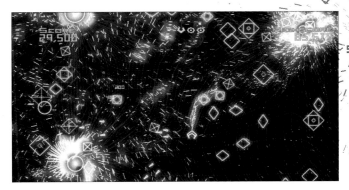

XBOX 360

Microsoft's second home console revealed the company's ambition to dominate not only the video game market, but also the family living room.

> **"This is a new era. This is a big jump – kinda like vinyl to CD to iPod."**
>
> J Allard, corporate vice president, design and development, Microsoft

Below: The Kinect add-on enables users to control and interact with the Xbox 360 by using gestures and spoken commands.

Microsoft's first foray into the video game hardware business had been costly but fruitful, the company overtaking Nintendo as the second most successful console manufacturer in the early part of the new millennium. But more valuable than the 24 million Xbox units sold around the world were the lessons learned in designing video game hardware and establishing Xbox Live, the company's innovative platform for online gaming.

In February 2003 J Allard, one of the key minds behind the original Xbox, began officially planning its successor, codenamed Xenon, holding an event for 400 developers in Bellevue, Washington to outline the publisher's plans for the system and recruit support. At the heart of the new Xbox ideology was the concept of connectivity, of delivering a powerful video game system that could seamlessly connect with a home PC network, streaming photos and playing music and movies for the wider family as well as delivering a leading-edge video game experience for the target demographic of 16- to 26-year-olds.

On 12 August 2003, semiconductor manufacturer ATI signed on to produce the graphic processing unit for the new console, while Microsoft commissioned a sculptor to design the casing for the machine in the hope that a simpler, more elegant design wouldn't date in the way that the bulky, cumbersome original Xbox had.

The success of a global launch in 2005 was spoiled by subsequent hardware issues, a damning 42 per cent hardware failure rate leading many to accuse Microsoft of shipping the console before it was adequately tested. But neither these issues (nor the estimated $1 billion cost of fixing broken consoles) could spike the console's long-term effects, which through the introduction of 'achievements', points-based trophies tied to a player's account to show their accomplishments in games, took high-score rivalries meta.

Even early support of the doomed HD-DVD high definition movie format via an add-on drive could not slow down the Xbox 360's inexorable sales in the US and Europe as Xbox Live's digital distribution capabilities delivered smaller, arcade-style titles and HD movies to the home across broadband connections.

In early 2011 Microsoft announced that it had sold over 50 million Xbox 360 units worldwide. This success was buoyed by the introduction of a Slimline model and a new, motion-sensing hardware add-on in Kinect.

MUST PLAY:
Red Dead
Redemption
Call of Duty: Modern
Warfare 2
BioShock
Rock Band 3
Super Street
Fighter IV

MONSTER HUNTER FREEDOM

The third entry to Capcom's hunter-gatherer sim became a Japanese phenomenon thanks to the PSP's capabilities that allowed people to team up and play in the street.

Year: 2005
Developer: Capcom
Publisher: Capcom
Original format: Sony PSP
Play today: Sony PSP

Despite a number of critical successes on Sony's PSP handheld, the system gave birth to few commercial winners. Capcom's *Monster Hunter* games are the exception to the rule, comfortably outselling any other series on the platform and reinvigorating multiplayer gaming across Japan. A gloomier take on *Pokémon*, *Monster Hunter* casts players in the role of a scavenger hunting fantastical beasts, before harvesting their hides and tusks in order to craft new weapons and armour.

While the game can be played as a solitary adventure, *Monster Hunter* comes into its own when played with others, the different 'classes' of hunter complementing one another to create powerful alliances that enable yet more fearsome beasts to be felled. *Monster Hunter Freedom* was the third game in a series that debuted on PlayStation 2. Despite the tortuous loading times, the marriage between game and handheld was a fortuitous one thanks to the PSP's ad hoc multiplayer capabilities that allow players to quest together wirelessly. The feature caused an explosion of

Below: *Monster Hunter* summer training camps were set up in Japan to train serious players.

popularity in Japan, players meeting in the street and in designated Monster Hunter cafés to play together, swapping items and exchanging the guild cards that keep track of the characters' stats.

The driving force behind the PSP game's success has been Yasunori Ichinose, the game's director who came to the series having worked on *Street Fighter III: 3rd Strike* and *Resident Evil Outbreak*, while much of the design work was handled by Ryozo Tsujimoto, son of Capcom CEO Kenzo Tsujimoto and brother to Capcom president Haru Tsujimoto, who became the series producer.

Despite the game's colossal success in its homeland, in contrast to *Pokémon*, the series has struggled to inspire devotion overseas. Arguably that's down to the unforgiving Japanese difficulty level, somewhat clunky interface and the way it demands dedication from any player who wants to scratch deeper than the surface. But most of all, it's a difference in culture. Where Japanese players will eagerly head out of their homes to group in public and play games together, in the West there is no such sense of public community, raising the barrier for entry to *Monster Hunter Freedom* too high for most.

"We consider deeply how we can ensure the game blends into players' daily routines without disrupting them."
Ryozo Tsujimoto, *Monster Hunter* series producer

[128]

OBLIVION

Year: 2006
Developer: Bethesda Game Studios
Publisher: 2K Games
Original format: Xbox 360
Play today: Xbox 360, PlayStation 3

THE ELDER SCROLLS IV: OBLIVION

A fully functioning fantasy world with hundreds of inhabitants going about their daily lives, *Oblivion* felt like the game that Tolkien himself might have written.

> **"Giving autonomy to a world can be a dangerous proposition. We've had to deal with everything from plot-essential characters being killed off to non-player characters breaking the economy by purchasing everything in a town."**
>
> Gavin Carter, game designer producer of *The Elder Scrolls IV: Oblivion*

I t's one of those moments of virtual epiphany, like the first time you ride across Hyrule on Epona under a shifting sky in *Zelda: Ocarina of Time*, or storm the beach with marines in *Halo*'s The Silent Cartographer. Stepping from the darkness of the city sewers into the hot brightness of verdant countryside in *Oblivion* is a moment happening outside reality that sticks in the mind with as much potency as any in real life. The orchestra swells and you blink in the rolling miles of countryside that lead to the feet of the hazy mountains, every step pregnant with possibility.

More rare still was the range of possibility on offer. Journey is as much story as narrative is story, and in *Oblivion* every metre travelled adds to your personal tapestry of experience, each conversation potentially leading to a new quest to undertake, each hillock potentially leading to a new cave network or curious settlement to uncover. There's a main quest to follow, of

course. But from the moment you step out from the sewers into the bright sunshine of Cyrodil, the only quest that really matters is your own.

Development began in 2002, immediately after its predecessor, *The Elder Scrolls III: Morrowind*, was published, with half of the *Elder Scrolls* team working on expansions for *Morrowind*, and half being assigned to begin preparatory work on *Oblivion*. The game was formally announced on 10 September 2004 as an Xbox 360 launch title, but slipped to early 2006 as the bug-testing process took longer than expected. Small surprise for a game of such scope and ambition, in which 1,500 non-player characters go about their daily lives within the game regardless of player input. For one of the first times in video games, Bethesda had succeeded in creating a world that did not revolve around its player, yet could still interface with the player's actions in beguiling ways. An adventure game in the true sense of the phrase.

Below and right: Players create a character such as a knight or mythical creature, then try to stop a cult opening the gates to the realm of Oblivion.

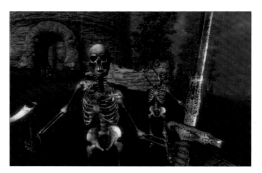

GEARS OF WAR

With its cast of oversized meathead marines, ludicrous guns and glistening gore, *Gears of War* typifies the adolescent power fantasy – albeit with rude style.

Year: 2006
Developer: Epic Games
Publisher: Microsoft Game Studios
Original format: Xbox 360
Play today: Xbox 360

Burly, gruff reformed ex-convicts that sweat testosterone and wield machine guns with chainsaws for their undercarriage: *Gears of War* is a characteristic, interactive blockbuster of the early 21st century. And yet there's more than mere dumb violence on offer in the planet Sera, as Epic Games' notable advertisement for its Unreal Engine technology borrows ingredients from action gaming's finest sources to create a distinguished concoction of its own.

The greatest debt is to Shinji Mikami's *Resident Evil 4*, the inspiration to which creator Cliff Bleszinki attributes *Gears of War*'s over-the-shoulder camera viewpoint, ornamental set design and lingering chainsaw kill cutscenes. Meanwhile *Kill Switch* and *Bionic Commando* inspired the game's point-to-point cover system, which introduces a layer of flank strategy that elevates the game above its peers.

Press the cover button when in range of a low wall or column and Marcus Fenix, leader of the COG group that has banded together to stem the invasion of the subterranean Locust Horde, will snap to the shelter. Press the button when a few metres out of range and he'll roll toward it, while holding the button down when out in the open. The camera will drop and shake as he sprints hunched over like a news

Below: The game focuses on Delta Squad as it fights to save the remaining human inhabitants of the planet Sera from a subterranean enemy known as the Locust Horde.

Above: The game cost $10 million to develop according to Epic's Mark Rein, with only 20 to 30 people involved at any time.

cameraman running after a fleeing war correspondent.

Epic Games was formed in in 1991 by Tim Sweeney in Rockville, Maryland under the name Potomac Computer Systems, making a name for itself releasing shareware games and publishing titles by smaller developers. In 1998 the company, now known as Epic MegaGames, released *Unreal*, a 3D first person shooter that soon expanded into a series. More successful than the game itself was the graphical engine that fired it, and the company began to sell Unreal licences to other developers to use in their games.

In *Gears of War*, Epic showed the potential of the engine with a parade of spectacular set pieces seasoned with a spattering of gore just as likely to inspire a giggle as a gag. Moreover, the developer proved it had the skill to shape the shooter genre from a design perspective, not merely a technological one.

"People didn't expect it to be as good or as much of a success as it is. I remember being on message boards and reading gamers claim there is no way the game looks as good as it did in those screenshots."

Cliff Bleszinki, creator of *Gears of War*

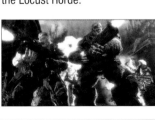

PlayStation®Move

MUST PLAY:
Little Big Planet
Demon's Souls
Flower
Uncharted 2
Valkyria Chronicles

PLAYSTATION®Network

Year: 2006
Manufacturer: Sony
Original Cost: ¥49,800

NOVEMBER 2006

[PS3]
PLAYSTATION 3

215

PLAYSTATION 3

Powerful, oversized and sleekly boisterous, the PlayStation 3's tortured development led to the resignation of Sony's video game architect, Ken Kutaragi.

The pressure on Ken Kutaragi to create a worthy successor to the PlayStation 2 was overwhelming. Yet the challenges from within Sony were just as tangible as those without the new system. The PlayStation's rise had coincided with a cultural shift in emphasis away from hardware engineering toward software engineering, one best exemplified by Apple's iPod music players.

Sony was a company built exclusively on hardware engineering, producing the gold standard in consumer gadgets such as televisions and tape players since the company's foundation. Its innovations focused on making products smaller and sleeker, with the software that fired them seemingly an afterthought. Despite the rise in PlayStation's importance to Sony the company had been slow to embrace the idea it needed to become a software developer as well as a hardware developer.

The issue had been seen in the PlayStation 2, which had been notoriously difficult to program. But the crack became a rift in Kutaragi's subsequent project, as the hardware team within Sony developed the PlayStation 3 in relative isolation, before handing a near-complete product to the software team. Sony's US president, Jack Tretton, would later identify this as the key issue for the PlayStation 3, a system hamstrung in its early days by the lack of collaboration between the hardware and software teams within Sony.

Kutaragi himself, a star executive within the company, didn't help the situation. The success of the PlayStation 2 had given the designer the position of renegade auteur within a Japanese company formed on teamwork and collaboration. When Howard Stringer became Sony's chief executive, Kutaragi hid the fact that development of the PlayStation 3 was over budget, a lack of communication that exacerbated issues.

Then, in September 2006, when Kutaragi announced to the press that Sony was halving shipments of the new PlayStation to the US and Japan, he blamed Sony's electronics group for failing to produce sufficient quantities of a critical component to meet demand. At a board meeting a few weeks later the designer told the assembled executives that he planned to reduce the price of the console by 20 per cent ahead of launch in order to make it more competitive, vastly increasing the amount of money the company lost on each console sold.

These tensions spilled into the PlayStation 3 launch as the system arrived in a squall of mixed messages. Kutaragi was keen to emphasize that the PS3 was a supercomputer for the living room, one that would eliminate the need for a PC in the home. Others stressed its capabilities as an affordable Blu-Ray player, Sony perhaps hoping to ape the PlayStation 2's success in shifting units as a cheap DVD player.

While Japanese consumers had ridiculed the original Xbox for being too bulky for Japan's modest living spaces, the PlayStation 3 was large, cumbersome and came with a noisy fan, a design shortcoming only redressed with the introduction of the Slim model three years later. Where once Sony had revolutionized, in the PlayStation 3 the company seemed to be playing catch-up, launching the PlayStation Network as a rival to Xbox Live, and aping the Microsoft system's multimedia capabilities. Almost immediately following the PS3's release Stringer reshuffled the Sony executive board, replacing the uncommunicative Kutaragi with Kaz Hirai as president of Sony Computer Entertainment.

Five months later, Kutaragi retired, taking up the role of honorary chairman. Despite the PlayStation 3's inauspicious launch, Sony's commitment to the system was unwavering. By 2007 Sony had reduced the production cost of the system by 70 per cent and by 2010 46 million units had been sold. But in the process, the PlayStation had lost its father and arguably some of its direction.

"We believe that the PS3 will be the place where our users play games, watch films, browse the Web, and use other computer functions. The PlayStation 3 is a computer. We do not need the PC."

Phil Harrison, president of SCE Worldwide Studios

Below: Backward compatibility with PlayStation games from earlier consoles was removed from later PS3 models, considered by Sony to add too much cost to manufacturing.

W

Manufacturer: **Nintendo**
Original Cost: **¥25,000**
US $249.99

NINTENDO WII

Originally codenamed the 'Revolution', the Wii removed Nintendo from the technological console arms race to present a different sort of games machine.

"Our ambition is to satisfy people's need to be happy, through our software. People want to play because human beings want to be human beings – and we are the only species on earth that loves to play."

Satoru Iwata, president of Nintendo

Unthreatening, uncomplicated. Compared to the trident prongs of an N64 pad or the cacophony of buttons that mark the face of a PlayStation Dual Shock, the Nintendo Wii's controller enjoys a zen-like simplicity, an angelic-white TV remote, light and comfortable in the hand. If the Nintendo DS saw the Kyoto company introducing new hardware features in the hope of introducing a new audience to gaming, the Nintendo Wii stripped the clutter away to broaden the player pool yet further.

Stand anyone from a child to a grandmother in front of *Wii Sports* tennis, and press a Wii remote into their hand and they instinctively know to swing it like a racquet. By removing the complication of analogue sticks and shoulder bumpers Nintendo removed the barrier to gaming at which so many fell. The Revolution, as the machine was known during development, was to be televised after all. And it came in the form of universal approachability: a controller that acted like a giant laser pointer stylus to your TV DS screen.

The inspiration for the system came from a growing view at Nintendo that the race to technological dominance in video game hardware, far from advancing the medium, was stagnating it. "Power isn't everything for a console," said designer Shigeru Miyamoto at the time. "Too many powerful consoles can't coexist. It's like having only ferocious dinosaurs. They might fight and hasten their own extinction." Work began on the system after the launch of the GameCube in 2001. While Sony and Microsoft forged ahead with their plans to create supercomputers for the living room, Miyamoto and veteran designer Kenichiro Ashida instead focused on creating a system that would be cheap to make, without the need for noisy cooling fans, and, crucially, that mothers would be happy to have sitting underneath the TV.

But when the system was unveiled at the Tokyo Game Show in late 2005, the reaction was one of confusion. Within the games industry, Nintendo's sidestepping of the technological arms race was perceived as imprudent. For those outside the games industry the Nintendo Wii represented a key step in gaming's evolution, and almost every month since launch it consistently outsold its competitors, becoming Nintendo's best selling home console – at least, until the launch of the Switch, in 2017.

MUST PLAY:
Wii Sports Resort
Super Mario Galaxy
Sin and Punishment:
Successor of the Skies
New Super Mario Bros
Wii
Little Kings Story

Right: The Wii's inventive controllers would be used again by Nintendo for its 2012 follow-up system, the Wii-U.

WII SPORTS

Better representing the physicality of its five sports than any game before, *Wii Sports* removed the barriers that had kept so many away from video games.

The best-selling video game yet made, *Wii Sports* overtook the aging *Super Mario Bros.* as the best-selling game in 2009. Sceptics will point out that it did so not on its own merits, but by piggy-backing on the enormous success of its host console, the Nintendo Wii, with which it was sold in every country bar Japan. But just as it's impossible to separate the sales of *Wii Sports* from the sales of the Nintendo Wii, so it is impossible to separate the appeal and success of each creation. *Wii Sports*, perhaps more than any other launch game, provides the perfect demonstration of the strengths, quirks and appeal of its hardware, a clutch of five straightforward sports-based minigames inextricably linked to the hardware on which they appear.

Tennis, more than any of the others, acted as an elegant statement of intent for Nintendo with their new machine. A redaction of the sport, players need only swing the Wii remote when the ball is close to their character to lob, slice or top-spin it back at their opponent. The characters move into position automatically, a simplification that

Below: The sound effect that accompanies any camera movements is taken from *Super Mario 64*.

Above: In *Wii Sports* bowling it's possible to release the ball on the back swing and frighten the characters standing behind you.

seemingly rewinds video game evolution past even *Pong*. But that, combined with a controller that requires you simply to mimic the real life actions of the sport it approximates, makes the game universally accessible. Each sport chosen by Nintendo's EAD is designed to show off a different way in which the controller can be used, the duck and jabbing motions of boxing wholly distinct from the smooth underarm swipe required by bowling, or the arcing sideways-on golf swings.

Producer Katsuya Eguchi, creator of *Animal Crossing*, intended Wii Sports to feature Nintendo's mascots, but the team found that players responded better to using their own Mii characters – created on the Wii dashboard from a palette of hairstyles and facial features. The joy of seeing a cartoon caricature of oneself (or a celebrity) striking out in baseball or cheering from the sidelines in tennis, exemplifies the family-oriented heart of the game and its hardware. A modern classic, *Wii Sports'* success is far from parasitic. Rather it is symbiotic, driving sales of the Nintendo Wii with kinetic force.

Year: 2006
Developer: Nintendo EAD
Publisher: Nintendo
Original format: Nintendo Wii
Play today: Nintendo Wii

"Our goal with Tennis wasn't to create a game that was challenging. We wanted a simple, pick-up-and-play idea. If we added the need for the player to run to the ball, that would add a level of complexity that would defeat the purpose of our initial goal."

Katsuya Eguchi, producer of *Wii Sports*

Below: In Japan, where *Wii Sports* was sold separately to the console, the game sold 176,167 copies in its first two days on sale.

Year: 2007
Developer: Realtime Worlds
Publisher: Microsoft Game Studios
Original format: Xbox 360
Play today: Xbox 360

"We kind of knew *Crackdown* would need as much help as it could get to get into players' hands... Like we've always said: It's a game player's game. It's not something that's going to sell in screenshot."

David Jones, creator of
Crackdown

Below right: The ability to drive the Agency SUV up a vertical wall when the player has maxed out his driving skill was originally a bug in the game.

CRACKDOWN

An open world game with minimal scripted story, *Crackdown*'s streets liberate the player just as the player seeks to liberate the streets.

For all its wonder and triumph, *Grand Theft Auto* is a series of games transfixed on cinema, borrowing the language and technique of film to sell its brutal stories. For Dave Jones, creator of *GTA*, *Crackdown* represents an attempt to strip the cinema out of the open world genre he helped create, instead offering the player a playground filled with dynamite and potential, one in which the player is almost the sole scriptwriter.

The set-up is as light as they come: you play as an interchangeable avatar known only as Agent, charged with freeing the various districts of Pacific City from the tyranny of their respective kingpin gangland bosses. But beyond the premise the story is all yours to write. Realtime Worlds tears down the walls of orthodox video game structure, pressing the keys to the city into your hands and allowing you to choose your own adventure, largely at your own pace.

The only paths are systemic ones, as your Agent's skill as a fighter, climber, runner and driver improve and develop in predetermined ways. But even these upgrades can be acquired in a loose order, your agent improving in those areas you choose to focus upon till he is the superhero sum of your choices. Development on the game began in 2002; a team of nine, many of whom had previously worked on the *Grand*

Theft Auto series, prototyping different mechanics in search of the perfect recipe for this new type of sandbox free from narrative constraints. In 2004 Microsoft approached the studio, asking that it consider making the game an Xbox 360 exclusive. Despite a tortuous second half of development, which saw a switch to a new game engine almost torpedo the project, a convincing downloadable demo, which accelerated the agent's speed of development to show players his later abilities, and Microsoft's decision to bundle a demo of *Halo 3* with the game, ensured *Crackdown* debuted to strong sales.

Arguably the game's most enduring legacy is to be found in the agility orbs scattered around its world. These 500 collectibles, found in alleyways and atop towers, kick-started a trend in 3D gaming for hidden trinkets, a designer's way to encourage players to explore off the beaten track that became prevalent throughout gaming in the wake of *Crackdown*'s popularity.

Left: *Crackdown* takes place in the fictional Pacific City, whose several districts are controlled by three crime organizations.

PEGGLE

Despite the saccharine presentation and decidedly mainstream appeal, *Peggle*'s origins lay in one of Japan's most peculiar pastimes.

The rise of the Nintendo DS and Wii had widened gaming's boundaries, introducing not only a new generation to the joys and frustrations of interactive entertainment, but also old ones who had been previously uninterested. In tandem with Nintendo's evangelistic work outside the confines of the gamer ghetto, a small army of PC and Flash games were serving non-traditional gaming audiences, those office workers looking for something to occupy their time during a quiet lunch break and young mothers looking for escapism while the baby was asleep. Chief among this new brand of game developers was PopCap, who had found global success on an unimagined scale with *Bejeweled*, popularizing the genre of so-called 'casual' gamers, the match-3 puzzle game.

But with the company's next global success, *Peggle*, the inspiration was in a most unlikely of nerdish niches. The game's producer Sukhbir Sidhu had imported a Japanese PlayStation game based on pachinko in the 1990s. *Pachinko*, a loose Japanese take on pinball, sees players drop ball bearings into a machine of clacking buzzers and bumpers, sitting back to watch the ball's descent through the inner workings of the machine. Thereafter Sidhu had always wanted to make a video game that elicited the same feelings in a player, but as *Pachinko* is based purely on luck

Above: The game's ten playable characters include Bjorn the Unicorn, Jimmy Lightning the Beaver, Lord Cinderbottom the Dragon, and Splork Sporkan (above).

rather than skill, the designer pushed it to the back of his mind. After joining PopCap, Sidhu was introduced to a 2D physics engine designed by one of the studio's coders, Brian Rothstein, one so perfect for this style of game that his vision was rekindled. In *Peggle* players fire a ball bearing into an arrangement of coloured pegs that disappear when struck. The aim of the game is to eliminate all of the orange pegs before your stock of balls runs out. Success and failure pivots on a curious balance of chance and design, but the pachinko-esque payoffs for success, including a blast of Beethoven's *Ode to Joy* upon completing a stage, make the game exuberantly satisfying.

Peggle was responsible for closing the gap between so-called 'casual' and hobbyist players, its accessible quality inspiring devotion in players of all ages and experience, cementing PopCap's reputation as the most serious of casual developers.

Year: 2007
Developer: PopCap Games
Publisher: PopCap Games
Original format: PC
Play today: Various

"Since it was important not to distract the player, the only real place to jam in nonsensical pachinko-style craziness was the end of the level. We started with just the words 'Extreme Fever' in giant letters, and Brian added 'Ode to Joy'. At first, these were just jokingly added as placeholders, but people who played seemed to react well, so we just added more and more."

Sukhbir Sidhu, creator of *Peggle*

Below: Kat Tut holds an Egyptian ankh and a stave, which are a sign of royalty in the game. She wants to be a circus performer.

Below: The climax to each level is accompanied by a rendition of Beethoven's *Ode to Joy*.

Year: 2007
Developer: Paul Preece
Publisher: n/a
Original format: Web
Play today: Web, Nintendo DS

"It didn't really exist as a genre yet. It was an underground clique. I could never claim credit for creating the TD genre, but for most people, the first one they played was *DTD*."

Paul Preece, creator of *Desktop Tower Defense*

DESKTOP TOWER DEFENSE

Perhaps the most recent genre to assimilate within video games, *Desktop Tower Defense* is the defining title in this idiosyncratic style of strategy game.

Although it did not give birth to the genre with which it shares two-thirds of a name, *Desktop Tower Defense* was the game that took the tower defence game mechanic (one that originated in a custom *WarCraft III* map), polished it, perfected it and then took it out to the mainstream. Not only was this Flash game responsible for popularizing gaming's youngest variety of game, but in securing 15 million plays in the four short months following its debut on the internet, it came to represent a new breed of game, one that combined the deep tactics of PC strategy games with the vast player figures of *Bejeweled* and the other leading 'casual' games.

Perhaps the key to the game's popularity – and today this is a game that has consumed the lives of tens of millions of players across the globe, both experienced game players and novices – is in its setting. Eschewing the orcs and Tolkien-style fantasy visuals of the *Warcraft III* mod from which it originated, designer Paul Preece instead settled upon the most mundane and familiar of settings: a desk.

A stretch of tan laminate, similar no doubt to the vast majority of Ikea-bought workspaces on which the game has been played since, with the side of a keyboard and mouse edging one side of the play area, and a scattering of small change and fluorescent marker pens on the other gives

Below: In *Desktop Tower Defense* the player must stop a set number of enemies, known as 'creeps', from reaching a set point on the playing field.

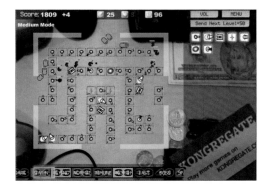

Above: Two of the desk settings that are used in the game *Desktop Tower Defense*.

the game area a routine, everyday feel. And yet, in the tiny biro-scrawl gun turrets you place upon the game board, and the blob-like creeps that you are charged with taking down, the essence of war is to be found in this most mundane of scenes.

Desktop Tower Defense began life as a reinterpretation of a *WarCraft* map named *Autumn Tower Defense* in which enemies would rush across the screen following predetermined paths while players set down turrets to stop them. Different styles of turret behave in different ways, and each one has its own individual cost and 'area of effect', the zone around the tower that will trigger its attacks when an enemy wanders within its bounds. The player must manage their limited resources, choosing the optimum placement and variety of towers in order to hold back the incoming waves of attackers. A mod for a six-year-old game, this strategy offshoot was known to only a handful of players around the world, of

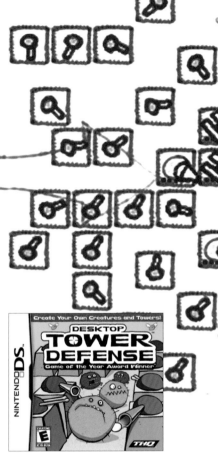

whom Paul Preece was one. Preece wanted to try his hand at making his own tower defence game, but he was a Visual Basic programmer and did not know how to code Flash. However, when his friend David Scott created *Flash Element TD* in 2007, a web-based standalone game using art and assets from *WarCraft III*, Preece decided to jump in himself, drawing upon Scott's knowledge and experience to help him code the game.

Preece began work in February 2007, coding the game in his spare time, incrementally adding new gameplay features as he learned his way around Flash. Within just four weeks his work was complete. Thanks to his basic art skills, he named the game's website, HandDrawnGames.com. Preece borrowed a number of design elements from other formative tower defence titles, such as the

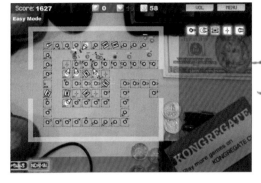

Above: Because of creator Paul Preece's lack of artistic ability he named the game's host site *HandDrawnGames.com*.

'area of effect' indicator that showed a tower's range. But he also introduced a number of key features that would go on to be genre standards, such as the button to send the next wave of attackers ahead of time, and an indicator showing which types of enemies would be included.

The game's genius lay in its relative simplicity. *Desktop Tower Defense* launched with just five types of tower, gameplay then consisting of arranging these in such a way as to deplete the creeps' health before they reached the level exit. The game manages to hit that sweet spot between accessibility and complexity that all classic titles exhibit, and thanks to its hardcore strategy heart, was responsible perhaps more than any other web-game before or since for taking a complex, abstract video game into the mainstream.

A few years later and tower defence games are ubiquitous, with most major publishers delivering their own take on the genre to every conceivable platform. Some offerings, such as Square-Enix's mobile phone hit, *Crystal Defenders*, simplify the formula, while others, such as Xbox Live's *Monday Night Combat*, mesh the core concepts with other action game mechanics. Part resource management sim, part maze-builder, *Desktop Tower Defense* reignited a long lost sense that a globally successful video game could be created by one man coding away in his bedroom, a reality the advent of Apple's iPhone would greatly amplify in the coming months.

Below: The game ends in defeat if the player's lives reach zero and provides no way to regenerate lost lives.

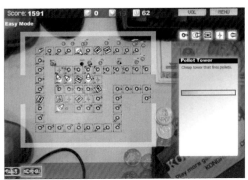

Above: By 2008, *Desktop Tower Defense*'s success had inspired a slew of tower defence games on video game consoles such as *Defense Grid: The Awakening*, *PixelJunk Monsters* and also *Savage Moon*.

THE KNOWLEDGE
The voice sample used when a player is asked to enter a score for the high score table is taken from the 1959 British animated television series *Ivor the Engine*.

ZOO KEEPER DX
touch edition
★ START ★

662M
000

108,650
HINT
MENU
0:02

CANABALT

9:41 AM
3G
7
Calendar
Photos
Camera
Messages
Stocks
Maps
Weather
YouTube
Utilities
iTunes
App Store
Notes
Settings
Phone
Mail
Safari
iPod

MUST PLAY:
Angry Birds
Canabalt
Solipskier
Infinity Blade
Game Dev Story

Year: 2007
Manufacturer: Apple
Original Cost: $599

JUNE 2007

[IOS]

I PHONE

223

iPHONE

Apple's much-anticipated mobile phone and its App Store enabled amateur and professional game-makers alike to present their game to a global audience.

On 9 January 2007 Steve Jobs, one-time junior technician at Atari, now CEO of a computer company with worldwide annual sales of $65.23 billion, announced the company's new product: the iPhone. Jobs described the device in a keynote address delivered at the Macworld Conference & Expo in San Francisco as a combination of three products: "widescreen iPod with touch controls"; a "revolutionary mobile phone"; and a "breakthrough Internet communicator". What Jobs didn't mention was that the iPhone was also a video game device, one that would, in the next two years, see more games released than any other hardware platform in video gaming's history.

Developed at a reported cost of $150 million over a 30-month period, expectations ahead of the iPhone's US release in June 2007 loomed tall. Hundreds queued outside Apple and AT&T retail stores for days before the device's launch and within an hour of release many retailers sold out. Meanwhile, the video game industry remained unconvinced of Apple's tentative steps toward its field. Apple computers had always played second fiddle to Windows machines, and the Pippin, the company's only attempt at creating a game console, had been a resounding failure.

Nevertheless, Xbox Live and PlayStation Network had proved the effectiveness of and market for digitally distributed games, whereby players could simple pay to download their games without needing to visit a bricks and mortar store. Likewise, the rise of mobile phone games, epitomized by the Nokia 6110 version of the classic 1970s computer game *Snake* (programmed in 1997 by Taneli Armanto, a design engineer in Nokia) meant that people who had never before owned a video game system were beginning to enjoy the games that came pre-installed on their phones.

The conduit for all of this potential came, not in the device itself, but in its software, specifically the App store. An iTunes for mobile phone games and applications, here was a new platform that gave everyone from the largest game publishers to the most humble bedroom coders access to the same audience, all for a straightforward 70/30 split in revenue share in the developer's favour. Creators could choose the price point, write the marketing blurb themselves and, after waiting a fortnight for their game to pass certification, see it released to the world.

It took time for developers to understand the best way to have players control their games using the device. Many tried to recreate traditional control schemes on the touchscreen, adding virtual control sticks for players to manipulate. But soon new ways of interacting were discovered, be it through the accelerometer that, for example, has the device tilted like a steering wheel in order to control a car in games such as *Firemint Racing*, or gesture controls that have the player painting arcane symbols with their fingers to incant spells in *Infinity Blade*.

While many independent developers saw the rise of the App Store as a gold rush, the difficult of gaining visibility among the huge numbers of games on the service has meant that only a handful of plucky upstarts have found their fortune there.

Nevertheless, within a short space of time, the iPhone proved itself the most disruptive technology seen in video games since the Nintendo Wii, shifting the business model of countless publishers, and inspiring Sony and Nintendo to reevaluate their future plans.

When announcing the iPhone, Steve Jobs boasted: "Apple is going to reinvent the phone." Few guessed Apple would also reshape the video game industry.

"The graphics capability is greater than the DS, we have multitouch, the screen is larger and there's an accelerometer. And we have the App Store. I think it's the future of gaming."

Greg Joswiak, Apple's vice president of worldwide iPod marketing

Above: GameCenter, an application that allows users to compare scores with friends and track their in-game achievements, was added in the release of iOS 4.1.

Year: 2007
Developer: Irrational Games
Publisher: 2K Games
Original format: Xbox 360, PC
Play today: Xbox 360, PS3, PC, Mac

"I want to make great games. I don't have a second career I'm trying to experience. I'm trying to make a video game, which allows me to concentrate on the storytelling capacity of video games, not just aping another medium."

Ken Levine, creator of *BioShock*

Below: Big Daddies are the hulking guardians of the Little Sisters, young girls who have been genetically altered to loot the corpses that litter Rapture's streets.

BIOSHOCK

The ruined undersea metropolis of Rapture provides the striking backdrop for this disquietingly intelligent first person shooter.

By the start of the new millennium the first person shooter had established itself as video gaming's most prevalent and successful genre. Some might accuse the medium's obsession with guns as being a symptom of the medium's ongoing fascination with the adolescent, the desire to upgrade the toy soldiers and Airfix fighter planes of boyhood, to render the miniature wars of the carpet in almost-life on screen.

Nevertheless, despite attempts by titles such as *Deus Ex* and *System Shock 2* to introduce complexity and introspection to their systems, gun games' ambition rarely stretched beyond a re-skinned virtual version of cops and robbers. But with *BioShock*, a developer demonstrated that it was possible for a blockbuster shooting game to feature thoughtful mechanics, intricate world building and a plot relevant to the destruction. In creator Ken Levine's waterlogged vision, for once the practical brilliance of the guns was matched by that of other elements, ones that games rarely prize.

A utopia project turned to dystopian ruin, the underwater world of *BioShock*'s Rapture is one of video gaming's most enduring locales. The game opens with a plane crash into the sea, your character swimming through the water aflame with fuel, to a nearby rock outcrop. There he finds a curious elevator leading down into a derelict, submerged colony. The art deco signage and 1930s fixtures and fittings that greet when you step out of the lift into Rapture are striking, the wear and tear bespeaking an ideology-driven utopia project gone wrong. Striking too are those survivors still living in Rapture, the splicers, murderous solvent-abusers, and of course, the Big Daddies, hulking monsters in bronze oversized diving suits, and the little sister, syringe-wielding orphans that they accompany.

Work began on *BioShock* soon after the release of *System Shock 2*, a cult PC game that shares many characteristics with *BioShock*. The plot for the game went through several significant changes before the game's announcement in 2004. Levine drew influence from the work of Ayn Rand, whose objectivist theories form the basis of Rapture's foundational ideology, while George Orwell's seminal *1984* provided inspiration for the dystopian decay that riddles the world. With a relatively small team of around 80 staff (many of whom worked on *System Shock 2*) and an equally modest budget, the setting of an underwater cosmos helped to limit the scope of the game world's geography.

The team rapidly iterated and released internal demos to help refine the moment-to-moment experience. When they felt the game was coming together, a group of

Above: Dr. Steinman, one of the game's most memorable antagonists, is a plastic surgeon driven to madness through pursuit of perfection. His surgeries end in the mutilation, and in many cases death, of his trusting patients.

Above: Players are able to use 'plasmids' to imbue their character with special powers. These powers range from telekinesis and hypnotism, through to the ability to blast flames, or ice, from the fingertips.

Above: The decrepit art deco grandeur of the ruined underwater city of Rapture acts as a constant reminder of just how far this civilization has fallen.

designers and producers took a demo to a focus test group who knew nothing about either the game or the company in order to gauge reaction. The response was brutal, with players criticizing the amount of dialogue and story and complaining that the first level was overly dense and confusing. The team went away and redesigned the entire first section of the game. In August 2007, just over a year after the first playable version of the game was shown to the public, *BioShock* was released to critical acclaim, the *Chicago*

Sun Times describing the title as "rare, mature video game that succeeds in making you think while you play".

In purely systemic terms *BioShock* is a game about shooting things while genetically upgrading your character's abilities. But to reduce the experience to its basic interactions is to ignore those aesthetic, narrative and ideological aspects that move the game into territory rarely investigated by video games. For once here is a satisfying game whose story and setting define the experience. In that sense, *BioShock* helped move video games one step closer toward maturity, proving that virtual guns and virtual smarts are not mutually exclusive.

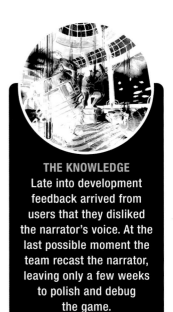

THE KNOWLEDGE
Late into development feedback arrived from users that they disliked the narrator's voice. At the last possible moment the team recast the narrator, leaving only a few weeks to polish and debug the game.

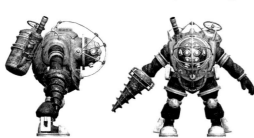

Year: 2007
Developer: EA Black Box
Publisher: Electronic Arts
Original format: Xbox 360, PS3
Play today: Xbox 360, PS3

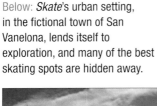

"We didn't want to copy Tony Hawk. We didn't want to waste one or two years of our lives just recreating something that, for what it was, had pretty much been perfected already."

Scott Blackwood, executive producer on *Skate*

Below: *Skate*'s urban setting, in the fictional town of San Vanelona, lends itself to exploration, and many of the best skating spots are hidden away.

SKATE

EA Black Box's straightforwardly titled *Skate* managed to teach an old dog of a genre some new tricks – each executed in a novel manner.

For nearly a decade Neversoft's *Tony Hawk* series of skateboarding video games had defined screen interpretations of the sport. Riotous, exhilarating and physics-defying, Activision's series sought to capture skating's showboating essence rather than its exacting detail, and players had long supported the approach. But midway through the first decade of the new millennium, the franchise was tired, its creators struggling to find new features with which to freshen a formula they had all but perfected. The environment was set for a challenger.

While *Skate*'s arrival may appear to have been the result of corporate precision targeting, EA delivering a game to take the crown from a beleaguered king, the game started life in a very different way. EA Black Box was a studio of skaters who had an idea to create a skating game in which the player controlled the avatar's feet, rather than the deck. The team was asked to wipe the slate clean, imagining that no one had ever made a skateboarding game before, in order to work out the ways in which they would approach the genre differently.

The result was a tech demo in which the analogue sticks were each mapped to one of the skater's feet. There were no graphics at this point; just a series of text read-outs on screen to indicate what move had been

triggered by what input on the stick. The system was ingenious. Flick the control stick down and up and the result would be an olly. Do the same movement across a diagonal and the result would be a kick flip. From this basic rearranging of the fundamentals, an entirely new approach was defined and built, one that feels both natural and precise.

Despite a steep learning curve, *Skate* established itself as the pre-eminent skateboarding game of the 2000s. At its best, the game has you plotting lines through dense urban environments, grinding along benches, weaving in and out of pedestrians and traffic in one long, glorious, uninterrupted flow. Thanks to the sober realism of the physics this kind of combo'ing is more satisfying than it ever was in a Tony Hawks game, even if it's far harder-won and less impressive to a casual observer. It's testament to the strength of the surrounding package that *Skate* continues to be a compelling place to inhabit even after the challenges are completed and the storyline tied up, and all that's left is the concrete playground with its playful edges.

Below: In contrast to its forebears, *Skate*'s control system requires that players utilize the controller's analogue sticks to perform tricks, spins and stunts.

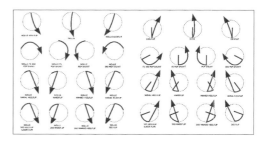

PORTAL

An inspirational puzzle game that sees the player take on the role of human guinea pig, pitted against one of the medium's most memorable antagonists.

For a game that started life as a throwaway Flash game, *Portal*'s greatness and influence belies its humble origins. You play as a lab-rat human, working your way through a series of test puzzle rooms under the watchful encouragement of Hal-like female sentient AI, GLaDOS. Ostensibly a first person shooter, *Portal* is transformed by way of its solitary projectile 'weapon', the Aperture Science Handheld Portal Device. Shooting the gun's 'bullet' against a flat surface opens up an oval portal door. Shooting a second bullet somewhere else in the environment opens up another door and stepping into one will see your character emerge from the other. From this single rule, a series of supremely ingenious puzzles emerges.

At its most basic level the game is about getting from here to there using lateral thinking and momentum to propel your character through each environment. But in time it presents more than just passive physics puzzles with more traditional 'enemies' that must be eliminated. However, as you only have the Portal gun, which is a passive tool and not a weapon at all, the way these opponents can be overcome is by turning their violence against themselves. Before *Portal* almost every first person shooter was about the one-man army gunning his way through insurmountable odds. Valve's game explores how it feels to be weak and weaponless, a rare position in a medium obsessed with power and control.

The idea for the game originated in *Narbacular Drop*, an independent game released by students of the DigiPen Institute of Technology in 2005. Valve was so impressed that it hired the entire team behind the game, pairing them with Erik Wolpaw, the writer behind *Psychonauts*, to expand the concept into a fully 3D spin-off to *Half-Life 2*. Wolpaw wrote using a text-to-speech programme on his computer, the dialogue providing much of the incentive to pull players through challenging puzzles.

A short, exquisitely crafted video game, *Portal*'s mechanical ingenuity is matched by its narrative. Smart, witty and at times affecting, *Portal* remains one of the medium's high points, melding story and systems with deft efficiency. While the pay-off of cake may never appear, nobody leaves *Portal* feeling short-changed.

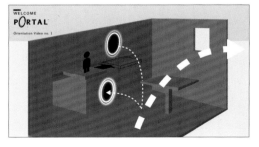

Above: The game's mindbending physics demand that players rethink the way they interact with their environment.

Right: As the game develops the puzzle rooms become increasingly hazardous, with the introduction of toxic gas, sentient gun turrets and deadly neurotoxins.

Year: 2007
Developer: Valve Corporation
Publisher: Valve Corporation
Original format: PC, Xbox 360
Play today: PC, Xbox 360, PlayStation 3, Mac

"We wanted an adversary personality that hadn't been done to death. I mean, GLaDOS does yell a lot and shoot rockets at you, which I guess is fairly traditional, but she's also kind of supportive and funny and sometimes she's a little sad and even scared."

Erik Wolpaw, writer of *Portal*

[137]
SUPER MARIO GALAXY

Year: 2007
Developer: Nintendo EAD Tokyo
Publisher: Nintendo
Original format: Nintendo Wii
Play today: Nintendo Wii

Above: Series composer Koji Kondo composed four pieces for the game while Mahito Yokota composed the rest of the orchestra-led soundtrack.

SUPER MARIO GALAXY

Mario had already conquered the world, but this joyfully imaginative entry into the much-loved series launched him headfirst into the video game stratosphere.

After the era-defining *Super Mario 64*, Mario's mascot laboured under a cloud of expectation. Its follow-up, *Super Mario Sunshine*, while at times brilliant, was too schizophrenic and confused to be considered a classic. Where next for the diminutive plumber? For Mario's debut on the Wii, Nintendo shared humanity's understanding that beyond the confines of our planet there lies a universe of opportunity and bright discovery. In this yearning for the stars the company broadened the horizon of its most treasured series. It was, perhaps, a logical leap. After all, once we've flown across *Super Mario World* where else can one go but the *Super Mario Galaxy*?

The result is a sugar rush of ideas, a pixel-perfect platform game set, not on the slopes and hills of dry land, but also on the stars and spheres that buckshot space itself. Mario loop-de-loops from plump patchwork planet to planet, each sphere a perfect, distinct capsule of game design with more inventiveness and sparkle than many games achieve across their entire experience. The presentation is nothing short of joyful, as Mario leaps into breathless flight between globes, collecting showers of Star Bits and leaving light trail in his sweeping wake.

The true evidence of Nintendo's creative dominance of the medium it helped define, is in the way in which its designers build a new structure and ideas around familiar and

Below: Mario's wardrobe of super suits had several new additions, including this bee suit.

Above: A second player can use the Wii remote to gather Star Bits and shoot them at enemies in order to aid the main player.

solid foundations. *Super Mario Galaxy* is a pure blood Mario game, yet one that manages to sidestep nostalgic indulgence, and instead captures the spirit of bold inventiveness that defines the series, without re-treading old ideas. Intoxicating in their imagination and variety, the ideas never let up, the ground constantly shifting beneath the player's feet, confounding expectations and delighting in equal, assured measure at every leap toward the conclusion.

The core idea for the game originated in the *Super Mario 128* tech demo shown at Nintendo Space World in 2000, designed to demonstrate the processing power of the Nintendo GameCube. The demo's director, Yoshiaki Koizumi, felt that the use of a spherical platform could be developed into a full Mario game, but supposed that such a thing would be technically impossible.

Meanwhile, Nintendo's EAD Tokyo studio began work on *Donkey Kong Jungle Beat*, an innovative platform game that used a plastic bongo drum peripheral as a controller. After work was completed on the project, Shigeru Miyamoto approached the team to ask what they would like to work on next. Takao Shimizu, a producer at Nintendo EAD Tokyo, suggested the team begin work on a new IP, but Miyamoto urged them to look at possibilities for the next Mario title.

As work began on the game, Koizumi returned to the idea of spherical platforms but time and time again the team came up

"I worked on this project thinking that I had taken on the role of the cook. First, I showed the recipe to everyone saying, 'I want to make a kind of dish like this on Wii', but nobody in the staff was able to imagine the finished plate."

Yoshiaki Koizumi, director of *Super Mario Galaxy*

against discouraging technical issues. Miyamoto, however, was insistent that this idea was the key to unlocking the direction of the next core Mario title, and the team pressed on, creating a demo in three months featuring a single spherical planet with its own gravitational pull that Mario could sprint around. From this proof of concept, Nintendo President Satoru Iwata and Miyamoto felt vindicated, and work began turning the core concept into a game.

One area in which the team placed a great deal of focus was in working out how best to handle a camera in 3D space. With *Super Mario 64* a group of players in testing reported they felt 3D platform games were just too difficult to control, while the decision to allow players to choose what type of camera they wanted to use on *Super Mario Sunshine* 'burdened' them, as Koizumi put it – with an extra decision. To answer these issues for *Galaxy* the team tested the game with a huge number of players, so many that the release of the game was delayed as they worked to solve an issue that Nintendo believed had been present in its 3D games for a decade.

The result is a 3D Mario game that is arguably as accessible as the 2D titles with which the company made its name. The simple structure asks merely that players find stars in order to open up new levels, fixing eyes on the next sparkling reward in the face of endlessly disruptive creativity. The only question that remains at the end of one of the medium's most cohesive and consistent experiences is where on earth – or beyond – could Mario possibly go next?

Above: Mario flees from the gaping jaws of a Mandibug, which is one of the game's many new enemies.

Above: The game's levels take the form of planets, each with their own gravitational pull that hold Mario, even when he appears to be walking upside down.

Above: Mario is launched from planet to planet, collecting tasty Star Bits as he goes gliding through the air.

Above: Mario must collect Grand Stars to power up the Comet Observatory and progress through the game.

THE KNOWLEDGE
The orchestral score was recorded at different tempos in order to perfectly synchronize with Mario's movement at any given point. The faster Mario runs the faster the music plays.

Year: 2007
Developer: Infinity Ward
Publisher: Activision
Original format: Xbox 360,
  PlayStation 3, Nintendo DS, PC
Play today: Xbox 360, PlayStation 3,
  Nintendo DS, PC

CALL OF DUTY 4: MODERN WARFARE

The first game in the *Call of Duty* series to explore modern conflict, *Modern Warfare* flits between James Bond fantasy and newsreel footage realism.

Like one of its own flashbang grenades, Infinity Ward's first break from the narrative shackles of World War II leaves you reeling. Leaping forward into the near future of warfare, *Call of Duty 4: Modern Warfare* is a rollercoaster ride through various dioramas of contemporary combat, equal parts exhilarating and distressing. One moment it offers pure James Bond-style thrills: an escape from a sinking cargo ship, the decks and walls tilting at drunken angles all around; a race against the clock to diffuse a terrorist nuclear missile; a crawl through tall grass in a ghillie camouflage suit in between the tracks of incoming enemy tanks. Then it presents, in dry, detached tones some of the most arresting replications of contemporary war seen in a video game.

The most memorable of these moments is Death From Above, an AC-130 bombing mission in which you man the turrets of a helicopter as it strafes above an unidentified Middle Eastern city. Set at night, the screen is a grey-greenish wash of night vision goggles, the bright luminous shapes of men running at full pelt for cover from your gaze, as realistic as a news report. In muffled silence, your shots land true, puffs of incandescent annihilation that leave bodies prostrate and fading in the aftermath. For the first time in video games, the lines between fantasy and reality were not so much blurred, as fully scrubbed away.

The third game from California-based Infinity Ward, *Modern Warfare* arrived at a time when the game industry was weighed down with World War II-themed first person shooters. The team at Infinity Ward was complicit in generating the sense of ennui surrounding the niche, as all 22 founding members of the studio had worked on *Medal of Honor: Allied Assault* while working at 2015, Inc. The studio's two initial

THE KNOWLEDGE
During development the team attended a live-fire exercise at Marine Corps Air Ground Combat Center Twentynine Palms, a training facility in the California desert, in order to better simulate the effects of being near an Abrams tank when it fires.

releases, *Call of Duty* and its sequel *Call of Duty 2* were two of the strongest World War II-themed first person shooters. By the time it came to start work on the developer's third title, both staff and players were desperate for a new setting.

The studio originated two games ideas as a way to end the virtual war but, rather than choosing between them, split the studio into two teams and began parallel development on each game side by side. Understaffed and overworked, both projects began to falter and Infinity Ward management took the decision to fold the second game's team into the *Modern Warfare* project midway through development. Despite a disappointing reaction to a demo some months before release, with players claiming the game was more of the same, just re-skinned away from the 1940s setting, *Modern Warfare* released to universal acclaim, in two short months securing the accolade of best-selling game of 2007 with more than seven million copies sold.

While *Call of Duty 4*'s enduring legacy includes establishing one of the most successful franchises in contemporary video games with the *Modern Warfare* name, it's the innovations Infinity Ward brought to the online aspect of the game that changed the design landscape. The introduction of RPG-style levelling elements, where experience points are earned for each headshot and kill, and guns unlock as you rise through the military ranks, add a meta-layer of objectives that earned the

game the Guinness World Record of 'Most Played Online Video Game' in 2009. The in-built option to form clans and fight other teams for ranking formalized a traditionally ad hoc aspect of online play in the framework of the experience. Meanwhile an overlay of bonus challenges (such as making 25 headshots with a certain weapon, or surviving a long fall), ensure that every action and reaction in the online portion of the game has meaning and value in its internal prestige economy.

The game has its detractors, those who criticize the feeble narrative set-up, or the uninspiring use of re-spawning enemies in order to create urgency and false challenge. But this is blockbuster war-gaming at its keenest, a rollercoaster ride through Hollywood replications of modern warfare that every now and again manages to make you drop the popcorn to pause for thought.

Below: The conflict is seen from the alternating perspectives of a US Force Reconnaissance Marine and a British SAS commando, set in exotic locales.

[139]

Year: 2008
Developer: Dimps/Capcom
Publisher: Capcom
Original format: Arcade
Play today: Arcade, Xbox 360, PlayStation 3

"Until the day of release, *Street Fighter IV* was an unwanted child. Nobody thought it would sell, so I had virtually no help from other departments – they were all reluctant, right up to the day of release."

Yoshinori Ono, producer of
Street Fighter IV

Below: *Street Fighter IV* takes place several months after the events of *Street Fighter II* (and is therefore chronologically set between the second and third games in the series).

STREET FIGHTER IV

A bold reimagining of a series that many – including its keepers – believed should stay in retirement, *Street Fighter IV* heralded a fighting game revival.

The eight years between 2000 and 2008 represented the longest amount of time the *Street Fighter* series had gone without a sequel or a spin-off. Was the series dead? Certainly there were those within Capcom who believed the venerable fighting game series was finished, the waning popularity of arcades combined with the rise of 3D fighting series such as *Tekken and Virtua Fighter* leading many to assume that the glory days of 2D fighters were lost. But for Yoshinori Ono, a producer who joined Capcom with the sole intent of one day working on a *Street Fighter* game, the dream was coiled and alive.

His pitch, made to Capcom R&D head Keiji Inafune in 2007, seemed to buck all prevailing trends. Ono wanted to reassemble the team responsible for Capcom's seminal fighting game, *Street Fighter II*, in order to create a game painted in 3D polygons, but that played out exactly like the 2D games of the genre's formative days. Capcom almost didn't green light the project. Ono, who had previously worked on *Street Fighter III 3rd Strike* as a sound management director and produced *Capcom Fighting Jam*, was hardly a safe bet to lead a project of such high profile, and the enormous risks involved in taking a failure to the arcades made many within the company uneasy. But the critical and commercial success of a high-definition

Above: The arcade version of the game includes the full cast of the original *Street Fighter II* and four entirely new characters to the series.

remake of *Street Fighter II Hyper Fighting* on Xbox Live Arcade led Inafune to consider whether the time was right for a *Street Fighter* revival and, thanks to Ono's persistence and enthusiasm, *Street Fighter IV* was moved into full production. Capcom began to work alongside the Osaka-based Dimps, a developer founded by many former SNK and Capcom staff who had worked on the brightest and best 2D fighters of the 1990s.

When the game released into arcades July 2008, it was clear that not only had Ono delivered an impassioned love letter to his favourite title in the series, *Street Fighter II*, but also he and his team had succeeded in rebuilding the genre for a contemporary audience. The furious spectacle of sprite-based fighting games is translated into

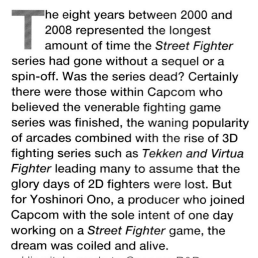

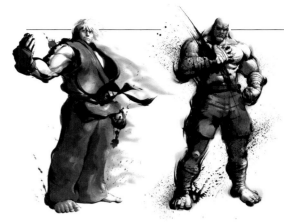

Above: Art director and character designer Daigo Ikeno opted for non-photorealistic character rendering with visual calligraphic stroke effects used during the fights.

Above: While Capcom's updates by way of the subsequent 'Super' and 'Arcade Edition' releases may have improved the template, it was 2008's release that sucker-punched *Street Fighter* back into the mainstream, and into the future.

3D with effortless ease. The iconography and comfortable, familiar rhythm of play succeeded in welcoming many gamers who had grown up with *Street Fighter II* back into a style of video game that had alienated them in subsequent years with its pedantic intricacy.

Alongside these returning prodigals, *Street Fighter IV* managed to jostle and inspire younger players. While Capcom may have overstated the game's accessibility to newcomers, there's no denying that, by simplifying move lists, lengthening the windows of opportunity for combos and making inputs far more forgiving in their timing, the barrier to entry is lower than just about anywhere elsewhere in the genre. The simplification of a style of game that was hitherto burdened by exclusive terminology had the effect of allowing a broader range of players to learn its language of play, which in turn widened the pool of players wanting to compete both in the arcades, and subsequently over Xbox Live and PSN.

Street Fighter IV arrived at a time when blockbuster games were becoming increasingly yoked to grand narratives.

By contrast, this game's story has a crisp purity. A single, recurring 99-second vignette: two characters sparring for dominance. It may be a short story with only two possible outcomes (three if you count the occasional Double KO), but it's one told in a hundred thousand different ways, each with its own nuance and pacing. Likewise, here was a game that 'levelled' the player, not the avatar. Play as Ryu and everyone will have the same set of abilities as everyone else: no in-game bonus or skill sways the fight one way or the other. Matches are won on a player's ability, giving the game a competitive clarity that, since *Call of Duty 4: Modern Warfare*'s meta-reward systems, had become somewhat clouded.

Play for any length of time and the characters on screen become pure ciphers for their player's intent, marionettes revealing the mind games that happen the other side of the screen. Video games are so often celebrated for allowing us to play out our fantasies on screen, making approximations of impossible or prohibitively expensive experiences available to anyone. There is no fantasy in *Street Fighter IV* (unless, perhaps you long to role play throwing fireballs from your palm). There's just technique, and mastery and a rabbit hole that leads from here to forever.

THE KNOWLEDGE
The original game concept, titled *Street Fighter IV Flashback*, was imagined in part by David Sirlin, the designer of *Super Street Fighter II Turbo HD Remix* but never made it past proposal stage. Flashback's proposed easy control system was later used in *Tatsunoko vs. Capcom: Ultimate All-Stars*.

Year: 2008
Developer: Number None, Inc.
Publisher: Microsoft Game Studios
Original format: Xbox 360
Play today: Xbox Live Arcade,
   Windows, Mac, PSN

> "I was excited about the game when I started, but what I ended up with was much better than the original idea. I don't think that happens very often in game development. I got lucky there. Usually, you have a great idea for a game, and you can't do all of it."
>
> Jonathan Blow, creator of *Braid*

BRAID

Braid imagines a series of worlds in which time behaves in different ways to our own, revealing the power of video games to construct truly alternative realities.

By 2008, the ability to manipulate in video games was a familiar trope. In a more immediate, effective way than any other medium, video games allow us to rewind the seconds in order to undo mistakes and rewrite the present, as games such as *Chrono Trigger*, *Blinx: The Time Sweeper* and *Prince of Persia*: *The Sands of Time* had explored with uneven success.

Independent platform game *Braid* chooses the same start point as these precedents, allowing the player to rewind time in order to, for example, undo a mistimed jump, drawing its protagonist off the spikes and placing his feet back on the soft grass. But what sets the game apart is the way in which the core mechanic is grown, evolved, riffed upon, and manipulated. Imagination and invention colour this world as much as the delicate

watercolour brush strokes that describe its backgrounds.

There are levels in which the movement of time is tied to the movement of the character, proceeding when he runs to the right, reversing when he runs to the left. Later it's possible to spawn doppelgangers who are unaffected by the time reversal, requiring you to solve puzzles by working together with previous versions of yourself. Likewise, the introduction of an object that pauses time for objects in its immediate vicinity, while the rest of the world moves forward at the speed of reality, facilitates some of the most ingenious puzzles yet seen in a video game.

Ostensibly a satire on *Super Mario*'s familiar tropes (the plumber swapped out for a besuited 21st-century man who must jump on his foes' heads and descend into

Above: Jonathan Blow claims that he designed the game to be a personal critique of contemporary trends in game development, funding the three-year project with his own money. The game has subsequently made him a millionaire.

green pipes in search of a princess). *Braid* is a puzzle game at its core. Its wonder and thrill derive from the release of pent-up infuriation at the moment you solve an irksome riddle for yourself. But it's also a love story, the ambitious allegorical riddle just as difficult to solve as the mechanical puzzles that reveal it, piece by piece.

Developed by US programmer Jonathan Blow, the idea for the game was conceived while the designer was in Thailand in December 2004. The influences were primarily literary ones: *Invisible Cities* by Italo Calvino, a series of short stories about fictional cities that have different kinds of reality, and *Einstein*'s *Dreams* by physicist Alan Lightman, which explores the repercussions of the behaviour of time in our universe. In April 2005, with Blow designing and coding solo, work began on a game that would take these themes and explore them via interactivity.

"Braid was a fascinating development experience for me," Blow would later say. "It became very clear that more ideas came out of the development process than I put into it as a designer. It was more like discovering things that already exist than it was to putting themselves together arbitrarily. Which is another way of saying: this is a game that designed itself. My role was knowing what questions to ask of the system."

By Christmas 2005, *Braid* had been pieced together from the answers to these questions, albeit using placeholder art. Artist David Hellman was then hired to create the final look of the piece, but it was two years before the game was ready for release on to Xbox Live. For a title with such lofty ambitions, lateral thinking mechanics and challenging writing, *Braid* was perhaps an unusual candidate for widespread success. But 55,000 people downloaded the game in its first week of release, fast becoming the second-highest selling Xbox Live Arcade title in 2008.

Games are at their most exciting when they subvert the laws of our reality rather than merely aping them. That's always been a feature of the medium, but most designers focus on merely exaggerating our present reality rather than twisting or pulling it apart completely. Through video games, we have the power to breathe new worlds to life and fill them with unfamiliar sets of laws of time and space; *Braid* is one of the few video games to imagine a world driven by a different sort of time, and one of the first games to prove that this approach, when handled elegantly, does not preclude commercial success.

Above: *Braid* features licensed music from Magnatune artists Cheryl Ann Fulton, Shira Kammen and Jami Sieber, chosen to reduce development costs.

THE KNOWLEDGE
Blow strongly discouraged players from using a guide to work their way through the game. He even created his own official "walkthrough" that promises to guide the player through the game but, when opened, simply restates that the player should work through the puzzles on their own.

[141]

Year: 2009
Developer: Mojang
Publisher: Mojang
Original format: PC, Mac
Play today: PC, Mac

"I replied to every email I got up until just a few weeks ago. Replying to emails was taking up an hour and a half per day."

Markus 'Notch' Persson, creator of *Minecraft*, after having sold 6,400 copies of the game. Twelve months later, it broke 1.2 million sales.

MINECRAFT

Minecraft reflects the story of man: survival, hunting, community and, eventually, hubris – all within a world of rudimentary blocks and boundless potential.

Every video game reflects the basic human instinct to practise survival through play: each 'Continue' a new birth, every 'Game Over' a final curtain. In *Minecraft* the metaphor is made wholly explicit in a game that returns to humanity's earliest battles for life. At the start of the game you are deposited in a unique, procedurally generated world built from a palette of coloured square building blocks comprising its mountains, valleys, lakes and clouds. Faced with this canvas, at first your task is mere exploration, charting the terrain around you.

Then night falls and monsters rise: dead-eyed zombies, skeletons, and camouflaged creepers that pursue you with terrifying single-mindedness. Now you are fighting for survival, digging a shelter with your bare hands and cowering in the dark until the sun shoos your tormentors back into hiding. The next morning you can choose to turn your cave into a castle, venturing out to gather the necessary raw materials to laminate your new abode's floor or to build a stove on which you can cook your meat. Or you can dig down to the centre of the earth, searching for rare materials

Below: In Creative Mode players are able to build projects without interruption from enemies and without the need to collect building resources beforehand.

Above: In late 2012 the Xbox 360 version of the game overtook *Call of Duty* as the most played online game on the service.

with which to fashion gleaming armour or indestructible pickaxes.

Or you could embark upon a more ambitious project, like, as some players have, building a full-scale replica of the Taj Mahal, or one of the Starship Enterprise, or perhaps to use sand and water to create logic gates that fire a giant rudimentary computer scrawled into the landscape. By offering the player exactly the tools they need to express themselves, and by constructing the world from square blocks, video game atoms that can be arranged in every imaginable combination, *Minecraft* is perhaps the closest we have to a true god game even if, regardless of how you choose to express your creativity and power, every night you must still retreat into your creation to hide.

For the game's Swedish creator, Markus 'Notch' Persson, this sense of disempowerment is key to the game's success. "Infinite power just isn't very interesting no matter what game you're playing," he's said. "It's much more fun

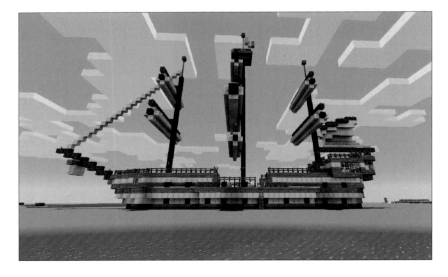

Above: *Minecraft*'s music and sound effects are produced by German composer Daniel Rosenfeld.

Below: In 2011, Persson split his £2.2 million company dividend among his employees at Mojang.

when you have a limited toolset to use against the odds." *Minecraft*'s extraordinary success has also confounded the odds for a game of rudimentary graphics. One of the most unlikely commercial successes of new millennium (it was released long before it was finished, requires a User ID to play and can only be bought over the Internet payment system) the game has sold in excess of 20 million copies since its release in 2009, earning armfuls of prestigious

Below: *Minecraft* sales across PC, Mac, Xbox 360 and mobile devices passed 100 million copies in 2019.

awards and secured merchandising deals with LEGO and other toymakers. It also earned its creator over one hundred million dollars by 2012.

Persson grew up in Edsbyn, a provincial town near Sweden's east coast, learning to programme by copying the code printed in the back pages of magazines into his Commodore 128 as his sister read it out to him. When his family moved to Stockholm when he was 13 years old, Persson became friends with other young programmers and, by the time he eventually left school he knew he wanted to make games for a living. Persson worked at a number of web-game companies over the next few years, working on his own projects in his spare time, including the popular free-to-play game *Wurm Online*.

When Persson began work on *Minecraft*, he knew that this was the game he had been waiting to make. He went part-time at his job in order to free up more time to work on his game and, after two months, handed in his notice on his birthday, 1 June.

He released the full version in 2009 and within 12 months the game had been downloaded more than six million times, and Persson was struggling to keep up with player requests for new features and bug fixes.

Through a combination of word of mouth and the appeal of a toolset with almost limitless potential, *Minecraft* turned its one-man creator into a multi-millionaire before the game was even out of Beta, while irrevocably changing the very landscape of gaming.

THE KNOWLEDGE
One intrepid player built *Star Trek*'s USS Enterprise spaceship in the game. On seeing this, Universal Studios sent Persson a Cease and Desist letter. "I had to explain that we didn't make this," said Persson. "It's a bit like sending a letter to Adobe because somebody drew a copyrighted image or logo in Photoshop."

Year: **2009**
Developer: **Naughty Dog**
Publisher: **Sony**
Original format: **PlayStation 3**
Play today: **PlayStation 3**

> **"We have a collapsing building where, as the building is collapsing, you're still in control of Drake and are still shooting. What other companies have in cutscenes, we wanted to have in the game, to let you play those big cinematic blockbuster moments."**
>
> Neil Druckmann, lead designer and writer on *Uncharted 2: Among Thieves*

UNCHARTED 2: AMONG THIEVES

Naughty Dog's *Uncharted* series may offer the player only limited freedom, but it's the closest a game has come to aping Hollywood's spectacle.

In their awkward grasps for maturity (marrying hyper-violence with de-saturated post-apocalyptic landscapes) and its celebration of the juvenile (plumbers who defeat foes with hops and stomps) video games have often failed to find the middle ground that, in cinema, is represented by the Saturday matinee blockbuster. That rip-roaring yarn, featuring stubbly, boisterous men, tomboyish yet alluring women and Indiana Jones-esque baddies has been a Hollywood staple for decades, and yet it was only in *Uncharted 2: Among Thieves* that video games received their first equivalent experience.

The second game to feature wisecracking, smooth-talking explorer Nathan Drake offered a more assured, technically accomplished experience than its forebear. In part this is thanks to the set pieces. While the first game excelled at gunplay and featured hardy *Tomb Raider*-style environmental puzzles, Naughty Dog's ludicrous ambition in the sequels'

spectacle makes *Uncharted 2* one of the most exhilarating slices of popcorn gaming yet seen. Cliffhanger follows cliffhanger, a parade of ever more impressive and unlikely crescendos, from escaping a tumbling multistorey building as it crumbles around you, to battling along the roof of a train as it winds its way through the jungle and up into the Himalayan mountains, only held back from parody by some expertly integrated downtime.

Naughty Dog removed numerous features and sections, preferring to increase the level of detail on a smaller number of chapters. The game's innovations are few, drawing inspiration and ideas from a range of sources, but the execution is unrivalled. By choosing to embrace youthful, paperback fantasies, rather than fleeing from them, the experience seems more at ease and comfortable in its character and identity than most, proving that there is gold in those clichés for a developer skilled and wise enough to pan it out.

Left: One hundred and one secret artefacts are hidden throughout the game, awaiting discovery by the player.

ANGRY BIRDS

Despite a simple premise (catapult the birds to topple the pigs) *Angry Birds* has become a ubiquitous mobile phone game and global character brand.

In just 12 short months, Finnish game studio Rovio Mobile's *Angry Birds* had been downloaded 50 million times. It's the kind of figure that one would expect of a mainline *Super Mario Bros.* game, or perhaps a new instalment to the *Halo* series. But for a new IP released on young hardware with almost no marketing promotion, this kind of result is unthinkable. Yet it illustrates the force with which Apple's App Store disrupted the games industry, making those hobbyist gamers who have long supported Mario and Master Chief a niche within a much larger family of players.

In 2003, three students from the Helsinki University of Technology, Niklas Hed, Jarno Väkeväinen, and Kim Diker, entered a competition organized by Nokia to make a real-time multiplayer game for mobile phones. The trio's game, *King of the Cabbage World*, won the competition, and the three men set up their first game company at the end of the year, named Relude. *King of the Cabbage World* was renamed *Mole War* and sold to a publisher to become the first commercial real-

time multiplayer mobile game. Over the next few years the team took on work-for-hire jobs, hoping to accrue enough reserves to fund an original IP. In January 2005, the team received investment funding, and the company changed its name to Rovio Mobile and began asking staff for ideas for its first in-house developed game.

Members of staff pitched their ideas to the rest of the company, but it was a legless animated angry bird, presented by designer Jaakko Iisalo, that caught the imagination. The team decided to design a game around this character, borrowing ideas from a number of Flash titles to create a simple puzzle game in which players catapult at pigs stationed on or within various structures, a humorous take on the swine flu epidemic that was making headlines at the time. Released for Apple's iOS *Angry Birds* became the top-selling paid application on Apple's UK App Store in February 2010, and reached the top spot on the US App Store in the spring. A port for Android devices followed and was downloaded in excess of 1 million times in the first 48 hours of release, inspiring a generation of smaller developers with its unprecedented success.

Year: 2009
Developer: Rovio Mobile
Publisher: Clickgamer Media/ Chillingo
Original format: iPhone
Play today: iOS, Android, PSP, PlayStation 3, Windows, Mac

"Many of the proposals that we got were really well thought out, but then we saw this one screenshot of an angry bird character just trudging around on the ground. Everybody in the room really liked the character. So we said: 'Okay, we should look at this character and come up with gameplay for it'."
Mikael Hed, CEO of Rovio

Below: Points are awarded for each pig defeated in addition to points for the damage that is inflicted on structures.

Below: The player is awarded between one and three stars depending on the number of points scored at any given stage.

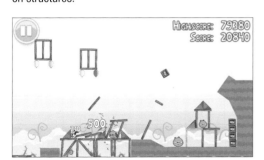

Year: 2010
Developer: Rockstar San Diego,
 Rockstar North
Publisher: Rockstar Games
Original format: Xbox 360,
 PlayStation 3
Play today: Xbox 360, PlayStation 3

Below: You primarily travel by horseback, the animal able to comfortably negotiate any type of terrain.

RED DEAD REDEMPTION

Set in the twilight days of the Wild West, no game has done sunsets and fiddles, stirrups and stubble with such assuredness as Rockstar's spaghetti western.

Since Rockstar's heaving together of cinema and interactivity in *Grand Theft Auto III*, the developer has been steadily perfecting the art of the film game, through the *Miami Vice*-esque pink neon streets of *Grand Theft Auto: Vice City* and the ghetto, *Boyz n the Hood*-style social brutality of *Grand Theft Auto: San Andreas*. But it was through the company's bold cowboy game that the flexibility of the *GTA* template was revealed. Liberty City, with its buffed taxis, resolute skyscrapers and air of affluence may appear a world away from this arid, adverse wilderness, but peel back the skin and the framework is identical. *Red Dead Redemption* is GTA: Wild West, a sandbox most familiar, albeit one, for once, filled with sand.

The game's brilliance is in how its makers twist their own conventions to suit the setting. Horses that must be lassoed, broken in and made your own replace the shiny cars. As you gallop over the game's parched canyons and tousled plains, across which steam trains puff their way into bruise-purple horizons, you form a deep bond with your steed. So too do the interactive missions match the setting. For those wearied by years of delivering drugs and stealing cars for Rockstar, the chance to herd cattle in a thunderstorm, act as an accomplice in a snake oil salesman's scam or shoot rabbits as they try to steal a friend's carrots at night, makes for a welcome, creative change.

Above and below: Slow-motion effects combine with the game's ragdoll physics to create the kind of iconic shooter-keeling-from-a-rooftop images that define the Western in cinema.

The game charts the exploits of John Marston, an outlaw turned police confidant, a cowboy who finds himself in the twilight days of the Wild West. The assured story leads to one of gaming's most satisfying conclusions while the emergent narratives that spring up during every horseback chase and saloon shoot-out ensure that each chapter feels like your own. Rockstar San Diego's skill in creating a believable, functioning world with a distinct, coherent and consistent atmosphere is peerless, and while the debt owed to cinema may make video gaming's purists uneasy, few other blockbusters come with such assuredness and clarity of vision.

"Tell a gritty crime drama with violence and profanity and call it *The Sopranos*, you're handed a load of awards to put up on the shelf. You do the same and call it a video game and you'll have certain organizations up in arms."

Lazlow Jones, developer on
Red Dead Redemption

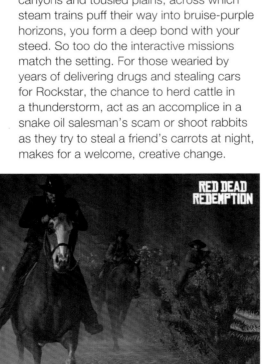

DARK SOULS

Dark Souls' captivating world may seem to work with clockwork-like logic, but it's a fantasy game that values hazy mystery as much as elegance.

DARK SOULS
PREPARE TO DIE EDITION

Year: 2011
Developer: From Software
Publisher: From Software/Namco-Bandai
Original format: Xbox 360, PS3
Play today: Xbox 360, PS3, PC

Despite the routine fantasy styling – the knights in tarnished armour, the clinking skeleton attackers, the testy dragons with scorched nostrils and flicking tails – *Dark Souls* delivers an ambience and reveals a core quite unlike any other. About as far from the churning mainstream of bellicose action games as one can trek, in *Dark Souls* you skitter through narrow sewers and dense forests while cowering behind a shield.

Your journey is one of hurried dashes, racing between the bonfires that punctuate the unforgiving world: a rare point of safety, a place to trade currency for upgrades and to plant a respawn point a little further into the game's hazy myth.

The second dark fantasy game from Japanese Hidetaka Miyazaki, *Dark Souls* builds upon the themes and ambience of its forebear *Demon's Souls* in fascinating ways: disempowering players, hurling them against overwhelming odds in the hope that they pick themselves up and tenaciously head back into the fray having learned a valuable lesson. Unlike so many popular games of the early 2010s, *Dark Souls* asks that players improve their own abilities, rather than those of their character, if they want to prevail.

Its world is expansive and diverse, and yet fits together with the elegance of a giant contraption, short cuts unlocking as you press deeper and see how it all fits together. Its grim yet beautiful landscapes are filled with terrible monsters, but there are also friendly factions here to pledge allegiance to and these provide the end game where players can eventually invade one another's worlds to better their covenant's standing. An extraordinary game that values the mysterious and unspoken, but which continues to attract endless debate and loyalty.

Below: Advice from other players is dynamically scrawled into the environment, clues that help explain the controls, or warn low-level players from heading into areas where they may be overwhelmed.

Below: Respite in the game is to be found at the bonfires that punctuate Lordran's landscape. These offer health-replenishing save points, but using one will bring all of the local enemies back to life.

"Some of my ideas seem impossible to implement at first, so I am grateful for a team who continues to strive to fulfill all of my requests. The way I work is only possible because I have such a loyal and trusting team around me."
Hidetaka Miyazaki

242

Year: 2012
Developer: thatgamecompany
Publisher: Sony Computer
  Entertainment
Original format: PS3
Play today: PS3

"To all intents and purposes, games should be more capable than film. But the fact is that gaming is still a subset of the film industry. It's tragic. I see so much potential. I feel like there is so much more I can do here."

Jenova Chen, co-creator
of *Journey*

Right: At one point in the game's development, *Journey* was a four-player game, but this feature was removed as Chen believed it's "much harder to create a meaningful four".

JOURNEY

Journey offers an artful reflection on life and its meanings, but its most powerful moments are those shared with another.

This journey is a pilgrimage of sorts: to the sleepy mountain that looms ever present on the game's horizon, a marker by which to set your bearings as you travel towards its base, hooded and hunched into the belting wind. But also into new creative territory where we witness what can happen when an indie game – or, at very least, a game that prizes indie ideals – is given a blockbuster budget and development period.

It's also a game about religion, death and a certain restraint: over the course of this three-hour journey your interactions are limited to walking and jumping through its sand-blown landscapes.

Your character, a mute, pin-legged traveller, wears a heavy cloak and flowing scarf, the latter of which acts as an indicator of how much energy you have for jumping, by shrinking in length as you use up the magical resource. Checkpoints are rendered as stone altars. Kneel before them and you'll save your pilgrim's progress. The flat, dusty scenery is pocked with craggy temples, the wind howling about their bellies and rounding off their time-nicked edges. The game's puzzles are straightforward, pulled from 30 years of game design, but obfuscated by whimsy, and executed with a serene, light touch that

disguises these influences to the point that they begin to feel like novelties.

All of this would be cause for heady wonder, but the game's most potent delight comes from its unique multiplayer element, seamlessly pairing your pilgrim with another. They appear as a shadow on your horizon and, after you run to one another for a silent greeting, you may quest together, keeping one another company for a short leg of the journey. Then one time you turn your back and, when you look for them again, find they are gone. *Journey* may have taken three years to develop, running vastly over schedule and budget, but the effort has resulted one of the most interesting spaces in a video game, one that allows for gentle communion with another human, a reminder both of the fleetingness of existence and of the importance of relationship within it.

PAPERS, PLEASE

Immigration hardly seems like ideal subject matter for video game treatment, yet Lucas Pope's game is an affecting portrait of where red tape meets compassion.

Year: 2013
Developer: Lucas Pope
Publisher: 3909 LLC
Original format: PC
Play today: iOS, macOS, PlayStation Vita, Linux

The dour, chunky pixels belie a game that is often more poignant than the most dazzling of blockbusters. So too does the setting: a cold and miserable border checkpoint of a fictional 1980s-era communist European country, Arstotzka. You play not as a typical video game protagonist – the plucky spy, trying to fool his way past the guards, or the rogue soldier, guns raised – but in the deskbound role of an immigration inspector. Your role is seemingly straightforward: deny entry to anyone who does not have the correct papers. It's a humdrum premise, and yet from the grim setting and simple rules, magic springs.

A huddled, shuffling line of would-be immigrants weaves back off screen and you must simply process as many as possible, checking their documentation before confirming or denying entry. While you hold power over all you process, this is no power fantasy. This is your job, and the size of your paycheck is dependent on both the number of people you process, and the accuracy of your decision-making. After work you return to your family, where, once you've paid your rent, you are forced to choose between spending your remaining earnings on heat, food or, in the event that a family member falls sick, medicine (who to nurse: wife, child or mother-in-law?).

The game's designer, Lucas Pope, complicates your job by forcing you to listen to the stories and pleas of the people who approach your desk. You meet, for example, a woman who holds the correct documentation but, behind her in line, stands her husband who does not. Do you uphold the bureaucracy, and split the marriage partners, or show mercy and allow them through, risking the wrath of your superiors?

Your choices have wider narrative consequences: allow a mother to reunite with her son even though her entry document expired a few days ago, and the Arstotzkan newspapers will report that the recent influx of immigrants is stealing jobs from locals.

Above: Pope reported that, by 2016, more than 1.8 million copies of the game had been sold.

Pope's game injects the vividly personal administrative context and in doing so achieves what few others manage: to cause the player to question the single-minded quest for mastery of a game's systems. In Papers, Please, you must consider the human cost of triumph within the game's structure and reality. You might win the game if you obey its rules, but what will be lost in the process?

"I'm naturally attracted to Orwellian communist bureaucracy."

Lucas Pope, creator of *Papers, Please*

Below: As the game progresses the criteria for entry become ever more stringent. Eventually pointing out that an entrant's weight does not match records is sufficient grounds to deny a person entry to Arstotzka.

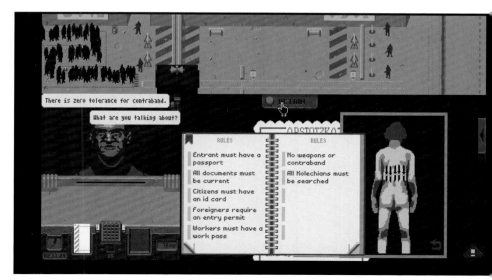

[148]

GRAND THEFT AUTO V

Year: 2013
Developer: Rockstar North
Publisher: Rockstar Games
Original format: PlayStation 3,
Xbox 360
Play today: PlayStation 4,
Xbox One, PC

"What we make is action adventure-games; they're not quite RPGs but it's getting harder and harder to say what the difference is between an RPG and what we do."

Dan Houser,
co-writer of *Grand Theft Auto V*.

Below: Run over Michael's wife and she later sends you a bill for her hospital treatment.

GRAND THEFT AUTO V

With a story that skewers everything from Hollywood excess to ultra clean-living, *GTAV* is never better than when simply recreating the baked majesty of California.

Los Santos, a dazzling recreation of California's Los Angeles, is not so much the backdrop for Rockstar's fifth Grand Theft Auto game, as its entire substance. The story of the game's three criminal protagonists, Michael, Franklin and the memorably unhinged Trevor, is merely something that passes through the city, one of many stories that you pick up every now and again, in between following your own sojourns and distractions. Long after the end credits have rolled, you can return to this city, and explore its forty-nine square miles. The developers reportedly conducted more than a hundred days of research in Los Angeles, taking thousands of photographs and countless hours of digital video, and the city's essence is all here, stretching from the Los Santos International Airport in the south of the city, through the central district, bordered by the Del Perro and La Puerta freeways and the Los Santos river, up through the Tongva valley, over the Tataviam mountains and back down to Blaine County and the lapping ocean beyond.

The possibilities here, in the sun-baked city, are almost endless. Want to hire a bicycle and pound your way along the coast, gasping in the sea air? Sure. Want to hijack a 747 and fly it into the Del Perro pier? You can. You can live the high life

Above: You save progress in the game by sending your character to bed. Each protagonist keeps a different sleep schedule lasting between six and twelve hours.

using the proceeds of your stock market investments, or become a property tycoon, or, if that sounds like too much work, play never-ending games of tennis along with the other luminary retirees of Beverly Hills (or 'Rockford Hills', in Rockstar's fiction). Los Santos, like its analogue Los Angeles, is a city of invention and reinvention: you give and take what you need.

This is also true of Grand Theft Auto V in general: a game of such scope that it allows us to see what you need to see. You can look at Rockstar's opus as a technological miracle, a game that recreates one of our species' great cities in sound and light. Or you can look at it like a holiday destination, a place to tumble about with friends (an enduring online mode is what has kept the game at the top of the charts for years, selling more than 90 million copies to make it, in 2018, the most profitable entertainment product of all time) racing mountain bikes or planning heists online. Or you can see it as a sandbox in which to

explore your darkest fantasies, all within a consequence-less reality.

You can see the game's missions as spectacular set-pieces, as you tear down the frontage of a penthouse using a tow truck, or attempt to reclaim your yacht and missing son from thieves in a highway chase. Or you can see these moments as failures of mimicry, which recreate the spectacle of television greats such as The Sopranos or The Wire, but fail to transpose their substance and meaningful human drama. You can look at the game as knowing satire. At times it successfully skewers western culture's excesses and failings. Or maybe you don't buy the satire, and see only weak jokes that throw punches in all directions, and land only a few.

The game's three protagonists – each of whom you can control at any given point, in order to take up their individual or collaborative criminal missions – are memorable, precisely because of their darkness. And perhaps the fact that their (and by association our) heroism is achieved through violence is a cultural failing, rather than that of the writers. The American idea of heroism is almost always linked to violence of some sort.

Grand Theft Auto V still defies straight-forward definition because it is simultaneously so many games all at once. Like all cities, as we enter Los Santos we bring with us our own perspectives, hang-ups, ambitions and fears and embrace or reject them accordingly. Los Santos is a mirror to Los Angeles, but also to the individual playing. This kind of projection happens with all art and entertainment, but perhaps more so with video games, the only form in which we take an active participant role. And especially in Los Santos, in which our freedoms are so broad and so generously accommodated.

Above: *Such is the attention to detail that the moon's phases change as the weeks progress, altering the quality of the light.*

Below: *Shave your head or keep your face clean-shaven, and, in time, stubble will grow.*

[149]

THE LEGEND OF ZELDA:
BREATH OF THE WILD

Year: 2017
Developer: Nintendo EPD
Publisher: Nintendo
Original format: Nintendo Switch,
Wii-U
Play today: Nintendo Switch

"Many times there were things that just weren't functioning at all. We'd have to remove everything and build back up again."
Takuhiro Dohta, *BOTW's* technical director

THE LEGEND OF ZELDA: BREATH OF THE WILD

After years of joyful but often conservative updates to a familiar format, here, at last, was a total reimagining of Zelda, with astonishing, medium-defining results.

When starting work on The Legend of Zelda: Breath of the Wild, series creator Shigeru Miyamoto told his team they could tear up Zelda's well-worn template and change anything they wanted. "We wrote down all of the stress points, the things that make Zelda games less enjoyable, and we replaced them with new ideas," said the game's director Hidemaro Fujibayashi. The result is astonishing, the first true reimagining of the thirty-year-old series, and a game that certainly enabled its host platform, the Switch, to become Nintendo's best-selling video game console yet made.

We're back in Hyrule, of course, but this version of the mythical land is a wilderness of hills and lakes and mountain peaks in which you are free to traipse wherever you please. Almost all of protagonist Link's abilities, most of which are new to this game, and which grant the player the wizard-like abilities to stop time, freeze water and levitate objects, are acquired within the first hour's play. Once collected, you are free to do as you please, even

Above: Shoot a fire arrow into grass while flying and you'll create a height-giving updraft.

trotting off to the final encounter with Link's perma-nemesis Ganon, ignoring everything else. Alternatively, you can while away the hours catching and training wild horses, or becoming a wildlife photographer, meticulously chronicling every animal, insect, and fish. Breath of the Wild is a game that contorts itself to accommodate every interest and predilection.

As well as beauty, the world of Breath of the Wild has an exhilarating cohesion, a chemistry-set-like quality whereby its very elements can be combined in interesting ways. Brandish a flaming torch in a patch of dry grass and the fire will spread. Wear a metal helmet in a thunderstorm and you may attract a head-wrecking bolt. In this Hyrule, the rain makes stone surfaces slick and difficult to climb. And in this Hyrule, Link can cook meat cut from the carcasses of birds and animals, combining it with fruit knocked from trees, or harvested mushrooms to produce life-restoring meals and ability-enhancing elixirs.

In Breath of the Wild Nintendo finally appeared to acknowledge the advances that have been made in mainstream game design during the preceding decade: the shift to open worlds and freeform gameplay. And its designers' careful calibration and improvements of the form built to a memorable and affecting paradigm shift.

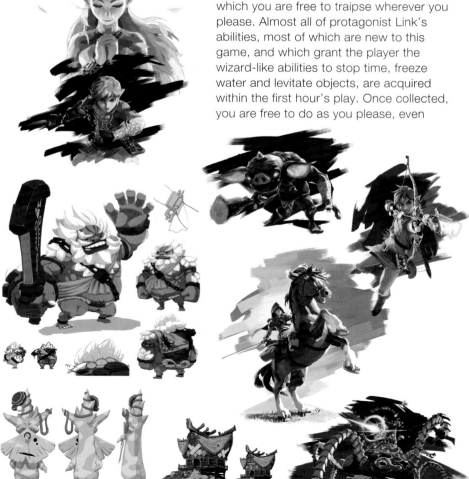

WHAT REMAINS OF EDITH FINCH

Studied, careful world-building and exquisite storytelling define an unforgettable game that examines family secrets, bereavement, and hope.

Above: The Finches' home has been haphazardly extended.

Year: 2017
Developer: Giant Sparrow
Publisher: Annapurna Interactive
Original format: PC, PlayStation 4
Play today: PC, PlayStation 4, Xbox One

What Remains of Edith Finch, a game about a young woman who returns to her childhood home on a forsaken island, was the first video game release from Annapurna Pictures, a film company founded in 2011 that has, in the years that have followed, shown a talent for choosing cinematic, characterful and, above all, quality video games that sit apart from the mainstream.

Edith Finch is the only surviving member of what one newspaper in the game described as America's "most unfortunate family." In seven decades no fewer than ten Finches died in or near to the family home. Now, after the death of the last, she returns to the house she has inherited in order to reminisce about her curious and idiosyncratic family. She finds a warren of memorials: each of its bedrooms, studies and basements sealed in time, as if waiting for an occupant to return.

After breaking in, you guide Edith around its corridors and rooms. The house has a higgled, chaotic character, with crazed extensions and weird protrusions where the family had added new rooms and wings as it expanded. Each bedroom in the house, left locked and untouched, reflects the character and, it follows, the destiny of its vanished relative. There's the child star betrayed by the arrival of puberty, the teenager's shrine to weed and video

games. As you discover mementos amid the dust and detritus, you enter a series of vivid flashbacks that slowly tell the story of the family and its demise. These vignettes have a magical-realist quality, and, quickly and efficiently reveal something about the character you momentarily inhabit, as well as, typically, how they met their end. This is not a horror game but there's a note of unsettling sadness that runs throughout the experience. "Whatever's wrong with this family," Edith says at one point, "goes back a long way."

Text plays a crucial role in the game, too. Much of the script is made incarnate, scrawled momentarily on a wall or a doorway. Letters then scatter like dandelion fronds in the wind, while sentences flutter like a kite's tail in the wind. The result is an elegiac, literary exploration of the way in which we inherit not only our ancestors' likenesses but also, sadly, their traumas and taboos.

> **"**My interest is in moments that shake people up a bit and present the world in a way people haven't considered before.**"**
>
> Ian Dallas, creative director, *What Remains of Edith Finch*

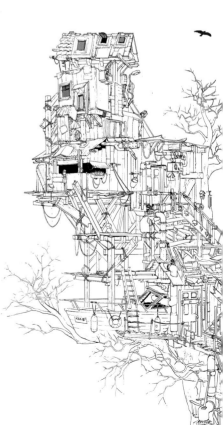

[151]

FORTNITE: BATTLE ROYALE

Year: 2017
Developer: Epic Games
Publisher: Epic Games
Original format: PlayStation 4, Xbox One, PC, Mac
Play today: PlayStation 4, Xbox One, PC, Mac, Nintendo Switch

> "It's the first shooter with a huge female population. Somebody estimated it at roughly 35 percent, which is unprecedented – why isn't it 50? – but it's unprecedented for anything like this. It brings together players in a social experience."
>
> Tim Sweeney, founder Epic Games.

FORTNITE: BATTLE ROYALE

Fortnite did not invent 'Battle Royale', where a hundred players compete to be the last survivor, but it popularized and, for some, perfected this emerging genre.

Above: Fortnite generated an estimated $2.4 billion in 2018 through sales of 'skins', cosmetics, and other in-game items, more than any other game to date.

It took less than six months for Fortnite, released without much fanfare in the summer of 2017, to become the most popular video game in the world. It is, now, a cultural juggernaut on a par with Star Wars, or Minecraft. Developed by one of the oldest companies in the business, Epic Games, Fortnite borrows the premise of the Japanese novel Battle Royale and The Hunger Games, in which contestants are sent to an island with nothing but the clothes on their backs, where they must then scavenge and fight one another until only one contestant remains.

In Fortnite: Battle Royale, you are dropped, along with 99 other players, from a flying bus, to parachute onto a candy-coloured island. Every few minutes a lethal electrical storm draws closer, herding you and the other survivors toward a final standoff until, finally, a sole victor is left standing. Over the 20 minutes that each game lasts, 100 small stories of bravery and cowardice, skill and haplessness accumulate and intersect. Matches are never anything less than exhilarating, unexpected but, for all but the victor, they are also, usually, indescribably maddening.

While Fortnite's style and rhythm are unique, the template closely follows that of PlayerUnknown's Battlegrounds, which dominated the PC game charts five months prior to Fortnite's release. PUBG's developer threatened legal action, but it came to nothing and, by mid-2018, Epic's game had, among the world's children at least, overtaken Battlegrounds as the game of the moment.

It's not a complete derivative. For one, Fortnite gives players the ability to harvest materials such as wood and rock from the environment, which can be used to build walls, stairs and shelters. Talented builders are able to construct towering fortresses in which to hide (at least, until a rival knocks the edifice down with a well-aimed rocket).

The game's world-conquering success is due to a variety of factors. For one, Epic Games is one of the industry's oldest outfits, experienced in building and maintaining online competitive video games since the dawn of the internet. While PUBG's updates have been slow and generally unexciting, Fortnite's updates launch with military-grade regularity and have introduced a flurry of new items and wild, one-off game modes (50 vs. 50, Sniper rifles only).

The game's aesthetic, which is bright, colourful and decidedly un-bloody, has also helped convince parents that this is a world of harmless, cartoonish violence. PUBG, by contrast, is brown and gory.

Then in March 2018 the musician Drake, the rapper Travis Scott and the American football player JuJu Smith-Schuster joined professional video game streamer Tyler 'Ninja' Blevins in a Fortnite squad. Footage of their play session, broadcast on the live-streaming service Twitch, broke the record for the most-viewed episode on the internet. In playgrounds, word of the game has spread virally, not only through excited recaps of the previous night's matches, but also, extraordinarily, via the Floss, a dance move that originated on YouTube in 2014 and was popularized by Fortnite. (The game allows players to aggressively perform a variety of dance moves at one another, either as a form of bonding or antagonism.)

Fortnite's business model is also quietly revolutionary. The studio makes money not from point-of-sale (it's free to download) but from selling digital costumes, known as skins, to the players. Each day a new wardrobe is put up for sale on the game's storefront, for a few pounds apiece. Players can dress their digital avatar as a ninja, a medieval knight, an Olympic skier, or a skeleton, to name but a few, and in this way stand out from the crowd. The men and women who design these costumes have become some of the most important members of Fortnite's development team: it

is through their fashion work that the game makes its money.

While, in the early months, professional players, Twitch streamers and YouTubers ignored the game, viewing it as too childish for their audiences, that soon changed. Blevins has reportedly made $500,000 a month from streaming the game, while daily videos posted by Ali-A, one of the most popular British YouTubers, routinely pass two million views in 24 hours.

Like so many other fads in video games, Fortnite's longevity, and the general popularity of Battle Royale-style games, is questionable. But for now, the nascent genre is here to stay. And while other developers rush to create their own Battle Royale games, it seems increasingly likely that Fortnite will be the last man standing.

Below: *Tyler Blevins, aka 'Ninja', reportedly earned $10 million in 2018 by live-streaming himself playing Fortnite.*

INDEX

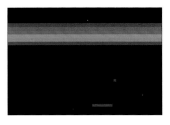

Bushnell, Nolan 10–11, 12, 21

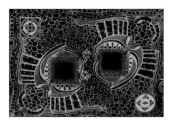

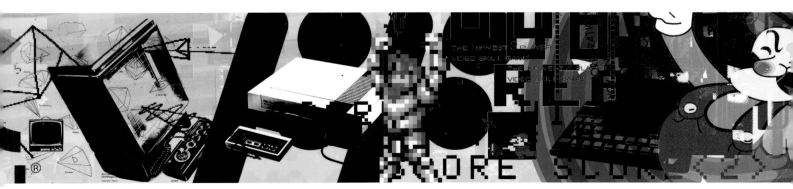

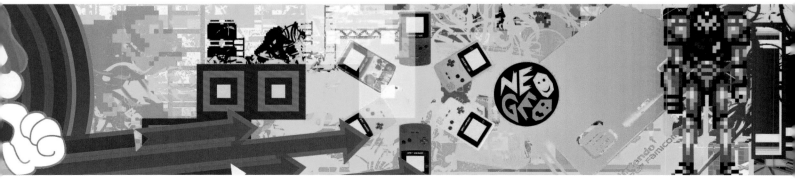

PICTURE CREDITS

Every effort has been made to credit the copyright holders of the images used in this book. We apologize for any unintentional errors or omissions and will insert the appropriate acknowledgement to any companies or individuals in subsequent editions of the book.

3909 LLC: 243; **Activision Blizzard:** 131, 156, 198–9, 208, 230–1; **Annapurna Interactive:** 247; **Apple:** 222–3; **Archetype Interactive:** 129; **Atari:** 12–13, 16, 17, 18–19, 20–21, 25, 30, 40, 48, 53, 67, 104; **Bally Midway:** 17, 98; **Broderbund:** 73, 102; **Capcom:** 59, 66, 88–9, 120, 169, 203, 207, 211, 232–3; **CCP Games:** 192; **Chillingo:** 239; **Cinematronics:** 41; **Commodore:** 37; **EA:** 72, 73, 100, 109, 116, 142, 158–9,

226; **Entertainment:** 204; **Epic Games:** 2489; **Hudson:** 86; **id Software:** 95, 106, 122–3; **Infogrames:** 188; **InterPlay:** 94, 143; **Irem:** 58; **Koei:** 192; **Konami:** 57, 137, 138, 140, 146–7; **LucasArts:** 61, 80, 81, 193, 205; **Magnavox:** 14, 15; **Melbourne House:** 49; **Microsoft:** 178–9, 180–1, 209, 210, 213, 218, 234–5; **Mojang:** 236–7; **NAMCO BANDAI Games Inc.:** 24, 28–9, 103, 196, 241; **Nintendo:** 16, 32–3, 44–5, 50, 51, 54, 55, 70, 71, 79, 82, 83, 84, 84, 92–3, 96–7, 108, 118–9, 121, 126, 127, 128, 129, 140–1, 152–3, 155, 157, 170, 172–3, 184–5, 191, 200–1, 206, 216, 217, 228–9, 231, 246; **Nipon Ichi Software:** 190; **PopCap Games:** 168, 212, 219; **Psygnosis:** 115, 149; **Red Octane, MTV Games:** 208; **Renegade:** 107; **Rockstar Games:** 176–7, 195, 240,

244–5; **Sega:** 43, 52, 64, 65, 90–1, 101, 105, 110, 111, 116, 128, 130, 150–1, 154, 157, 167, 171, 182–3; **Sierra Studios:** 148; **Sinclair:** 34, 35; **SNK:** 76, 77; **Sony:** 112–3, 117, 132–3, 134, 135, 144–5, 147, 162–3, 174–5, 177, 202, 206, 214–5, 240, 238, 242, 247, 248; **Square Enix:** 56, 62, 63, 99, 130, 134–5, 136, 139, 164–5, 167, 186, 187; **Taito:** 22–23; **Tetris Company:** 68, 69; **THQ:** 222, 223; **2K Games:** 207, 212, 224–5; **Ubisoft:** 189, 194; **Valve:** 150, 166, 168, 197, 227; **Vectobeam:** 24; **Virgin Interactive:** 114; **Williams:** 31, 36.

Illustrations by Terry Stokes appear on the following pages: 1–7, 8–9, 26–27, 74–75, 162–163, 250–251, 252–253, 254–255, 256, plus game icons and icons for endpapers.

ACKNOWLEDGEMENTS

Special thanks to the team at Anness Publishing for their belief in the project, and to Arcade Flyers for their assistance in sourcing images.

This edition is published by Lorenz Books an imprint of Anness Publishing Ltd
info@anness.com
www.lorenzbooks.com
www.annesspublishing.com

© Anness Publishing Ltd 2019

Publisher: Joanna Lorenz
Editors: Anne Hildyard, Daniel Hurst
Designer: Terry Stokes
Design support: Alvin Weetman
Picture Researcher: Darren Phillips
Production Controller: Ben Worley

Publisher's note
Although the advice and information in this book are believed to be accurate and true at the time of going to press, neither the author nor the publisher can accept any legal responsibility or liability for any errors or omissions that may have been made.

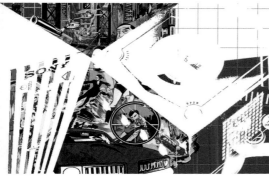

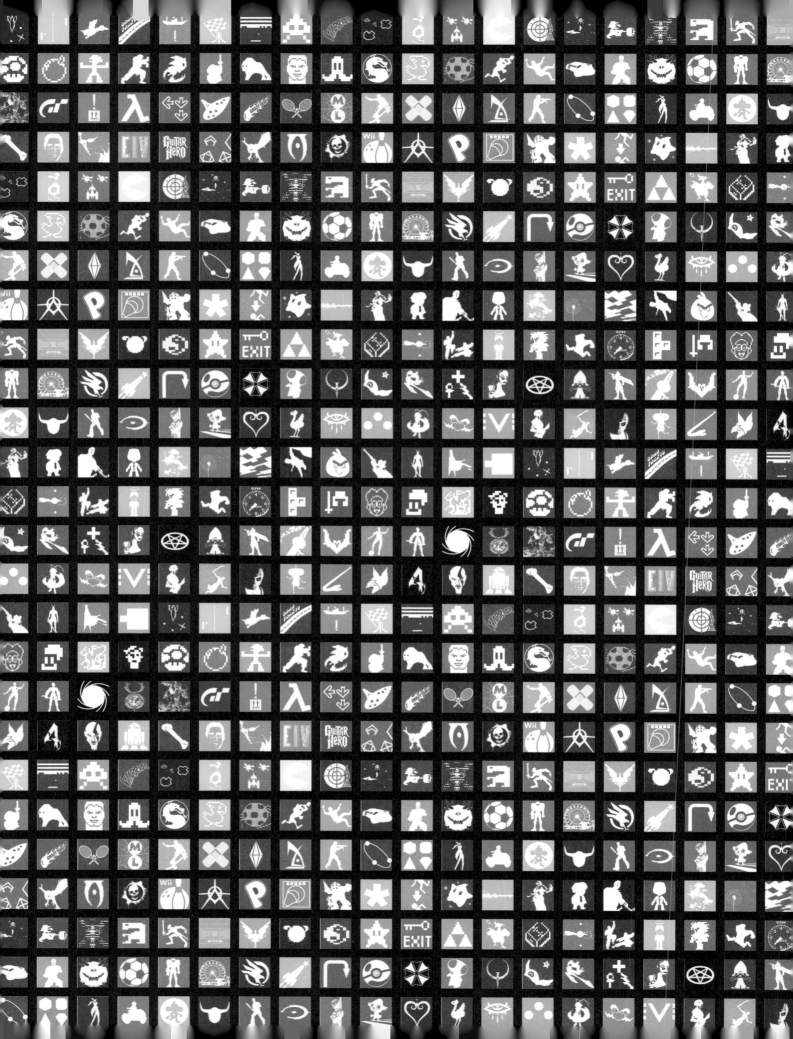